ENVIRONMENTAL ARCHAEOLOGY

Other books by the same author

Archaeological sediments, Butterworths 1975
Geoarchaeology: Earth science and the past (edited with D. A. Davidson), Duckworth 1976
Rocks and man, George Allen & Unwin 1978
Neanderthal man, Duckworth 1980

ENVIRONMENTAL ARCHAEOLOGY

Myra Shackley
Department of Archaeology, University of Leicester

London
GEORGE ALLEN & UNWIN
Boston   Sydney

George Allen & Unwin (Publishers) Ltd.,
40 Museum Street, London, WC1A 1LU, UK

George Allen & Unwin (Publishers) Ltd.,
Park Lane, Hemel Hempstead, Herts HP2 4TE, UK

Allen & Unwin Inc.,
9 Winchester Terrace, Winchester, Mass 01890, USA

George Allen & Unwin Australia Pty Ltd.,
8 Napier Street, North Sydney, NSW 2060, Australia

First published in 1981

British Library Cataloguing in Publication Data

Shackley, Myra
    Environmental archaeology.
1. Environmental archaeology
I. Title
930.1   CC81
ISBN 0–04–913020–X
ISBN 0–04–913021–8 Pbk

Library of Congress Cataloging in Publication Data

Shackley, Myra L.
    Environmental archaeology.
Includes bibliographical references and index.
1. Environmental archaeology.   2. Animal remains
(Archaeology)   3. Plant remains (Archaeology)   I. Title.
CC81.S5   930.1   81–7996
ISBN 0–04-913020–X   AACR2
ISBN 0–04-913021–8 (pbk.)

Set in 10 on 12 point Plantin by Nene Phototypesetters Ltd, Northampton
and printed in Great Britain
by Mackays of Chatham

Preface

Environmental archaeology is an integral part of archaeological science with archaeologists acting as co-ordinators for the products of a large number of different disciplines. The applications of the biological sciences (bioarchaeology) and earth sciences (geoarchaeology) combine with archaeometry to extend the scope of archaeological research and blind us with new names (palaeoethnoparasitology is my current favourite). We cannot divorce the study of man from the study of his environment, their mutual interaction and the tangible evidence of that interaction. Archaeological data is composed of structural information, artefacts and ecofacts linked by a complex of factors which can never be fully understood. Archaeology is, after all, human palaeoecology in its truest sense, from the very first appearance of man (itself a controversial point) to yesterday. All ecological systems are dynamic, each component influencing the others to varying degrees. It might be argued that human communities have a far greater effect on this balance than any other life form, and that this effect increases with time. This is partially true, and one can divide human evolution into successive stages starting with a point at which the first hominids were merely an ineffective food source for carnivores, and ending with the stage we have reached at present, where we are cheerfully obliterating other species which even momentarily compete with our 'progress'. 'The later the date and the more sophisticated its technology, the greater the effect a community has on its environment' is an idea that is both true and false: true in that man can create his own conditions, but false in that he must still exploit the rest of the biosphere for the raw materials of his existence. The results of such exploitation are the province of environmental archaeology, down to the last chicken bone thrown over someone's shoulder.

In an ideal world (a contradiction in terms, anyway) the excavator requires an on-site expert in each subdiscipline present for the duration of the work and the necessary post-excavation analysis. This is clearly impossible and in the best cases is replaced by pre-excavation consultation (to design research and sampling strategies) and post-excavation analysis and interpretation. The actual sampling and site description should not be left solely to the excavator as this will result in a reversal to the limp environmental appendix model for excavation reports. The days of the general purpose on-site environmentalist are coming, a species which has evolved either from an archaeological training with experience in another science, or from the corollary. He must take decisions on what categories of information *may* be revealed, what *should* be sampled and what *must* be recorded. The ghastly vision of potted specialists armed with a copy of this book has haunted my nightmares for some time, since such a phenomenon has been present in recent years with the result that some sources of data must be very carefully checked. An obvious Catch 22 exists. Excavators need to be aware of problems, potential and requirements for environmental work for project design and costing but cannot possess this information without knowing something about the subject. On the other hand, if they know too much, will they get carried away and start trying to write their own bone reports or boiling up pollen samples over a gas ring? I hope not.

Think of this book as a signpost. It should be read at two levels: as a guide to the subject and an indicator of the locations of specialist literature, and secondly as a reference book for details of procedures and laboratory techniques. It is *not* designed to produce potted specialists. Perish the thought! The internal organization of each chapter is the same, to aid students who are chasing information of a specific type (for example, on comparative recovery procedures), except in some cases where this has not been possible as the subject matter is very diverse (Chapter 2) or does not fit conveniently into any single information category (Chapter 9). Soils and sediments have been amalgamated into one chapter and archaeozoology divided into three by a triumph of logic dictated by the fact that in the first case the sampling, descriptive procedures and information yielded from both is very similar and in the second that the different problems posed by fish, bird and mammalian assemblages justify the division. Each chapter finishes with several short accounts of work in its field, chosen from easily accessible papers making specific points, which also contained good bibliographies and provided indicators of the scope of research. These topics are, obviously, not intended to be an exhaustive and comprehensive survey.

In several cases the subject matter of each chapter has already been covered by one or more high-level textbooks. The student can do no better than consult them for detailed information. Where this is the case, the chapters tend to be rather short, but if the information is scattered in dozens of unlikely journals (as is the case with micro-organisms), more space for discussion has been allowed.

There are just a few books which will be mentioned constantly, the two textbooks by John Evans (*Introduction to environmental archaeology* and *The environment of early man in the British Isles*) being the most recent. Karl Butzer's *Environment and archaeology* is differently slanted but comprehensive, his examples being drawn from Pleistocene material. The collection of papers edited by Brothwell and Higgs (1969) under the title *Science in archaeology* remains of outstanding importance, and more recent primary publications may be found, especially in the *Journal of Archaeological Science* and *Archaeometry*. There is, as yet, no specific journal for environmental archaeology, but the recently established Association for Environmental Archaeology circulates a newsletter which lists new publications and current research projects.

It is early days, as yet, to see lasting trends emerging in modern environmental archaeology and its practitioners, or to set down a *codex* which will stand for all time. I can do no better than present for a general aim the *credo* of Dr W. Groenman-van Waateringe, contained in the 1979 Beatrice de Cardi lecture to the Council for British Archaeology:

The task of the environmental archaeologist in this whole set-up is not merely the documentation of still surviving information from the past, nor merely the recording of the information before it is lost; he should be able to present the sum of all the information derived from the specialist reports in the various disciplines within its relevant archaeological setting. And, furthermore, it must be his concern to help seek out new paths towards natural and environmental management.

If this book contributes in any way to such a grand design it will have served its purpose.

Myra Shackley
October 1980

Acknowledgements

The completion of this book is the result of the help, criticism and co-operation of so many people that to detail each individual's contribution would take many pages. I hope that everyone in the following list will forgive me for not being more precise about what I am thanking them for; be assured it is lack of space, not lack of gratitude.

Peter Addyman
Keith Barber
Jan Bay-Petersen
Peter Beaumont
Andrew Best
Jennifer Bourdillon
Don Brothwell
Kay Campbell
John Coles
Marius Cooke
Jennie Coy
Barry Cunliffe
Donald Davidson
Geoffrey Dimbleby
John Evans
Gary Fry
Richard Hall
Philip Holdsworth

Ian Horsey
Andrew Jones
Roger Jones
Harry Kenward
Richard Klein
Erica Klarenberg
Cheryl McCormick
Euan MacKie
Deirdre O'Sullivan
Bruce Proudfoot
Peter Sneath
Ken Thomas
Pam Thornett
Giovanna Vitelli
Harry Voss
John Wacher
Ann Woods

The following organizations and individuals are thanked for permission to reproduce illustrative material, figure numbers in parentheses:

Figure 1.2 reproduced from *Analytical archaeology* (Clarke 1978) by kind permission of Methuen & Co.; Figure 1.5 reproduced by kind permission of Munsell Color, 2441 N. Calvert St, Baltimore, MD 21218, USA; Figure 1.9 reproduced by kind permission of G. Bibby and the Royal Society; Figures 1.11 and 1.12 reproduced from *World Archaeology* 9, 334–46, by kind permission of L. E. Stager and Routledge & Kegan Paul; R. A. M. Gardner (1.13); D. A. Davidson (1.19); Figure 1.20 reproduced with permission from H. Keeley, *J. Archaeol. Sci.* 1977, copyright by Academic Press Inc.

(London) Ltd; Figure 2.2 reproduced from *Plants: a scanning electron microscope survey* (Troughton & Sampson 1976), copyright John Wiley and Sons Ltd; M. J. Jansma (2.3, 2.4); the Editors, *Journal of Applied Bacteriology* (2.8, 2.9); Figure 2.10 reproduced from *An atlas of recent British foraminiferids* (Murray 1971) by kind permission of Heinemann Educational Books; John Wiley and Sons Inc. (2.11); Figures 3.3 and 3.4 reproduced from *British mosses and liverworts* (Watson & Richards) by kind permission of Cambridge University Press; Figures 4.1 and 4.5 reproduced from *Textbook of pollen analysis* (Faegri & Iverson) by kind permission of Munksgaard International; R. Jones (4.2); J. R. Pilcher and the Editor, *Ulster Journal of Archaeology* (4.4); Sir H. Godwin (4.6); the Royal Society of Antiquaries of Ireland (4.7); Figure 4.8 reproduced from *Proc. R. Soc. B* **161**, by kind permission of J. Turner and the Royal Society; the Editor, *New Phytologist* (4.9); Figure 4.11 reproduced with permission from Greig & Turner, *J. Archaeol. Sci.* 1974, copyright by Academic Press Inc. (London) Ltd; Alfred A. Knopf Inc. (4.12); Figure 5.1 reproduced by kind permission from *The living plant* (Allen Brook), copyright Edinburgh University Press; R. Morgan (5.2); Figure 5.3 reproduced from C. Keepax, *J. Archaeol. Sci.* 1975, copyright Academic Press Inc. (London) Ltd; York Archaeological Trust (5.4–5.6, 8.2, 8.3); D. H. French (6.3); R. Ellison (6.5); D. G. Wilson (6.6); J. G. Evans (7.1a, 7.2, 7.4, 7.5); Figures 7.1a, 7.2 reproduced with permission from *Land snails in archaeology* (J. G. Evans), copyright by Academic Press Inc. (London) Ltd; Figure 7.1b reproduced from *Land invertebrates* (Cloudsley-Thompson & Sankey) by kind permission of Methuen & Co.; Society of Antiquaries of London (7.3); G. W. Dimbleby (7.4); Leicester University Press (7.4, 7.5); Council for British Archaeology (7.7); H. Kenward (8.2, 8.3); the Roman Society (8.4); Figure 10.2 reproduced with permission from *The study of animal bones from archaeological sites* (M. Chaplin), copyright Academic Press Inc. (London) Ltd; S. Hirst and RESCUE (10.5); John Wiley and Sons Inc. (11.2); Figures 11.3, 11.4 reproduced with permission from *Fish remains in archaeology* (R. Casteel), copyright Academic Press Inc. (London) Ltd; Norfolk Museums Service (11.5, 11.6); the Prehistoric Society (11.7); V. M. Bryant and W. H. Freeman & Co. (12.3).

Contents

CONTENTS

List of tables

1 Sediments and soils

One cannot doubt that, somehow, good
Shall come of water and of mud;
And, sure, the reverent eye must see
A purpose in liquidity.

(Rupert Brooke, *Heaven*)

1.1 Introduction

The volume of archaeological data increases each year, partly due to the steadily growing number of 'rescue' (salvage) excavations on sites threatened by development, but the subject still suffers from the lack of a unified methodology, which has led firstly to an unsystematic borrowing of techniques from other disciplines and secondly to the creation of 'archaeological science' which attempts to integrate them. An important step forward was the realization that human communities did not exist *in vacuo* and that information about them could not be obtained simply by a study of cultural debris. It was realized that archaeological information comes in three forms: artefacts, structural remains and ecofacts. Clarke (1978) used the phrase 'environmental subsystem' to describe the interrelationships of the many branches of ecology which comprise the human environment, and a consequent improvement in excavation design and techniques resulted in increasingly sophisticated site description and sampling populations of organic material (ecofacts). The idea that sociocultural systems were inextricably linked to, and in many cases controlled by, their environments has become of increasing importance and palaeoenvironmental reconstructions, the study of crop domestication, dietary variations and disease now form a major part of archaeological science.

Any archaeological site must be seen in its context. The geology of the region controls to a great extent the landscape, soil fertility, vegetation and agriculture. One could represent this relationship very simply as an ecological pyramid (Fig. 1.1) with each layer dependent on the one below, but a better

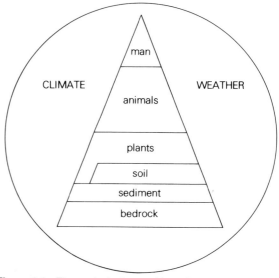

Figure 1.1 The ecological pyramid – a simple model.

model would be the self-regulating system of Clarke (1978) (Fig. 1.2) and Haggett *et al.* (1977).

Barker (1977, p. 274) states that: 'There is a regrettable tendency for the importance of environmental studies to be in inverse proportion to the archaeological results from a site'. This is very true, and it often happens that an excavator who finds much less than he predicted turns to environmental work in order to justify the excavation and make the final report look a little more like value for money. A corollary to this is the regrettable tendency to concentrate on environmental work in inverse proportion to the age of the site, working on the basis that the later the site the more artefactual and/or structural information was likely to be available and the less it would need to be 'boosted' by environmental studies. The later and more complex the

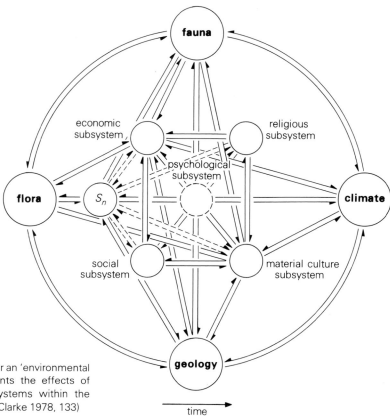

Figure 1.2 Model for an 'environmental system'. Sn represents the effects of alien sociocultural systems within the same territory. (from Clarke 1978, 133)

society the more complex its relationship with its environment (and the more difficult it is to arrive at the correct interpretation of environmental material). On a Palaeolithic site faunas are likely to represent either hunted animals, the remains of the animals that hunted man or 'background' fauna. In the early stages of human evolution man was limited by his environment, but with the advent of food production, tool-making, fire and complex societies he became to a certain extent able to control it. One might argue that after this stage an understanding of the man–environment relationship becomes less critical for our interpretation of the society concerned, but this is far from being the case. Just as Nature abhors· a vacuum, it is impossible to make an interpretation of archaeological evidence without seeing it in its environmental context. The man–land relationship is always important, whatever the age of the site.

The early development of environmental archaeology was assisted by the borrowing of techniques from the biological sciences. It took a longer time for the potential contribution of the Earth sciences to be realized, despite the close relationship between archaeology and geology which has existed since the time of Lyell and Darwin. The final amalgamation of Earth sciences and archaeology has created a field of 'archaeological geology' called, more commonly, **geoarchaeology** (Shackley 1979).

Gladfelter defined 'geoarchaeology' as 'the contribution of Earth sciences, particularly geomorphology and sedimentary petrography, to the interpretation of archaeological contexts' (Gladfelter 1977, p. 519). This means an integration of the Earth sciences and the human past. Geoarchaeological research has been well represented in papers delivered to, for example, the Geological Society of the USA (Hassan 1979) and a division of 'archaeological geology' has now been established within this organization. The discipline is composed of two main fields: first, a study of the **environmental context** of a site and secondly a consideration of the

sedimentary matrix of the archaeological material. Much work has been done on site location and classification. The relationship between site and environment is summarized, for example, in classic studies like Butzer (1971) as well as more recent papers by the same author (Butzer 1974, 1975). Table 1.1 shows a classification of some site contexts, best defined by considering all surviving features of the landscape.

Table 1.1 Geomorphological contexts of sites (after Gladfelter 1977).

	Morphological situation (habitat)	Depositional setting	Principal agent of deposition
interfluve	aeolian sites	open air	wind (volcanics, loess)
	cave sites	open air or protected	mass-wasting
mid-slope	colluvial sites	open air or protected	mass-wasting; solifluxion
	alluvial sites	channel, overbank, basin; deltaic; fan	fluvial
lowland	lacustrine sites	marginal lacustrine; insular	waves
	littoral sites	foreshore, backshore, storm beach, lagoonal–tidal	waves, currents, wind
	(aeolian as above)		

A model for the scope of geoarchaeology is shown in Figure 1.3. Many people have surveyed the application of geomorphological studies (site location, surface topography, geomorphology, drainage patterns, etc.) to archaeology but this falls outside the scope of this book. Here only one field will be considered: the recording, description, sampling and analysis of soils and sediments.

On the sedimentological side much work has been done on the analysis of archaeological deposits and their associated sediments (Hassan 1978) for palaeoenvironmental reconstruction (Farrand 1973, Butzer 1975) and depositional history (Lubell *et al.* 1976). Palaeoenvironmental reconstructions may be based on the geomorphological, stratigraphic and

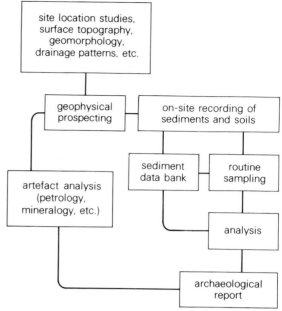

Figure 1.3 A model for **geoarchaeology**; Earth science applications in archaeology.

sedimentological studies in conjunction with the study of soils, fauna, macrobotanical remains and pollen, the first task being to reconstruct the sedimentary environment. The second requirement is a consideration of the climatic-morphogenic environment (tropical, desert, periglacial) and the prehistoric palaeogeography (Kraft *et al.* 1975). Regional stratigraphic studies such as those of Haynes (1968) and Hay (1976) may be used in conjunction with sedimentological analyses, to help understand site-forming processes.

Most people are therefore agreed on the desirability of having some species of 'Earth scientist' in attendance on excavations. The question is, who? What sort of training should they have had and where are they likely to have come from? This matter has been the subject of some interesting survey work carried out in North America in the spring of 1977, by sending out a questionnaire to 193 known 'archaeological geologists' complemented by a list of people who attended conferences or symposia in archaeological science (Society for Archaeological Science 1978). Of the respondents, 58% were university lecturers and a further 40% were employed by the government, in, for example, museums. The most common background disciplines were geomorphology and historical geology (36%), mineralogy and petrology (19%), palaeontology and zoology (14%) and archaeology (13%). This last figure is especially interesting since it differs from the British situation where geoarchaeologists tend to be either university lecturers in archaeological science or archaeology, professional field archaeologists or people with a primarily archaeological background. There are exceptions, however, and some of the most important British geoarchaeological work is published by geographers and pedologists. The questionnaire also asked about the interest and tasks in archaeology-related projects and people cited one or more special concerns as shown in Table 1.2. Only 10% of the respondents were essentially full-time geoarchaeologists and a primary problem was a lack of close consultation before the design of excavations and research strategies. The actual time in which geoarchaeologists attended the field side of their projects was frighteningly small, averaging two weeks per project for 42% of the respondents.

Table 1.2 Geoarchaeological concerns (from Society for Archaeological Science 1978).

	%
palaeoenvironmental reconstruction	58
site stratigraphy	48
geochronology	44
palaeo-geomorphology	40
feature identification/interpretation	20
artefact analysis or general prehistoric question	16
geophysical site prospecting	9
remote sensing	6
other	9

Of course the limitations of this survey for our purposes are immediately obvious. Firstly, it was confined to North America, where the archaeological work and research funding is carried out on quite a different basis from Great Britain. Less use is made of volunteer help, more attention is paid to specialist co-operation in excavations and the appropriate funding is more readily available. Secondly, it was dealing with the whole field of geoarchaeology, including the study of sediments and soils, and we do not have a statistical breakdown of the number of people specifically engaged in this work. Thirdly, the survey was project-orientated, whereas in

Britain much geoarchaeological work tends to be site-orientated, a situation that is a direct result of the emphasis on rescue (salvage) excavation over research projects. The survey does tend to illuminate a very important difference, exemplified in a paper by Rapp (1975), who argued that geologists, if given sufficient archaeological training, are better equipped than anyone to deal with all the problems posed by the stratigraphy of a site. Few would deny that, but in Britain we tend to view archaeological scientists (including geoarchaeologists) as archaeologists with scientific tendencies rather than scientists with archaeological tendencies. In the United States the opposite is true. However, in both countries problem orientation, whether of fieldwork, excavation or environmental studies, has replaced the random approach of the 1950s and 1960s, as a result of increasingly sophisticated techniques, more knowledge, larger scale operations and an increasingly constricted budget.

Archaeological excavation differs from other scientific research in that postulated theories cannot be tested by the setting up of exact duplicate experiments. The development of excavation techniques from the simple keeping of structural records to excavations with drawn baulk-sections was an important step forward, but more recent trends towards a concentration of recording emphasis on plans rather than sections has produced problems. Whilst plans are clearly vital to give a whole picture of what is happening on site, the section is equally vital to see the stratigraphic sequence; it is almost impossible to visualize (let alone sample) a sequence without having it in front of you. A combination of methods, the cumulative section of Barker (1977, p. 80), is the answer, as a reasonable alternative to a permanent on-site sedimentologist/pedologist.

Understanding of the principles of stratigraphy is fundamental to excavation and to interpretation but comparatively little is known about the process actually involved in the build-up of a site: the gradual (or sudden) accumulation of the many different kinds of sediment or soil which must be peeled off by the excavator to reconstruct the sequence. Although artefacts and structures can be used as a means of obtaining relative dates for sequence accumulation, little is known about the calibration details of accumulation. Recent experimental work on earthworks and pits (see Section 2.3) has shed some light on process types and rates in closed contexts but much remains to be done. We all know, for example, that an earthwork will settle, a wall will crack and the contour of a feature will change, but if these processes are gradual then calibration of change rates is difficult. In some cases one can extrapolate backwards. The writer has observed monasteries in the Far East which were constructed of sun-dried mud brick, tied together by mud mortar and keyed together by a system similar to that used on the bricks of pre-pottery Neolithic B buildings at Jericho and the lintels of Stonehenge. The monasteries were abandoned at a known date during the Revolution (1929–31) and it would be possible, by excavating them, to observe the disintegration of a building and the accumulation of material in a known climatic régime over a short period of time. All the necessary evidence is present, the climatic records, plans of the former structures and details of the functions of precise buildings, even eye-witness accounts of the way in which the site was used. However, an unrealistic element is introduced since the sites have been unoccupied since their abandonment, meaning that the disturbance and compaction which would have been most important in the gradual build-up of long term urban sites are absent. It is suggested, however, that such studies may be useful in forming a basis for sediment accumulation calibration on sites, as well as to complement studies of building decay similar to those already undertaken in Africa, but it will be difficult to generalize from such observations to reconstruct site formation processes.

Various questions can be asked of each archaeological deposit. First, where did the material come from? Secondly, how did it reach the site? Thirdly, how long did it take? A fourth question is rarely considered except in cases where there is obvious compaction or some evidence of chemical change, for example the formation of an iron pan. This question is, what happened afterwards? All post-depositional (diagenetic) processes are important since they affect the nature of the sediment which we see, and the answers to the first three questions posed above. Diagenetic processes will often be important due to their effect on buried artefacts. It is unfortunate, but true, that 99% of archaeological effort is expended on structures (*sensu lato*) and artefacts. Of the remaining 1%, most is concentrated on the recovery and interpretation of biological material and very little on a study of the actual dirt surrounding the artefacts. Yet it is this pay-dirt which we so carelessly throw away which may answer a series of vital questions. A geologist does not attempt to describe a fossil without reference to its surrounding material, and one should not consider either artefacts or structures without their sedimentary context. Regrettably, since our understanding of the processes at work is limited, much provision must be made for future better-informed workers in a variety of ways: leaving sites partially unexcavated, emphasizing the standardization of recording techniques and ensuring that the most detailed quantifiable recording system possible is used to perform the function of a data bank for the future. The initiation and use of standardized on-site recording methods for sediments and soils is one of the most important geoarchaeological developments of recent years (p. 12). The system chosen must use standard terms, compatible between sites and indeed between countries. It must be easy to work with, simple to understand by untrained labour, easy to record, capable of infinite extension, complemented by a visual record and stored permanently as part of the site records. The systematic recording of 'dirt' is a first stage; the second stage is to decide what problems are posed by the stratigraphy and how they may best be solved. This will involve reasoned, careful, problem-orientated sampling followed by reasoned, careful, problem-orientated laboratory analysis. The results will be significant not only to solve existing archaeological problems but also to produce a *corpus* of new hypotheses.

A sediment is a collection of mineral or rock particles which have been weathered or eroded from their primary context and redeposited elsewhere. The nature of a sediment depends on the nature of the parent rock, the distance and means of transport, the environment of deposition and post-depositional processes (diagenesis). Literature is to be found in the journals of geomorphology, sedimentary petrology and pedology (if the sediment has been modified to form a soil (p. 7)).

We may define an archaeological sediment as 'a deposit which is directly or indirectly related to past human activity' (Shackley 1975). This descriptive definition includes a wide range of sediments produced, influenced or modified by man, from loess deposits to occupation floors in urban sites. Figure 1.4 illustrates some of the questions asked of archaeological sediments. 'Forensic' geoarchaeology often involves the analysis of an individual deposit in answer to a request for information concerning (generally) its mode of deposition or origin (Fig. 1.4). The archaeologist may also want to know how long a particular deposit took to form, whether or not it could have been influenced by cultural factors in the neighbourhood and what influence it exerted over artefact preservation. One is frequently asked to give a rough idea of the formation rate of deposits within complex stratigraphic sequences and in some cases this may be possible. In some cases it is vital to know the source of the deposit. Although it is rare for the material at a given point on an archaeological site to be absolutely allochthonous, yet its point of origin may be only a metre or so away. It is thus important to distinguish materials brought

from some distance, either by man or by some natural agency. An example of such a study may be seen at Carthage, where excavations on the Ilôt d'Amirauté (see Section 1.5.3) revealed the wooden foundations for Punic ship-sheds which would once have surrounded the island.

Autochthonous deposits are also of interest, especially when they occur in locations (such as caves) where one may be relatively sure that they have been undisturbed. Cave sediments were among the first archaeological deposits to be investigated (Bonifay 1962) because caves were preferred living sites for early man. Splendid examples of interdisciplinary research projects may be seen in the caves of central and southern France, where teams composed of archaeologists, Earth scientists, palynologists and zoologists have combined to produce detailed and complex records of palaeoenvironmental fluctuations during the Riss and Würm (Bordes 1972, de Lumley 1972, Laville 1973). Although it has been pointed out that under certain environmental conditions cave sedimentation may bear little or no relationship to palaeoclimatic variations (Shackley 1978b), this is the exception rather than the rule in European climates. Each feature of an ancient environment is relevant to the archaeologist who is studying the remains of cultures already biased by the vast sampling errors introduced by time and preservation.

It is very important to differentiate 'natural' from man-made sedimentary contexts, since this is clearly vital when evaluating archaeological material or sites. Particle size analysis has been one of the tools most frequently used, together with an examination of grain surface texture and sediment fabric (see Section 1.5.3). The survey mentioned above (p. 4) also produced information on the various laboratory techniques used by geoarchaeologists (Table 1.3) and it was found that some 62% of the time allowed for each individual project was spent in the laboratory.

Of those using particle size analysis for archaeological sediments, 70% employed dry sieving, 44% wet sieving, 39% pipette analysis and 35% hydrometers. These methods are discussed in detail below (see Section 1.3).

Soil has been defined in many ways, for example as a 'medium in which plants grow', or 'products of

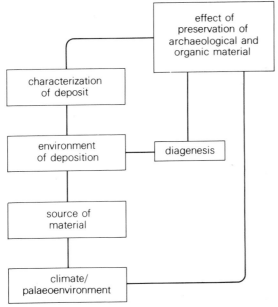

Figure 1.4 Jobs for geoarchaeologists. The most frequent questions asked concern the nature of a deposit ('what is it'), how it arrived at the site (environment of deposition) and where it originally came from (source of material). The effect of diagenesis must be taken into account and linked to any modification of buried artefacts and ecofacts since their deposition.

Table 1.3 Techniques used in laboratory analysis (after Society for Archaeological Science 1978).

Laboratory techniques	%
ceramic/glass analysis, mineralogy, petrography, optical microscopy, scanning electron microscopy, X-ray	40
isotopic dating	38
particle size analysis	24
palynology/botany	12
non-isotopic archaeometric dating	10
palaeontology	3

the decomposition of the land surface under the influence of weather and vegetation'. A soil is a sediment which has been weathered and altered *in situ* and whose vertical section shows interior zonation, horizontal divisions as a result of the movement of constituents through the profile. The zones are characterized as follows:

(a) A horizon. Often humus rich. An eluvial zone where leaching and other processes remove the components by washing through.
(b) B horizon. Illuvial zone of accumulation of the components removed from the A horizon.
(c) C horizon. Weathered but intact bedrock.

Subsidiary horizons are given numbers and letters. All soils are technically sediments but not all sediments are soils, unless they have been subjected to the processes of pedogenesis which include the addition of organic matter from plant growth. Soils are grouped together into classes on the basis of shared characteristics (see Section 1.3.6). The interpretation of palaeosols (soils formed in a past landscape) rests on an understanding of how soil-forming processes operate in modern soils and at what speed (Burhmans 1973). Four types of map are important when studying sediments and soils: maps of the solid geology, drift geology, soil and topography, but they are not available everywhere. The archaeologist may be fortunate enough to be working in an area where the soils have been surveyed, and soil maps produced together with their accompanying memoirs. Those of the Soil Survey of Great Britain, for example, are very helpful indeed and are based on the 1 : 25 000 and 1 : 63 360 Ordnance Survey Maps. (This last is in itself a great advantage – anyone who has tried matching up the

old Geological Survey maps of Great Britain with topographic Ordnance Survey maps will have noted differences in scale and projection which are incredibly frustrating and require much juggling.) Soil maps are available for many other countries in the world but are often printed on a smaller scale. Their availability is also subject to 'Murphy's law', which states (among other things) that the likelihood of something being available decreases in relationship to the amount that you need it. However, if such maps are available they will generally be found to be published by the government department concerned. Excellent reference collections may be found in England in the central libraries of the Royal Geographical Society and the Geological Society of London, with subsidiary collections in county archives and university libraries. Every map published in Britain is available at the copyright libraries (e.g. the Bodleian Library, Oxford) and the reference collections of the Ordnance Survey at its Southampton headquarters. The greatest benefit may be obtained from such maps if they are taken out into the field and studied in relationship to the actual appearance of the ground, digging small test pits to examine the profiles where necessary or possible and making use of accidental exposures in ditches or quarries. The Soil Survey of the United States, CSIRO (Australia) and CSIR (South Africa) also have very large soil map collections. As in Britain, most soil survey work is carried out by government departments whose staff are often very helpful in providing advice and occasionally equipment.

1.2 Fieldwork and sampling

1.2.1 Field description

Close co-operation between Earth scientists and archaeologists is required in the study of archaeological deposits. Such study requires, primarily, good field description and recording, sampling and the posing of questions followed by selective problem-orientated laboratory analysis. The results of such work are then available to assist in the interpretation of the site or project being worked, and in the framing of new questions. Such work requires either full-time collaboration on site or pre-excavation consultation, collaboration in the design of recording and sampling strategies and post-excavation analysis and feedback. The former is much the better course but generally impractical in terms of time and funding.

Two schools of thought exist over the nature and use of site recording systems for archaeological sediments. One, the pessimists, say that 'accurate' on-site recording is impossible and therefore should not be undertaken since by the time the information is published it is already obsolete. The optimists argue that it is important to try and record all relevant sediment characteristics at the time of the excavation in order to give the maximum amount of potential data for synthesis and interpretation. If it is not possible for the Earth scientist to be available throughout the excavation, a programme of description and sampling should be worked out and full visual coverage such as drawings and photographs must be provided. In many cases the questions asked from the sediments will be very simple. Excavators often first require confirmation (or denial) of visual interpretations, for example whether two layers are indeed very similar in composition or whether a layer which appears on a different part of the site is identical or not to one which is regarded as a continuation of it. The contents of the sediments may be important; the identification of often microscopic fragments of building materials, or industrial debris, may be of great help to the excavator. Simple questions such as, 'Is the black colour of this layer due to burning or does it represent the remains of organic material?' require only a microscopic examination and perhaps one or two chemical tests. More complicated questions such as, 'Is this material wind-blown and if so where did it come from?' may involve a whole battery of tests including particle size analysis and an examination of heavy mineral content. It is not for the excavator to specify the tests; he merely asks the questions and provides the necessary background information. But it is difficult and quite undesirable for an Earth scientist to work on material seen only out of context. Site visits (including pre-excavation planning) are essential, as is mutual understanding of the recording and sampling methods to be used, and of the type of information which may be obtained. Various hallowed archaeological terms will be dis-

carded during the course of such collaborations, for example the ubiquitous use of the word 'the natural' (meaning undisturbed rock or subsoil) will provoke hoots of laughter from Earth scientists unused to the terminology who will point out, correctly, that most archaeological sediments and soils are natural. However, the term is part of the intrinsic vocabulary of the subject and seems unlikely to be replaced. Its use is discussed by Limbrey (1975), but it must be avoided if possible.

Full description of sediments or soils requires only a pair of hands, a set of standard terms, some common sense and a collection of Munsell charts. The idea of using standard descriptions is to reduce the range of subjective assessment of sediment and/ or soil characteristics. All Earth scientists will be aware of the widespread ignorance of simple facts; silt, for example, is a term used to describe a specific particle size grain of sediment *not* a mode of deposition. Such errors can be avoided by using the standard terminology which avoids such descriptions as the famous colours quoted by Cornwall (1958).

Colour. Sediment colour may be primary (from the source material) and/or diagenetic (through alteration), for example as a result of the effect of groundwater phenomena such as oxidation–reduction mottling, or subaerial processes such as biochemical alteration. The Munsell soil colour charts are undoubtedly the best method of describing colour, although cheaper Japanese versions are available. The possession of a set of Munsell charts should be a first priority with excavators, even if this is difficult, since they are far from cheap. Reading a colour from a chart may make one miss out on the charming (if subjective) verbal descriptions but it standardizes and quantifies the colour by reference to three properties: the **hue** (dominant spectral colour), **value** (lightness), and **chroma** (degree of greyness). The sediment is compared with colour chips on the cards (Fig. 1.5) (protected by a plastic film) until the chip nearest in colour is found. The notation is read off and the corresponding verbal description given. A set of charts is available bound in a ring-binder and sufficient for most British sediments; additional sheets may be bought to cover more exotic areas with a wider colour range. Most British soils fall within

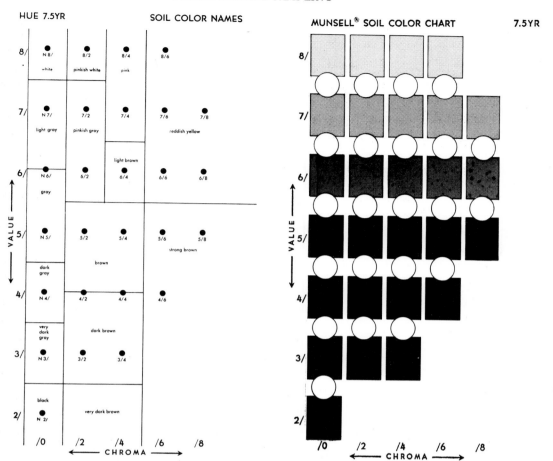

Figure 1.5 Sheet 7.5 YR, Munsell soil colour charts. A sediment sample is compared with the coloured chips on the right-hand side of the chart and a notation to describe the colour read. This may then be translated into a verbal description by consulting the categories on the left.

the red (R) and yellow (Y) hue ranges, a separate card being available for each hue. The notation of colour is made using the formula

hue value/chroma, description.

Thus a soil colour might be noted as 7.5YR 7/2, pinkish grey. Variables are introduced by the light in which the colour is being studied, the dampness of the sediment and operator variability. No two people see colour the same way and tests have shown that even just one person will record different notations for the same sediment at different times of day. Minimum error is introduced by having all colours recorded by the same person, preferably at the same time of day and in similar conditions of dampness. In British conditions it is easier to record site colours from damp sediments than dry, but the moisture content of the sediment should be noted. The best time is in the mid-morning when there is optimum light and the operator has not yet tired of the process (repeatability of results declines sharply after lunch). The colour must always be recorded from a freshly broken (not smeared) chunk.

Texture. Field determination of sediment texture may be made by hand using the results expressed on the scale (Table 1.4). Grain shape may be described and considered in relation to transport, erosion and weathering (Farrand 1975) to assess transport conditions and different kinds of gravel types. The arrangement of particles using petrofabric analysis

Table 1.4 Scales for particle size analysis.

d_A (mm)	φ scale	Udden (1914)	Wentworth (1922)	British Standard
64	−6		cobbles	cobbles
45.3	−5.5	boulders		
32	−5			
22.6	−4.5		pebbles	gravel
16.0	−4			
11.2	−3.5			
8.0	−3	gravel		
5.65	−2.5			
4.00	−2			
2.82	−1.5		granules	
2.00	−1			
1.41	−0.5	coarse	very coarse	coarse
1.00	0			
0.700	+0.5	medium	coarse	
0.500	+1	sand	sand	sand
0.354	+1.5	fine	medium	medium
0.251	+2			
0.178	+2.5	very fine	fine	
0.124	+3			fine
0.088	+3.5	very coarse	very fine	
0.062	+4			
0.044	+4.5	coarse		coarse
0.031	+5	silt		
0.022	+5.5	fine	silt	silt
0.016	+6			medium
0.011	+6.5	very fine		
0.0078	+7			
0.0055	+7.5	very coarse		
0.0039	+8	clay		fine
0.0028	+8.5	coarse	clay	
0.002	+9	fine		clay
0.0014	+9.5			

may produce information on sediment and/or artefact movement (Section 1.5) and surface textures of quartz grains are related to depositional environment (Section 1.5.3). The classification of sediment texture is accomplished by assessing the 'feel' of the damp material and calculating relative proportions of coarse sand, fine sand, silt and clay, and the soil given its texture name according to the proportion of these groups present. The material is worked between the fingers and thumb and a textural description made. The basic types are characterized as follows (Shackley 1975) and further refinements may be found in Avery and Bascomb (1974):

(a) *Sand*. A loose and clean-grained material, of grain size 4–0.5 φ. If a dry sample is squeezed in the hand, it will fall apart when the pressure is released. Coarse sand (grain diameter 1–0.5 φ) has grains which 'grate' against each other in the hand sample, and which can easily be detected visually. In fine sand this effect is much less obvious, but the individual grains should still be distinguishable.

(b) *Silt*. Silt is finer-textured than sand and has rather a 'silky' feel. It may be slightly gritty, but the individual grains will not be distinguishable without the aid of a hand lens. The sediment will form a 'sludge' when wet.

(c) *Clay*. A clay forms hard lumps or clods when dry, but when moist is sticky, cohesive and plastic. It will form excellent casts, and has a grain diameter less than 8 φ.

The presence of a great deal of organic matter in a sediment tends to make it feel more clay-rich, and the presence of much calcium carbonate, as in very chalky deposits, imitates the feel of silt. It is rare to find sediments composed entirely of sand, silt or clay, rather than combinations of the three in different proportions.

(d) *Sandy loam*. A sediment which contains mostly sand but has enough silt and clay to make it cohesive. It will form a cast when moist, but the cast is easily broken. A true sandy loam contains 50% sand, 30% silt and 20% clay.

(e) *Loam*. Loam feels rather gritty in the hand, but has a reasonably smooth texture and is rather plastic. The moist sediment will form a good cast, and is composed of nearly equal parts of silt and sand, with about half their amounts of clay.

(f) *Silt loam*. This has a slightly silky feel, and will form clods when dry. The lumps are easily broken, the resulting material being rather soft and floury. Wet silt loam will form a thick 'sludge' and make good casts. It contains at least 50% of sand and silt together with 12–25% clay.

(g) *Clay loam*. A clay loam is a fine-textured deposit which will readily break up into clods or lumps that are hard when dry. The moist sediment is plastic and cohesive, and contains nearly equal amounts of sand and clay.

Coherence and cementation. **Coherence** is the strength of the bonds between the individual grains, measured on the scale in Table 1.5. **Cementation** is a measure of the degree to which the grains have been chemically bonded together by something other than clay minerals (Table 1.6). Common cementing media are calcium carbonate or iron oxides. An iron or manganese pan (p. 31) is an example of a very strong cementation.

Table 1.5 Coherence.

A. *moist sediments*
0 = non-coherent
1 = very friable (crumbles under gentle pressure)
2 = friable (crumbles under moderate pressure)
3 = firm (crumbles under moderate pressure, with noticeable resistance)
4 = very firm (crumbles under strong pressure but is difficult to crush between the fingers)
5 = extremely firm (crumbles only under very strong pressure and must be broken apart bit by bit)

B. *dry sediments*
0 = loose (non-coherent)
1 = soft (weakly coherent and fragile, breaks under light pressure)
2 = slightly hard (weakly resistant to pressure and easily broken between thumb and fingers)
3 = hard (resistant to pressure. Can be broken in the hand but difficult to break between thumb and forefinger)
4 = very hard (only broken in the hand with difficulty)
5 = extremely hard (cannot be broken in the hand)

Table 1.6 Cementation.

(a) *weakly cemented* (brittle and hard but can be broken in the hand)
(b) *strongly cemented* (brittle but cannot be broken in the hand)
(c) *very strongly cemented* (will require a strong hammer blow to break)

Structures. Figure 1.6 shows some typical soil *structures* (defined as ways in which soil materials arrange themselves). Such structures may be developed to various extents and some soils will be structureless, consisting simply of a coherent mass. The nature of the boundaries between horizons must be noted, which may sometimes be blurred and indistinct where mixing has been taking place while on other occasions it will be very sharp. Care must be taken to distinguish between the identification of a true boundary between stratigraphically distinct layers and the identification of a pan (e.g. iron, manganese or calcite) which occurs within a bed (p. 31).

Boundaries between beds are best described by reference to the nomenclature of the USDA 7th Soil Approximation (United States Department of Agriculture 1960), which has four categories of vertical distinctiveness.

Recording. Various aids are available for drawing sections, including the use of standard symbols, which must of course be adjusted in size in relation to the scale of the drawing. The use of filters may assist in bringing out various sediment colours in photographic recording, a yellow–green filter being especially useful. The use of a blue filter can bring out post-holes as darker stains, or this may sometimes be achieved by damping. Olsen (1968) in the excavation of the Viking fortress of Trellbørg used a method of staining the sediment with hydrochloric acid and potassium sulphocyanate, which goes red in the presence of ferric iron. White (1971) discussed the difficulty of illustrating the kind of detail shown in soil pits and suggested that this could be overcome by using selected grey density slices of original photographs. The technique involves the separate printing of a particular shade of grey from the original and picks out the detail required – helpful for 'marker' layers. A wide angle lens may be required for distance shots and a macro lens for close work. White and Hayes (1961) described the use of stereo-colour paired photographs as a means of recording, but this is too sophisticated for most archaeological work, and too expensive except in special cases. Brongers (1965) describes a method of recording a soil silhouette (p. 34) with ultra-violet light which relies on the presence of uncremated bone fluorescing and showing on the print. The photographic recording of sediments is also dealt with in general works on archaeological photography (see, for example, Conlon 1973).

There are two distinct schools of thought concerning precisely which member of an excavation team should be responsible for on-site recording. Limbrey, for example, is of the opinion that the recording of sediments and soils should be carried out by the trowellers who are in intimate contact with the material, rather than by more remote supervisors or directors (Limbrey 1975). The advantages of having sedimentary changes recorded by trowellers are legion but so, unfortunately, are the

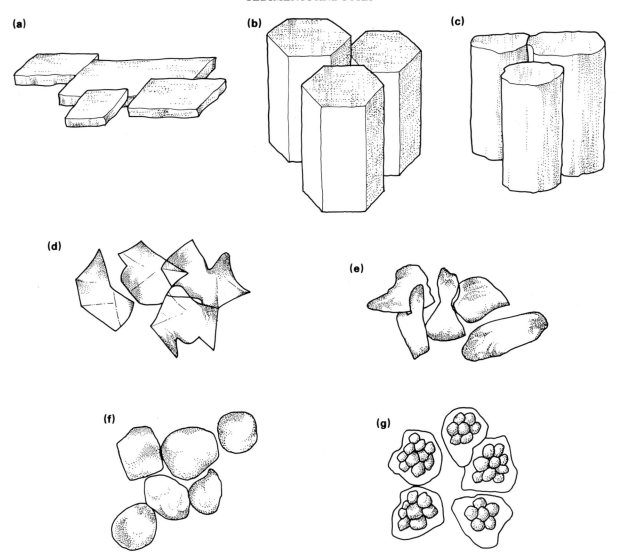

Figure 1.6 Shapes of particles used in soil and sediment description. (a) Platy; (b) prismatic; (c) columnar; (d) angular blocky; (e) subangular blocky; (f) granular; (g) crumbs.

disadvantages. The main objection is that by having many people recording sequences there is a lack of standardization; no two people, for example, record colour in the same way. The likelihood of record cards and sheets being poorly or inaccurately filled in is greater if this is carried out at below supervisory level. It also slows up the pace of work. In the writer's opinion it is better to have one person with overall responsibility for environmental recording and sampling, a combination of archaeological technician and specialist liaison officer with (preferably) some training and a good awareness of the problems involved. With all environmental sampling being co-ordinated by one person the likelihood of missing record cards, badly packed samples and inadequate interdisciplinary co-ordination is reduced. Because of financial problems it is unlikely that such a person will be able solely to do this job, except in very large excavations, but it is better combined with a 'dry' job (planning or small finds) rather than a 'wet' one (trowelling).

Site recording systems are either visual (drawings,

DOE Central Unit **Context Record**

01 Grid ref	02 Site sub div	03 Site code	04 Context no.

05 Category

06 Length	07 Width	08 Diameter	09 Height/depth

Soils	10 Matrix colour
	11 Matrix texture
	12 Matrix consistence
	13 Coarse components

Structures	14 Matrix
	15 Constituents

16 Description

Relationships	17 Part of
	18 Contains
	19 Same as
	20 Below
	21 Above
	22 Cuts
	23 Cut by
	24 Uncertain
	25 Butts
	26 Butted by
	27 Bonded to

28 Interpretive comments

29 Plan no.	30 Section no.	Photo (M)	Photo (C)
Super	Excav	Passed	
Flotation	Samples	Continuation sheet	

Figure 1.7 A record card for archaeological contexts. This format is used by the central excavation unit (after Hirst 1976).

sections, photographs) or written (record cards, notebooks, punched cards, etc.). The chosen system must make the storage, interpretation and publication of data as easy as possible and maximize the understanding and use of the data by others. A standard sediment-recording format should be used for each site, adapted to particular needs and problems. General information to be recorded on each record card will include details of position, site name, grid reference, locality and date, stratigraphic location and numbers, shape, dimensions and character of the layer and name of person responsible for the record. Simple descriptions of texture and colour may be reinforced with notations of other factors, e.g. included stone size or degree of disturbance, and the presence or absence of root holes. The participants at many large excavations are now finding it easier to computerize their data, including layer descriptions, which may either be done in the field directly on to computer coding sheets or cards, or after the excavation from notebooks. The former is greatly preferable. In the main, computerized schemes are most popular where the site consists largely of 'closed' collections of stratigraphic units such as pits, post-holes or ditches, rather than the vast areas of interdigitating vertical strata composing an 'open' site. At Hamwih (Holdsworth 1980) separate record cards were kept for animal bone and pit records (the latter including coding for pit type, volume and relationships) and pottery. For each layer, details of the samples taken and the presence or absence of various categories of information and small finds were noted. It is essential to store information such as the plan number, photograph numbers, section and sample numbers with the sediment descriptions and a preliminary interpretation of the deposit. Barker (1977, p. 144) describes a system for recording a single context (or feature) sheet using just a space for 'Description of context', the Munsell numbers and details of position, interpretation and finds. Feature cards used at the Cadbury–Congresbury excavation go into more detail (Fig. 1.7). A similar system was used at the pilot scheme for the Iron Age hillfort site of Danebury (Hampshire), where coding systems were devised for pit fill types, layer shapes, relationships and various physical parameters in an effort to understand the relationship between the shape and fill of a large collection of Iron Age pits (Shackley 1975). After various questions had been asked of the pilot scheme it was found possible to simplify recording methods for integration into a central computerized scheme while retaining very detailed information about stratigraphy in a separate computer subroutine to be recalled if necessary. Jeffries (1977) describes the methods used by the Central Excavation Unit for recording sediments, adapted from Hodgson (1964). Characteristics recorded include colour, texture, consistency and coarse components – the recording form (Fig. 1.7) being accompanied by a manual to assist excavators.

1.2.2 Sampling

The sampling methods required by Earth scientists are often at odds with the excavation techniques of 'area' or 'plan' type such as those of Barker (1977). It is sometimes possible (if unpopular) to leave a column for sampling but infinitely preferable to

have the earth scientist present for the whole duration of the dig. In a masterpiece of understatement Limbrey (1975, p. 273) said that 'a well studied section should have a ragged and well-used appearance, not the smart and polished look so beloved of some excavators. Obviously, photographs of the whole rather than of details have to be taken before the beginning of detailed examination.' At the 1978 meeting of the Society for American Archaeology a notice was posted which announced the formation of a soil 'bank'. Its purpose was to acquire a research collection of soil samples from a wide variety of cultural sites and environmental settings and to encourage biogeochemical work on archaeology-related material. The bank will act as a clearing house for soil standards, analytical data files and information on related research, new instrumentation and facilities. These collections are available to members and will operate like an ordinary bank. The Society has also compiled index and details of geoarchaeologists with lists of publications and research interests, an important step towards good collaboration. The 'bank' system has been tried before on various sites, for example the excavations at Carthage (p. 23), where the writer recommended the establishment of a sediment data bank where samples are automatically kept from each archaeological stratum. This has proved invaluable where it was impossible for the Earth scientist to be present during the whole excavation and where post-excavation questions are asked of strata that are, of course, no longer present. This might be called

Figure 1.8 Excavations at the Ilôt de L'Amirauté at Carthage, Tunisia, showing the line of postholes filled with clean beach sand.

'forensic' geoarchaeology – questions asked include such topics as the presence of building or industrial debris which is important in, for example, the detection of destruction levels or gaining some indication of the use of a particular structure.

Stout plastic bags, a tape, clean trowel, spatulae, ample supplies of packing materials, labels and kitchen roll are all the equipment necessary for sampling. An alternative sampling method is the monolith tin (p. 31), preferably an aluminium tin lined with plastic measuring approximately 500 mm × 150 mm × 150 mm and hammered into the face. Orientation must be marked on the tin, which is then sealed with foil and placed in a large plastic bag. Such a monolith is sometimes useful for an especially interesting or tricky profile but should not be used for coarse material or unconsolidated deposits or where there is a very great distance to be traversed with the sample, which may be very heavy. Limbrey (1975) recommends the packing of soil samples in aluminium foil to prevent the structure being mashed, before bagging for transport. The orientation of the sample can be marked on the foil and the soil allowed to dry out slowly in the laboratory. This has many advantages over the plastic bag method for the study of consolidated sediments as well as for soils, but for loose material two layers of plastic bags (stout, heavy duty) with a label in between the layers and another tied round the neck of the bag cannot be improved. Labels should *never* be placed inside bags and the necks of plastic bags should never be knotted but fastened with string or bag closures. Details of the United States preferred methods for on-site description and sampling may be seen in the USDA bulletin (United States Department of Agriculture 1960). The size of the sample required is directly proportional to the coarseness of the sediment; the finer the sediment the smaller the sample. The laboratory test requiring the largest sample size is grain size analysis, so, if a sufficiently large sample to permit accurate measurement of the particle size distribution is taken, the addition of a little more should be sufficient for all routine tests. Approximate sample sizes and particle coarseness values are given in Table 1.7. It is much better to take a larger bulk sample and split it in the laboratory with a riffle box or rotary sample splitter than to take small sub-

samples in the field and have to recombine them. Samples should be taken with clean tools from a freshly cleaned, unsmeared, vertical section, sampling from the bottom upwards at predetermined intervals. A general rule is that the faster the sediments have been deposited the wider apart the sampling intervals may be. When sampling at, for example, 100 mm intervals it is important that the sampling point should be dug *into* the face and not taken from around the point by surface scraping, as this reduces the interval and increases the error. Samples may also be taken by augering or coring if this cannot be avoided. A simple screw-auger may be very useful in giving a rough indication of the nature of the underlying material or the depth at which bedrock is likely to be reached. Laboratory samples should not be taken from augered sediment since they will have become contaminated in the process of extraction. The difficulty of turning a screw-auger increases with depth and sediment consistency; in order to probe through thick clay to anything over 1 m several people will be required. Wet deposits are also not suitable for augering. Pollen samples are frequently obtained by peat borers (Fig. 4.2) which may also be used for obtaining samples of inorganic sediments. Many different models are available (West 1968, Faegri & Iversen 1965, Wright *et al.* 1965) for different types of sediment and different sampling situations. It is rare but not unknown that deep bore samples are required in an archaeological context; when this is the case hand-held samplers have generally been used in preference to more sophisticated (and expensive) rig-mounted systems. In certain rare cases it may be either necessary or desirable to preserve the surface layers of a section by applying a chemical and peeling off the dried film with its adhering thin layers of sediment. This can never be used to replace either section drawing or sampling, but has been useful when, for example, a profile with dramatic impact has been required to illustrate some specific point. It is not a routine procedure. For small sections a monolith tin will be perfectly adequate, but in some large excavations, for example in Near Eastern **tell** sequences (Franken 1965), the hundreds of very thin superimposed layers have been recorded in this way. The deposits must be fine grained and without salient pebbles. The chemicals used to produce a peel include celluloid + acetate mixture, polyvinyl acetate (West 1968) and commercial plastics of the type used for sealing floors.

Table 1.7 Approximate sample sizes required for accurate particle size analysis of sediments.

Particle diameter (mm)	Minimum weight required (kg)
64	50
50	35
40	15
25	5
20	2
12.5	1
10	0.5
5	0.2

1.3 Laboratory analysis

The various techniques useful for the laboratory analysis of archaeological soils and sediments have been described elsewhere (Shackley 1975) but are summarized here to provide a background for understanding the analytical applications considered below (Section 1.5). A preliminary step is the examination of a sample under a binocular microscope for the presence of included material (ash, burnt debris, slag, building material, bones, etc.). This is best done in two stages, after the sample has been dried (in a slow oven at 50 °C if it does not contain organic material) and secondly after the fine clay fraction which coats the rest of the grains has been removed by wet sieving through a 63 μm sieve. Other necessary preliminary treatments may include ultrasonic disaggregation (never used if the grain surface texture is to be examined), dispersion in suspension using sodium hexametaphosphate in 10% solution, removal of organic matter with 15% hydrogen peroxide (H_2O_2), of carbonates using 10% hydrochloric acid (HCl) and iron oxides with aluminium and concentrated oxalic acid (Catt & Weir 1975). Further tests may be *physical* or *chemical* and on the whole the latter will require more sophisticated apparatus.

1.3.1 Surface texture

The surface texture of a grain may help to distinguish its origin and depositional history. For this the high magnification of a scanning electron micro-scope rather than a light microscope is needed. Krinsley and Doornkamp (1973) provide characteristics and specimen photographs of the surface textures of sand grains from a wide variety of environments (Table 1.8). Brown (1973) casts doubt on their working hypotheses but archaeological applications have been made on cave sediments and pottery (p. 23). After pretreatment 50 grains less than 200 μm (2 φ) in diameter are mounted on a specimen stub with silver paint or glue and a thin coat of gold applied in a vacuum evaporator before insertion in the scanning electron microscope.

1.3.2 Particle size analysis

Particle size analysis of a sediment is one of the most useful ways of obtaining information about its

Table 1.8 Diagenetic surface characteristics of quartz sand grains (after Krinsley & Doornkamp 1973).

marine, fluviatile and lacustrine environments

High-energy (surf)	medium- and low-energy
(a) V-shaped patterns of irregular orientation	(1) 'en echelon' V-shaped indentations at low energy; as energy increases, random orientated V-patterns replace them.
(b) straight or slightly curved grooves	
(c) blocky conchoidal breakage patterns	

aeolian

tropical desert	coastal dune
(a) meandering ridges	(1) meandering ridges
(b) graded arcs	(2) graded arcs
(c) chemical or mechanical action giving regular pitted surfaces replacing the above features in many cases	(3) disc-shaped depressions
(d) upturned cleavage plates and well-rounded grains	

glacial

normal	glacial-fluvial
(a) large variations in size of conchoidal breakage patterns	(1) rounding of the normal glacial patterns
(b) very high relief	
(c) semi-paralleled and arc-shaped steps. Parallel striations of varying length	
(d) imbricated breakage blocks which look like a series of steeply dipping hogback ridges	
(e) irregular small-scale indentations associated with conchoidal breakage patterns	
(f) prismatic patterns	

characteristics. Accurate analysis produces information on the **agent** of deposition (wind, water, sea), the **process** and **environment** of deposition and **diagenesis**. Dozens of methods are available but the technique is no longer so fashionable now as it was, geologists having progressed out of the doldrums of the 1960s when a particle size analysis was a general panacea for all ills. Articles in recent issues of the *Journal of Sedimentary Petrology* discuss problems which were not at first taken into account, but it is generally accepted that a good particle size analysis may certainly be a means to a conclusion, but not an end in its own right. The questions being asked of archaeological sediments are often similar to those demanded of sediments which have never been affected by man, but man is an unquantifiable influence in sedimentation and any sediment that has been connected in any way with human activity will not be in a 'natural' state. Some allowance must be made for this fact when processing the results of analyses. It is rare that particle size analysis is used alone; there are many instances of it being combined with micromorphological examination or various chemical tests to sort out difficult sedimentary sequences (see Section 1.5.2).

Particles of sediment differ from each other by minute size gradations along a continuum which may be divided somewhat arbitrarily into grades which refer only to particle *sizes* not mineral types (Table 1.4). For a granulometric analysis the sample is first split, pretreated, analysed and then the results are evaluated. They may be expressed on a triangular diagram (Folk 1954) or a semi-pictorial graph (Shackley 1972), or as statistical measures of the size distribution curve obtained by plotting the results of the analyses on arithmetic probability paper, producing a curve and describing its shape statistically (Fig. 1.15). There is a vast literature on the interpretation of such graphs, often with conflicting views, and by far the majority of such archaeological work has been carried out on cave sediments. The many techniques available include dry sieving, wet sieving, pipette analysis and hydrometer analysis for suspensions of fine sediments. Dry sieve analysis is best for particles coarser than 63–100 μm (sand and gravel) using either a stack of American ASTM series sieves or British Standard sieves, 8 in (203 mm) in diameter

and spaced at ½ φ intervals, mechanically shaken. The sediment is poured in at the top of the deck of sieves and the weight retained on each sieve is noted after shaking. The same set of sieves must never be used for wet sieving and all sieves should be cleaned by gentle brushing. The percentage of the sample retained on each sieve may be easily calculated and the fine fraction (silt and clay) which passes the last sieve may be analysed in suspension by pipette or hydrometer. Wet sieve analysis is generally used only for removing this fine fraction (< 63 μm) since if it is used for the complete run a modified shaker with a shower head must be made, and each sample dried before weighing.

The analysis of sediment suspensions uses Stokes law, which governs the frictional resistance of a fluid to a particle falling through it. It is possible to calculate the particle diameter from the equation

$$V = 2gr^2(D_1 - D_2)/9\eta ,$$

where V is the particle velocity, g the acceleration due to gravity, D_1 the relative density of the falling sphere, D_2 the relative density of the sedimentation liquid or gas, η the viscosity of the liquid, and r the radius of the sphere. For a particle size analysis it is the particle radius (r) which is required. The settling times and fall heights may be measured, atmospheric pressure assumed and gravity acceleration taken to be 9.8 m s^{-2}; water or other suspending liquid may be kept at a constant temperature using a water bath and the relative density of quartz (2.65) assumed, which simplifies the calculations. If the sediment is water then the viscosity is known. The method is not nearly so complicated as it seems from the equation; tables are available for all the variables and standard computer programs have been written to assist in the operation. The two basic analytical methods involve different principles. **Pipette** analysis measures the concentration changes which occur in a settling suspension by withdrawing samples at fixed depth and time intervals. It works on the principle that if two particles start settling out from a suspension at the same time the larger falls to the bottom of the sedimentation cylinder faster than the smaller, according to Stokes law. One can therefore calculate the particle size distribution by dispersing the mixture (stirring) and withdrawing samples from known depth and height to correspond to particular particle sizes. The **hydrometer** method, arguably less accurate but certainly less trouble, measures concentration changes in the density of a settling suspension using direct readings from a hydrometer floated on the top of it. Various automatic and semi-automatic devices are also used, the best being the Coulter counter, an electronic particle sizer (see Section 1.5.3).

1.3.3 Chemical analysis

Chemical analysis methods for sediments and soils are listed in the classic textbooks of Jackson (1962) and Hesse (1971). The most important ones for archaeological work include the quantitative determination of carbonates, humus, phosphates, iron and the identification of trace elements, by wet chemical analysis, colorimetry, X-ray diffraction for clay minerals and atomic absorption for trace elements. Problems met in the chemical analysis of archaeological sediments are discussed by Catt and Weir (1975).

1.3.4 Use of mineral identification

Minerals with a relative density greater than 2.9 ('heavy' minerals) may be used to identify their parent rocks or sediments by noting the presence and abundance of the various types. Less weathered sediments will contain a higher proportion of heavy minerals than very heavily weathered ones, and there is a close relationship between heavy mineral assemblages and grain size. It is usual to study only one size fraction, the very fine sand. Pretreatment is followed by the separation of the heavy and light fractions using a heavy liquid of suitable density. Bromoform with a relative density of 2.80–2.90 is the usual choice and the process must be carried out in a fume cupboard under supervision. The heavy mineral fraction, usually 2–3% of the total minerals, is removed by crushing and pretreating the sediment followed by heavy liquid separation. Grains are collected, washed and mounted on microscope slides for identification and counting and the heavy liquid may be recovered and recycled. Details are given by Allman and Lawrence (1972) and there have been numerous applications to the study of pottery fabrics. An example of an application to archaeological sediments may be seen in the analysis

of the tufa sequences of the australopithecine breccias and tufas at Taung (Boputhatswana) by Butzer (1974).

1.3.5 Thin sections

Thin sections of sediments may assist in the description and interpretation of micromorphology and microfabric, for example in examination of the structure of palaeosols (Section 1.4). Mineral identification and quantification of particle size and shape is carried out in thin section, together with descriptions of texture, fabric, fossil content and diagenesis. If the material is hard, then it may be sectioned using a diamond saw and lap wheel, but a soft sediment must first be impregnated with a suitable resin mixture under vacuum before being cut, cemented to a slide and ground using a diamond lap wheel and carborundum powders to achieve a uniform 30 μm thickness (Allman & Lawrence 1972).

1.4 Soils

The soils associated with archaeological sites are the result of a complex series of depositional and pedological (soil forming) processes. The questions asked of a soil are very similar to those already outlined for sediments, namely the **origins** of the material, **method** and **environment** of deposition and **intensity** and **type** of post-depositional processes. Soils found in archaeological contexts will either be relatively modern (surface) examples, which may be mapped, sectioned and studied, or else they will be buried. If a soil is buried, then the process of covering it will disturb the top layers and various processes will be initiated. Much depends on the depth and characteristics of the material which has covered the buried surface. If only a thin layer of material is present, the buried surface will be affected by processes related to the more modern surface; earthworms, for example, will continue to mix up the organic material and add to it from the modern surface. If the soil is buried very deeply, no more organic material can be added and gradually all organic activity will cease. This process may be studied experimentally on the short term at experimental earthworks such as Wareham, Dorset (Evans *et al.* 1974) which is built on a buried podsol. Iron and manganese pans may form in buried surfaces, related to burial depth and the movement of water as well as to the characteristics of the buried soil. Soils buried beneath earthworks are of particular interest since it is possible to compare the buried surface with the modern one which has developed on the top. The earthwork settles and erodes and the character of the buried surface changes. In order to comment on the buried soil one must, of course, take into account post-depositional processes such as the intensity of worm activity, oxidation, hydration and solution, or the development of new horizons as a result of burial. If the earthwork is shallow, the formation of a new soil will have an effect on the buried soil (see above), including increased earthworm and root activity. The whole question of earthworm activity in archaeological contexts has been considered by Atkinson (1957), who noted that it was possible for earthworms to remove entire humic horizons from a buried soil altogether. Dimbleby and Speight (1969) reported a discussion during a British Association meeting at Dundee over the precise meaning of the term 'buried soil'. It was agreed that a buried soil could be taken as 'a once exposed geological substrate in which biological activity has taken place and which is now under a later deposit'. Many complex changes may take place in a soil when it is buried by material, either through natural causes (hillwash) or human activity (earthworks) and if the soil is truncated it may be difficult to recognize. The whole question of the formation, importance and classification of soils is dealt with in the excellent survey of Limbrey (1975) which deals comprehensively with many of the questions posed by soils which occur in archaeological contexts.

The soil contains information about the environment under which it was formed and changes since its formation making it a data bank of information about dynamic ecological conditions and a means of reconstructing the extent of human influence. Soils in archaeological contexts are evidence, unlike sediments, of past stability situations; a soil cannot form and mature under conditions of marked erosion or very active deposition. The formation of a soil profile is gradual and may be interrupted many times in the soil's cyclic history of development. The soil will contain material (e.g. pollen) which is both contemporary with its formation and diagenetic (arriving after its formation) and in order to reconstruct past environmental changes it is obviously necessary to disentangle the two (Section 4.5). The same is true, to a lesser extent, of included artefacts which may have arrived post-depositionally through worm action, rabbits, moles, roots, cracks or other forms of disturbance. If a soil is burnt then its organic component may be either completely incinerated or slightly charred, depending on a ratio of the amount of oxygen which was available in the fire to the amount of organic matter being burnt. Charred organic matter is black and, if a soil is poor in organic matter, the iron compounds in the soil remain in a reduced state. If the soil is highly organic, the iron compounds are oxidized and the characteristic red colour of haematite (ferric oxide $Fe_2O_3 . H_2O$) is seen, a colour change missed in tropical, desert and Mediterranean soils which often tend to be red and haematite-rich anyway. Close examination of the quartz sand grain surface textures will show whether or not the soil itself has been burnt, or whether (as is often the case) a little burnt material such as charcoal has contaminated the unburnt material. Burnt sediment shows characteristic fractures of the quartz sand grains, and it may even be possible to give a rough estimate of temperature and intensity of burning (Shackley 1975). Some examples of the application of soil studies to archaeology are given below.

1.5 Applications and case studies

1.5.1 Petrofabric analysis

Petrofabric analysis is the study of the spatial relations of the units that comprise a rock, including a study of the movements that produced these elements. Over the past 40 years the technique has been widely used in the study of sediments such as glacial till, outwash sediments and solifluxion deposits. The writer (Shackley 1978) discussed the application of petrofabric analysis techniques to the study of the behaviour of palaeolithic artefacts deposited in Pleistocene river gravels.

Particles which have been deposited in a moving medium tend to orientate themselves with their longest axis (*a* axis, Fig. 1.9) parallel to the direction of flow and the shortest (*c*) axis transverse to it. This is useful when studying depositional histories and on site these directions may be measured on a coarse pebble deposit by cleaning fine material from the interstices and marking the direction of the *a* and *c* axes on each pebble with a chalk line. The length of each dimension is recorded, together with the inclination (dip) of the pebble from the horizontal, completed by drawing the horizontal line across a suitable face of the pebble (by lining it up with a small spirit level) and measuring the declination of the *a* and *c* axes with an inclinometer (Fig. 1.9). The orientation of the *a* and *c* axes is then noted using a prismatic compass, sighting along the measured drawn lines. Inclination and orientation are expressed by plotting them on a stereographic net, using a base model such as the polar equi-area net of Phillips (1971) which has a centre point representing a pole at right angles to the plane of projection, with concentric circles for angular declinations from this pole at 10° intervals (Fig. 1.9). The radial rays represent the azimuths and a horizontal particle would therefore lie at the outside of the circle. The method is most suitable for linear or tabular rocks and its accuracy decreases with increased sphericity and roundness.

At the Iron Age hillfort of Danebury (Hampshire) a flint concentration at the foot of the interior of the rampart was tested to see if it represented tumble from the rampart or a deliberately placed material, perhaps serving as the foundation for some structure. In the former case a preferred orientation should be seen and in the latter random directions. The three axial lengths, inclinations and azimuths of 80 pebbles were noted and a polar equi-area net completed using the orientation of the *a* axis. The dot diagram was converted to contours (Fig. 1.9) for ease of interpretation, and a strong preferred northeast to south-west orientation was observed which corresponded to the direction which would have resulted had the material fallen from the rampart. A minor north-west to south-east mode followed the slope of the ground in the interior of the fort. The hypothesis of deliberate packing was thus rejected (Shackley 1975). A contrasting conclusion was reached by Bibby (1974) in his work on the stone pavement at Kintraw (Argyll). The site had produced a stone pavement which could either be the result of natural geomorphological agencies or the activities of man. Natural pavements are known from hill areas (Mitchell & Jarvis 1956) sometimes caused by the upward movement of coarse particles accompanied by downward movement of fine materials by frost heaving (Corte 1962). At Kintraw the possibility also existed that the pavement represented a scree accumulation. Two areas of pavement each 0.5 m × 0.5 m were chosen and at each a sample of 100 stones of size greater than 30 mm in diameter (smaller stones were difficult to measure) were chosen. The *a* axis was located, its inclination measured with an Abney level and azimuth with a prismatic compass. The pebbles were mostly of mica schist, dominantly tabular or wedge-shaped. Results were plotted on a polar equi-area net (Fig. 1.9a and b) showing a wide variation in the dip of the *a* axis and generally low angles of inclination. Figure 1.9d may be seen as a contrasting case, taken from a natural scree, and Figure 1.9e shows the results of similar measurement on a stone pavement produced by frost action and modified by solifluxion. On the scree diagram there was a marked correlation between slope direction and inclination but the opposite was observed on the solifluxion pavement. There is a very marked difference between the Kintraw diagrams (Fig. 1.9a and b) and the natural pavements (Fig. 1.9d and e). A control test was made on a man-made pavement identified at the Sheep Hill vitrified fort (Milton, Dunbarton) seen in Figure 1.9c, which has a strong resemblance to Figure 1.9a and b, despite contrasting parent materials. The conclusion was reached, based on this evidence, that the Kintraw pavement was man-made.

Figure 1.9 Petrofabric diagrams after Bibby (1976). (a) Lambert polar equi-area net. (b)–(f) Contoured petrofabric diagrams with contour intervals of 2%. (b) Kintraw 1, direction of slope 240° (mag.); angle of slope 21°. (c) Kintraw 2, direction of slope 240° (mag.); angle of slope 21°. (d) Man-made pavement (Sheep Hill Fort, Dunbartonshire, Scotland), direction of slope 163° (mag.); angle of slope 5°. (e) Scree (Broad Law, Peeblesshire, Scotland), direction of slope 175° (mag.), angle of slope 37°. (f) Soliflucted stone horizon (Broad Law), direction of slope 305° (mag.); angle of slope 16°.

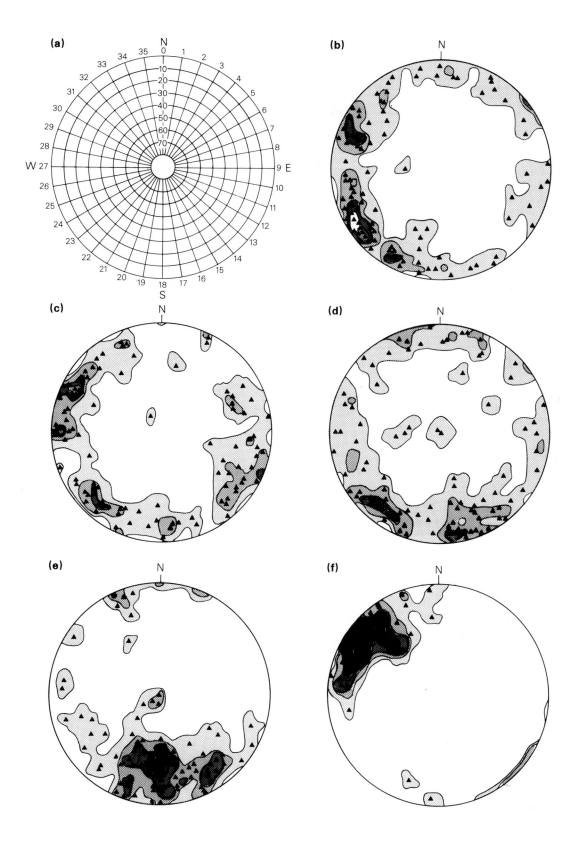

1.5.2 Grain surface textures

Rogers and Tankard (1974) described the surface textures of some quartz sand grains from the west coast of southern Africa, examining modern depositional environments and identifying relect grains from previous cycles. The latter author illustrated some applications of the technique to archaeology in the examination of sand grains 0.45–0.55 μm in size from the cave sediment sequence at Die Kelders 1. At the base of the column (Fig. 1.10) wave-generated beach boulders with coarse to medium grained interstitial sand were overlain by alternating successions of Middle Stone Age occupation and sterile layers (5–15, Fig. 1.10). On top of these layers there were boulders resulting from roof collapse due to an earthquake shock. After the Middle Stone Age the cave had been abandoned for a long period, with weathering of the rock debris followed by deposition into standing water (3, Fig. 1.10). The growth of a dune at the cave entrance produced talus in the cave itself and the return of the shoreline to its present position was marked by shelly sands (2, Fig. 1.10) with foraminifera and complete echinoid spines. Sand grains in this layer show characteristic littoral features. Quartz grains from the interstitial sands of the boulder layer (17, Fig. 1.10) show conchoidal gouge marks on the edges as a result of grain collisions in a high energy environment of deposition with seawater surging through the cave. Such high energy (produced in a very dynamic environment) littoral textures appear only on grains from 1, 2 and 17 (Fig. 1.10) and never in combination with low energy (produced in relatively quiescent conditions) features. Layers 3–16 (Fig. 1.10) produced grains of aeolian origin with diagenetic surface alterations attributable to the highly active chemical environment of the cave (pH 7.9–8.7). The results of the sedimentary analysis concur with the archaeologists' evaluation of the stratigraphy (Tankard & Schweitzer 1975). After the lowering of the sea level and increasing distance from the sea during the Würm the cave was occupied by Middle Stone Age people in several phases separated by sterile sands. During the Würm maximum cold the shoreline was approximately 20 km distant, still being exploited by man as is evidenced by the occasional seal and penguin remains. The period of non-occupation marked by the top iron-stained sands dates from

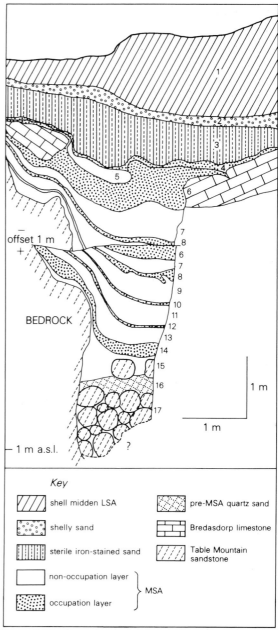

Figure 1.10 Cross section of the stratigraphy at the cave of Die Kelders 1 Cape Province, South Africa (after Tankard & Schweitzer 1976).

40 000 to 6000 BP, when the shelly sands with different grain surface textures indicate a return of the shoreline to its present position. This prolonged abandonment was probably due to dampness in the cave (plus occasional standing water) and much additional sand on the continental shelf left by the

22

Würm marine regression which resulted in the accumulation of a dune field in front of the cave associated with increased wind activity. The correlation of the results of particle size analysis and a high magnification examination of grain surface texture provided some explanation for the discontinuous archaeological sequence and elucidated the sedimentary history of the cave.

A very different application of the method was described by the writer (Shackley 1975) in the analysis of a potting clay fabric from 'Carrot' amphorae (Camulodunum form 189) which were imported into Britain during the first century AD and are found at various Continental sites such as Pompeii. Neither thin section nor heavy mineral content was helpful in establishing their provenance, but the scanning electron microscope showed that the included sand grains had characteristic features such as upturned quartz plates affected by the solution and precipitation of silica, typical of desert conditions. A hot sandy dune environment was indicated, confirmed by a control examination of amphorae from the Palestinian site of Tell Faras (fifth century BC) and a short list of potential origins for the form could be produced, the most likely source areas being either Cyrenaica (Libya) or Jericho (Israel).

1.5.3 Micromorphology

A fine example of the application of the micromorphological examination of archaeological sediments may be seen in the work of Goldberg (1979) who made a study of the sediments from the important Palaeolithic site of Pech de l'Azé (Dordogne, France), comparing his results and palaeoclimatic interpretation with those of classic sedimentological analyses carried out on the same deposits (Laville 1973). Micromorphologically based interpretations were, on the whole, in close agreement but had several advantages. Comparatively little work has been done on the micromorphology of archaeological sediments and soils, despite a seminal paper by Dalrymple (1958). The detailed stratigraphy of the Pech de l'Azé site was described by Laville (1973) and Goldberg collected samples 60 mm × 50 mm × 50 mm in size (in blocks where possible) which were oven-dried at 60 °C and vacuum-impregnated with cold polyester resin. After

hardening and curing sections were cut and the slides examined in stratigraphical order under the microscope, features being described quantitatively using the terminology of Brewer (1964). Micromorphological elements identified and counted included **skeleton grains** (both sand and silt sized, mainly quartz but with a small proportion of heavy minerals), lithological **relicts** of bedrock fragments, rounded **phosphate** grains and bone fragments. The phosphate grains were further examined by X-ray diffraction producing patterns identified as hydroxaptite or dahllite (Goldberg & Nathan 1975), probably representing the decayed coprolite of large carnivores such as bear or hyaena. **Voids**, the presence of **organic matter** and various **pedological features** such as clay cutans were described and counted. Results were expressed in tabular form by point counting of features and it proved possible to describe the structure of the sediments in great detail, including the identification of a fluvial component and some cryoclastic activity. The advantage of micromorphology over particle size analysis as an analytical tool is that it gives information about the spatial organization of the components and how these are distributed, as well as revealing the sequence of processes and full details of texture. It examines the hypotheses produced by other techniques very critically and generates more ideas.

1.5.4 Environments of deposition

The definition of a particular depositional environment is one of the most frequently required pieces of information. We have already seen (Section 1.5.1) how this may be accomplished by an examination of sand grain surface textures, but it is more commonly carried out by some form of particle size analysis. Changing depositional environments may be important sources of archaeological information, and a good example of this can be seen in the study of the early sedimentary sequence at Carthage (Tunisia). The site of Carthage exemplifies many of the problems presented by large and complex urban excavations, and is at present being examined by archaeologists from several countries under a Unesco plan. The British team has been working on several sites both in the interior of the town and near the Punic naval and commercial harbours which were described by Appian. They have now been identified and work at Carthage has concentrated on the development of the port and its environmental setting. From the fourth to the third century BC the port was sited to the south-east of the city nucleus in the flat or gently undulating coastal plain, approximately 2–3 m above present sea level. The many changes in the topography of the area since antiquity include the growth of the La Goulette–Le Kram tombolo (sand bar) and the erosion of the east-facing part of Carthage (Fig. 1.11). The study of the natural sedimentary sequences beneath the ancient occupation levels shows that in antiquity the area of the late Punic port had also been subject to many changes, summarized by Hurst and Stager (1978) from work at three sites, the Ilôt de l'Amirauté at the centre of the circular harbour, the west side of the rectangular harbour 300 m to the south of the Ilôt and the Tophet, some 50 m west of the rectangular harbour (Fig. 1.12). The environmental sedimentary sequences at these three sites was virtually identical and it has proved possible to make some general observations on the evolution of the harbour

site. A sequence of dry land–lagoon–marsh–dry land conditions was observed, starting with a fine yellow aeolian quartz sand in beds up to 2 m thick, probably a dune sand and texturally quite different from a marine sand. Above this was found a lithified crust of caliche representing exposure to subaerial conditions (Evans 1973, p. 102) capped by a 100–200 mm thick dark brown or black calcareous clay which contained marine molluscs (e.g. *Cerastoderma glaucum*). A shallow lagoonal environment was indicated, confirming a rise in sea level to above the level of the caliche crust. It seems probable that a tombolo partially blocked the eastern end of the rectangular harbour (Fig. 1.12), restricting the flow of the open sea and producing lagoonal conditions. The succeeding marsh phase is represented by a layer of black organic clay and seaweeds, marine grasses and snails. On the Ilôt d'Amirauté this was succeeded by wind-blown sand before the first occupation. The dating for the end of this sequence of natural changes was seen at the Tophet where cremation urns from the fourth century BC were set in pits cut

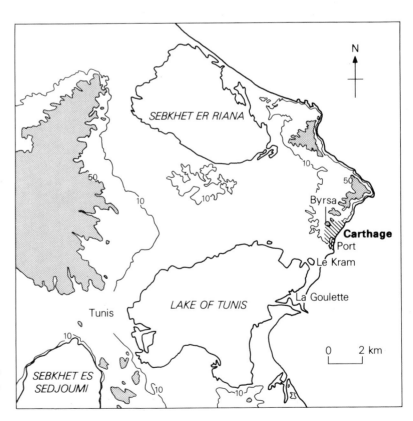

Figure 1.11 Location of the ancient city of Carthage in relation to the modern coastline (after Hurst & Stager 1978).

into the lagoon and marsh clay. On the rectangular harbourside levels of the same date containing metalworking debris overlie the marsh clays. A water channel 15–20 m wide and approximately 2 m deep (Fig. 1.12) represents the earliest harbour construction work. It was cut into the natural sand and unlined, its final silting dating to the fourth century BC. The reasons for its construction are not known but seem likely to have been an attempt to drain the marsh. The channel extended north to south across the Ilôt and south to the west die of the

rectangular harbour (Fig. 1.12), the presence of marine molluscs and sediments suggesting that it was linked with the open sea and possibly used for navigation since it could have held an estimated 1.6 m of standing water. A high concentration of undigested fruit seeds suggests that it also received some sewage. The excavators were of the opinion that it probably had quite a short life span and was excavated in response to a particular set of environmental conditions. The reasons for the sudden change from a rather barren marsh to a well popu-

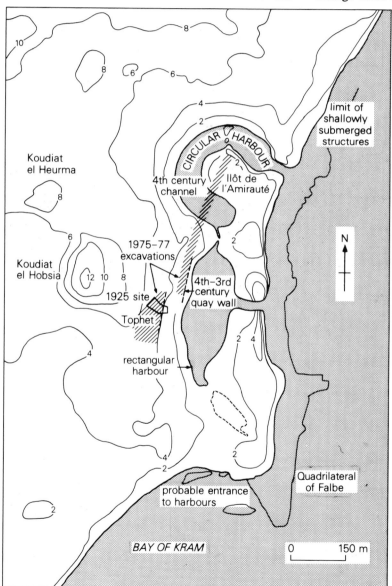

Figure 1.12 Topography of the harbour area of Carthage showing the location of sites mentioned in the text (after Hurst & Stager 1978).

25

lated port with international trading connections are complex. A response to changing environmental conditions is possible, perhaps accompanied by sea-level change or drying-out of the area, making the marshy site more attractive, but this was undoubtedly combined with urban expansion on a large scale. On the Ilôt a fill of yellow sand occurs over these channel sediments followed by successive timber building plans marked by individual round post-holes or trenches for lines of posts (Fig. 1.8). At least six successive phases are present and the fill of the post-holes has provided an interesting sediment-ological problem. The holes are filled with a clean beach sand, texturally identical to modern foreshore deposits sampled from nearby beaches. The sand is quite different from either the underlying dunes or muddy redeposited channel sediments. It is difficult to speculate on the reasons behind this behaviour pattern; why was it necessary to fill these particular post-holes with beach sand which had to be brought from some distance away? The only explanation seems to be that it assisted in drainage but this is most unsatisfactory.

Quite a different type of problem was tackled by Gardner (1977) who describes the analysis of a deep series of sediments near Tell Fara (Israel) which yielded artefacts dating from 70 000 to 14 000 BP in the top 19 m. It was generally accepted that the artefact-rich sediments were aeolian in origin, although Yaalon and Dan (1974) suggested that some of the Negev loess had been locally redeposited by stream action. Gardner's analysis proved that neither hypothesis was correct; the sediments were fluviatile in origin. Small scale cross-bedding was observed in the section, very rare in loess but more common in fluviatile and lacustrine sediments. Gravel-sized particles in the lower levels also argue against a loessic origin and 75 particle size analyses were undertaken using dry sieving for the coarse fraction and photo-extinction for the silt and clay (Shackley 1975). Loess is characterized by the bulk of the sediment falling in the 4.5–5.5 φ range, with at least 80% of the sediment by weight in the silt grade. Of these 75 samples only 47 had 21–60% silt and only one more than 80%, with no visible trends in silt increase or decrease through the section. Results were shown on a triangular diagram (after Doeglas 1949) (Fig. 1.13), and as cumulative

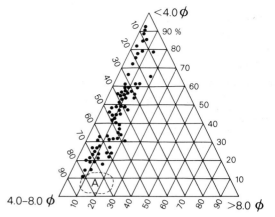

Figure 1.13 Triangular diagram showing the composition of possible loess samples from Tell Fara. The axes show the percentage of clay (>8.0 φ), silt (4–8 φ) and sand and gravel (<4 φ) but only one sample has the actual characteristics of loess whose textures should occur within the area marked 'A' (after Gardner 1977).

particle size distribution curves with loess controls. Scanning electron microscope examination proved to be of limited value in this case and the hypothesis of fluvial redeposition of loess was rejected due to the lack of any aeolian characteristics and no sedimentary structures which might, for example, be the result of slopewash. The sediments seem to represent fluvial deposition of a series of gravels, sands and silts from the headwaters of the Beer Sheva drainage basin, producing a concentration of sediments and palaeoliths of the greatest importance in evaluating the environmental archaeology of the Fara area in the Pleistocene.

A similar problem was tackled at the site of Hamwih (southern England) (Shackley 1980) where extensive deposits of 'brickearth' underlie the Saxon town, resting conformably on Pleistocene gravels at heights of between 0 and 3 m OD. The deposit is orange-brown in colour, and often rich in silt. No evidence of soil development has been observed, although the presence of a thin decalcified *braunerde* is attested from other sites. The excavator required a description of the texture and composition of the material, together with an indication of the environment of deposition. Crawford (1949) suggested that there might have been a tidal lagoon in the area, and it was therefore vital to establish from an analysis of the composition of the 'brickearth' whether it could be the product of estuarine conditions. Eight samples of 'brickearth' were taken from six of the excavations. The object of the analysis at Hamwih (Fig. 1.14) was to define and compare the depositional environments of the 'brickearth' samples, isolating discrepancies and drawing general conclusions concerning the nature of the sediments. The

analysis of samples 1 and 2 was carried out using an electronic particle sizer, the Coulter counter (Shackley 1975, pp. 142–6). This instrument, first developed for industrial purposes, counts and sizes the particles composing a sediment, and this was the first time that it had been utilized for archaeological

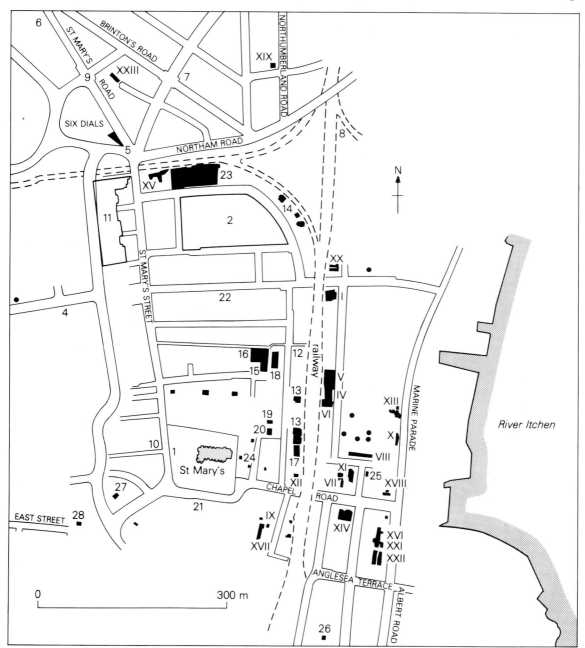

Figure 1.14 Hamwih (Saxon Southampton): excavations and the location of 'brickearth' samples.

samples. Particle size distributions of the remaining samples were obtained by the more conventional methods of dry sieving the gravel and sand fractions (sizes > 4 φ, 63 μm), and pipette sedimentation of the silt and clay (< 4 φ). Table 1.9 shows that samples 1 and 2 were remarkably similar in composition, both consisting of over 50% silt, the re-

mainder being fine sand and clay. Samples 3–6 were, however, quite different in character. None contained more than 12% total mud (silt and clay), most of which was clay, whereas the mud fraction of samples 1, 2, 7 and 8 had been mostly silt. The gravel fraction of these samples varied between 8 and 50%, the highest value coming from the base of

Table 1.9 Description of samples taken at Hamwih.

Sample no.	Weight processed (g)	Particle sizing method	Gravel (%)	Sand (%)	Mud (silt/clay) (%)	Description (after Folk & Ward 1957)				
						Mz	φI	Sk	Kg	Description
1	—	Coulter counter	0	24.00	76 total mud	0.40	2.139	0.377	6.557	very poorly sorted, positively skewed, extremely leptokurtic
2	—	Coulter counter	0	22.00	78 total mud	0.45	1.932	0.136	7.259	very poorly sorted, positively skewed, extremely leptokurtic
3	135.61	dry sieve and pipette	8.41	84.95	6.64 total mud	2.283	1.188	+0.024	1.629	poorly sorted, nearly symmetrical, very leptokurtic
4	63.44	dry sieve and pipette	26.85	67.02	6.94 total mud	0.690	3.391	−0.518	0.941	very poorly sorted, very negatively skewed, mesokurtic
5	41.18	dry sieve and pipette	14.53	73.47	11.90 total mud	1.910	2.870	−0.257	1.318	very poorly sorted, negatively skewed, leptokurtic
6	91.278	dry sieve and pipette	50.37	44.95	4.67 total mud	−0.70	3.225	−0.428	0.558	very poorly sorted, very negatively skewed, very platykurtic
7	122.040	dry sieve and pipette	27.049	21.525	35.265 16.139 51.424 total mud	2.439	5.550	−0.190	0.938	very poorly sorted, negatively skewed, mesokurtic
8	89.630	dry sieve and pipette	8.122	53.275	23.512 10.04 38.603 total mud	3.565	3.680	0.204	1.392	very poorly sorted, positively skewed, leptokurtic

Table 1.10 Location of samples taken at Hamwih; see also Figure 1.14.

Sample no.	Site	Grid reference	Location	Notes
1	SARC IV	428150/117900	top surviving 'brickearth'	site 2 (Shackley 1975, sample A)
2	SARC XIII	429320/11716	top surviving 'brickearth'	site 3 (Shackley 1975, sample B)
3	SARC XVIII	429000/115780	top surviving 'brickearth'	site 4
4	SARC XVIII	429200/116200	top surviving 'brickearth' depth 0.98 m	site 5
5	SARC XVIII	429200/116200	middle surviving 'brickearth' depth 1.14 m	site 5 — depth below present ground level. Some 'brickearth' lost due to building and disturbance
6	SARC XVIII	429200/116200	base surviving 'brickearth' depth 1.26 m	site 5
7	SARC V	428150/117800	top surviving 'brickearth'	site 6; probably 250–300 mm below original brickearth surface
8	SARC XX	428350/119500	top surviving 'brickearth'	site 7

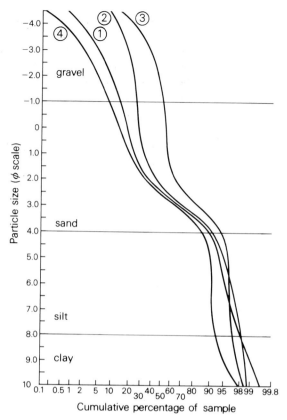

Figure 1.15 Cumulative percentage frequency curves for Southampton 'brickearth' samples. The diagrams, plotted on arithmetic probability paper, have the cumulative percentage of the sample on the horizontal axis and the particle size grades on the vertical axis.

the 'brickearth' where it had presumably been in contact with the terrace gravels (Fig. 1.15). Samples 3–6 were principally composed of sand, with a major mode in fine sand (2–4 φ) and a small minor mode in gravel (> −0.5 φ). The high kurtosis values of Group 1 (samples 1, 2, 7 and 8) indicate either an estuarine or an aeolian (wind-blown) environment, but the unimodal nature of the size distribution and the poor sorting values would support the latter. Such a high silt content and general size distribution was taken by Pitcher *et al.* (1954) as typical of aeolian-deposited loess. The slight differences in texture between the samples of Group 1 may very probably be attributed to differential weathering *in situ*, and Cornwall (1958) noted that the percentage of clay in loess tended to increase at the expense of the sand fraction as the material was weathered.

Samples 7 and 8 are not, however, pure loess, and seem to have been affected by contact with the underlying gravels which have contributed the coarse fraction. No features of the Group 2 samples (3–6) suggest a similar origin, although the high percentages of fine sand are within the particle size range capable of being wind transported. The origins of these sediments seem to have been complex. It is suggested that the sand fraction was probably deposited by water, under medium velocity flow conditions. This was sufficient to impart negative skewness values but insufficient to remove all the fine material. The gravel fraction could again be derived from the underlying material, and the mud laid down in slowly moving water. This composition suggests conditions similar to those of a small tidal creek, but not an open beach or a strongly tidal estuary. In the former case the percentage of mud would be lower and in the latter the percentage of clay would be higher. The theory that the Saxon town was bounded on the south-west by a tidal creek leading to a lagoon (Crawford 1949) has led several writers to interpret the 'brickearths' as the products of this lagoon. Excavations at sites 25 and 26 (Addyman & Hill 1968, p. 75) produced material described as 'presumably lagoon silts' and 'fine apparently waterlain silts above gravel'. These may well be references to sediments similar to those of Group 2, since the sampling points are close to the area of the proposed creek. However, none of the samples remotely resemble lagoonal deposits and, if a lagoon existed, it must have been located considerably to the south of any of the provenances sampled. The results of these analyses suggest that the majority of the 'Hamwih' 'brickearths' consist of redeposited loess, but that in the extreme south the former presence of a small creek may be inferred.

1.5.5 Sediment accumulation and distribution; rates and problems

Atkinson (1957) attacked the tacit assumption made by many excavators that once an object (large or small) has come to rest in or upon a deposit it remains in that position for ever. Natural agencies of disturbance include the various forms of weathering and the action of worms; the latter can displace up to 36 tons of topsoil per acre per year (14.8×10^3 kg ha^{-1} a^{-1}), burying surface objects, displacing finds and confusing stratigraphic distinctions. Man himself disturbs the archaeological deposits that he has helped to accumulate but this is very difficult to recognize. Sometimes the disturbance is deliberate and on a very large scale (for example when clearing debris for new buildings or graves), but occupational disturbance caused by people just walking around on a deposit is more difficult to see. Mixing occurs near the surface of the deposit and decreases rapidly with depth after 300 mm, but this figure depends on the nature and intensity of the disturbance as well as the texture of the sediment. Stockton (1978) experimented with vertical displacement of material in Australian rockshelters containing dry coarse sand by spreading glass on the surface, trampling the area for a day and then excavating. Glass fragments moved down to a maximum depth of 160 mm but more than half the total number actually moved upwards. Any abrupt cultural changes would therefore have been obliterated by mixing – a fact with horrifying repercussions for European sites with very tightly pottery-controlled stratigraphy. Radiocarbon dates for such sites suggest that their accumulation of debris may be measured in a few centimetres per century, as happened at Devil's Lair, south west Australia (Shackley 1978b). If sites are disturbed in 200 mm zones then this could account for the lack of sharp stratigraphic lines in many Australian sites. Exca-

vation is best undertaken in 'spits' (arbitrary stratigraphic units) and it is impossible to be too precise on cultural events or dating. Hughes and Lampert (1977) give examples of such sites, noting that disturbance is minimized if the loose deposits are bound together by shell or organic matter. Devil's Lair had an interesting example of this, christened the sputnik effect (Shackley 1978b) (Fig. 1.16). Diagenetic precipitation of calcium carbonate from dripping water had percolated into the quartz sands, forming a knobbly rind around the individual grains. These rough surfaces interlocked, giving stability to the whole series, and eventually the grains were bound together both chemically and physically. A similar case where abundant shell and precipitated calcium carbonate were observed was at the Seton deposit (Hughes & Lampert 1977) and at both this site and Cave Bay Cave (Bowdler 1976) occupation deposits were separated by sterile layers which helped to protect them from disturbance.

Other agents of disturbance include frost action, which is of importance for two reasons: it can disturb archaeological material and produce geomorphological phenomena which may be relatively easily confused with the product of human action (Atkinson 1957, Limbrey 1975). Williams (1973) discusses the deceptive frost-caused features (such as ice-wedge casts, wheel patterns and involution) which can resemble archaeological phenomena.

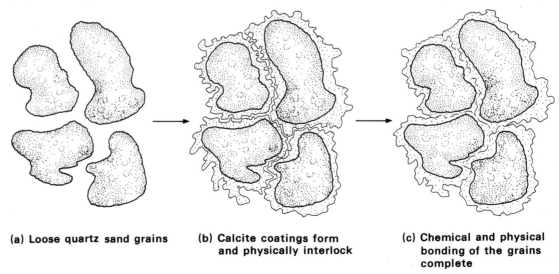

(a) Loose quartz sand grains **(b) Calcite coatings form and physically interlock** **(c) Chemical and physical bonding of the grains complete**

Figure 1.16 The 'sputnik' effect. Loose quartz sand grains (a) become coated with calcite (b) which eventually acts as both a chemical and physical means of bonding them together (c).

This is especially important in cave sites where crysturbation may also damage the edges of artefacts.

1.5.6 Barrow construction and soil interpretation

The excavation of a middle Bronze Age bell barrow at Canford Heath (Dorset) (Fig. 1.17) revealed the remnants of the old ground surface, a mature humus–iron podsol with the topmost organic L-H layers missing (Fig. 1.17b). The barrow was circular with a diameter of 8.5 m, surviving to a maximum height of 0.6 m and with its centre approximately coinciding with the centre of curvature of a partly surrounding bank and ditch (Horsey and Shackley 1981). A date of 3060 ± 110 BP was obtained. The old land surface carried a heathland vegetation, probably burnt before the construction. A shallow ditch had been dug to deliminate the barrow and the underlying yellow gravel had been used to cover the berm, making the barrow more conspicuous. The sealed palaeosol was described *in situ* and three monoliths were taken from the south-west quadrant for laboratory examination (Fig. 1.18, which shows Munsell colours). The removal of the topmost L-H layers suggests some preliminary clearance of the site and the structure of the basal podsol is shown in Figure 1.18. The basal layer of monolith 87 represents the Bs horizon of the buried soil, a yellowish-brown illuvial layer rich in iron and very acid (pH 3.2) sealed by the Bfe horizon, a very compacted indurated sandy gravel, virtually an iron pan, slightly less acid at pH 4.4. Over this pan layers 3–6 formed part of a complex Bh horizon, dark grey in colour and rich in illuviated organic matter which had been leached through the soil. Layer Ea was open textured, bleached light grey, nearly pure sand from which nearly all the mineral salts and organic matter had been removed by leaching. It was strongly acid (pH 3.5) and merged gradually into layer 8 (the A horizon) which is seen most clearly in monolith 86 layer 1. Some panning was also visible in this layer. The A horizon consisted of mixed mineral and organic matter, dark grey in colour with pH values from 4.0 to 4.2. The podsol had formed as a result of leaching acting on the very sandy sediments under a vegetation of heath plants which would have contributed the missing topmost *mor* humus layer.

The barrow mound was constructed of spade-sized clods, heaped up at an acute angle in at least five different layers, each clod comprising the A–Ea layers of the original buried soil. The method of construction must have been similar to that which would have resulted from digging a spade 6 in (152 mm) into the soil and heaping the resultant clods into a mound. Each clod consisted of the topmost layers of a soil identical to the palaeosol underneath the mound, containing the A–Ea horizons (Fig. 1.18), with occasional traces of the missing humic L–H layers. All sections through the barrow show this interesting sequence of podsol segments although some of the clods appear to have been inverted when the barrow was stacked and a certain amount of settling has taken place. The construction method of the barrow had included the initial digging of a shallow central pit dug slightly to the south-west of the centre of the mound, cut through the old ground surface. The pit fill is composed of redeposited topsoil, possibly missing L–H layers of the podsol with some sparse botanical material. An element of ritual is certainly present here and the barrow is far from unique; other examples of constructions with central pits clearly not intended for a burial may be seen at Kinson (Knocker 1958) and Brenig (North Wales). The most reasonable explanation of this curious rite is that the barrow represented a cenotaph.

1.5.7 Soils as landscape remnants

The reconstruction of former soil landscapes may be made either by the study of palaeosols or by an analysis of the remains of landscape degeneration. There is little doubt that the soils of, for example, the Aegean and indeed the whole Mediterranean area have been transformed during the last 3000–4000 years. Extensive and varied evidence of this exists, for example in geomorphological investigations of the present day landscape which show the dominance of erosional processes (Harris & Vita-Finzi 1968). Major soil changes can also be suggested from the palaeobotanical record. The Bronze Age site of Phylakopi on Melos has been examined by Renfrew (Davidson *et al.* 1976) within the framework of a project designed to study the evolution of the settlement pattern and economy of the island in a geographical manner, implying a need to

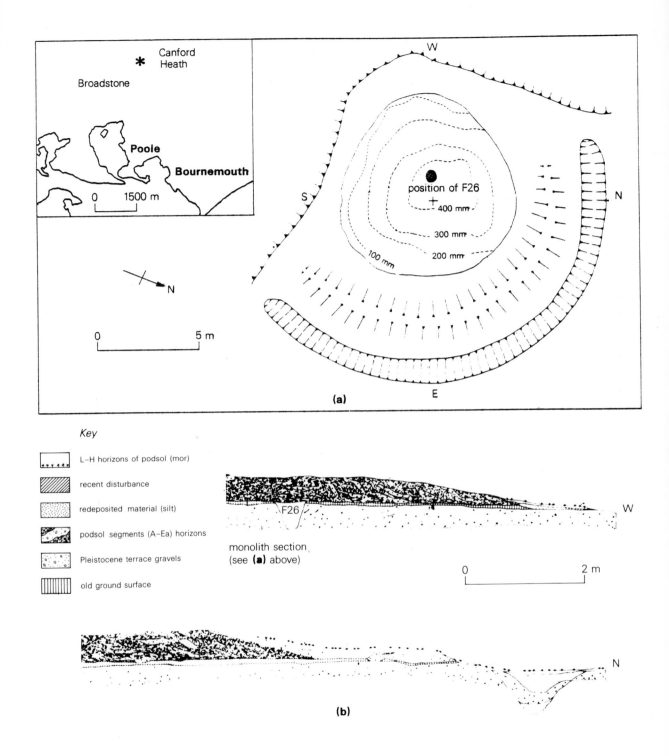

Key

- L–H horizons of podsol (mor)
- recent disturbance
- redeposited material (silt)
- podsol segments (A–Ea) horizons
- Pleistocene terrace gravels
- old ground surface

position of F26
+ 400 mm
300 mm
200 mm
100 mm

(a)

monolith section
(see **(a)** above)

0   2 m

(b)

Figure 1.17   Location of the Canford Heath barrow on a spur of gravel overlooking Christchurch harbour.

Soil unit	Soil horizon interpretation	Colour	Monolith section
soil 5	mixed/disturbed	10YR 6/1 grey	
	A horizon	10YR 4/1 dark grey	
	bleached elluvial horizon	10YR 6/1 light grey	
soil 4	A horizon	10YR 5/1 grey (mottled)	
	Ea horizon	10YR 6/1 light grey	
soil 3	A horizon	10YR 4/1 dark grey	
		10YR 5/1 grey	
	Ea	10YR 6/1 light grey	
soil 2	A	10YR 4/1 dark grey	
	A	10YR 5/1 grey	
		10YR 4/1 dark grey	
		10YR 5/1 grey	
	Ea	10YR 6/1 light grey	
soil 1	A	10YR 5/1 grey	
		10YR 6/1 dark grey	
top of buried soil	A	10YR 3/1 very dark grey	
all part of buried soil	base of A horizon	10YR 6/2 light brownish grey	
	Ea horizon	10YR 7/1 light grey	
	Bh	10YR 3/1 very dark grey	
	part of Bh	10YR 6/2 light brownish grey	
	Bh	10YR 3/1 very dark grey	
	transition zone	mottled and mixed layer	
	Bfe	7.5YR 4/4 dark brown	
	Bs	10YR 5/8 yellowish brown	

monolith 86

monolith 87

1 m

0.5 m

0 m

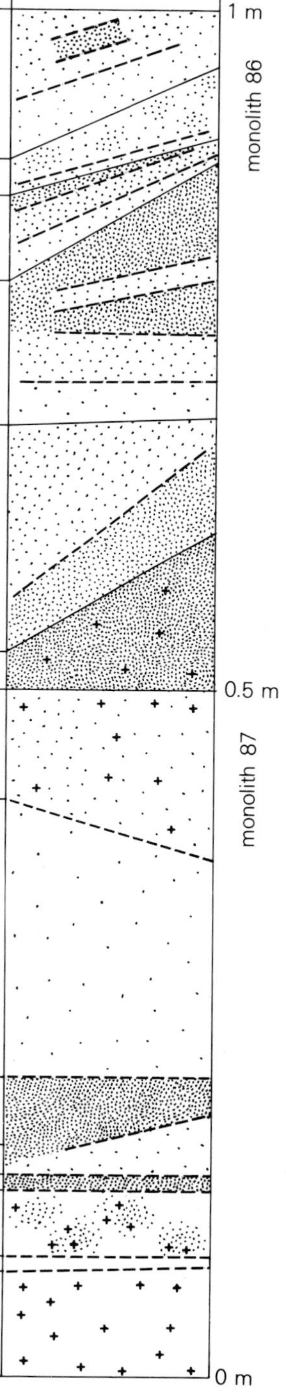

Figure 1.18 Section through the mound and buried soil from Canford Heath to show the structure and succession of podsol horizons.

reconstruct the Bronze Age environment. By making inferences on the basis of vegetation information the Melos site dates from the beginning of the early Bronze Age (c. 3000 BC) to the late Bronze Age (c. 1100 BC). Results include the fact that towards the end of the occupation on the site rapid soil erosion was accompanied by deforestation, its effect probably being compounded by the devastating explosion of the island of Thera some 100 km to the east-south-east. During the Bronze Age itself deep well-drained soils existed but there is little evidence of them now (Davidson 1978). An examination of the Thera sequences shows that the pumice and tephra fall-out from the eruption effectively sealed remnants of the old ground surface which existed during the Late Minoan period. These remnants were examined at several localities, found stratified beneath a fine pellety pumice (Davidson 1978). The land surface remnants have often been thought (e.g. by Money 1973) to include a relict Minoan palaeosol, but this is now known not to be the case. They consisted principally of a narrow band of dark brown loamy sand, but no evidence of a fertile, well developed soil was found, the existing soil remnants being rather poorly developed and very similar to modern soils derived from the tephra. The organic content of these soils was low or non-existent, and on the steeper slopes the soil was not found at all. It is clear that the landscape of Thera was already being severely eroded by 1500 BC, evidence which agrees with that from Melos. Davidson (1978) also considered the 'buried soil' described by Money (1973) as a humus-like layer which had developed between the ruins of the late Minoan 1a town of Acrotiri on Thera and thick deposits of pumice and ash from the eruption of the volcano which destroyed the island and desolated east Crete in the Late Minoan 1b period. The development of the 'soil' was formerly thought to represent an interval between the destruction of the Late Minoan 1a buildings by an earthquake and their burial by the volcanic explosion, indicating two separate periods of tectonic activity with some intervening vegetation growth. Money (1973) suggested that the thin humus layer which he found was an indicator of a period of stability of some length between these events. A contrasting view was expressed by Doumas (1974) who argued that the 'soil' was very discontinuous

and probably a result of site clearance. The Acrotiri section shows a pocket of dark material above building rubble, its stratigraphic position being illustrated in Figure 1.19. The 'soil' contains much silt (23%), some clay (8%) and some included organic matter. Davidson suggested that in fact it consisted of material washed in from the immediate vicinity, judging from the natural hollow in which it collected and the high clay content (probably indicative of selective inwashing of fine materials rather than *in situ* weathering). Thus it is not necessary to postulate a substantial period between the two volcanic events.

1.5.8 Phosphate and manganese in archaeological soils

Phosphorus is present in all ecosystems, its ultimate source being the breakdown of phosphate minerals in the soil's parent materials. Human activity may disrupt the cycle, which involves transference from soil to plants to animals and then back to the soil (with some loss by leaching) by producing a net phosphate loss (for example by overgrazing) or gain (by increments of material from livestock dung). Soil phosphorus is very stable. Major sources of phosphates may come from archaeological material and refuse, plant and animal remains and excreta and the deliberate application of fertilizer (Proudfoot 1975a).

The phosphate content of soils on archaeological sites is therefore generally higher than on unoccupied adjacent areas due to increments of material from occupation, and some of them may be rendered insoluble and thus be retained in the soil. Use has been made of this fact to locate archaeological sites (especially graves) by phosphate survey, methods which have been reviewed by Dauncey (1952) and Cook and Heizer (1965). The latter authors described the amounts of phosphorus likely to be excreted by human or animal populations, arriving at 62 kg a^{-1} for a group of 100 people, a figure which will vary with life styles and between groups but which will be added to by phosphates from refuse, farming and industrial activities. Many variables exist, for example the phosphate content of plants, which is dependent on soil type, growth conditions and on species (Black 1968), and even within the plant itself the phosphorus is unevenly distributed.

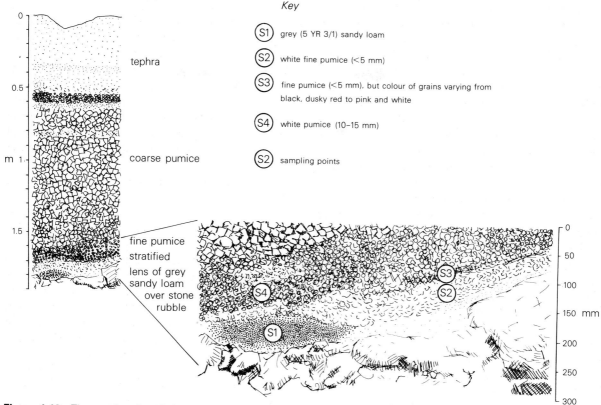

Figure 1.19 The stratigraphy of the archaeological site at Acrotiri (Santorini) showing a section through deposits above a tumbled wall. (after Davidson 1977).

In bodies the phosphorus contents depend on age, sex and food supply, among other factors. Bibliographies of these have been prepared by Thompson (1952), Just Nielsen (1972) and McQuitty and Barber (1972). Allowing for all the above variables the Cook and Heizer 100 person unit occupying a 0.81 ha site might contribute as much as 146 kg ha^{-1} a^{-1}, perhaps 10% of the phosphorus already present in the soil. Chemical analysis of soil phosphorus to determine the amount present in the soil must firstly establish the amount available for plant growth (finding some index of phosphorus fertility) and secondly separate the phosphorus present into its components. The *total* soil phosphorus contains both an organic and inorganic fraction (Black 1968). Most of the inorganic phosphorus is contained in the clay fraction and when organic matter (e.g. plant debris) is added to a soil it begins to decompose, the organic phosphorus present in the organic matter being gradually converted into inorganic soil phos-

phate by a complicated series of processes (Proudfoot 1975a). The organic phosphorus may remain in the soil for a long time, as is shown by the soil buried beneath the Roman amphitheatre at Winterslow which had one-third of the original organic phosphorus still present which had survived into modern times (Mattingly & Williams 1972). There is some mobility of phosphorus in soils and not all the phosphorus that is added remains at the surface. In sandy soils and peats phosphorus may be leached rapidly through until no evidence of the initial input remains.

The body of a 68 kg man contains some 630 g phosphorous, 86% of which is in the skeleton. In a burial this is concentrated in a very small area, resulting in local high phosphorus values which form the basis of phosphate 'prospecting'. Nunez (1975) describes a simple project at the Mesolithic site of Kilteri (Finland) approximately 12 km north of Helsinki. The site had a lithic industry of the

Suomusjärvi Culture, dated to 5000 BC and the underlying soil was an iron podsol. A series of 'graves' had been discovered, important since the acid Finnish soil very rarely preserves bone. Phosphate analysis of the grave-like structures was undertaken, 518 samples being analysed (251 from within the graves and the rest as controls). The samples were oven-dried and sieved to see if particle size composition had any effect on the phosphate concentrations which were then obtained using the finer fraction (< 1 mm) with colorimetric determination of total phosphate (P_2O_5) from molybdenum-blue solution in sulphuric acid (Black 1968). Results were expressed as milligrams of phosphorus yielded by 1 g of dried sieved sample. The method was pioneered in Scandinavia by Arrhenius (1931) and other Scandinavian applications include the work of Ilvonen (1974) in Finland. As stated above nearly 1% of the weight of the human body is phosphate and the presence of inhumations enriches the phosphate contents of the soil. Solecki (1951), amongst others, had shown that it was possible to identify graves from high phosphorus concentrations as was done here. The grave-like structures had higher phosphorus contents than the surrounds and in control samples the soil profiles showed normal distributions (decreasing with depth – higher phosphorus values at the surface and at the B horizon below which the phosphorus decreased with depth). Grave phosphorus reached a maximum at certain depths, suggesting that this was not a surface enrichment from fertilizers. An example of this was seen in Grave I, photographed in infra-red light to show a human-shaped lens of darker colour. The same phenomenon recurred in Grave 3 and the phosphorus maxima in both graves coincided in depth above the shapes. The work at this site concluded that it was clearly impossible to allow for variations in phosphate content due to such intangibles as different burial rites. It confirmed that the phosphorus values of sediment in these prehistoric graves is higher than that of the surrounding soil, the phosphorus profiles of such graves producing a sharp clear maximum at certain depths which coincide with the level at which the body was laid.

Keeley *et al.* (1977) worked on soil 'silhouettes', examining their mineral constituents. These 'silhouettes', which may represent the penultimate stage in the disappearance of bone material, were thought to be phosphate-rich (Johnson 1954), although the work of Biek (1957) on soil samples from the silhouette at the Great Barrow, Bishops Waltham (Hampshire) suggested that manganese concentrations were higher in areas of body stains than in the surrounding soil but that phosphates were of less significance. More positive correlations had, however, been obtained elsewhere (Bascomb 1957). At Mucking, Essex (Jones 1968) results from the analysis of Anglo-Saxon silhouettes suggested that only in very localized areas were the phosphate concentrations higher than in the surrounding soil. Sometimes the silhouette has ten times as much manganese as the rest of the grave, but only where the phosphorus concentration is greater than 1% (Werner & Hughes 1971). Keeley *et al.* (1977) chose two graves which were sampled to confirm this manganese/phosphorus relationship, selecting one for even more detailed work. This grave (no. 963) had a fifth century Saxon burial at 0.6 m depth after the topsoil had been removed but had produced very little bone (Fig. 1.20). Samples were taken at 50 mm vertical intervals and three horizontal positions to 0.5 m depth, then at 25 mm intervals for a further 75 mm. At 0.6 m depth samples were taken from fixed positions in the silhouette and a further three taken below it. Samples were oven-dried at 105 °C for 4 h and sieved to remove the coarse material. The analytical method chosen was emission spectroscopy followed by quantitative atomic absorption analysis on samples of special interest. The phosphorus was determined colorimetrically using the vanadomolybdate methods of Hesse (1971). The silhouette had higher concentrations of phosphorus, manganese and copper than the soil, and phosphorus values were very high where bone had survived. The sample contents of these elements was correlated. The manganese in the sample from the silhouette was higher than the values usually found in bone and the copper values lower. In conclusion it may be seen that there is no evidence for copper accumulation, but it was probably retained preferentially in the acid soil due to fixation by organic matter (the body). Low manganese values in the soil immediately above and below the silhouette suggest manganese withdrawal. Mishra (1973) had shown that manganese availability in soils is affected by the

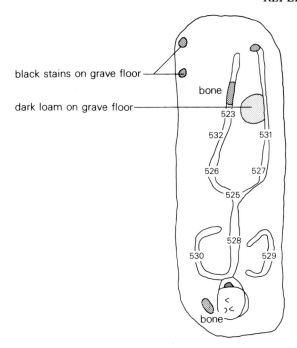

black stains on grave floor

dark loam on grave floor

bone

523

532   531

526   527

525

528

530   529

bone

Figure 1.20 Grave 963 at Mucking, Essex, showing sampling positions from the silhouette level (after Keeley *et al.* 1977).

the light of current knowledge about phosphates.

Much research has been carried out on the composition of phosphate compounds and their mode and rate of formation, but considerable uncertainty still exists. Some methods give different results on different soils and (especially with inorganic phosphates) the different fractions isolated are of little help when trying to understand the formation of phosphate compounds. Much lateral variation exists and one of the major archaeological needs is to ensure that the total horizontal and vertical range of sediments present on the site is examined. New analytical methods need to be developed and care taken in evaluating the results of phosphate analysis of archaeological contexts by traditional methods since these may be producing values which represent only a certain type of soil phosphorus.

addition of different sources of soluble and insoluble phosphates. The manganese and some other 'biophile' elements accumulate in areas of microbial activity and high organic matter content as in graves. Manganese values are more use in showing a silhouette than phosphorus or copper contents which depend on the soil composition.

The site of Goodland (Co. Antrim, Northern Ireland) consisted of a series of houses and field systems of medieval and late medieval date together with a Neolithic complex of pits, ditches and postholes. Proudfoot (1958) linked the archaeology of the area with its soil development and it was hoped that phosphate analyses would show whether or not the features contained phosphates which might have derived from material stored in them, and whether variations in phosphate values outside and inside the huts might indicate use patterns. A wide range of values was found, partially derived from different parent materials and degrees of soil development with the variable introduced by occupation superimposed on it. No significant amounts of phosphorus-rich debris were found from the huts, confirming the difficulty of interpreting data in

References

Addyman, P. V. and D. H. Hill 1968. Saxon Southampton. A review of the evidence, part I. History, location, date and character of the town. *Proc. Hants Field Club Arch. Soc.* **25**, 61–93.

Allman, M. and D. F. Lawrence 1972. *Geological laboratory techniques*. London: Blandford.

Arrhenius, O. 1931. Markanalysen i Arkeologius Tjänst. *Geol. Stockh. Förhand.* **3**, 42–59.

Atkinson, R. J. C. 1957. Worms and weathering. *Antiquity* **31**, 219–33.

Avery, B. W. and C. L. Bascomb 1974. *Soil survey laboratory methods*, Soil Survey Technical Monograph 6. Harpenden: Rothamsted Experimental Station.

Barker, P. 1977. *The techniques of archaeological excavation*. London: Batsford.

Bascomb, C. L. 1957. In Ashbee, P., The Great Barrow at Bishop's Waltham, Hampshire. *Proc. Prehist. Soc.* **23**, 137–66.

Bibby, J. S. 1974. Appendix. Petrofabric analysis. *Phil. Trans R. Soc.* A **276**, 191–5.

Biek, L. 1957. Appendix D: The silhouette. In Ashbee, P., The Great Barrow at Bishop's Waltham, Hampshire. *Proc. Prehist. Soc.* **23**, 137–66.

Black, C. A. 1968. *Soil–plant relationships*, 2nd edn. New York: Wiley.

Bonifay, E. 1962. *Les terrains quaternaires dans le sud-est de la France*. Bordeaux: University of Bordeaux.

Bordes, F. 1972. *A tale of two caves*. New York: Harper and Row.

Bowdler, S. 1976. Hook, line and dillybag: an interpretation of an Australian coastal shell midden. *Mankind* **10**, 248–58.

Brewer, R. 1964. *Fabric and mineral analysis of soils*. London: Dent.

Brongers, J. A. 1965. Ultra-violet fluorescence photography of a soil silhouette of an interred corpse. *Ber. Rÿksdienst oudheik Bodemonderz* 15–16, 227–8.

Brown, J. E. 1973. Depositional histories of sand grains from surface textures. *Nature* 242, 396–8.

Butzer, K. W. 1971. *Environment and archaeology*. London: Methuen.

Butzer, K. W. 1974. Paleoecology of South African Australopithecines: Taung revisited. *Curr. Anthropol.* 15, 367–82, 413–16.

Butzer, K. W. 1975. The ecological approach to archaeology: are we really trying? *Am. Antiquity* 40, 106–11.

Catt, J. A. and A. H. Weir 1975. The study of archaeologically important sediments by petrological techniques. In *Geoarchaeology: Earth science and the past*, D. A. Davidson and M. L. Shackley (eds), 65–92. London: Duckworth.

Clarke, D. L. 1978. *Analytical archaeology*, 2nd edn. London: Methuen.

Conlon, V. M. 1973. *Camera techniques in archaeology*. London: Baker.

Cook, S. F. and R. F. Heizer 1965. *Studies on the chemical analysis of archaeological sites*. Univ. Calif. Publs Anthrop. no. 2.

Cornwall, I. W. 1958. *Soils for the archaeologist*. London: Phoenix.

Corte, A. E. 1962. *The frost behaviour of soils: field and laboratory data for a new concept. 1. Vertical sorting*, US Army Cold Regions Res. Engng Lab. Res. Rep. no. 85.

Crawford, O. G. S. 1949. Trinity Chapel and Fair. *Proc. Hants Field Club* 17, 45–55.

Dalrymple, J. B. 1958. The application of soil micromorphology to fossil soils and other deposits from archaeological sites. *J. Soil Sci.* 9, 199–209.

Dauncey, K. D. M. 1952. Phosphate contents of soils on archaeological sites 1, *Advmt Sci., Lond.* 9, 33–6.

Davidson, D. A. 1978. Aegean soils during the second millenium BC with reference to Thera. In *Thera and the Aegean world*, vol. 1, 725–39. London: Bishopsgate Press.

Davidson, D. A., A. C. Renfrew and C. M. K. Tasker 1976. Erosion and prehistory in Melos: a preliminary note. *J. Arch. Sci.* 3, 219–27.

Dimbleby, G. W. and M. C. D. Speight 1969. Buried soils. *Advmt Sci., Lond.* 26, 203–5.

Doeglas, D. J. 1949. Loess, an aeolian product. *J. Sedim. Petrol.* 19, 112–7.

Doumas, C. 1974. The Minoan eruption of the Santorini volcano. *Antiquity* 48, 110–5.

Evans, G. 1973. Recent coastal sedimentation: a review. In *Marine archaeology*, Colston Papers no. 23, D. J. Blackman (ed.), 89–112. Bristol: John Wright.

Evans, J. G., S. Limbrey and H. Cleere 1974. *The effect of man on the landscape: the highland zone*. London: Council for British Archaeology, Research Report 11.

Faegri, K. and J. Iversern 1965. Field techniques. In *Handbook of paleontological techniques*, B. Kummel and D. Raup (eds). New York, London: Freeman.

Farrand, W. R. 1973. New excavations at the Tabun Cave, Mount Carmel, Israel 1967–72: a preliminary report. *Paleorient* 1, 151–83.

Farrand, W. R. 1975. Sediment analysis of a prehistoric rock shelter: the Abri Pataud. *Quaternary Res.* 5, 1–26.

Folk, R. L. 1954. The distinction between grain size and mineral composition in sedimentary-rock nomenclature. *J. Geol.* 62, 344–59.

Folk, R. L. and W. C. Ward 1957. Brazos River bar, a study of the significance of grain size parameters. *J. Sedim. Petrol.* 27, 3–27.

Franken, A. J. 1965. Taking the baulks home. *Antiquity* 39, 140–2.

Gardner, R. A. M. 1977. Evidence concerning the existence of loess deposits at Tell Fara, Northern Negev, Israel. *J. Arch. Sci.* 4, 377–86.

Gladfelter, B. G. 1977. Geoarchaeology: the geomorphologist and archaeology. *Am. Antiquity* 42, 519–38.

Goldberg, P., 1979. Micromorphology of Pech-de-l'Azé II sediments. *J. Arch. Sci.* 6, 17–47.

Goldberg, P. and Y. Nathan 1975. The phosphate mineralogy from el-Tabun Cave, Mt Carmel, Israel. *Mineralog. Mag.* 40, 253–8.

Haggett, P., A. D. Cliff and A. Frey 1977. *Locational analysis in human geography*, 2nd edn. London: Edward Arnold.

Harris, D. and C. Vita-Finzi 1968. Kokkinopilos – a Greek badland. *Geog. J.* 134, 537–46.

Hassan, F. A. 1978. Sediments in archaeology: methods and implications for paleoenvironmental and cultural analysis. *J. Ad. Arch.* 5, 197–213.

Hassan, F. A. 1979. Geoarchaeology: the geologist and archaeology. *Am. Antiquity* 44, 267–70.

Hay, R. L. 1976. *Geology of Olduvai Gorge: a study of sedimentations in a semi-arid basin*. Berkeley: University of California Press.

Haynes, C. V. 1968. Preliminary report on the late Quaternary geology of the San Pedro Valley, Arizona. In *Southern Arizona guidebook III*, 79–96. Tucson: Arizona Geological Society.

Hesse, P. R. 1971. *A textbook of soil chemical analysis*. London: Murray.

Holdsworth, P. 1980. *Excavations at Melbourne St, Southampton 1970–76*, Southampton Archaeological Research Committee/Council for British Archaeology Research Report no. 33.

Hodgson, J. M. 1964. The low level Pleistocene marine sands and gravels of the West Sussex coastal plain. *Proc. Geol. Assoc.* 75, 547–61.

Horsey, I. and M. L. Shackley 1981. Excavation of a barrow on Canford Heath, Dorset (forthcoming).

Hughes, P. J. and R. J. Lampert 1977. Occupational disturbance and types of archaeological deposit. *J. Arch. Sci.* 4, 135–40.

Hurst, H. and L. E. Stager 1978. A metropolitan landscape: the Late Punic port of Carthage. *Wld Arch.* **9**, 334–46.

Ilvonen, E. 1974. Muinaisen Ulvilan Kapungin Sijaintipaiken Määrittäminen Fosfaattigeokemian Avulla Karhunaammas 1. *Turun Yliopiston Arkeologian Iaitos.*

Jackson, M. L. 1962. *Soil chemical analysis.* London: Prentice-Hall.

Jeffries, J. S. 1977. *Excavation records techniques in use by the Central Excavation Unit.* Department of the Environment Occ. Pap. 1.

Johnson, A. H. 1954. Appendix II. In Piggot, S., Excavations in passage-graves and ring cairns of the Clava Group 1952–3. *Proc. Soc. Antiq.* **88**, 173–207.

Jones, M. U. 1968. Crop-mark sites at Mucking, Essex. *Antiq. J.* **48**, 210–30.

Just Nielsen, A. 1972. Deposition of calcium and phosphorus in growing pigs determined by balance experiments and slaughter investigations. *Acta Agric. Scand.* **22**, 223–37.

Keeley, H. C. M., G. E. Hudson and J. Evans 1977. Trace element contents of human bones in various states of preservation. 1. The soil silhouette. *J. Arch. Sci.* **4**, 19–24.

Knocker, G. M. 1958. Excavations of three round barrows at Kinson, near Bournemouth. *Proc. Dorset Nat. Hist. Archaeol. Soc.* **80**, 133–45.

Krinsley, D. H. and J. C. Doornkamp 1973. *Atlas of quartz grain surface textures.* Cambridge: Cambridge University Press.

Laville, H. 1973. *Climatologie et chronologie du Paléolithique en Perigord étude sedimentologique de depôts en grottes et sous abris.* Thèse de Doctorat d'Etat ès Sciences Naturelles, Université de Bordeaux.

Limbrey, S. 1975. *Soil science and archaeology.* London: Academic Press.

Lubell, D. F., F. A. Hassan, A. Gautier and J.-L. Ballais 1976. The Capsian Escargotieres: an interdisciplinary study elucidates Holocene ecology and subsistence in North Africa. *Science* **191**, 910–20.

de Lumley, H. 1972. *La grotte de l'Hortus.* Marseille: Université de Provence, Laboratoire de Paléontologie Humane et de Préhistoire.

McQuitty, J. B. and E. M. Barber 1972. *An annotated bibliography of farm animal wastes.* Ottawa: Water Pollution Control Directorate, Environmental Protection Service.

Mattingley, G. E. G. and R. J. B. Williams 1962. A note on the chemical analysis of a soil buried since Roman times. *J. Soil Sci.* **13**, 254–8.

Mishra, P. L. 1973. Role of organic acids and phosphates on the forms of soil manganese. *An. Inst. Nac. Invest. Agron.* **2**, 213–8.

Mitchell, B. D. and R. A. Jarvis 1956. *The soils of the country round Kilmarnock,* Mem. Soil Surv. Great Britain. London: HMSO.

Money, J. 1973. The destruction of Acrotiri. *Antiquity* **47**, 50–3.

Nunez, M. 1975. Phosphorus determination of the graves of Kilteri in Vantaa, Southern Finland. *Empaunos-Suomen Museo* 18–25.

Olsen, D. 1968. *Om at Udgrave Stolpehuller.* Nationalmusats Arbiydomark.

Phillips, F. C. 1971. *The use of stereographic projection in structural geology*, 3rd edn. London: Edward Arnold.

Pilcher, W. S., D. J. Spearman and D. C. Pugh 1954. The loess of Pegwell Bay, Kent. *Geol Mag.* **91**, 308–14.

Proudfoot, V. B. 1975a. The analysis and interpretation of soil phosphorus in archaeological contexts. In *Geoarchaeology: Earth science and the past*, D. A. Davidson and M. L. Shackley (eds), 93–114. London: Duckworth.

Proudfoot, V. B. 1958. Problems of soil history. *J. Soil Sci.* **9**, 186–90.

Rapp, G., Jr 1975. The archaeological field staff: the geologist. *J. Fld Arch.* **2**, 229–37.

Rogers, J. and A. J. Tankard 1974. Surface textures of some quartz grains from the west coast of southern Africa. *Proc. Electron Microsc. Soc. S. Afr.* **4**, 55–6.

Shackley, M. L. 1972. The use of textural parameters in the analysis of cave sediments. *Archaeometry* **14**, 133–45.

Shackley, M. L. 1975. *Archaeological sediments: a survey of analytical methods.* London: Butterworths.

Shackley, M. L. 1978a. The behaviour of artefacts as sedimentary particles in a fluviatile environment. *Archaeometry* **20**, 55–61.

Shackley, M. L. 1978b. A sedimentological study of Devil's Lair, Western Australia. *J. Proc. R. Soc. West Aust.* **60** (2), 33–40.

Shackley, M. L. 1979. Geoarchaeology: polemic on a progressive relationship. *Naturwiss.* **66**, 429–33.

Shackley, M. L. 1980. The 'Hamwih' brickearths. In *Excavations at Melbourne Street, Southampton 1971–6*, P. Holdsworth (ed.), 3–7. London: Council for British Archaeology Research Report 33.

Society for Archaeological Science 1978. Geoarchaeological questionnaire from University of Chicago, *Soc. Arch. Sci. Newsletter* (1) 3.

Solecki, R. S. 1951. Notes on soil analysis and archaeology. *Am. Antiquity* **16**, 254–6.

Stockton, E. D. 1978. Shaw's Creek shelter: human displacement of artefacts and its significance. *Mankind* **9**, 112–7.

Tankard, A. J. and F. R. Schweitzer 1975. Textural analysis of cave sediments: Die Kelders, Cape Province, South Africa. In *Geoarchaeology: Earth science and the past*, D. A. Davidson and M. L. Shackley (eds), 289–316. London: Duckworth.

Thompson, L. M. 1952. *Soils and soil fertility.* New York.

United States Department of Agriculture 1960. *Soil classification: a comprehensive system (7th approximation).* Washington, DC: Soil Conservation Service.

Werner, A. E. and M. T. Hughes 1971. *Report on (a) an experiment to test the retention of phosphate by soil of the Sutton Hoo Ship burial; (b) phosphate analysis of soil from*

Grave 662 at the Anglo-Saxon cemetery at Mucking, Essex. RL File no. 3093, unpublished report – British Museum Research Lab.

West, R. G. 1968. *Pleistocene geology and biology, with especial reference to the British Isles*. Harlow: Longman.

White, E. E. and R. J. Hayes 1961. The use of stereo-colour photography for soil profile studies. *Photogr. J*. **101**, 211–5.

White, L. P. 1971. A new technique for soil pit illustrations. *J. Soil Sci*. **23**, 58–61.

Williams, R. B. G. 1973. Frost and the works of man. *Antiquity* **47**, 19–31.

Wright, H. E., D. A. Livingstone and E. J. Cushing 1965. Coring devices for lake sediments. In *Handbook of paleontological techniques*, B. Kummel and D. Raup (eds). New York: Freeman.

Yaalon, D. H. and J. Dan 1974. Accumulation and distribution of loess-derived deposits in the semi desert and desert fringe areas of Israel, *Z. Geomorph*. Suppl. **20**, 91–105.

2 *Micro-organisms*

The microbe is so very small
You cannot make him out at all,
But many sanguine people hope
To see him through a microscope.

(Hillaire Belloc, *The Microbe*)

2.1 *Introduction*

All living things are basically similar, being composed of protoplasm (a colloidal organic complex consisting largely of protein, lipids and nucleic acids). All have membranes for cell walls and most have nuclei with surrounding membranes (with the exception of bacteria). Micro-organisms, or microbes, include the bacteria, rickettsiae, fungi, algae of the Plant Kingdom and the protozoa and viruses from the Animal Kingdom. The position of viruses is doubtful and extremely controversial, but in this book the *International code of nomenclature of bacteria and viruses* (1975) is used, together with *Bergey's manual of descriptive bacteriology* (Breed *et al.* 1974). The problem of microbial classification is discussed by Ainsworth and Sneath (1962), who give names of institutions which maintain reference collections of organisms and present a general bibliography on classification. Pelczar and Reid (1972) deal with identification and staining methods, and discuss different applications of microscopy. It must, however, be emphasized that the preparation and identification of micro-organisms requires techniques, expertise and reference collections outside the normal range of environmental archaeology. Archaeological microbiology is a specialized job, and the justification for including it in a work such as this is that it is a field where great work remains to be done with, alas, few people interested in doing it.

The Plant Kingdom has conventionally five divisions, listed below:

I Protophyta (primitive plants, including bacteria)
II Thallophyta (moulds, yeasts and algae)
III Bryophyta (mosses and liverworts)
IV Pteridophyta (ferns and club mosses)
V Spermatophyta (seed-bearing plants).

Of these the first two divisions contain micro-organisms, together with the protozoa from the Animal Kingdom. Some micro-organisms are plant-like and some more like animals, but some, unfortunately, have the characteristics of both. Viruses are even more complicated since they are sometimes classified as living and sometimes as inanimate. The difference between a plant and an animal, so obvious with higher forms, may not be readily apparent in micro-organisms. The following distinctions have been suggested by Pelczar and Reid (1972):

(a) plant cells have rigid walls whereas animal cells are bounded by flexible membranes
(b) plants are not actively mobile but most animals are mobile
(c) only plants contain chlorophyll and perform photosynthesis (making carbohydrates from carbon dioxide and water in the presence of sunlight); animals cannot do this and form a high level in food chains, obtaining their nourishment from organic matter of plant origin
(d) plants store their food reserves as starch but animals have glycogen and fat as their principal food reserves.

It is now becoming accepted that the bacteria and the blue-green algae are a specialist group of organisms called prokaryotes, and are very different from other organisms, called eukaryotes. This may ultimately lead to a revision of the simple division into animals and plants.

Bacteria, fungi and algae may for most purposes

41

be included with the bryophytes in the general heterogeneous category of non-vascular plants, which differ from vascular (higher) plants by not possessing lignified water-conducting tissue. They are therefore defined, like the invertebrates (Section 2.7) by a negation. Some of these simple plants are unicellular and microscopic and show a morphological diversity resulting from adaptation to their particular environment, but branched and unbranched chains of cells (filaments) also occur. The most highly differentiated non-vascular plants have leaf-like, root-like and stem-like structures, for example the large group of seaweeds which may grow to over 60 m in length yet are morphologically quite simple. Archaeological sites have yielded little evidence of any non-vascular plants since the fleshy non-skeletal parts do not preserve well, and in many cases their presence is only identified by the incidence of spores (Section 2.3).

Some explanation of the species classification may be required. A species name is composed of two words, the first being the genus (e.g. *Yersinia*) and the second a description of some kind (e.g. *pestis*), making the species name *Yersinia pestis* (the bacillus of bubonic plague). Species are grouped into a genus and genera into a tribe; families are composed of groups of related tribes or genera, and orders of groups of related families. On a higher level the orders are grouped successively into classes, phyla and finally into kingdoms (plant or animal) but may be subdivided into sub- or super-families or genera where necessary.

In 1866 E. H. Haeckel proposed a third kingdom of Protista for all unicellular organisms, both plant and animal, in addition to the two main kingdoms. It was to include all organisms characterized by a lack of definite cellular arrangement as well as a lack of differentiation of cells for specific metabolic functions. This terminology has not been adopted here as its use seems to cause some confusion and it does not agree with the more modern prokaryote–eukaryote concept.

All micro-organisms need energy: carbon and nutrients in utilizable forms. The energy sources are widely varied – for algae and photosynthesizing bacteria energy comes from light, and for chemoautotrophic bacteria, for example, from hydrogen. Micro-organisms may obtain their food in different ways. A heterotrophic micro-organism (which obtains energy from the oxidation of organic matter) may either use dead tissue (in which case it is classified as *saprophytic*) or living matter (parasitic). Similarly, modes of subsistence, dispersal and reproduction are almost incredibly varied.

Bacteria which produce respiratory infections, for example, are expelled in vast quantities during sneezing or coughing and may be transported some distance. Air-transported plant pathogenic (disease-bearing) fungi like *Puccinia graminis* (p. 51) release millions of spores to increase their chances of survival. Some micro-organisms require a **vector**, which is an individual of one species that transmits propagules of another from place to place. It may serve as a mechanical transmitter, a simple carrying agent, or it may have some physiological or pathological association with the cell which it transports. When the identity of the vector is known the means of dispersal is established and transmission by a vector increases the likelihood of individuals from a population finding a new, favourable habitat. If the micro-organism has a vector, then less propagules are needed; therefore in bacteria or fungi transmitted by insect vectors or carried, for example, on the surface of seeds, less numbers are reproduced. This, of course, lessens the chances of detecting them in archaeological deposits. Some species reduce dispersal risks not by their numerical superiority but because at one stage in their life cycle most or all individuals are resistant to their environment and can survive, inert, for varying periods (p. 51).

Micro-organisms are, by definition, very small, and may be identified archaeologically in one of three ways:

(a) By direct culturing of viable organisms obtained from an archaeological deposit (p. 55) using laboratory cultures which may produce thousands or millions of individuals, grown in special culture media which contain various nutrients compounded to favour growth. A pure (axenic) culture is one in which an organism is reared in an environment free from any other living organism. Mixed cultures are composed of two or more kinds of organisms. The organisms are usually grown as colonies, not individuals. A colony may be seen by the naked eye but individual cells will need high magnification, the use of a light microscope up to ×1000 or even an electron microscope at magnifications of up to ×10⁶ in some cases. Measurements are made in micrometres. Films or smears of the culture are examined, either stained or unstained, and it may be necessary to supplement the light microscope with ultra-violet or phase microscopy. For viruses or rickettsiae living host cells (a tissue culture) are needed. Some require oxygen, others do not, but all need the appropriate micro-environment. Aids to identification include staining, the most important method being that of Gram staining where a fixed bacterial smear is subjected to the following solutions in order: crystal violet, iodine solution, alcohol (as a decolourizing agent) and safranin or some other suitable counterstain. Bacteria stained by the Gram method are divided into Gram positive (which retain the crystal violet and thus appear deep violet in colour) and Gram negative (which lose the violet and retain the safranin, thus appearing red).

(b) Not all organisms in a sample are viable and thus not all can be cultured. A further method of identification, also direct, is used where a hard shell is preserved, calcareous in the protozoans called foraminifera (Section 2.6.3) and siliceous in the group of algae known as diatoms (Section 2.2.2). Microscopic identification of microorganisms by direct examination of spores (p. 51) is sometimes possible.

(c) A third method of identification may be referred to as the indirect (or secondary) method, as, for example, when the plague-bearing black rat (Section 2.4.3) is found in archaeological deposits, or when an outbreak of plague is recorded by historical sources (p. 59). The existence of the plague bacillus *Yersinia pestis* may be inferred, but not confirmed. All literary and historical references (frequently but not always ambiguous) are included in this category.

2.2 *Algae*

2.2.1 *Introduction*
Algae are photosynthetic non-embryo-producing plants, subdivided on the basis of their colour (red,

blue-green, etc.) which is due to the different proportions of pigments in the cells. Inevitably, all specialists do not agree on their classification. Most algae are aquatic although some live in the soil. Most are free-living but some are symbiotic (for example those which combine with fungi to produce lichens). All need water, carbon dioxide and light for growth and some need one or more specific organic compounds as well. Sizes range from microscopic unicellular algae to highly differentiated multicellular organisms such as the seaweeds. Archaeologically the most important algal group is the Chrysophycophyta (*chryso* = golden) algae, which includes the yellow-green or golden brown algae and the diatoms, the latter having a siliceous cell wall. Chrysophyta include both unicellular and colonial forms, planktonic algae which live in a wide range of conditions from marine to freshwater and have an important role as photosynthesizers and starting points for food chains. The division Chlorophycophyta (*chloro* = green) of green algae includes the species *Pamellococcus*, famous for its destructive effect on the Lascaux cave paintings. The opening of the cave to the public in the early 1950s created an upheaval in the atmosphere which, combined with damp conditions and carbon dioxide exhaled by human visitors, produced disintegration of the calcite crystals under the paintings, a re-precipitation of a calcite film on top of them and a favourable growth environment for *Pamellococcus*. Despite the closure of the cave and many attempts at conservation the future of the paintings is uncertain.

Various species of algae have been used as food plants and Farrar (1966) showed that the Aztecs of Tenochtitlan (Mexico City) ate large quantities of a blue-green algae *Cyanophyta*, which at certain seasons covered the brackish lake surrounding the town. When dried and made into cakes it had a salty, cheesy flavour and kept well (Dimbleby 1978). *Exodus 16:* 14–15 has a description of the 'manna' which sustained the Israelites in their wanderings in the desert, and physiologists suggest that it might have been a blue-green alga belonging to the genus *Nostoc* (Pelczar & Reid 1972). Other sources (Dimbleby 1978) suspect that it was a lichen, probably *Lecanora esculenta*, which grows in semi-desert areas of northern Africa and western Asia. Doubt has been cast on this because of the vast quantities of algae or lichen that would have been required. If the Biblical figures on the number of Israelites are to be taken seriously then the estimated 2–2½ million people would require 2000–9000 tons of lichen per day (Moldenke & Moldenke 1952), but a less literal interpretation might at least support the possibility that lichens provided an ancillary food source. Lichens, a symbiotic union of fungi and algae were certainly eaten by some North American Indian tribes, and have other uses as bedding, dye-stuffs, etc. They are characterized by leafy thalli, the simplest being relatively few fungal cells forming among the algal cells, but fungus is usually the dominant organism and the thallus has a definite internal structure. The algal component may be either green or blue-green algae, but very little work has been done on cultures. Another reference to algae in the Old Testament was mentioned by Pelczar and Reid (1972), again from *Exodus* (*7:* 20–21) where the river Nile is referred to as turning into a 'river of blood'. This was probably a 'red tide' or 'water bloom' of red algae, commonly reported by sailors. Macroscopic algae, particularly the division Rhodophyta (red algae) are more commonly used for food than the blue-green variety, and even today the Japanese cultivate and harvest the species *Porphyra* which in parts of Britain (especially Wales) is used to make the delicacy laverbread. This seaweed 'bread' may also be made from a green alga *Ulva* sp., but apparently the flavour is much inferior. Other economic uses for algae are many and varied – extracts are used in food manufacture and seaweeds have a history of utilization for the caulking of boats, the earliest examples being those from the Bronze Age plank-built boats from North Ferriby, Yorkshire (Wright & Churchill 1965). Brown algae (Phaeophyta, *phaeo* = brown), most common in cold marine waters, include large species called kelp, a major source of iodine with modern derivatives used in everything from the production of salad dressings to the manufacture of waterproof cloth.

2.2.2 Diatoms

Introduction. Diatoms are microscopic unicellular or colonial algae with a siliceous cell wall, often well preserved and forming the basis for identification, using the same type of method as pollen analysis

(Section 4.4). They have both chlorophyll and fucoxanthin pigmentation like the golden algae but an additional third pigment which participates in photosynthesis. Diatom cells consist of two overlapping highly sculptured halves, rather like the top and bottom of an old-fashioned pillbox (Fig. 2.2). Vegetative cells are radially or bilaterally symmetrical and have no flagellae. Some diatom vegetative cells are capable of movement even if non-flagellated, and these are characterized by a longitudinal striation (rafe) on the surface (Fig. 2.1a). Diatoms absorb silica compounds from water and deposit them in the cell wall continuously throughout their life, irrespective of the amount of available light or whether or not the cell is actively in the process of dividing. After the cell dies the wall begins to disintegrate but if conditions are favourable massive thicknesses of diatomaceous deposits may accumulate – over 1200 feet (*c.* 370 m) having been recorded, composed almost entirely of the remains of the diatoms shells. Such deposits are mined for their industrial uses, as a filtering agent, abrasive and insulation.

Diatoms can move in the currents of oceans and rivers or be transported by man, for example *Biddulphia sirensis* which was transferred from the Far East to European seas on the hulls of ships (MacNeil 1977). Distinct geographical patterns are usual among the marine algae, for example *Thalassiosira antarctica* which is characteristic of Antarctic

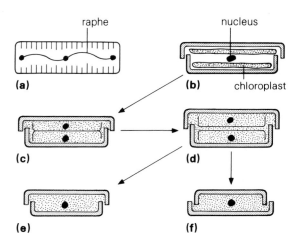

Figure 2.1 The diatom cell. (a) Top view; (b) side view; (c)–(f) stages in division.

Figure 2.2 Scanning electron photomicrograph of the diatom *Melosira* (× 2300).

waters while *Thalassiosira hydralis* is limited to the Arctic. Diatoms, being exclusively aquatic, may be used to distinguish particular environments of deposition, for example changes in the silting patterns of an estuary or in the type of deposits forming in a lake. Early work on diatoms was pioneered by Pennington (1943) in her study of the diatom succession of Lake Windermere, and much attention has been focused on Quaternary sediments (Clark 1975). A number of analyses of archaeological importance have now been carried out, although the field is a comparatively new one. In the Netherlands archaeologists have been concerned not only with distinguishing the depositional environment of sediments *in situ* but also of the potting clays made from them, giving clues to the provenance of the finished pot. Voorhips and Jansma (1974) carried out a pollen and diatom analysis of a shore section of the former Lake Wervershoof (Holland) to reconstruct local and regional occupation and vegetation history. The lake sediments were deposited between 1800 BC and AD 850, and their study complemented the excavation of a Carolingian settlement nearby. Bakker *et al.* (1976) undertook an interdisciplinary investigation of the ecology and archaeology of an agrarian settlement at the Middle Bronze Age site of Hoogkarspel-Waterforen, which comprises a complex of houses, barrows and field systems in western Friesland. The project, which integrated diatom evidence with that obtained from pollen, molluscs, seeds, fruit, animal bones, geomorphology and pedology, produced the earliest known system of ditch-surrounded fields recorded from Holland and a correlation between areas of prehistoric farming and different preferred soil types. The enclosure ditch system, which conformed remarkably well to the soil type and micro-relief, lasted several centuries with a continuous process of slight shifts and re-allotment. The pioneering work of Jansma (1977) illustrated the potential use of diatom analysis for provenancing pottery, especially in coastal areas where local clays of marine origin were used, with important implications for early trade patterns.

Site sampling. The sampling method used for diatomaceous sediments is the same as that for pollen samples (Section 4.2) with an equal emphasis on great cleanliness in sample-taking to minimize the risk of contamination.

Laboratory preparation. The following method is recommended but may be adapted for different types of sediments:

(1) Boil the sample with 30% hydrogen peroxide (H_2O_2). Wash and decant as for pollen analysis (Section 4.3).
(2) Repeat using 30% hydrochloric acid (HCl). Wash. Decant.
(3) Wash the sample gently through a 63 μm (4 φ) 3 in (76.2 mm) sieve. The sieve will retain the sand and coarse particles, which may be thrown away. The silt and clay should be collected in a beaker.
(4) Voorhips and Jansma (1974) recommend that the fine clay fraction (particle diameter < 2 m, 9 φ) be removed to avoid 'coating' the diatoms which makes identification more difficult. This may be done by dispersing the residue in the beaker in a large measuring cylinder of water, shaking it and then allowing it to settle for about 8 h at a temperature of 20 °C (Shackley 1975). The liquid fraction must then be siphoned off, retaining the fine clay in suspension. The residue should be dried at a low temperature in a slow oven.

Identification and counting. Diatom identification is extremely laborious since, after the residue is mounted on slides, the identification and counting must be carried out at a magnification of × 1000, counting by species until a total of at least 300 specimens per preparation has been reached. Species are identified on the basis of size and surface texture of the silicified cell walls (thecae) and the counting procedures outlined for pollen analysis may be found useful. Reference specimens must be used.

Presentation of results. The diagram shown in Figure 2.3 presents the results of the analysis of Voorhips and Jansma (1974), although only those parts of the diagram which showed essential differences in composition and were therefore counted for both whole and broken specimens are reproduced. The principle of the diagram is exactly the same as for a pollen diagram, expressing relative values as a percentage of the total counted per sample. Some variation of the horizontal scale is necessary for species such as *Melosira granulata*, which, because of its frequency, is reduced by a scale of 1 : 10. In the case of a pottery analysis not all the clays examined will prove to contain diatoms, and in any case a selective preservation factor may be operating since diatoms from brackish water have thicker thecae than those from purely fresh or purely salt water, being subject to greater fluctuations. The firing temperature is also critical – the siliceous thecae cannot survive more than 1000 °C. The shape of the diatom scale is also important (Fig. 2.3). Despite their resistance repeated transport will cause the long pendant thecae to fracture while compact rounded scales remain intact. Jansma (1976) noted that the occurrence of large numbers of broken specimens suggested redeposition, possibly into a different environment, and, if a mixture of allothonous and autochthonous material is found, the latter will show less broken specimens. A deposit with a high pH value may dissolve the diatoms, evidence of such attack being marks of dissolution on the surface of the diatoms. It may also fragment the coarser specimens and even completely remove the less well silicified, as at Lympne (p. 49). In the case of clays formed under similar environmental conditions over a large region, a similar diatom content is likely, which can be used to establish the precise nature of the ancient depositional environment. In the case of pottery the diatom analysis of sherds can at least

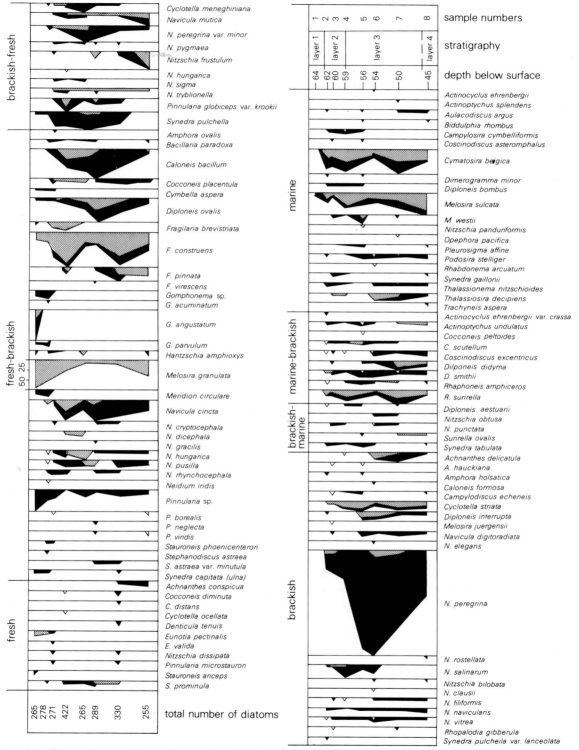

Figure 2.3 Diatom diagram of the sediments from Medemblik (after Voorhips & Jansma 1967), showing the gradual change from maribe to fresh water conditions.

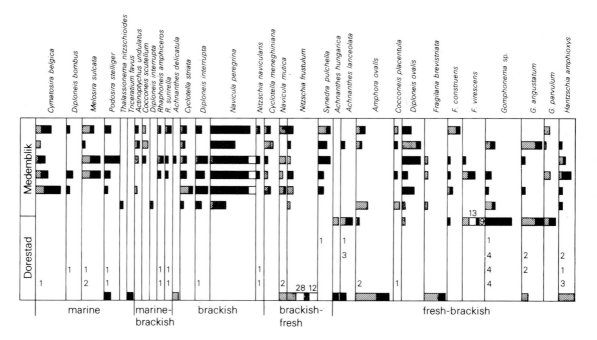

establish the possibility that the sherd was made from a particular clay, or the certainty that it was not. However, if the clay from another region was brought to the site, the pot may have been made there from imported material, implying a trade in raw material rather than in finished products, rather like that outlined by Peacock (1977) for pottery on the basis of heavy mineral analysis.

2.2.3 Applications of diatom analysis

Lake Wevershoof, Medemblik (Voorhips & Jansma 1974). Figure 2.4 shows diatom analysis at Lake Wevershoof, Medemblik in Holland. The base line of this diagram shows, from left to right, a transition from marine to brackish/freshwater forms, with many intermediate stages. The total number of diatoms preserved was rather small (2375), especially in the marine and marine–brackish range. *Melosira granulata*, a freshwater–brackish type, represented over half the counted species and, together with *Fragilaria construens* (of similar habitat preference) was present as whole individuals, suggesting *in situ* accumulation in calm freshwater. Some species (e.g. *Navicula peregrina*) which prefer brackish conditions almost always occurred broken and this, together with other features of the deposit,

suggests that an inflow of disturbed material, originating in marine–brackish conditions, took place, the brackish diatoms being redeposited in the freshwater habitat. The fresh–brackish and freshwater forms return later to dominate the diagram. The authors suggest that this mixing was occasioned by the Dunkirk III marine transgression into the then essentially freshwater lake, which also effected a break in the occupation of the area. Towards the end of the diagram (Fig. 2.4) a temporary break in the transgression is indicated, where the lake conditions again became fresh and the Carolingian farmers (ninth century AD) could return to the area and resume the growing of rye, the pollen of which is once more prominent in the pollen analysis which accompanied the diatom work. In this case the archaeologist is studying the material remains of settlement, the diatom analyst is charting the major changes in a sedimentary sequence and the palynologist is providing a detailed breakdown of floral changes. Together, this illustrates man's activities in the area and presents a full causal interpretation of palaeoenvironmental change.

Diatom analysis of pottery (Jansma 1977). Some Dutch Neolithic sherds of TRB (Funnel Beaker) type were used for preliminary analysis, done by

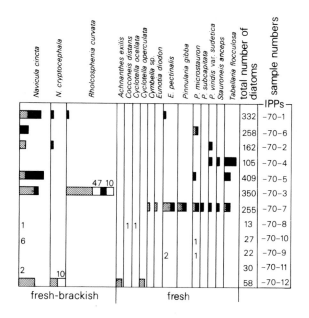

Figure 2.4 Diatom diagram of specimens obtained from the analysis of pottery from Medemblik and Dorestad (after Jansma 1977).

qualitative comparison and not the type of quantitative analysis outlined above (p. 46). They were compared with three other groups of Dutch Neolithic pottery with variable results. The pottery from sites located on Pleistocene deposits was found to have been made either from boulder clay without diatoms or from freshwater clays with sparse diatoms. Inland sites on Holocene deposits frequently yielded diatomaceous clays and when this was not the case it seems likely that either the pottery was imported or else the raw material had been traded. A quantitative analytical study was undertaken on a series of Neolithic Vlaardingen (VL) sherds, and some from the stratigraphically differentiated and later Bell Beaker (BB) sherds from the Vlaardingen site. The difference in the diatom content of these two groups of pottery was associated with a comparable change in the diatom content of the site section, showing that the diatoms of the VL sherds corresponded to those of the fill of a small creek bed in the site which would have contained brackish water. The BB shells contained mainly allochthonous marine and brackish species which corresponded to the characteristics of the clay deposited just before the Beaker occupation by periodic flooding.

Other diatom analyses have been used to prove local pottery production, as at Medemblik (Besteman 1979) and Dorestad, both of which produced Medieval Kugeltöpfe wares, the former being a coastal site and the latter an inland one. The comparative diagrams are shown in Figure 2.4. At the former site the diatom spectrum could be matched with a local clay characterized by equal proportions of marine, brackish and freshwater species, suggesting redeposition. Six sherds of Kugeltöpfe pottery from Dorestad were processed, all of different types, differently fired and tempered with different materials. Two produced reliable spectra, one with almost exclusively freshwater–brackish to freshwater diatoms and the other with so few marine–brackish diatoms that coastal clays could not be the source. In the latter case the diatoms probably accompanied the shell temper which *would* have been brought from the coast. Local production of Medieval Kugeltöpfe is suggested on the basis of this (admittedly restricted) analysis.

Estuarine silting at Lympne, southern England. During the spring of 1976 a series of borings was made from estuarine deposits which had formed part of the gradual silting of Romney marsh, at the foot of the Roman fort of Lympne. This silting resulted in the present position of the Saxon Shore

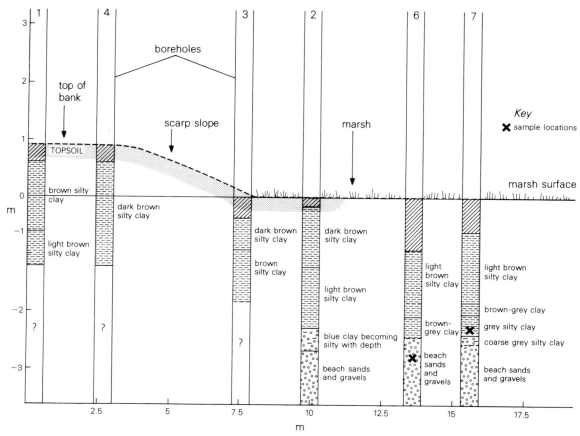

Figure 2.5 Location of boreholes for diatom samples from the edge of Romney marsh at the foot of the Saxon shore fort of Lympne.

Fort, once a thriving port and now separated from the sea by some three miles (*c.* 4½ km) of marsh. It was hoped that an analysis of the marsh diatoms might assist with an interpretation of the duration of this post-Roman silting, accompanying excavations on the actual site of the fort carried out by Professor B. W. Cunliffe. Figure 2.5 shows the location of the various boreholes. Several samples were examined from each core by Mr N. I. Hendey, who reported on the included diatoms (N. I. Hendey, personal communication). The results, summarized in Table 2.1, show, surprisingly, fully saline conditions (where salinity is greater than 30%) throughout the sequence with no evidence of brackish water, which, is strange in view of the nature and topography of the present-day marsh. The only non-marine species was *Scoliopleura tumida*, which is sometimes found in salt-marshes and suggests at least reduced

salinity, but was very rare in the material examined. The two species of *Rhaponeis*, *R. amphiceros* and *R. surirella*, are described as marine–brackish by Voorhips and Jansma (1974), but with such a small sample it is not really possible to correlate diatom succession with palaeoenvironmental change. The high pH value, 9, had certainly destroyed some of the most delicate specimens and invalidated the results of the analysis.

2.3 Fungi

Fungi are plants which are not differentiated into roots, stems and leaves. They have no chlorophyll and are therefore heterotrophic (p. 42), either obtaining food from non-living matter (saprophytes) or from living tissue (parasites). Nearly 100 000

Table 2.1 Diatom list from Lympne.

Species	Coarse grey silty clay at 1.80 m	Very coarse grey silt and beach sand at 1.98 m
diatoms		
Actinoptychus senarius (Ehrensberg)	×	×
Aulacodiscus argus (Eh.) (Schmidt)	× M	×
Melosira westii Wm. Smith	× M	×
Paralia sulcata (Eh.) Clere	×	×
Podosira stelliger (Bailey)	× M	—
Trachyneis aspersa (Eh.) Clere	×	×
Triceratium favus (Eh.)	× M	—
Scoliopleura tumida (de Brébisson ex Kützing) Rabenhorst	× ?brackish	× ?brackish
Cystosira belgica Grunow	× M	×
C. lorenziana Grunow		×
Biddulphia rhombus (Eh.) W. Smith	× M	×
Dimeregramma minor (Gregory) Ralfs	—	×
Rhaphoneis amphiceros (Eh.)		×
R. surirella (Eh.) Grunow		× } *
Surirella recedens Schmidt		×
Thalassiosira sp.		×
foraminifera		
Silicotextulina deflandrei frenguelli	×	×
coccolithophores		
Coccolithus pelagicus (Wallich) Schiller	×	×

×, present; M, marine species.
* These species taken as marine–brackish by Voorhips and Jansma (1974).

species are known, occurring everywhere and often having a profound influence over their environment. They resemble plants in some ways and animals in others, with differences sufficiently pronounced to complicate their classification. One school of thought (followed here) says that fungi are true non-vascular plants, another believes them to be animals and yet a third places them in the kingdom Protista with other microscopic thallophytes. The most widely accepted classification is that of Alexopoulos (1962) who puts fungi into the division Mycota within the kingdom Protista, dividing them into two subdivisions, the true fungi (Eumycotina) and the true slime moulds (Myxomycotina), further subdivided into classes and orders. The true fungi include many widely diverse morphological types, some of great economic importance and others which produce disease.

The thallus of a fungus is differentiated into the vegetative portion and the reproductive structures, although in many fungi one can only see the latter since the former grows within the substrate. The vegetative part may be unicellular (yeast-like) or filamentous (mould-like). Fungal filaments are called hyphae and are usually highly branched to form the mycelium of the organism (Fig. 2.6). Growth of the hyphae is restricted to the tip of the filaments and the most common type of reproduction is the spore, a small usually unicellular unit which becomes detached from the parent plant, either during sexual or asexual reproduction.

The classes of fungi are differentiated on details of sexual reproduction and the form of flagellated cells, when present. The so-called Fungi Imperfecti (where sexual reproduction is never found) are grouped into an artificial class of organisms with a different taxonomic meaning, identified on details of asexual reproduction. They produce diseases such as 'ringworm' and athlete's foot.

Spores (the microscopic bodies released by non-flowering plants as part of their reproductive cycle) are often identifiable. There may be several different types of spore produced by one species at different stages of its reproductive cycle if this is very complex. The teleutospore of the wheat rust fungus *Puccinia graminis*, for example, was discovered in a

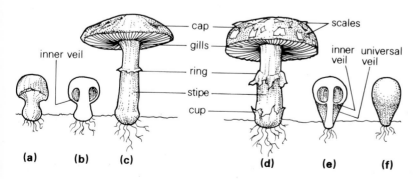

Figure 2.6 Stages in mushroom growth. *Agaricus* type: (a) button; (b) section through button; (c) mature fruiting body. *Amanita* type: (d) button; (e) section through button; (f) mature fruiting body.

coffin in the Great Barrow at Bishops Waltham (Ashbee 1957), which suggested that the coffin had been lined with wheatstraw. Fungal spore identification is very difficult and a matter for the specialists. Vast quantities of spores may be produced – *Puccinia graminis* might yield 26 million uredospores per square metre and certain puffballs (below) produce $7–10^{12}$ spores (Gregory 1961), meaning that individual fungal populations might disperse very efficiently and widely. *Puccinia graminis* spores can travel 970 km and are wind-borne, but the spores are subject to the effect of rain and topographic variations, which means that not all will find a suitable *locus* for germination. Fungal spores may be vertically transported within the soil by water, gravity or natural channels. Algae, too, may be carried to great depths where they are unable to produce food by photosynthesis. Fungi have been noted at depths of half a metre in sand and soil, arriving at an ecological dead end with very low nutrient content.

The class Ascomycetes (*askos* = sack) is a group of economically important fungi which include the food-spoilage moulds and the powdery mildews, which are plant parasites. Morels and truffles belong to this class and form an important food resource. Truffles, *Tuber* spp., consist of a mass of ascospores and mycelia covered by a thick knobby rind. They are found below the soil surface in association with trees such as oaks and beech, detected by their characteristic odour, detectable by specially trained pigs and dogs. Food-spoiling moulds such as *Claviceps purpurea* (ergot of rye) were recognized by the Greeks and Romans. This mould will produce gangrene and death if ingested in large quantities with its cereal host, but infected plants have medicinal uses in the control of haemorrhage and in treating migraine. Fungal diseases of plants have been recorded from several archaeological locations. Helbaek (1958) found evidence of such plant diseases in the Tollund and Graubelle bog corpses (Section 6.5), including ergot, sclerotia and the spores of various smuts (*Ustilago* spp.) which attacked wild grasses and weeds. Crop diseases included one brought about by a fungus from the family Dematiaceae, which includes seed-borne cereal parasites and the covered barley smut (*Ustilago hordei*). Studies of plant pathology in archaeology are, regrettably, few and far between,

but there can be little doubt that similar examination of collections of plant material might produce equally interesting evidence of disease. One of the most important plant diseases of all, so-called Dutch elm disease, is a fungus which belongs to the class Ascomycetes and is spread by bark-boring beetles. It is, regrettably, little studied from archaeological contexts.

The class Basidiomycetes includes the mushrooms, toadstools, puffballs and bracket or shelf fungi, many of which are saprophytic. It also includes some rusts and smuts which have many points of similarity with Ascomycetes. Both, for example, are mycelial with central pores in hyphal septa, but Basidiomycetes have a club-shaped basidium (a cell in which nuclear fusion and meiosis occurs) which is unicellular in mushrooms, puffballs and bracket fungi and septate in rusts and smuts. A mushroom is simply an edible basidiomycete that has a fruiting body differentiated into cap, stipe and gills (Fig. 2.6). The toadstool morphology is similar, but it is inedible. Localized areas of hyphal growth enlarge to produce a mass of compacted hyphae called a button; later enlargement by water uptake gives the formation of the mature fruiting body. Basidia line both surfaces of the gills and forcibly discharge basidiospores when mature. Certain members of this class are poisonous, *Amanita*, for example, which has an additional structure called a universal veil which encloses the immature fruiting body. Remnants of this occur as scales on the cap and a basal cup on the immature mushroom (Fig. 2.6). The fruiting body of puffballs (which are edible before spore formation) originates like a mushroom's and differentiates structurally as basidia and basidiospores remain enclosed until maturity.

There are many different dispersal methods for fungi. *Calvatia* (the giant puffball which may measure more than 450 mm in diameter) has an outer layer which disintegrates and the spores are passively dispersed by the wind.

Rusts differ from the rest of this group since they have septate basidia which are not produced in a fruiting body. They are obligate plant parasites, often needing two different hosts to complete normal development, and they may produce up to five different types of spores. *Puccinia graminis*, the black stem rust of wheat, has already been mentioned and is perhaps the most important plant parasite known to man. It interferes with the normal growth of the wheat and uses the sugar synthesized with the result that the cereal produces smaller than normal grain sizes and less yield per hectare.

Edible fungi and other wild foods no doubt figured very importantly in the life of pre-Neolithic hunter–gatherers, but it is rare indeed that the evidence of such activities survives. Virtually no plant material survives from Mesolithic or Palaeolithic contexts except pollen grains, the rare plant finds being made by chance. However, plentiful evidence for the utilization of wild plants is provided by ethnographic evidence. No doubt a far greater range of plants was used to supplement the diet than is used today, and this was especially the case in pre-farming communities who would have had extensive and detailed knowledge of the plants and other food resources within their hunting territories. More fungi would have been eaten. It is interesting that in England today we virtually restrict ourselves to the edible mushrooms, *Boletus edulis* and *Tricholoma* spp., while other countries exploit a far greater range, for example the beefsteak fungus (*Fistulina hepatica*), a massive bracket fungus which grows on trees, and the little apricot-coloured *chanterelles* (best served with parsley butter in a little stock). The spectacular *Amanita caesarea*, splendid in scarlet and orange, is served in Italy *in umido* (cut in thin slices and stewed in oil with garlic and herbs), and the rubbery yellow mushroom *Cantharellus cibarius* (add thick cream and garnish). Leader (1888) illustrates the vast range of available fungi of which comparatively little use is made. According to the same author, at the time of writing there was a village in the Appenines (Piteglio) which had neither butcher nor baker and where mushrooms formed the basis of the peasant diet, over 3000 lb (1360 kg) a day being gathered from the immediate area around the village! White truffles grow most plentifully in Piedmont, with a season which lasts from October to March. Their flavour is quite different from the black truffle of Perigord. David (1970) recommends a purée of white truffles in small sandwiches, preferably accompanied by a dry white wine, as an excellent restorative for the temper.

In addition to the numerous fungi which are known to be poisonous some also produce hallucinations. The fly agaric (*Amanita muscoides*) was traditionally used by the Vikings as an aid to becoming 'berserk' in battle. John Allegro speculated on the role of the hallucinogenic mushroom in the development of Christianity, but his thesis lacks conviction. The earliest known find of a fungus in archaeological association is, interestingly enough, not a food but the species *Fomes fomentarius*, a tree parasite which was used as tinder and has the property of smouldering for a long time and being able to be fanned into flame. It occurs on several Upper Palaeolithic sites in France and also at the Mesolithic site of Starr Carr, in Yorkshire (Clark 1952). Seaward (1976) notes specimens of the puffball *Bovista nigrescens* from strata II and III of the pre-Hadrianic occupation deposits at Vindolanda, a fungus also reported in relatively large numbers by Watling (1974) from layers in the Skara Brae (Orkney) midden dated to between 155 BC and AD 225. This suggests that the Skara Brae puffballs were of some economic importance, but since the fruiting bodies were fully mature they had not been gathered for food. Watling (1974) suggested that the fungus was simply used to block up draughty holes, but alternatively it may have been used medicinally (as a styptic) or as tinder (Grieve 1931).

2.4 Bacteria

2.4.1 Introduction

The bacteria are a primitive group of organisms which were already in existence in the pre-Cambrian (> 5000 Ma ago), belonging to the class Schizomycetes conventionally included in the Plant Kingdom. They are very common in almost every available habitat and are the smallest organisms with definite cellular organization. No double-membrane structures such as nuclei or mitochondria are present, the whole cell being the basic operational unit (a 'primitive' characteristic). The cell wall (Fig. 2.7b) contains both carbohydrates and amino acids and commonly has a 'slime layer' which helps prevent it from drying out. If this layer is thick and rigid the cell is referred to as a capsule, for example that bacterium which produces pneumonia

(a)

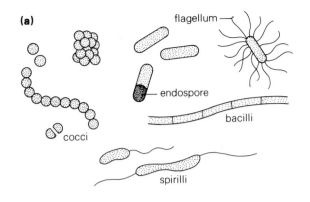

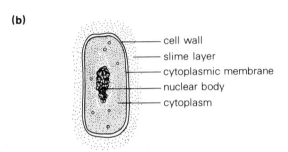

(b)

- cell wall
- slime layer
- cytoplasmic membrane
- nuclear body
- cytoplasm

Figure 2.7 Shapes of bacterial cells (a) and diagrammatic representation of a bectrial cell (b).

(*Klebsiella pneumoniae*). The capsule is a form of protection against the body defences. Bacteria may be autotrophs (making organic compounds from carbon dioxide and obtaining energy from light and inorganic reactions) or heterotrophs (needing to obtain organic compounds and energy from a surrounding medium as parasites or saprophytes). Bacterial shapes are simple: a rod (bacillus), sphere (coccus) or helical (spirillium) (Fig. 2.7a). Some form colonies of characteristic shape and others (for example the actinomycetes) are filamentous. They are physiologically and chemically diverse, species being identified on the basis of their metabolic characteristics, in a culture. These will include appearance, colour and odour. It therefore follows that the archaeological detection of bacteria is restricted to recovery in culture of a few species that can survive in a dormant state for long periods or inferred from historical sources or the presence (in the case of pathogens) of the appropriate vector.

Some bacteria can transform themselves into small, highly resistant, oval or spherical *endospores*,

most spore-forming genera occurring among the actinomycetes. Endospores are very resistant to chemical and physical decay and when in a medium and environment favourable to growth they germinate by rupturing the spore wall so that the spore can develop into a new vegetative cell. The endospores have been identified in archaeological contexts (p. 55).

Some parasitic bacteria, in common with some viruses, protozoa and simple multicellular creatures, cause disease, and these are referred to as *pathogens*. Some will cause acute disease in the host which will kill it, while others produce an immunity reaction by activating the defences of the host body and this results in their own destruction. Sometimes the organism is contained within the host's body so that it acts as a carrier, capable of infecting another member of its species without itself becoming very sick. A parasite which kills its host makes a crisis for itself and needs to find a replacement in order to continue with the chain of life. Optimum conditions of symbiosis are clearly required for optimum growth; these may be found, for example, in the human lower intestine, where massive amounts of bacteria perform their own particular tasks without killing either their hosts or their fellow parasites.

Many bacteria, including pathogens, retain their viability for considerable periods of time – up to 2000 years in the case of actinomycetes' endospores. Some pathogenic bacteria may survive in dust, dirt and occupation deposits for a short while and can infect a new host at some later date. Dispersal methods are varied; the hides of infected animals are the source of the aerially dispersed *Bacillus anthracis* spores and droplet infection is the means of spread of the viruses which cause diseases such as mumps, measles, influenza and tuberculosis.

2.4.2 *Bacteria identified by culturing*

Introduction. Bacteria belonging to the thermophilic actinomycete genus *Thermoactinomyces* can be relatively easily isolated and identified. The precise classification of thermophilic bacteria and actinomycetes has, until recently, been a subject of much dispute. A consensus of opinion has now agreed that they are true bacteria but differ morphologically, being filamentous or mycelial and producing spores very similar to those observed in fungi which accounts for the heated debate over whether or not they should be classified as fungi or bacteria (Cross 1968). They have been isolated from a wide variety of habitats, especially compost and dung, and may be found in most soil samples, being especially common in plant litter where temperatures in excess of 30 °C can be achieved either as a result of microbial activity or from sunlight. High numbers of spores are produced where vegetation is stored, or where cereal crops have been harvested or processed. Their resistant endospores have been used as proof of the longevity of bacterial endospores, since the studies of Cross and Attwell (1974) suggested that in anaerobic lake muds survival was in excess of 1500 a. Such spores have been recorded from archaeological sites, notably from occupation debris at the Roman fort of Vindolanda, Northumberland (Seaward et al. 1976). The concentrations of spores at this site were correlated with particular types of sediments, emphasizing the need to study such relationships (p. 57). A related project was undertaken by Lacey (1971), who studied the microbiology of grain stored underground in Iron Age-type pits as part of an experiment sponsored by the Ancient Fields Research Committee of the British Academy and the Council for British Archaeology's work on primitive agricultural practices. This particular experiment involved digging four pits in chalk downland near Salisbury, Wiltshire, lining and preparing them (Bowen & Wood 1968), filling them with barley grains and sealing with different substances. The stored grain was then sampled after periods of one or two years and the level of microbiological activity noted.

Sampling methods. The sampling methods used at Vindolanda were described by Seaward (1976), Seaward et al. (1976), and Unsworth et al. (1977). Sections about 130 mm long (7×10^{-4} m^3) were cut from a freshly cleaned trench wall and stored in tightly sealed polythene jars at room temperature. Samples for microbial analysis were removed from the centre of each section after slicing it with a sterile knife, approximately 10 g being required for each analysis. Sims (1973) described a similar sampling procedure for removing microbial samples from a

sample tube from Seamere lake, the core sample involved having been obtained using a Livingstone piston corer (West 1968).

Thermoactinomycetes may be detected by spreading agar medium with dilutions of the sediment and incubating aerobically at 50–55 °C, preferably in a humid incubator. Relatively simple bacteriological media such as nutrient agar or yeast extract–glucose agar can be used as the bacteria are not nutritionally demanding. Some species will give visible colonies after incubation for 24 h but others require 2–3 days. Other media formations have been recommended by Uridil and Tetrault (1959) and Tendler (1959) but these seem to have few advantages.

For the Vindolanda samples, 1.0 g subsamples were transferred to sterile plastic bags with a sterile scalpel and a suspension produced in 5 ml quarter-strength Ringer solution containing 0.01% (w/v) gelatin (Straka & Stokes 1957) with the aid of a Colworth stomacher (Unsworth et al. 1977). Aliquots (0.2 ml) of the suspension were spread on the dried surface of the modified thermoactinomycete isolated agar (Cross & Attwell 1974) and the petri dishes incubated for 48 h at 50 °C in a humid environment. A problem with this culture method is that the growth of other thermophilous bacteria and fungi can 'swamp' the actinomycetes making detailed counts impossible. However, Gregory et al. (1964) used an Andersen sampler (Andersen 1958) in a wind tunnel (Gregory & Lacey 1962 1963) where the dry spores were detached from the substrate being tested in a wire basket and diluted in a stream of air which is sampled for a definite time period. The number of spores per gram of substrate may be calculated from the initial weight of the substrate present and the volume of air passing the sampler. In experiments done with hay (Gregory et al. 1964) viable counts as high as 2×10^5 spores g^{-1} were reached. Cross (1968) describes a simpler modification of this apparatus which involves shaking the sample in a tin of known volume and allowing the larger particles to settle. The small actinomycetes' spores remain suspended for very long periods and a known volume is then sampled using an Andersen sampler connected to a small vacuum pump. Certain physiological properties of *T. vulgaris* make it possible to develop a selective

(a)

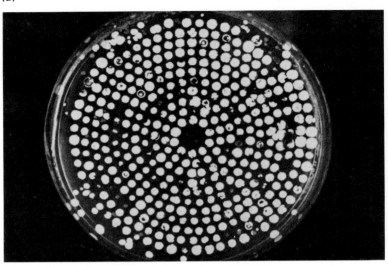

(b)

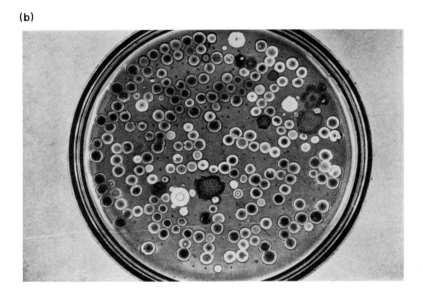

Figure 2.8 Culturing bacteria. (a) *T. vulgaris* colonies from hay, grown on half-strength nutrient agar incubated for 24 h at 55°; (b) *Streptomyces* sp. colonies and isolated conolines of *T. vulgaris* and *Bacillus* sp. from hay. Yeast extract glucose agar incubated for 48 h at 55° (from Cross 1968).

medium to optimize culture growth, enabling the recovery of high numbers of spores (Cross 1968, and Fig. 2.8).

Identification and counting. The identification and counting of the thermoactinomycetes is best carried out by the method of Cross and Goodfellow (1973), employing direct microscopy. *Thermoactinomyces* belonging to the species *T. vulgaris*, *T. sacchari*, *T. dichotomica* and *T. candidus* whose characteristics are described below (Table 2.2) having been sub-

cultured for further study. The dry weight of the suspension was determined after drying for 18 h at 95 °C in a vacuum oven and, in the case of the Vindolanda surface soils (Fig. 2.9), 1.3×10^5 thermoactinomycetes per gram dry weight were obtained. Interestingly, detailed studies of certain isolates from both Vindolanda and the Seamere deposit mentioned above (p. 55) differed from those considered typical of the recognized species. Some *T. dichotomica* strains from Vindolanda showed orange reverse colour and a bright lemon

Table 2.2 Characteristics of *Thermoactinomyces* species and variants recovered from Vindolanda and Seamere deposits (from Unsworth *et al.* 1977, p. 49).

	Aerial mycelium colour *	Reverse colony colour *	Sphorophores	Amylase activity †	Aesculin hydrolysis ‡
typical *T. vulgaris*	white	dark cream or tan	−	+ +	−
Seamere variants	grey–white	grey–yellow	+	+	+
T. candidus-like strains	thin white	cream	+	−	+
typical *T. dichotomica*	white to pale yellow	lemon–yellow	+	+ +	NT
orange variants	lemon–yellow	orange	+	−	NT
small white variants	white to pale yellow	lemon–yellow	+	−	NT

*Observed on isolation medium incubated at 50 °C.
†Aliquots of 1% (w/v) starch added to isolation medium: CSL/starch medium (Cross *et al.* 1968) used for *T. dichotomica*.
‡Aliquots of 0.1% (w/v) aesculin + 0.05% (w/v) ferric citrate scales added to Trypticase Soy Agar (BBL).

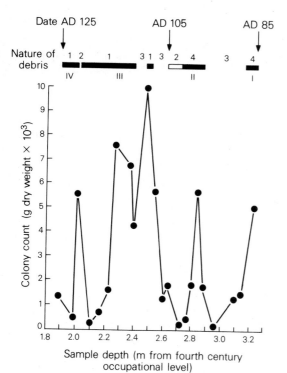

Figure 2.9 The relationship of thermoactinomycetes recovered from Vindolanda to the position of the major organic layers. (1) Highly organic, composed mainly of straw and moss; (2) less organic with some mineral soil; (3) compacted clay; (4) highly organic composed mainly of straw, bracken and moss. The major occupation strata are marked I–IV (from Unsworth *et al.* 1977).

fered too; neither of the variants was able to hydrolyse starch while reference and typical strains showed strong amylase activity. The *T. vulgaris* strains from the Seamere cores (p. 55) included a new variant, greyish-white colonies on isolation agar with a grey-yellow reverse colour, and other isolates resembled the newly described species *T. candidus*.

Interpretation of results. Taxonomic investigation showed that the relative frequency of the *Thermoactinomycetes* spp. differed markedly at Vindolanda between the pre-Hadrianic deposits (Fig. 2.9), dated to AD 85–110 and characterized by a very high organic content (61–89% dry weight), and recent soil strata. Over 98% of the species from surface soil were *T. vulgaris*, whereas the buried organic layers had far more *T. sacchari*. *T. dichotomica* was present in the organic deposits but not in the surface soil, suggesting that the thermoactinomycetes recovered from the ancient organic layer were genuine representatives of the Roman actinomycete population. In layers of the Seamere cores which were especially rich in cereal and associated weed pollen (Sims 1973) the occurrence of thermoactinomycete spores had been predicted since the investigators had expected to find them associated with cereal growing and storage (Lacey 1972). A high incidence of *T. vulgaris* spores in cereal-rich layers was indeed found, suggesting again that the fauna was a relict one. *T. vulgaris*, frequently associated with modern bracken litter, was predicted in the pre-Hadrianic layers at Vindolanda, since they consisted almost entirely of *Pteridium* (Seaward 1976a, b). It is, perhaps, surprising that such small and very fragile organisms could survive for this length of time. Unsworth *et al.*

yellow aerial mycelium in contrast to the reference strains which were pale (*T. dichotomica* Agre 127 CUB 394). Some strains from Vindolanda were similar in colour to the reference strains but differed in forming small colonies. Chemical activities differ

(1977) suggested that the reason for the Vindolanda survival was to be found in the presence of compacted clay layers within the deposit which (together with the low temperature and high water table) inhibited the processes of decay. At Seamere similar cold anaerobic conditions were present. Contamination by modern populations is ruled out by the nature of the material and uneven vertical distribution of the endospores.

The studies of the grain stored in pits also produced some interesting results (Lacey 1971). After the first winter over 40 species of fungi and actino-

Table 2.3 Fungi and actinomycetes from grain stored underground, and also from straw* and basketry† lining the pits (from Lacey 1972, p. 152).

Fungi

Absidia corymbifera (Cohn) Sacc. and Trotter	Mucor pusillus Lindt
Aspergillus candidus* Link	Papulaspora coprophila (Zukal) Hotson
A. flavus Link	Penicillium cyclopium Westling
A. fumigatus Fres.	
A. terreus Thom	P. decumbens Thom
A. versicolor (Vuill.) Tiraboschi	P. lanosum Westling
	P. piceum Raper and Fennel
Botrytis sp.	P. rugulosum Thom
Cladosporium spp.	Unidentified Penicillium spp.*
Fusarium sp.*	Scopulariopsis brevicaulis* (Sacc.) Bainier
Humicola lanuginosa (Griffon and Maublanc) Bunce	Sporotrichum sp.†
Microascus desmosporus (Lechmere) Curzi	Thermoascus crustaceus (Apinis and Chesters) Stolk
Mucor fragilis Bainier	Trichoderma viride*† Pers. ex Fr.
Mucor miehei Cooney and Emerson	Trichothecium roseum† Link Yeasts*

Actinomycetes

Micropolyspora faeni Cross, Maciver and Lacey	S. thermoviolaceus Henssen
Nocardia madurae* (Vincent) Blanchard	Thermoactinomyces vulgaris* Tsiklinsky
Streptomyces albus (Rossi-Doria) Waksman and Henrici	Thermomonospora viridis (Shuurmans, Olson and San Clemente) Küster and Locci
S. griseus (Krainsky) Waksman and Henrici	

Species from basketry or straw only

Fungi

Acremoniella atra* (Corda) Sacc.	Doratomyces stemonitis† (Pers. ex Fr.) Morton and Smith
Aspergillus nidulans* (Eidam) Wint.	Hypocrea sp.†
Cephalosporium sp.*	Rhizopus sp.*
Chaetomium spp.*†	Stachybotrys sp.*

mycetes were recovered from the grain, which had survived its burial remarkably well except in one pit where it had rotted and germinated so no results could be obtained. Most of the fungi occurred towards the edge of the grain mass in the pits, where the grain was moderate to very mouldy and consequently germinated badly (Table 2.3). The spore content of these areas varied from 23.2×10^6 to 105.3×10^6 spores per gram in comparison with the mean spore content of freshly harvested grain from another investigation which was stated by Lacey (1971) to be 5×10^6 spores per gram. After a second winter increased decay was evident in all pits, and in Pit 2 a wet surface layer of rotted grain capped cereals that had heated and contained very abundant fungi (20×10^6 spores per gram dry weight) and actinomycetes (92.2×10^6 spores per gram dry weight), while even more species grew on the basketry lining and straw floors of the pits. The experiment proved that although the underground storage of grain in pits was feasible if the pits were adequately sealed to prevent deterioration, damp grains at the outside of the pit would cause problems with germination; penetration of damp through the seal would also cause much spontaneous heating and spoilage of the crop.

2.4.3 Bacteria identified from secondary sources

An excellent example of a bacterium identified only from historical sources and the presence of its vectors is the plague bacillus *Yersinia pestis*. It normally affects rodents and their fleas, only occasionally humans. In rodents it assumes a stable pattern of infection and recovery, but when it infects a previously unexposed rodent or human population the infection may become lethal. It is estimated that nearly one-third of the total population of Europe died between 1346 and 1350 as a result of the bubonic plague caused by this organism which, even if the numbers are overestimated, must certainly make it the most lethal organism ever encountered by man. Rats will pick up the infection by the interchange of fleas, and also by exchange with wild rodents which harbour *Yersinia pestis* on an ongoing basis. There are still areas of the world where plague is endemic in the local rodents, and it is interesting to note how the human populations cope with this problem. During recent travels in Outer Mongolia accompanying the nomad population the author asked on what grounds they selected marmots for shooting (since the killing of these attractive rodents for fur and food forms part of the traditional way of life). Ancient Mongol tradition states that a marmot must never be trapped or snared but always shot, formerly with the compound bow but now with a bolt-action rifle. The appearance of the animal and its behaviour conditions whether or not it is fair game; a marmot that seems slow or sleepy must be left alone and the hunter concentrates on those animals which are most frisky (and present the most difficult targets). This, it seems, is a simple precaution against plague since the first sign of an outbreak in the marmots is the appearance of slow, lethargic animals, and if the rodents are shot rather than trapped this minimizes the risk of personal contact with an infected host. Since the population of the area is so sparse (1½ million people in an area half the size of Europe) the risk of human infection is remote, but even if this occurs the area can be rapidly evacuated and the risk of the disease spreading is slight. Such an outbreak did, in fact, occur in Mongolia during the writer's visit, but no human fatalities occurred. It is a very different matter in overcrowded insanitary urban conditions. Rackham (1979), in an article on the introduction of the black rat into Britain, quoted the recent find of a black rat skull, mandible, maxilla, humerus, premaxilla, etc., representing a minimum of two individuals from a Roman timber-lined well at Skeldergate in York (Addyman 1976). It had previously been thought that the black rat was introduced into Britain by the Normans, as a result of the species returning from the Near East with the Crusaders. The context of this find suggests that the rats were thrown in as dead animals and date from before the eighth century AD, at least 400 years *earlier* than the accepted date of introduction. The animals were either contemporary with the backfill of the well (dating between the fourth and eighth centuries AD) or residual in the deposits which were used to fill it (implying a much earlier date). The excavator concluded from various features of the deposits that the well had been filled by the fourth century. Black rats were the principal European carriers and transmitters of the primary vector of the bubonic plague, the flea *Xenopsylla cheopis* which carries the plague

bacillus. Although, as already mentioned, other rodents and other varieties of flea may carry the plague, Hirst (1953) is of the opinion that epidemics only occur in urban situations where the black rat is present, and that the disease is only sustained where the rat population is well established. It is possible to plot the distribution of the black rat from archaeological finds (like that from York), together with historical references about outbreaks of plague, the latter occurring from the first century BC onwards. The pandemic disaster which occurred in the reign of Justinian was recorded by the historian Procopius, who gives an astonishing (and doubtless much exaggerated) figure of 10 000 dead each day in the Byzantine empire between 542 and 588 AD, totalling 100 million lives. However, as Shrewsbury (1970) pointed out, there is little doubt that these figures are exaggerated. Plague was known from the Mediterranean coasts from 300 BC (diagnosed from later historical sources) and seems to have spread to Britain by the beginning of the fifth century AD as a result of the ship-borne dispersal of rats to Roman military and commercial ports. This no doubt solves the previously inexplicable problem of plague outbreaks which have been suggested for Anglo-Saxon Britain (McArthur 1949, 1959).

2.5 Viruses

Viruses are the smallest and simplest of known organisms. Only the largest can be seen with a light microscope, requiring an electron microscope for identification; over 300 kinds are known, producing diseases in a wide variety of organisms. It follows that they will be recoverable from archaeological contexts in only one of two ways, by culturing viable specimens (which is not yet possible as their period of survival is too short) or by their effect, for example in the production of diseases. Since viral diseases usually affect the soft tissue and leave no skeletal evidence, it is clear that their presence is going to be deduced only from historical references. A single type of virus will usually infect only one specific kind of host, and the viruses are very simple in form and structure, consisting of plain geometrical shapes such as the brick, rod and needle. Since virus infections deduced purely from historical sources fall outside the terms of reference of this book it is not proposed to deal with them in detail, but merely to note in passing that such infections may have the greatest demographic and historical significance. An epidemic of smallpox (*Variola* virus) was raging in Mexico City on the night when the Aztecs succeeded in driving Cortez and his men out (McNeill 1977). This no doubt explains why the Aztecs did not pursue their retreat-

ing and numerically much smaller enemy but gave them time to rest, regroup, acquire Indian allies and set siege to the city. The Spaniards having recovered from smallpox in their youth were immune and the psychological implications of a disease which killed only Indians and left the Spanish unharmed are tremendous, so it is not surprising that the disease was regarded as a supernatural manifestation and was recorded as secondary archaeological evidence

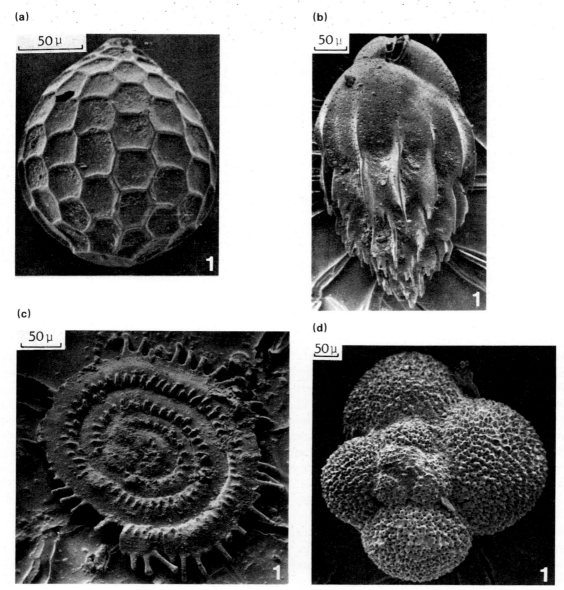

Figure 2.10 Scanning electron photomicrographs of foraminifera. (a) *Oolina hexagona* (Williamson); (b) *Bulimina cf. alazensis* (Cushman); (c) *Sejunctella earlandi* (Loeblich and Tappan); (d) *Globigerina bulloides* (d'Orbigny).

in the form of pictures. By 1568 (less than 50 years after the Spaniards arrived) the population of Central Mexico had shrunk to three million, about a tenth of the pre-Conquest figure, and the disease progressed rapidly for another fifty years reaching a low of 1.6 million by 1620. Recovery did not start for another thirty years and the population remained very low until the eighteenth century. It is unlikely that such a rapid population decline is entirely attributable to war and smallpox but those factors certainly started it. It has, however, been argued that the assessment of the enormous post-Conquest decline was proposed partly on the basis of mistaken premises in the identification of sixteenth and seventeenth century pottery.

2.6 Protozoa and rickettsiae

2.6.1 Introduction

Protozoa are the simplest of all animals. They usually occur as single cells and are predominantly microscopic in size. The name derives from the Greek *protos* (first) and *zoon* (animal). Hundreds of species are known, widely varied, the phylum Protozoa being divided into subphyla according to means of locomotion. The simplest forms are the amoeboid protozoa (Class Sarcodina) which have pseudopods for locomotion and are mostly free-living, although the group includes some parasites. Some free-living protozoans of archaeological importance are foraminifera and radiolaria. The Order Foraminifera produces a chalky shell with numerous chambers. They are marine and obtain food by the action of their pseudopods which extend through pores in the tiny shells. The chalk cliffs of Dover and the chalk beds of Mississippi and Georgia are deposits of billions of these shells. Radiolaria, like foraminifera, are marine, but most of them construct shells of silica with radiating spines.

2.6.2 Pathogenic protozoa

The genus *Entamoeba* includes a large number of species found in the alimentary canal, three of which are common in man, including *Esherichia histolytica* which causes amoebic dysentery. Possible cysts of *E. coli* were recovered from the mummified body of a young boy described by Pizzi and Schenone

Figure 2.11 Barley, diseased by the fungus *Ustilago.*

(1954). *E. coli* and *E. histolytica* cysts also occur in 1800-year-old human coprolite from the Dead Sea, together with cysts of *Giardia lamblia* and *Chilomastix mesnili* (Section 9.3) and have been recorded from various Egyptian mummies (Szidat 1944).

Dunn and Watkins (1970) examined 286 samples of coprolite from Lovelock Cave in the Great Western Basin, as well as the intestinal contents of a sample from Pyramid Lake, Nevada, but found no evidence of parasitic infection. They did, however, note Charcot–Leyden crystals in the sample which might be indicative of an infection by *E. histolytica*, although no cysts were recovered.

Plasmodium, which belongs to the Class Sporozoa, causes malaria, a disease which accounts for a large proportion of deaths caused by parasites. In fact the malarial plasmodium is probably one of the oldest of human parasites. Four species can affect man, of which *Plasmodium falciparum* is especially virulent. It is possible that this form is the latest arrival and that it is not as well adjusted to human hosts as the others, since, as pointed out above (Section 2.1), an organism which kills its host defeats its purpose. In the case of the malarial plasmodium it is obviously a necessary part of the life cycle that the mosquito (*Anopheles* sp.) which acts as a vector for the parasite remains unaffected by it, since it must be healthy enough to carry it to a new host.

2.6.3 Foraminifera

Foraminifera may be recovered simply by field inspection using a hand lens, although this will bias the sample towards larger specimens (diameter > 1 mm). They may be removed from sediments with a fine paint-brush, but are unlikely to occur if the material has been much redeposited or heavily weathered, or if it contains much gypsum or limonite. They are also unlikely to occur in acidic sediments since the calcareous tests are dissolved. A better method is to place the sample in a container and soak for a few hours in water to disaggregate. Stir, decant the liquid and air dry the residue. Dry sieve it through a nest of sieves spaced at mesh 10, 35, 60, 120 and 230 (or 1.5, 2.5, 3.5 and 4 φ intervals) and place the residue from each under a microscope for examination. Wet sieving methods can also be used, as can sodium hexametaphosphate as a dispersant (Shackley 1975). Froth flotation (Section 6.3) is also a good method for retrieving forminifera.

Isolated occurrences of foraminifera from archaeological contexts are quite common, often being detected almost by accident and recorded in a general table of environmental finds. An example may be seen in the list by Wilson and Connolly (1978) of the macro-fossils identified from estuarine clays surrounding a Saxon boat; these include various foraminifera including *Jadammina macrescens* Brady 1870, some ostracods and insect fragments, but the forams are of no archaeological importance.

2.6.4 Rickettsiae

The rickettsiae are a small group of parasites of arthropods such as fleas, lice and ticks which they inhabit without injury. They have many points of similarity with bacteria and some are pathogenic for man. Their archaeological importance is again deduced from historical sources, evidence of diseases such as typhus which is caused by *Rickettsia prowazekii*.

References

Addyman, P. V. 1976. *Excavations at York 1973–4: second interim report.* York: York Archaeological Trust.

Ainsworth, G. C. and P. H. A. Sneath 1962. *Microbial classification.* Cambridge: Cambridge University Press.

Alexopoulos, C. J. 1962. *Introductory mycology*, 2nd edn. New York: Wiley.

Andersen, A. A. 1958. New sampler for the collection, sizing and enumeration of viable airborne particles. *J. Bact.* **76**, 471–84.

Ashbee, P. 1957. The Great Barrow at Bishop's Waltham, Hampshire. *Proc. Prehist. Soc.* **23**, 137–66.

Bakker, J. A., R. W. Brandt, B. Van Geel, M. J. Jasma, J. J. Kuijper, P. J. A. Van Mensch, J. P. Palc and G. F. Ijzereef 1977. Hoogkarspel-Watertonen: towards a reconstruction of ecology and archaeology of an agrarian settlement of 1000 BC. *Ex Horreo* Cingula IV, 188–224.

Besteman, J. C. 1979. Carolingian Mendemblik. *Bericht. Rijks. Ondheid. Bordemorderzoek* **24**, 43–106.

Bowen, H. C. and P. D. Wood 1968. Experimental storage of corn underground and its implications for Iron Age settlements. *Bull. Univ. Lond. Inst. Arch.* **7**.

Breed, R. D. S., E. G. D. Murray and N. R. Smith 1974. *Bergey's manual of determinative bacteriology*, 8th edn. Baltimore: Williams and Wilkins.

Clark, J. G. D. 1952. *Prehistoric Europe: the economic basis.* Cambridge: Cambridge University Press.

Clark, J. G. D. 1975. *The earlier Stone Age settlement of Scandinavia.* Cambridge: Cambridge University Press.

Cross, T. 1968. Thermophilic actinomycetes. *J. Appl. Bact.* **31**, 36–53.

Cross, T. and R. W. Attwell 1974. Recovery of viable thermoactinomycete endospores from deep mud cores. In *Spore research 1973*, A. N. Barker, G. W. Gould and J. Wolf (eds). London: Academic Press.

Cross, T. and M. Goodfellow 1973. Taxonomy and classification of the Actinomyiles. In *Actinomycetales: characteristics and practical importance*, G. Sykes and F. A. Skinner (eds), 170–94. London: Academic Press.

Cross, T., P. D. Walker and G. W. Gould 1968. Thermophilic actinomycetes producing resistant endospores. *Nature* **220**, 352–4.

David, E. 1970. *Italian food.* Harmondsworth: Penguin.

Dimbleby, G. W. 1978. *Plants and archaeology*, 2nd edn. London: Baker.

Dunn, F. L. and R. Watkins 1970. Parasitological examination of Prehistoric human coprolites from Lovelock Cave, Nevada. *Contrib. Univ. Calif. Arch. Res. Fac.* **10**, 176–85.

Farrar, W. V. 1966. Tecuitlatl: a glimpse of Aztec food technology. *Nature* **211**, 341–2.

Gregory, P. H. 1961. *The microbiology of the atmosphere.* London: Hill.

Gregory, P. H. and M. E. Lacey 1962. Isolation of thermophilic actinomycetes. *Nature* **195**, 95.

Gregory, P. H. and M. E. Lacey 1963. Mycological examination of dust from mouldy hay, associated with farmer's lung disease. *J. Gen. Microbiol.* **30**, 75–88.

Gregory, P. H., G. N. Festenstein, M. E. Lacey, F. A. Skinner, J. Pepys and P. A. Jenkins 1964. Farmer's lung disease: the development of antigens in moulding hay. *J. Gen. Microbiol.* **36**, 429–39.

Grieve, M. 1931. *A modern herbal.* London.

Helbaek, H. 1958. The last meal of Grauballe man. *Küml*, 83–116.

Hirst, L. F. 1953. *The conquest of plague.* Oxford: Clarendon Press.

Jansma, M. J. 1977. Diatom analysis of pottery. *Ex Horreo* Cingula IV, 78–85.

Lacey, J. 1971. The microbiology of moist barley storage in unsealed concrete staved silos. *Ann. Appl. Bact.* **69**, 187–212.

Lacey, J. 1972. The microbiology of grain stored underground in Iron Age type pits. *Stored Prod. Res.* **8**, 151–4.

Leader, S. 1888. *Tuscan scenes and sketches.* London: Fisher Unwin.

McArthur, W. P. 1949. The identification of some pestilences recorded in Irish annals. *Ir. Hist. Stud.* **23**, 169–88.

McArthur, W. P. 1959. The medical identification of some pestilences of the past. *Trans R. Soc. Trop. Med. Hyg.* **53**, 423–39.

McNeill, W. H. 1977. *Plagues and peoples.* Oxford: Basil Blackwell.

Moldenke, H. N. and A. L. Moldenke 1952. *Plants of the Bible.* New York: Ronald Press.

Peacock, D. P. S. 1977. *Pottery and early commerce.* London: Academic Press.

Pelczar, M. J. and R. P. Reid 1972. *Microbiology*, 3rd edn. New York, London: McGraw-Hill.

Pennington, W., 1943. Lake sediments: the bottom deposits of the north basin of Windermere with special reference to the diatom succession. *New Phytol.* **42**, 1–27.

Pizzi, T. and H. Schenone 1954. Hallazho de hueros de *Trichuris trichiura* en contenido intestinal de un cuerpo arqueologico ineaico. *Boll. Chile Parasit.* **9** (73), 58–71.

Rackham, J. 1979. *Rattus rattus:* the introduction of the black rat into Britain. *Antiquity* **53**, 112–20.

Seaward, M. R. D. 1976. *The Vindolanda environment.* Haltwistle, Northumberland: Barcombe Publications.

Seaward, M. R. D., T. Cross and B. A. Unsworth 1976. Viable bacterial spores recovered from an archaeological excavation. *Nature* **261**, 407–8.

Shackley, M. L. 1975. *Archaeological sediments: a survey of analytical methods.* London: Butterworth.

Shrewsbury, J. F. D. 1970. *A history of bubonic plague in the British Isles.* London: Cambridge University Press.

Sims, R. E. 1973. The anthropogenic factor in East

Anglian vegetational history: an approach using APF techniques. In *Quaternary plant ecology*, H. J. B. Birks and R. G. West (eds). Oxford: Blackwell Scientific.

Straka, R. P. and J. L. Stokes 1957. Rapid destruction of bacteria in commonly used dilutents and its elimination. *Appl. Microbiol.* 5, 21–5.

Szidat, L. 1944. Uber die Erhaltungsfähigkeit von Helmintheneiern in vor-und frühgeschichtlichen Moorleichen. *Zentbl. Bakt. Parasit Kde.* 13, 265–74.

Tendler, M. D. 1959. Studies on thermophilic actinomycetes. *Bull. Torrey Bot. Club* 86, 71.

Unsworth, B. A., T. Cross, M. R. D. Seaward and R. E. Sims 1977. The longevity of thermoactinomycete endospores in natural substrates. *J. Appl. Bact.* 42, 45–52.

Uridil, J. E. and P. A. Tetrault 1959. Isolation of thermophilic streptomycetes. *J. Bact.* 78, 243–6.

Voorhips, A. and M. J. Jansma 1974. Pollen and diatom analysis of a shore section of the former Lake Wevershoof. *Geol Mijnb.* 53, 429–35.

Watling, R. 1979. Prehistoric puffballs. *Bot. Soc. Edinb. Newsletter* 14, 12–13.

Wilson, D. G. and P. Connolly 1978. In *The Graveney Boat: a tenth-century find from Kent*, V. Fenwick (ed.). Oxford British Arch. Report 53.

Wright, E. V. and D. M. Churchill 1965. The boats from North Ferriby, Yorkshire, England, with a review of the origin of the sewn boats of the Bronze Age. *Proc. Prehist. Soc.* 31, 1–24.

3 *Ferns and mosses*

To carry the Fern seeds about one's person
was to possess the secret of making oneself invisible.

(J. R. Crossland and J. M. Parrish, *Wild flower folklore*)

3.1 Introduction

The Division III (Bryophyta or mosses and liver-worts) and Division IV (Pteridophyta, the ferns and club mosses) of the Plant Kingdom may conveniently be taken together since they are represented in the archaeological record rather differently from species placed in Division V (seed-bearing plants). In bryophytes the water loss is modified by the presence of a cuticle on the outer surface of the plant with waxy substances impervious to water. They are most abundant in moist places but will survive under a wide range of conditions. *Sphagnum* moss, for example, grows in bogs where acid conditions and low oxygen availability decrease the rate of bacterial and fungal decay of organic matter and permit the accumulation of extensive deposits. It is used as a fuel, a wound dressing (notably during World War I) and a soil conditioner. The *Sphagnum* mosses have spores which can usually be identified, but since the spore production of mosses is less regular than the flowering of higher plants there are fewer records. There are three groups of bryophytes: the hornworts, liverworts and mosses. All have alternation of generation in which a multicellular long-lived gametophytic generation alternates with a multicellular short-lived sporophytic generation in which the sporophytic plant remains permanently attached to the gametophyte. The three groups are differentiated by their manner of sporophyte growth (Fig. 3.1). The reproductive system of hornworts is an erect structure differentiated into a capsule, region and basal foot embedded within the gametophyte. A meristem (zone of actively dividing cells) occurs in regions between foot and capsule and as the meristem divides the capsule increases in length. In liverworts it is

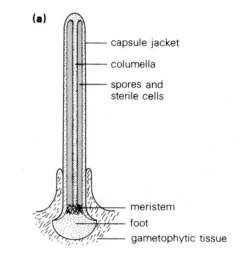

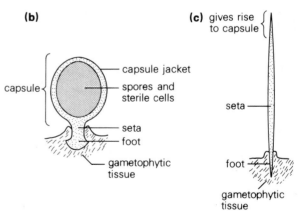

Figure 3.1 Morphology of bryophytes. (a) Hornwort; (b) liverwort; (c) moss.

differentiated into capsule, seta and foot, with no localized meristematic activity and in mature moss there is a sporophytic capsule, seta and foot with growth at apex during development.

Subfossil liverworts are uncommon, probably as a

65

Table 3.1 Bryophytes from some British archaeological sites (data from Dickson 1973).

Species	1 Barnsley Park	2 Bunny, Notts	3 Carpow, Perthshire	4 Godmanchester, Hunts	5 Holme Pierrepont, Notts	6 Little Paxton, Hunts	7 Newgrange, Co. Meath	8 North Ferriby, Yorks	9 Shippea Hill, Cambs	10 Upper Brook St, Winchester	11 Winetavern and High Sts, Durham
Amblystegium riparium			+								
Anomodon sp.										+	
Anomodon viticulosus	+										
Antitrichia curtipendula						+				+	
Brachythecium rivulare			+								
Brachythecium rutabulum		+					+				
Brachythecium velutinum											+
Bryum sp.		+									
Calliergonella cuspidata		+		+						+	+
Campylium stellatum		+									
Ceratodon purpureus			+	+							
Cirriphyllum pilferum											
Cratoneuron filicinum	+	+							+		
Ctenidium molluscum		+								+	
Dicranum scoparium			+		+						
Drepanocladus sp.			+								
Eurhynchium praelongum			+								+
Eurhynchium speciosum									+		
Eurhynchium striatum		+		+				+		+	+
Eurhynchium swartzii	+		+						+		
Fissidens adianthoides		+									
Fissidens bryoides			+								
Fissidens sect. bryoideum	+										
Homalothecium sericeum	+					+			+	+	
Hylocomium splendens			+		+						
Hypnum cupressiforme			+		+				+		
Isothecium myurum		+	+							+	
Neckara complanata	+					+					
Neckara complanata								+	+		+
Neckara crispa											+
Orthotrichum sp.			+								
Plagiochila asplenoides											+
Plagiomnium affine											
Plagiomnium undulatum			+				+				
Pleurozium schreberi			+		+						
Polytrichum commune			+		+			+ (rope)			
Pseudoscleropodium purum		+									
Rhytidiadelphus sp.						+					
Rhytidiadelphus squarrosus			+		+						+
Sphagnum subg. Litophloea						+					
Thamnobryum alopecurum	+									+	+
Thuidium delicatulum			+								
Thuidium tamarsicinum	+	+	+								+
Tortula sp.	+										

1. Well No. 2, Romano-British villa.
2. Roman well.
3. Roman fort.
4. Roman ditch.
5. Canoes and wheel caulking.
6. Late Saxon pit.
7. Turf horizon below Neolithic burial chamber.
8. Bronze Age boat.
9. Mesolithic and Neolithic horizons in peat.
10. Tenth century organic layer.
11. Eleventh century cess pit.

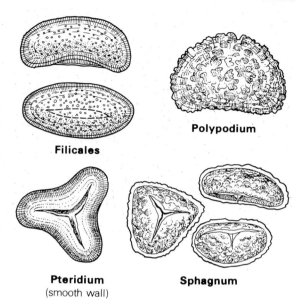

Filicales

Polypodium

Pteridium
(smooth wall)

Sphagnum

Figure 3.2 Morphology of some Pteridophyte spores.

result of differential preservation, and there are only 30 species recorded from Quaternary deposits (Dickson 1973). The most important archaeological find comes from a prehistoric boat at Brigg, Lincolnshire (Sheppard 1910) where 23 species of bryophyte were identified from the plants used as caulking (Wright & Churchill 1965), including 11 species of liverworts (Table 3.1).

There are a number of reports on mosses in archaeological deposits, varying from isolated occurrences such as that mentioned by Wallace (1956) to syntheses such as that of Seaward and Williams (1976), but Williams (1976a) considers that these are not representative of the true frequency with which mosses occur in archaeological deposits as excavators are unaware of the potential value of such material and the biological sampling is inadequate. He considers that since a high percentage of the bryophytes studies are from chance discoveries a major sampling error must be present.

Fern spores are much more likely to appear in the course of a pollen analysis than the spores of mosses but are frequently indistinguishable. Some (e.g. *Polypodium vulgare*) have distinctive features, as do the bracken spores (*Pteridietum*) and these, together with the club mosses, such as various species of *Lycopodium* and *Selaginella*, are often identifiable down to species.

Lycopodium spores formed part of the experiment in movement and preservation of organic material under an experimental barrow at Overton Down, southern England. These spores were chosen since they are very resistant to decay and it was found that after a period of only a few years their vertical and horizontal spatial distribution had changed, presumably due to the action of earthworms.

3.2 Site sampling

Sampling for bryophytes is done along similar lines to those used for any other plant macrofossils, taking samples from areas posing specific questions. Mosses are best preserved in anaerobic waterlogged conditions which should be sampled in a stratigraphic column and may be noticed when the material is broken open along bedding planes. They are generally of a rich brown colour. Any specially large quantities of moss should be bagged separately and the biologist notified. Williams (1976a) wrote an excellent article dealing with the sampling, processing and identification of bryophytes in archaeology.

Sometimes particular areas such as the Ebor trench (Seaward & Williams 1976) will be very rich in a single species of moss, probably representing material laid down on a floor or deposited in a pit and in such a deposit care and several subsamples should ensure that the full range of species has been sampled by taking subsamples from different areas of the moss 'pocket'. A combined volume of $5 \times 10^{-4} - 10^{-3}$ m^3 is suggested.

Ferns may either be sampled as macroscopic remains or as spores which will be identifiable in a pollen analysis.

3.3 Laboratory analysis

Paraffin (kerosene) flotation, employed for the extraction of insect remains (Section 8.3) is unsatisfactory for moss, although it will retain seeds, since most of the larger pieces of material do not float and the breakdown of the sediments in sieving causes fragmentation of the moss. The method of Williams (1976a), successfully used at York, is as follows:

Figure 3.3 *Polytrichum commune* moss, with capsules.

(1) Visual examination of sample with extraction of any visible moss fragments.

(2) Some samples require treatments with weak acids or alkali (Dickson 1970) to disintegrate them but this will often also disintegrate the moss leaves. Gentle washing with water is preferred and samples must in any case be kept moist.

(3) Wash the sample through a stack of sieves of mesh sizes 10 mm, 5 mm and 0.3 mm, removing all twigs, stones and large plant debris.

(4) Invert sieves into bowls of water and gently agitate until mosses detach themselves; collect them by straining off the water. This method also recovers large seeds and fruit stones which do not float (e.g. *Prunus* sp.).

(5) Carry out a standard paraffin (kerosene) flotation (Section 8.3) to recover small moss

fragments. Even more may be recovered by dry sorting the residue.

(6) Mosses should be kept in water with a fungicide added but preferably stored in absolute alcohol.

3.3.1 Identification

Dickson (1973) gave measurements for mosses recovered from archaeological sites (Table 3.1) showing that most are less than 20 mm long. With better processing larger fragments and whole plants should be recoverable and better chances of good identification obtained – stated simply, there is a general rule that the smaller the fragment the more time it will need to identify it.

3.4 Applications

Dickson (1973) emphasizes the importance of mosses from archaeological sites since their collection by early man was relatively unsystematic and a large range of possible habitats may be represented. In addition, mosses have very specific habitat requirements and much information on habitat conditions can be obtained. Mosses will seldom be found where they grew, except as isolated occurrences, such as at the Roman well at Barnsley Park (Dickson 1973). Some have been found in the construction of prehistoric monuments including Silbury Hill (Williams 1976b) and New Grange (Dickson 1973). On urban sites mosses will certainly be redeposited.

Specific uses of mosses include rope, made, for example, from *Polytrichum commune* Hedw. for the North Ferriby boat (Table 3.1). *Hylocomium splendens* (Hedw) B., S. & G., and *Rhytidiadelphus triquetrus* (Hedw) Fleisch., are both very common in archaeological deposits, probably as packing material. Pits filled or lined with moss occur at Winetavern Street, Durham (Dickson 1973) and York (Williams 1976a). *Polytrichum commune* (the hair moss) makes a fine fibre used for clothing (Clark 1952).

The mosses recovered from the turf stack in the middle of the Silbury Hill mound (Williams 1976b) appeared to have grown *in situ*. The majority of species were characteristic of moderately grazed,

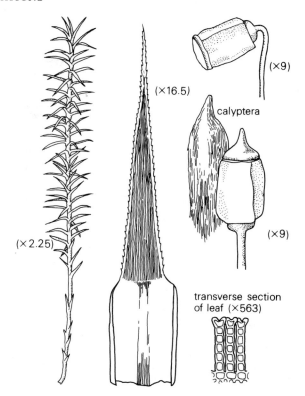

Figure 3.4 *Polytrichum commune* calyptera and part of a transverse section of leaf showing three lamellae.

mature chalk grassland, suggesting that the local environment at the time of construction (2145 ± 95 BC (I-4136)) was similar to that of the present-day South Downs.

A very fine example of the identification of bryophytes comes from pre-Hadrianic organic layers at the Roman fort of Vindolanda (Section 2.4). The most abundant species (55% of the bryophytic material analysed up to 1976) was composed of *Hylocomium splendens* (Seaward 1976a) among the most common Pleistocene and recent mosses. The good branching material at Vindolanda was up to several centimetres long and present in such quantity that Seaward (1976a) suggested an economic value, perhaps for bedding purposes or for packing the gaps in interwoven partition walls. The next most common species was *Acrocladium cuspidatum*, which is usually found on clay soils in moist habitats, as opposed to *H. splendens* which prefers acid and peaty soils amongst grass and heather. Other mosses from the pre-Hadrianic deposits included *Brachythecium rutabulum*, which lives in moist grassland or woodland, *Pleurozium schreberi* (an associate of *H. splendens*), *Rhytidiadelphus squarrosus* (an associate of *B. rutabulum* and *P. schreberi*), *Thuidium tamariscinum* (characteristic of both woodland and open situations and associated in various combinations with all the other species) and *Mnium undulatum*, which prefers humus-rich soils in woodlands. This wide variety of preferred habitats suggests that the Vindolanda mosses indicate very diverse vegetation in the immediate area of the settlement. The deposits in which these mosses had been enclosed consisted largely of bracken, and Seaward (1976a) suggested that bracken-harvesting was a major occupation of the community since for the 30 m² of rooms excavated at least 1 h (2.5 acres) of *Pteridietum* would have been required. It seems likely that the deposits were primarily animal bedding material, perhaps serving a secondary purpose in tanning leatherwork. Certainly the organic material thus produced yielded a plethora of different types of biological material. Bracken was also used by the North American Indians as food (Welch 1948), the fronds being eaten in the unexpanded state, but it can be fatal to some animals (Forsyth 1968). Tracheids of ferns, especially bracken, are also recorded from chalk sites, again probably the remains of the mucking-out of cattle bedding (Dimbleby & Evans 1974).

References

Clark, G. 1952. *Prehistoric Europe: the economic basis.* London: Methuen.

Dickson, C. A. 1970. The study of plant macrofossils in British Quaternary deposits. In *Studies in the vegetational history of the British Isles*, D. Walker and R. G. West, (eds), 223–54. Cambridge: Cambridge University Press.

Dickson, C. A. 1973. *Bryophytes of the Pleistocene.* Cambridge: Cambridge University Press.

Dimbleby, G. W. and J. G. Evans 1974. Pollen and land-snail analysis of calcareous soils. *J. Arch. Sci.* **1**, 117–33.

Forsyth, A. A. 1968. *British poisonous plants.* London: Methuen.

Seaward, M. R. D. 1976a. Observations on the bracken component of the pre-Hadrianic deposit at Vindolanda, Northumberland. *Bot. J. Linn. Soc.* **73**, 177–85.

Seaward, M. R. D. 1976b. *The Vindolanda environment.* Haltwistle, Northumberland: Barcombe Publications.

Seaward, M. R. D. and D. Williams 1976. An interpretation of mosses found in recent archaeological excavations. *J. Arch. Sci.* **3**, 173–7.

Sheppard, T. 1910. The prehistoric boat from Brigg. *Trans E. Riding Arch. Soc.* **17**, 33–54

Wallace, E. C. 1956. *Hylocomium splendens* (Hedw) B. & S. at Verulamium, Hertfordshire, *Trans Br. Bryol. Soc.* **3**, 127.

Welch, W. H. 1948. Mosses and their uses. *Proc. Indiana Acad. Sci.* **58**, 31–46.

Williams, D. 1976a. Bryophytes in archaeology. *Sci. Arch.* **18**, 12–14.

Williams, D., 1976b. A Neolithic moss flora from Silbury Hill, Wiltshire. *J. Arch. Sci.* **3**, 267–70.

Wright, E. V. and D. M. Churchill 1965. The boats from North Ferriby, Yorkshire, England – with a review of the origins of the sewn boats of the Bronze Age. *Proc. Prehist. Soc.* **31**, 1–24.

4 *Pollen analysis*

*The days of man are but as grass; for he flourisheth
as a flower of the field.*

(Psalms 113: 15)

4.1 Introduction

There are various techniques in palaeoecology
which utilize the study of very small (frequently
microscopic) organisms. These include foraminifera
and radiolaria (p. 62), diatoms (p. 48) and, most
important, the study of pollen and spores to give
information about an early flora.

Pollen analysis (palynology) is concerned only
with seed-bearing plants (phanerogams) which produce pollen in the male gamete (anther) or with the
spores, which are asexual reproductive cells, of
cryptogam plants (without obvious flowers and
seeds). The interior of the anther is sporogeneous
tissue which produces pollen mother cells. The mass
of pollen is surrounded by a wall which ripens,
liberating the pollen, which is transferred to the
pistil of another flower by wind, weather or some
animal vector, where it will be fertilized. Far more
pollen is produced than is necessary for propagation
of the species, and this vast mass falls as a pollen
'rain' which, when recovered from the enclosing
sedimentary matrix, will give information concerning the changing palaeoenvironment of the site.

Angiosperm (flowering plant) pollen grains have
three concentric layers, the centre being a living cell
covered by the middle layer (intine) principally
composed of cellulose, and an outer skin (exine)
which is itself composed of two distinct inner and
outer coats: the *en*dexine and *ex*texine. The pollen
exine, made of sporopollenin, is one of the most
resistant substances known, and it is this property
which forms the basis of preparing a sample for
pollen analysis – treatment of sediments with concentrated acids and bases will eventually remove
everything else (sometimes including the test-tube,
Section 4.3), but leave the pollen exine. Pollen

grains have been found in Paleozoic rocks some
500 Ma old, and may be heated to 3000 °C without
being destroyed. The only environments which have
an appreciably destructive effect on pollen are
oxidizing or calcareous ones, meaning that optimum
preservation is achieved in acid waterlogged bogs,
and minimum preservation in well-drained alkaline
deposits. The acidity of the deposit is very important
and 'mor' (raw humus) will preserve pollen even if it
is quite dry, the acidity destroying the bacteria and
fungi which produce decay. The large quantities of
pollen produced and their great resistance are two
very important factors in the use of pollen analysis
as a tool in the reconstruction of ancient vegetation;
the third being the fact that the pollen of each
species is distinctive and relatively easy to identify
by examination of grain surface texture and morphology, grain size and the number, position and
arrangement of apertures (pores and furrows).
Pollen grains vary in size from *c.* 5 to 200 μm,
although the size may be affected by some recovery
treatments and it may be necessary to apply con-
version factors to relate fossil and modern pollen. If
recent pollen is immersed in 10% KOH for a few
hours, grains of the same size as the fossil ones are
produced. Of the very large quantities of pollen
produced, not all arrive on the stigmata of the pistil.
The method of transference from anther to stigma
is important, and flowers pollinated by particular
methods develop their own characteristics, for
example the nectar flowers which produce large
quantities of pollen to lure animals (Section 4.5).

Pollen grains are not always present in sediments,
even when the conditions are suitable. They may
have been destroyed by abrasion, oxidation or
bacterial action, or be so rare that in order to recover
a statistically reliable sample (Section 4.5) such vast

quantities of sediment must be processed that the results become unrepresentative and useless. In any pollen analysis great attention must be paid to the characteristics of the deposits, watching for disturbance or redeposition or any form of distortion of the sequence. The action of earthworms in soil may mix the pollen – examination of worm casts show that pollen can pass through the gut unchanged. Persistent earthworm action can remove all pollen stratigraphy over quite a short time, as was shown by the Overton Down experiment (Jewell & Dimbleby 1966) which also illustrated the continuity of such processes beneath a large mound.

The use of pollen analysis is twofold: dating and palaeoenvironmental reconstruction, emphasis having shifted from the former to the latter in recent years. The technique is almost entirely restricted to Quaternary sediments, since in earlier material the species may now be extinct and the pollen and spores merely useful as zone fossils. In the Quaternary the technique not only aids in the reconstruction of former vegetation but also with illuminating the impact of man on the vegetation, since the pollen can be identified at least to genus or family level, and sometimes to species of the producer plants.

In archaeology pollen analysis has mainly been confined to late Pleistocene and Holocene sequences, although the technique has been used for earlier archaeological deposits (Solecki 1972, Horowitz 1979) and to illuminate the different phases of the Quaternary as a background for the evolution of man. The work of Godwin (1956), correlating large-scale analyses of Postglacial peat bogs in Denmark, Scandinavia and Britain, provides a round picture of vegetation change, particularly by studying changes in the forest composition, enabling comprehensive syntheses, like that of Pennington (1964), to be produced. Early work was particularly concerned with tree pollen and some of the early diagrams describe tree pollen only. The system of pollen zones, established following the work of Godwin and tightly subdividing the postglacial vegetation changes on a chronological basis, was eventually extended backwards to the late stages of the Pleistocene. The pollen zones are synchronous over a wide area and generally closely related to climatic change. This provides a method of relative dating for archaeology by analysis of deposits integrally associated with archaeological material. The use of palynology as a relative dating technique was largely superseded by the development of radiocarbon dating, although it is important for interglacial deposits and thus for a number of Pleistocene archaeological sites, for example at Hoxne (East Anglia).

The early emphasis on the study of changes in forest composition has now been supplemented by much work on the pollen of herbs and shrubs, often of greater interest to the archaeologist. This has provided a mass of data concerning the influence of man of the flora (and the limiting effect of the local flora on human activities), the introduction of new species, domestication of crops, forest clearance, and other such matters. Pollen analysis is now one of the most useful tools for studying palaeoenvironmental changes.

4.2 Fieldwork and sampling

4.2.1 Introduction

All pollen analyses are totally dependent on reliable fieldwork and sampling, meaning that unless great care is taken the results will be uncertain and the interpretation difficult. Before samples are taken the stratigraphy, sedimentology and geomorphology of the deposit must be recorded in detail to provide background information concerning, for example, the presence of allochthonous (redeposited) sediment with included plants and the relative importance of autochthonous (in situ) sediments such as peat or soil profiles which would hopefully contain the remains of vegetation that once lived in the area. In pollen analysis it is vital to distinguish between locally produced pollen and pollen which represents the region as a whole, and, in addition, since the nature of the sediments may well affect the preservation of pollen (p. 84), this should be noted. Sets of standard symbols are commonly used for recording sediments, for example those of Jones and Cundhill (1978) or Faegri and Iversen (1975) (Fig. 4.5). The latter authors discuss the problems of choosing a location for sampling. In many archaeological contexts this is not relevant since the choice may be limited to a small patch within a site, but if the vegetation of a region is being studied, it is

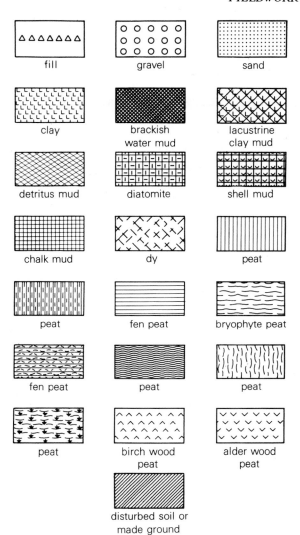

Figure 4.1 Sediment symbols.

between the locally produced material and grains which have travelled further, for example by identifying the local aquatic or bog plants, but there may be problems of stratigraphic interpretation where an hiatus or area of redeposition has not been distinguished. The latter will sometimes show up as a very mixed flora, and may also be detected from the sediments (Shackley 1975).

4.2.2 Sampling from an open section

Whenever possible it is best to sample from an open section, rather than use a peat borer. A primary reason is contamination since with a carefully sampled section this can be reduced to a minimum, and the section will also show variations in the sequence and the best place to sample. Ground rules are principally as follows: to use the utmost care never to touch the sample; always to use clean tools or containers; never to let material from one layer contaminate another; and always to sample from a freshly cleaned face, cleaned by horizontal knife-cuts to avoid contamination. After the face has been cleaned it should be drawn and photographed. Samples may be taken by one of three methods.

Sample tubes. Sample tubes may be pressed into the section, then sealed with paraffin wax and labelled with the name and depth. A tube 50 mm × 20 mm in size is optimum; it may be made of glass or plastic, and round bottomed.

Monolith tins. A monolith tin of stainless steel (or aluminium, which is lighter, cheaper but less robust) is lined with polythene and hammered into the sections. A convenient size is 500 mm × 150 mm × 150 mm, and the larger amounts of sediment removed may in some cases aid interpretation (e.g. at Shide Bridge, p. 151), and may also provide additional material for radiocarbon dating or analysis of some other aspect of the site ecology (e.g. macrofossil plant remains). The monolith should be removed from the section, labelled and sealed in plastic.

'Grab' samples. Samples may also be taken with broad smooth forceps or a spatula, care being taken to sample from the base of the section upwards (to avoid contamination) and to clean the sampling

important to choose a location where the sedimentary matrix has affected preservation or composition as little as possible. Thus the state of preservation will be better in lakes than peat bogs, but these will be less interesting from the point of view of human activity. The smaller the lake or the peat bog the greater the likelihood that it will reflect only local vegetation. On some archaeological sites where the question being asked is, 'What plants were growing here?', this does not matter, but in large-scale studies (for example those undertaken in the Somerset Levels, Section 5.9), it is of vital importance. It is frequently possible to distinguish instruments very thoroughly with some disposable material.

In the early days of pollen analysis a sampling interval of 250 mm was used, but this is far too large and a 50 mm interval is now customary. If the sediment has accumulated very slowly even closer intervals (25 or 10 mm) are recommended. Tubes must be kept moist and are therefore sealed with paraffin wax, possibly adding a little glycerol to the sample to prevent desiccation. An alternative method is deep-freezing, and some analysts oven-dry their samples.

4.2.3 Coring

It may often be impossible to obtain an open section, in which case a sampling device must be used. If the area to be sampled is small (e.g. a small peat-bog), one core may be sufficient, but if it is large then a profile is required. As Faegri and Iversen (1975) stated, one of the rules of pollen analysis field procedures is that the more complex the sequence the shorter the distance between sections (or boreholes). The appropriate tool depends, in theory, on the sediment and the depth required, but in practice, especially with archaeological work, which tends to be rather small scale, it depends on what can be borrowed from friendly departments of botany, or how much money and manpower is available. West (1968), Shackley (1975), Jones and Cundhill (1978) have reviewed the properties of various types of peat-borers, but one that is common to all is their propensity for getting buried or lost, necessitating the use of specialized recovery methods such as those of Clymo (1964). The general principle of a borer is a closed chamber of stainless steel attached to rods which can be rammed into the sediment to the required depth before the chamber is opened. The ordinary soil auger is not a tool for pollen analysis but may be useful in the initial penetration of dry deposits or just to give some idea of stratigraphy. Problems arise with compaction of deposits, subsurface impacts or unsuspected large boulders and, inevitably, with contamination. The hand-driven samplers such as the Hiller borer or Russian sampler (Fig. 4.2) are the most common, their properties and problems being described in detail by Jones and Cundhill (1978). The Abbey corer (Walker & Lowe 1976) is an alternative, but it is

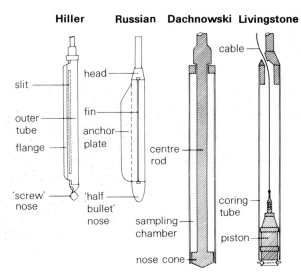

Figure 4.2 Coring devices for pollen samples (after Jones & Cundhill 1978).

both heavy and expensive. The stationary piston-type Livingstone corer is also used but disturbs unconsolidated material. More sophisticated equipment is required for lake sediments, for example the compressed-air Mackereth samples (Mackereth 1958). Core samples should be retrieved in plastic drainpipe segments, commercially available, which are ideally sealed and frozen as with hand samples.

4.3 Sample preparation

There are two cardinal rules for the preparation of pollen samples; firstly that it is only undertaken under appropriate supervision and secondly that the utmost care is exercised with the various chemicals involved. The highest standards of safety must be observed. Ideal conditions are a sterile laboratory with an air-filtering system but these are not often available. A large and powerful fume cupboard which can cope with the fumes of acetone and hydrofluoric acid is essential, as is a sink not lined with lead. Further items include a centrifuge, capable of speeds of at least 3000 rev min[-1] and with interchangeable swing-out heads to carry 8, 15 and 50 ml tubes. Other large items of equipment include a hotplate and a sample mixer. Since six, eight or twelve samples are prepared at once (depending on the type of centrifuge available), adequate supplies of tubes and stands (the former of polypropylene), glass vials 50 mm × 10 mm, sieves (3 in (76 mm) diameter, 180 μm mesh (2.5 φ) for the removal of coarse debris), stirring rods, funnels, beakers, petri dishes, de-ionized water and Analar grade chemicals, microscope slides, coverslips and (of course) a good microscope with electrical counter, laboratory identification manuals and standard record sheets being essential. Pollen analytical procedures are given in detail by the following authors: Faegri and Iversen (1975), Kummel and Raup (1965), Brown (1960) and Erdtman (1969). The object of the analysis is to concentrate the pollen and spores and remove any extraneous matter. Some substances of similar chemical properties to the pollen exines cannot be removed (e.g. chitin) and others (such as carbon and pyrite) tend to be left behind. The process involves the step-by-step removal of carbonates, humus, silica, cellulose, etc., by the appropriate methods, separated by washing with de-ionized water and concentration using a centrifuge, followed by mounting, staining and identification. Good supervision and great care with chemicals is absolutely essential. Numerous different methods are employed and slight variations are necessary to cope with different kinds of sediments. One important point is the need for careful labelling of all pieces of equipment which will come into contact with the samples, and the keeping of a laboratory notebook. The process is not difficult but it is finicky and time-consuming and requires the use of very noxious (and dangerous) chemicals. The following method is compounded from that used by the writer and that of Jones and Cundhill (1978).

4.3.1 Initial treatment

Chemical abbreviations: HCl, hydrochloric acid; HF, hydrofluoric acid; KOH, potassium hydroxide; K_2CO_3, potassium carbonate; HNO_3, nitric acid; H_2SO_4, sulphuric acid.

(1) The sample is examined and, if necessary, pebbles or plant parts are removed by wet-sieving.
(2) Concentration by centrifugation, which is repeated with rinsing and concentration after treatment between any of the following stages. Centrifugation is carried out at 3000 rev min⁻¹

for 5 min for 50 ml tubes and 3000 rev min⁻¹ for 2 min for 15 ml tubes, the centrifuge head being balanced as necessary and the supernatant liquid carefully poured off after each stage in the process.

4.3.2 Removal of carbonates and alkali-soluble humic compounds

(1) Place about 0.5 cm³ (2 g) of sample in a 50 ml polypropylene boiling tube. Add a little 10% HCl and fill tube to two-thirds unless violent reaction.
(2) When the reaction is complete and effervescence stops, centrifuge and decant.
(3) Add a few drops of 10% NaOH to residue, mix, add a further 20 ml and place in a boiling water-bath *in a fume cupboard* for 10 min to 1 h.
(4) Stir well to break any remaining lumps or use a sample mixer.
(5) Filter through a sieve into a polypropylene centrifuge tube. Wash the sieve residue with distilled water and add this water to centrifuge tube.
(6) Centrifuge and decant. If the supernatant liquid is still dark, humic material is still present and the sample must be washed, centrifuged and decanted until the liquid is clear.
(7) Wash the residue on the sieve towards the centre using a jet of water. Invert sieve on petri dish, washing out debris.

This will remove most of the plant debris if the deposit was organic, and concentrate the pollen. If so, then the sample may be prepared for mounting (below). If larger amounts of silica or plant debris (cellulose) are present, it is necessary to remove them by treatment with hydrofluoric acid and then acetolysis. Rubber gloves, goggles and a laboratory coat are vital, all procedures using concentrated acids being carried out in a fume cupboard which has been officially certified as able to cope with their fumes. Adequate supervision is *essential* and a first-aid kit recommended. Hydrofluoric acid dissolves glass and has a horrible effect on human skin requiring immediate intradermal injections of calcium gluconate. Damage is permanent and the necessity for taking adequate safety precautions cannot be overemphasized.

4.3.3 Removal of silica by hydrofluoric acid digestion

(1) A few drops of de-ionized water are added to the residue in the polypropylene centrifuge tube and thoroughly mixed.

(2) An aliquot (20 ml) of 40–60% HF is added to tube and placed in a boiling water-bath for 20–60 min. Stirring with a (polypropylene!) stirrer will detect when the silica grains are no longer present.

(3) Centrifuge and decant into the fume cupboard sink while water is being flushed continuously into it. Capped centrifuge tubes are advisable.

(4) Add a few drops of 10% HCl. Mix, add a further 20 ml of 10% HCl and place in boiling water-bath for 15 min. This removes colloidal silicon dioxide and silicofluorides.

(5) Centrifuge and decant.

(6) Add a few drops of 10% NaOH to the next washing water, centrifuge and decant.

(7) Wash, centrifuge and decant.

4.3.4 Acetolysis to remove cellulose

(1) Add 10 ml of glacial acetic acid to the residue in the tube. Mix, centrifuge and decant into the fume cupboard sink while flushing with water.

(2) Repeat.

(3) Prepare acetolysis mixture by adding 1 ml of conc. H_2SO_4 to 9 ml of acetic anhydride in a measuring cylinder. Stir in a fume cupboard to prevent heat build-up.

(4) Add a few drops to the sample, mix and fill the tube with 20 ml of mixture. Put it in boiling water-bath for 3 min, stirring carefully. Do not leave stirring rods in tubes or let water into tubes, as this gives a violent reaction.

(5) Centrifuge and decant into *a large beaker of water in the fume cupboard*.

(6) Add glacial acetic acid. Mix, centrifuge and decant into the sink.

(7) Add distilled water containing a few drops of 10% NaOH. Mix, centrifuge and decant. Repeat using distilled water only.

4.3.5 Grain mounting

After all the preparation reagents have been extracted from the sample it must be mounted and (if desired) stained. The decision whether or not to stain is a matter of personal opinion, but staining brings out structural details and stops one overlooking fragmentary or badly crumpled grains. The chosen stain should give the maximum contrast with short-wave light, meaning that neutral red, safranin or basic fuchsin are the most useful stains in glycerol or glycerol jelly. Grain mounts may be either permanent or temporary. The latter, being liquid, enables grains to be turned and moved around the slide, or even removed for special identification (for example with the scanning electron microscope).

4.3.6 Temporary mounts (glycerol)

(1) Add a few drops of distilled water to the residue, then one or two drops of safranin or fuchsin stain. Mix, centrifuge and decant.

(2) Invert the tube over a filter paper and carefully allow it to drain.

(3) Add three to six drops of glycerol and mix thoroughly. (The exact amount required depends on the pollen concentration and the amount of residue, which should be tested by preparing a trial slide using the principle that it is better to have too little glycerol than too much.)

(4) Using a small spatula or wooden applicator, transfer a small drop of material to a clean glass slide. Cover with a cover slip (either a 22 mm × 40 mm × 1.0 mm or 18 mm × 18 mm × 1.0 mm). Label with sample number, site notation and depth in profile. Prepare three or four slides for each sample.

(5) Seal and cover with clear nail polish, taking care not to get pollen on to the brush.

(6) Transfer any remaining material to a small labelled glass specimen tube with a polythene stopper. Store.

4.3.7 Permanent mounts (silicone fluid)

Silicone has a high viscosity and therefore will not allow the grains to be moved. It has the advantage of not drying or altering the pollen grains' size but is a longer technique.

(1) Add distilled water, centrifuge and decant.

(2) Repeat.

(3) Add 1 ml of distilled water and 5 ml of 100% ethanol. Centrifuge and decant. Add one or two drops of safranin if required.

(4) Add 100% ethanol, mix, centrifuge and decant.

(5) Add 1 ml of toluene and pour the mixture from the centrifuge tube to a labelled glass tube sealed with a polythene top *in the fume cupboard.*

(6) Lower the tube(s) into the centrifuge with forceps and great care. Centrifuge at *750 rev min⁻¹* (and no faster) for 10 min.

(7) Decant into a beaker in the fume cupboard.

(8) Add two to six drops of silicone fluid (200/200 cSt viscosity) and stir well or else the grains will clump together.

(9) Allow excess toluene to evaporate – 24 h in the fume cupboard.

(10) Make up slides and fix the coverslip with four blobs of varnish in the corners. There is no need to seal it completely.

4.3.8 Alternative procedures

Variations on these themes are published by Dimbleby (1961) who worked on mineral soils, oven-drying his samples to 105 °C after collection using a slightly different analytical technique to that outlined by Faegri and Iversen (1975). He mentions bromoform separation (Waterbolk 1954), which may clear most suspensions, but the HF method is preferable. Lignin may be removed by oxidation and Wilson (1971) describes a method for pollen preparation with extremely calcareous sediments which involves heavy liquid flotation. Guillet and Planchais (1969) discuss the extraction of pollen from soils using heavy liquids, commenting on their progressive disaggregation.

4.3.9 Absolute pollen analysis

Absolute pollen analysis is used to assist in the easier interpretation of results as percentages of fossil pollen grains independent of each other. The procedures involved are lengthy and have been described by Pennington and Bonny (1970) and Bonny (1972).

4.4 Identification and counting

Pollen grains and spores are very small, between 5 and 50 μm in size. It is therefore necessary to use a high-powered microscope with objectives at ×10, ×20, ×40 and an oil-immersion lens at ×100. This gives total magnification of up to ×1000. A mechanical stage for systematic traversing of the slide is also important and a bank of electromagnetic counters will facilitate record-keeping. The eyepiece adjustment and illumination should be adjusted to a comfortable level and the slide traversed in a straight line. Each grain should be identified on encounter and marked on a standard form (or entered in a counter bank). If a pollen grain is difficult to identify and the mount is a temporary one, the grain may be rotated by gentle touches of a needle. A ×40 objective should be sufficient for most grains, although some will require higher magnification. If the transects are correctly spaced at standard intervals, the mechanical stage will show the number of transects counted. The eyes will require frequent short rests or there is a corresponding loss in accuracy. A dictaphone (pedal-operated) may be used instead of a counter bank or forms, but the record has then to be read back and this wastes time.

The recognition of pollen requires practice, tuition, good keys and illustrations and a series of type-specimen slides which may be prepared using the methods of Faegri and Iversen (1975). Drawings, although helpful (Fig. 4.3) cannot be used alone and photomicrographs such as those of West (1968, 1971), Sparks and West (1972), Hyde and Adams (1958) and Erdtman *et al.* (1961) are more useful. Faegri and Iversen (1975) give a key of external pollen morphology (Fig. 4.3) but this requires detailed technical knowledge. The actual number of different pollen varieties encountered in any analysis is actually fairly small, and the major tree pollens are readily recognizable with practice. Some of the basic types of tree and herb pollen may be seen in Figure 4.3.

4.4.1 Electron microscopy

One of the problems in palynology is presented by the fact that many groups of pollen cannot be reliably separated by the optical microscope, but identification to species level is possible with the electron microscope and enables the separation of pollen which looks the same, for example the bog myrtle, *Myrica gale*, and the hazel, *Corylus avellana*, which grow in quite different environments (Pilcher

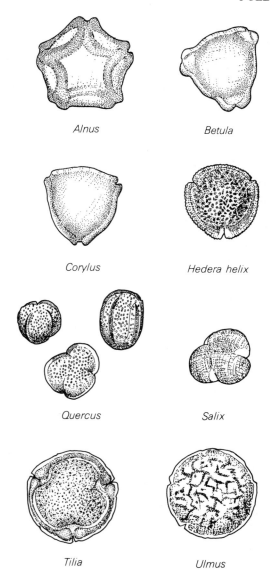

Alnus *Betula*

Corylus *Hedera helix*

Quercus *Salix*

Tilia *Ulmus*

Figure 4.3 Morphology of some pollen grains.

1968). The transmission electron microscope was already used for pollen analyses beginning with the work of Erdtman (1964) on thin sections, and further advances were made by the application of replica techniques (Muhlethaler 1955, Bradley 1958). Tsukada (1967) used the electron microscope on fossil maize pollen and later used replica techniques to distinguish between the pollen of the families Chenopodiaceae (Fig. 4.3) and Amaranthacae (Fig. 4.3) which often form a high percentage

of pollen from arid area deposits (Tsukada 1967). Replication techniques for the electron microscope are, however, difficult and impractical except for rare pollen grains.

The scanning electron microscope does not require thin replicas as objects can be mounted directly on the specimen stage. The process merely requires the dehydration of pollen and sealing with a metal film. Pollen from an ordinary preparation may be used, suspended in silicone fluid (Section 4.3). It is washed in benzene and dried on to the specimen holder in absolute ethanol. A whole preparation may be used or merely a single grain. The value of this method was recognized by Thornhill *et al.* (1965), Echlin (1968), and Heslop-Harrison (1968). Scanning electron microscope pictures are very clear (Fig. 4.4) although the scanning electron microscope is not practical for anything except the low magnification analysis of a few samples from each deposit to give closer identification of the most important pollen types. Figure 4.4 shows *Myrica* and *Corylus* pollen from a study by Pilcher (1968). The fossil samples are from the Beaker and Neolithic site of Ballynagilly, Co. Tyrone, where the scanning electron microscope was used to study pollen spectra of rejuvenated woodland following Neolithic clearance.

4.4.2 Counting the grains
It is a truism that the more grains counted the more the sample is likely to represent the real populations, and after a count of 800–1000 grains the sample should remain constant (Faegri & Iversen 1975). In practice, however, it is not usual to count so many grains and a figure must be arrived at where sufficient grains are counted so as not to conceal regularities by sampling errors (or the reverse), but also not to require an unreasonable amount of work. In the early days of pollen analysis it was usual to count until 150 grains of tree pollen had been reached, but this was a function of the climate of thought at the time where the primary academic interest lay with tree pollen (Dimbleby 1961). Barkley (1934) said that statistically there was no need to exceed 200 grains for a total count, and since then innumerable papers have been published discussing the statistically significant count. Dimbleby (1957) proved that by counting two samples of 700 and 900 grains, all

(a)

(b)

(c)

(d)

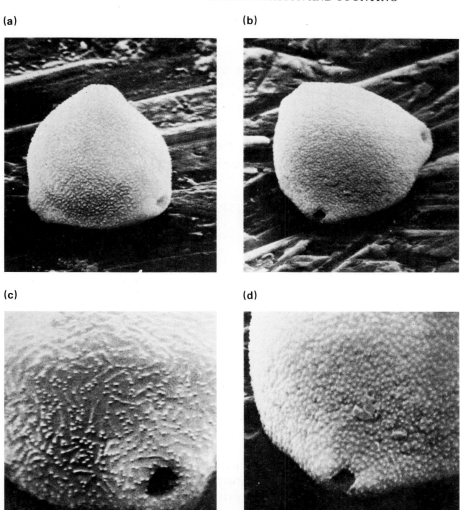

Figure 4.4 Scanning electron photomicrographs of *Myrica* and *Corylus* pollen from Pilcher (1968).

the pollen taxa which had a final percentage greater than 1% of the total pollen were identified within the first 250 grains, but if one taxon is dominant, total pollen numbers would have to exceed 250 to ensure that all major taxa were identified. Later authors have sometimes recommended larger amounts, for example the work of Handa and Moore (1976), who use a total of 500 grains. The standard method still in use is to count until 150 total tree pollen grains have been reached, but at the same time other pollen and spores are counted until the total reaches over 500. This method is very satisfactory for studying vegetation changes in north-western Europe, but less so in areas where arboreal pollen is not important and that of shrubs and herbaceous plants is.

The method of counting must be such as to ensure that no grain is counted twice, which is one of the reasons for the evenly spaced traverses made with a mechanical stage. If insufficient pollen is found on the first slide, the count is continued on further slides from the same sample, and more are made up from the stored reserve if necessary. If the required number of grains is reached in mid-traverse, then the count must continue to the end of that traverse, as errors can result from the differential movement of grains under the coverslip. An example of this is frequently seen in ericaceous grains, which tend to concentrate in the centre of the slide while the more mobile grains are evenly distributed. It is usual to express frequency of each individual pollen type as a

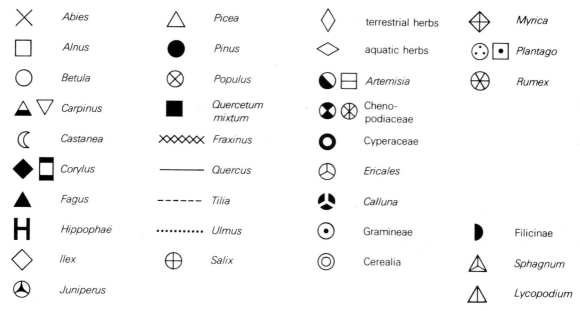

Figure 4.5 Symbols of pollen and spores used in northern Europe (after Faegri & Iversen 1975).

percentage of the whole (total pollen sum), but sometimes percentages are calculated as percentages of the tree pollen only.

4.4.3 Pollen diagrams

Pollen diagrams of different styles are used to express visually the percentage values obtained from the study of a pollen profile. One of the simplest forms of diagram (Fig. 4.6) shows at the left vertical a section through the deposits. At each level each sample is represented by a horizontal line, the percentage present being recorded on the sample line and each layer being distinguished by the conventional symbols (Fig. 4.1). Each horizontal line, therefore, equals a pollen *spectrum* and the different species from different levels complete the pollen *diagram*. Intervals of 10% are always shown and the graph should be drawn on an arithmetic not a logarithmic scale. Even if no single sample reaches more than 50%, the percentage lines for each species should reach 100% for legibility and comparability. Another form of pollen diagram may be seen in Figure 4.8 which is much easier to read, widely accepted and easy to interpret. The percentages of pollen present at each level may be shown either as 'sawblades' (Fig. 4.7) or histograms/bar graphs (Fig. 4.8), the former being easier to draw but the

latter a more objective presentation of the material. Simmons (1969) produced bargraph diagrams where the thickness of the bars was equal to the width of the sample taken from the peat profile and Pennington (1964) used a combination of 'saw-edge' and 'bargraph'. Diagrams may show the total pollen or just the arboreal pollen. An alternative method of presentation is the sector diagram (Godwin 1956), where each species or group is shown as a segment of a circle with different symbols for each. This 'pie-diagram' presentation cannot replace the complete diagram for interpreting the flora from a site, but may be used to show such matters as regional differences or similarities or the distribution of particular species.

4.4.4 Numerical methods and computing

Gordon and Birks (1972) made the trenchant observation that during the last 20 years ecology has changed from being almost entirely qualitative and observational to a science which will yield statistically analysed and quantifiable observations and conclusions. Numerical methods have the great advantage of forcing the operator to recognize the properties of his data. This does not eliminate inherent difficulties but ensures repeatability of results and may stimulate conceptual and methodo-

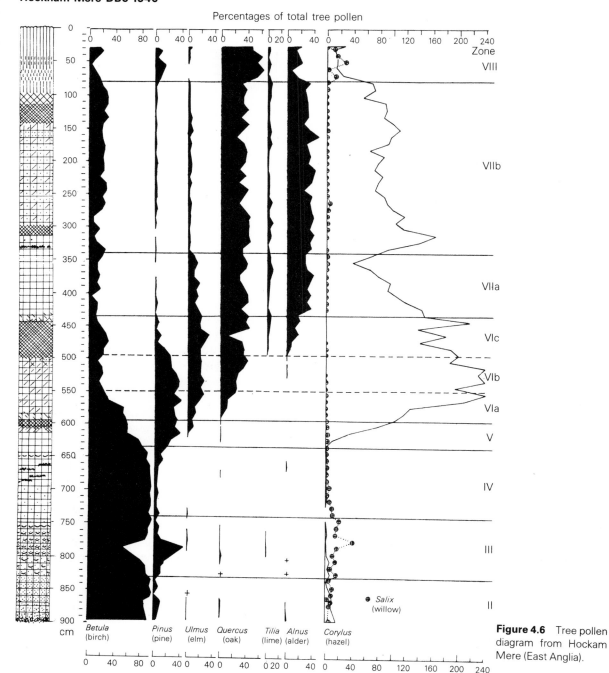

Percentages of total tree pollen

Betula (birch) Pinus (pine) Ulmus (elm) Quercus (oak) Tilia (lime) Alnus (alder) Corylus (hazel)

Salix (willow)

Zone VIII, VIIb, VIIa, VIc, VIb, VIa, V, IV, III, II

Figure 4.6 Tree pollen diagram from Hockam Mere (East Anglia).

logical controversies. Sokal and Sneath (1963, p. 49), in discussing the aims of numerical taxonomy, say that 'we hope by numerical methods to approach the goal where different scientists working independently will obtain accurate and identical estimates of the resemblance between two forms of organisms given the same characters on which to base their judgment'. Computerized numerical methods are often used to handle and process complex and diverse stratigraphic data objectively, and the techniques used for biofacies, lithofacies and biotope analysis in pre-Quaternary palaeontology

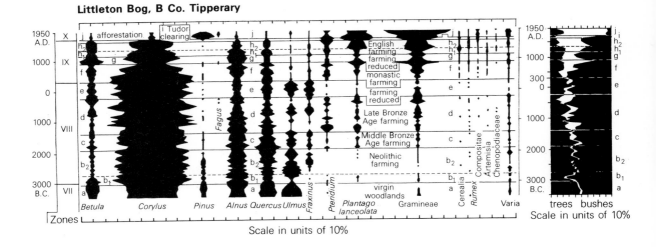

Figure 4.7 Pollen diagram from Littleton Bog, Co. Tipperary.

are reviewed by Buzas (1970) and Olsen (1970).

The most useful unit subdivision of the vertical dimension of a pollen diagram is the pollen **zone**, defined by Birks (1972) as 'a body of sediment with a consistent and homogeneous fossil pollen and spore content that is distinguished from adjacent sediment bodies by differences in the kind and frequency of its contained fossil pollen and spores'. Gordon and

Birks (1972) tested the accuracy of pollen zone divisions using computerized measures of uncertainty. He found that the pollen diagrams' original zonations and numerical analyses gave similar stratigraphical divisions, with minor differences in the exact location of zone boundaries. For example, visually determined zones were not consistently delimitated by numerical procedures but

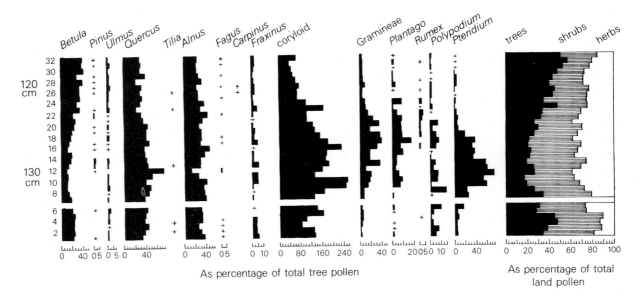

Figure 4.8 A 'small temporary clearance' from Tregaron Bog. This section of the profile was formed between 700 BC (170 cm) and 400 BC (82 cm) and shows three successive phases of clearance, occupation and forest regeneration.

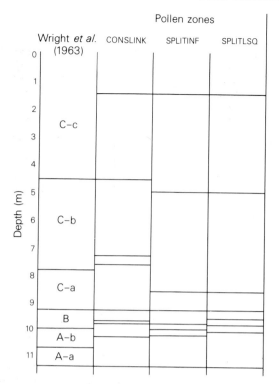

Figure 4.9 Comparison of pollen zonation schemes derived from observed stratigraphy and different computer-processed pollen analysis of samples from Kirchner Marsh (from Gordon & Birks 1972).

cards, but the volume of material soon became too great. The printout gives:

(a) document number
(b) family, genus or species of fossil
(c) site data
(d) part identified; radiocarbon date
(e) pollen significance; archaeology
(f) sediment type; zone
(g) climate; stage
(h) geology; data source
(i) environment; correlated with fauna

which may be used, for example, for studying the fossil record of a particular taxon, the distribution of taxa during different stages of the Quaternary, or the complete fossil flora for a particular stage, pollen zone or cultural phase, in the British Isles as a whole or region by region. It is also possible to compare the range of frequency of a pollen taxon in different pollen zones or of the frequency ranges of the different pollen taxa within the same zone, and one can plot the distribution of pollen taxa and map the frequencies of each tree pollen taxon during the postglacial. It is a basic tool for subsequent analysis and interpretation of observed varieties in the fossil flora and vegetation of the British Isles in space and time.

can be recognized on several sites and are of regional significance. There were some instances where numerical procedures deliminate pollen zones not recognized by the original investigator or dismissed as of little importance in a regional pollen study (Fig. 4.9).

Summaries of further work of this nature are listed, for example, in the Annual Reports of the Sub-department of Quaternary Studies (Botany School, University of Cambridge), which also contain very useful bibliographies.

A further application of numerical methods and computing in palaeobotany is described by Deacon (1972) who describes the computerized data storage system used at Cambridge which now contains a bank of pollen and macrofossil records abstracted from 500 papers and giving a comprehensive survey of the existing literature. Up to the time of the publication of the *History of the British flora* by Godwin in 1956, the data had been stored as edge-punched

4.5 Factors affecting the composition of an assemblage

Various factors affect the identifiable composition of a flora and the relationship which it bears to the original vegetation and/or pollen rain of the area. The pollen diagram will, for example, only show flowering plants and if a tree has been regularly cut before flowering it will not register. The method by which the pollen is transported is most important. A few aquatic plants are pollinated underwater, but have no exine and are under-represented in the diagrams, as are flowers whose pollen is not exposed. Some of the domestic cereals (e.g. wheat) are also under-represented in comparison with others (e.g. rye), even though their pollen is exposed. If the plant is *zoogamous* (animal-pollinated) it may be highly specialized to a particular species of insect, bird or bat which alone can remove the pollen. Unless the animal has died in the place where the pollen is being studied or the whole flower has dropped, little pollen will be preserved. The surface of the grains of zoogamous species is often sticky (like the threads which bind the pollen units together in *Rhododendron*) which mean they will disperse as a unit and may be difficult to record unless the soil beneath the actual plant is sampled. Twenty-five to forty per cent of grains stick into clumps in *Quercus*, *Acer*, *Larix*, *Salix* and *Pinus*. Pollen may be over-represented if a heavy pollen producer is in the immediate vicinity, *Corylus* (hazel) being the classic example, although other species (e.g. *Alnus* at New Shide Bridge, p. 150) do the same thing. One anther of hemp may produce 70 K pollen grains but the number of grains produced by insect-pollinated species is usually less, with the exception of the nectar flowers which produce much pollen in order to lure animals. Wind-pollinated species generally produce a lot of pollen, most of which is lost. The amount of pollen actually produced is amazing and Faegri and Iversen (1975) concluded that the spruce forests of south and central Sweden produce 75 000 tons of pollen per year when flowering freely. Much of this will fall into lakes and the sea and sometimes drifting masses may be accumulated by surface currents or be preserved as a sediment, *fimmenite*. If the pollen is easily transported it may be over-represented, and altitude will also affect the composition. Vertical transport of pollen tends to carry grains into lower regions where they do not belong and since the plants of the higher altitude vegetation belts produce less pollen and therefore have more sensitive vegetation spectra the opposite distortion is easy. Differential decomposition may also be important. It is clear that the quantity of pollen deposited per unit area does not only depend on the frequency of species in that area, but also on matters such as wind, turbulence, dispersal mechanisms, the absolute pollen produce of the species, frequency of flowering years and sedimentation rate of the deposit.

Dimbleby (1957, 1961) did an interesting study of the frequency of pollen in soils, often thought to be small but now known to be comparable with aquatic deposits with frequencies of *c*. 1.5 million per gram. Absolute pollen frequencies fall off rapidly down the soil profile and the pollen present depends both on any residual pollen in parent material and pollen deposits from *in situ* nearby vegetation. The two can sometimes be distinguished, for example if there is much pine pollen and also pine stomatal thickenings are present then pine was probably growing there. As Dimbleby says: 'One cannot argue that because a certain species is only present in very small quantities it never grew on the site, but on the other hand, if any species is represented in considerable quantities it almost certainly did grow there.' (Dimbleby 1957, p. 17). He investigated the relationships between pollen frequencies and pH from sites of pH 3–8, noting that if the pH was greater than 6, the soil is virtually useless. With pH values of 5–6, the pollen is present but in small numbers, often too scarce for reliability. With pH values of less than 5, frequencies of the same order (and sometimes greater) than in peat may be found. A summary is shown in Table 4.1.

Other detailed discussion of problems associated with the interpretation of pollen data may be found in Tinsley and Smith (1974), Davis and Goodlet (1960), Peck (1973), Tauber (1965) and West (1971).

4.6   Pollen in mineral soils

As Dimbleby (1961) pointed out, it has now been realized that palynological analysis of mineral soils may, if the conditions are reasonable, be just as informative as a study of peat bogs. Exceptions are found, as in the case of the mineral layers of heath soils where much pollen has been destroyed by fire, but even acid tropical soils bursting with micro-biological activity yield surprising quantities of pollen. The distribution curve of each species of pollen through the soil profile forms a characteristic shape related to the length of time the pollen has been in the soil, owing to gradual downward movement of pollen under the influence of gravity and leaching. This surprisingly slow process may, of course, be altered by the action of earthworms or by disturbance. The vertical distribution of pollen decreases with depth, the highest concentrations being found (as expected) in the top 1 in (25 mm) despite the intense microbiological activity, (buried surfaces may often be detected by high pollen frequencies), but seems unrelated to pollen size. Dimbleby (1961) gives a rate of 150 mm per 5000 years, probably connected with the downward movement of humus. If the soil is acid the pollen will persist for several millenia, although differential decomposition of species has been suggested. The greater the soil acidity the less the effect of soil-moving fauna, but the longer the pollen is in the soil the greater the chance that it may be destroyed.

Table 4.1 Pollen from different soil pH classes (from Dimbleby 1957). Values are given in absolute frequency per gram of oven-dry soil.

Place of origin	Vegetation type	pH	Pollen count
University Park, Oxford	grass	6.5–7	
Tubney Wood, near Oxford	mixed hardwoods	5	464 K
Forge Valley, Yorkshire	oak/bracken	3.7	196 K
Silpho Moor	oak/hazel	3.6	276 K
north-east Yorkshire	heather	3.1	437 K raw humus 21 K mineral soil
British Guiana★	kakaralli forest	3.6	11 K
North Rhodesia★	tall grass savannah	5.1	12 K

★ Tropical terrestrial soils with much charcoal.

In a paper comparing results achieved by pollen and snail analysis on calcareous soils, Dimbleby and Evans (1974) noted that after eight months some pollen types are almost entirely destroyed and all but the most resistant grains (e.g. fern spores) may lie in the soil for only 2–3 years. In alkaline soils the pollen is almost entirely coeval and without stratification – a vertical distribution of recent pollen rain. It is therefore justifiable to treat this as a direct reflection of contemporary pollen rain and the resulting spectrum as a reflection of the most recent ecological episode.

Much ecological information has been gained for archaeology by the study of buried surfaces, either by examination of molluscan faunas (Section 4.7) or by palynology. Before the surface was buried, it was actively accumulating pollen and, if the pH is above 5.5, sufficient will be preserved to be informative. Dimbleby (1978) illustrated the application of pollen analysis for buried surfaces by making a hypothetical model of a round barrow (Fig. 4.10) with turf core and perimeter ditch. The old land

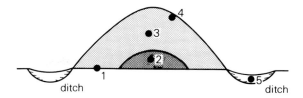

Figure 4.10 Sampling locations for pollen analysis of a round barrow with turf core and perimeter ditch.

surface (1) will, if the profile is complete, reveal the contemporary vegetation and perhaps the activities of man. The turf stack (2) will often complete the original profile, which may have been truncated by the cutting of the turves. In the body of the mound (3) the material is likely to be mixed, but at the surface (4) a recent vegetation record may be obtained, up to 200–400 mm deep, merging into the pollen of the mound (Thompson et al. 1957). The fillings of ditches present more complex problems since their pollen content is again likely to be mixed, as has been shown by the notable experiments at the Overton Down and Wareham earthworks (Jewell & Dimbleby 1966, Dimbleby & Evans 1974). A mound made of topsoil scraped up from the surrounding area will be rich in pollen (Dimbleby 1978), whereas one made from ditch excavation will be poor.

4.7 The study of a particular species

Simmons and Dimbleby (1974) presented an interesting paper on ivy (*Hedera helix* L.), an evergreen climbing plant belonging to the family Araliaceae, whose members prefer warm climates. North-western Europe is the edge of its range, making it a good climatic indicator. It is an insect-pollinated plant flowering between October and November, whose distribution in Denmark was related to climate by Iversen (1960) and van Zeist (1959). Although normally representing less than 10% of the tree pollen, some archaeological pollen analyses have shown an amazing 1000% of the tree pollen, indicating that the sample did not represent a natural pollen rain. Early studies by Troels-Smith (1960) suggested that ivy might have been used as an evergreen winter fodder for sheep, cattle and goats, since if collected at the beginning of winter it would be in flower, accounting for the high pollen concentrations. This is supported by analysis of Neolithic sites of the Swiss Michelsberg centre at Weir, where stable manure occurs yielding 37% of ivy pollen, a phenomenon recurring at various Bronze Age sites. Even more interesting occurrences have been noted at Mesolithic sites like Oakhanger (Rankine *et al.* 1960), where at one level 269 out of 309 grains were ivy. Simmons and Dimbleby (1974) note that in some hundreds of pollen analyses of terrestrial sites, the senior author had never found abnormal ivy percentages *'unless the site was an occupation site'* (present author's italics). This has important implications for the Mesolithic economy since, as red deer were known to be an important factor in Mesolithic economy and they are fond of ivy, it suggests the possibility that they were tethered and semi-domesticated. Several sites support this hypothesis, for example the Swiss rock-shelters of Balmes, where the Mesolithic occupation level had continuously heavy ivy counts. Clark (1972) and Jarman (1972) both suggest that ivy would permit the herding of red deer into a semi-permanent camp, an interesting possibility which makes it necessary to redefine the terminology for the beginning of animal husbandry in north-western Europe.

4.8 Climate, man and landscape evolution

Greig and Turner (1974) discuss the factors accounting for vegetation changes in Postglacial pollen diagrams from Greece (Fig. 4.11). At Lake Kopais (Fig. 4.11b) cores were obtained through several former lakebeds and at Phillipi (Fig. 4.11a) pollen diagrams were already available for some 50 000 years of vegetation history, although with little detail for the archaeologically important last 8000 years. The Phillipi peats and marls were prepared using acetolysis and hydrofluoric acid digestion by the methods already described (Section 4.3), identifications being carried out using reference slides and the key of Mediterranean pollen grains by Beug (1961). The Lake Kopais sediments were more difficult, requiring the development of a method utilizing 'Calgon' (sodium hexametaphosphate). Three diagrams were obtained, two for Phillipi and one for Lake Kopais, to compare these regions

which could possibly be typical of north and south Greece as a whole. In the north this work and that of Wijmstra (1964) showed thick oak forest which had developed by 7000 BC with little change in the Neolithic or later periods, although an unpublished diagram from Thrace shows regular deforestation in the medieval period which reduced the vegetation to its present degraded state. In the south the forest was apparently much reduced by the Bronze Age at the latest, giving the landscape its present appearance of treeless plains but with well-wooded hillsides. In classical times timber was imported from northern to southern Greece, providing a good historical correlation.

The climate was different in the two regions, with Macedonia being more favourable for forest which could regenerate after clearance because of extra rainfall (especially in the summer) but in the south severe erosion and a drier climate prevented re-growth. Greig and Turner (1974) suggest, however, that the difference in vegetation development between the two regions was probably a function of the population, since Neolithic tells are found in Thessaly and Macedonia but Bronze Age sites exclusively in central and southern Greece. If the tell occupation did not involve too much clearance, either because the population was quite small or because there was sufficient empty land available due to the river courses, then this might explain the forest. The rapid and final deforestation of southern Greece might similarly be explained by the increased Bronze Age populations which is suggested from the archaeological evidence.

4.9 Caves and coprolites

Caves present different problems for the pollen analyst since only in the entrance and twilight zone are plants likely to have actually been growing, the other fractions of the pollen rain being contributed from some difficult-to-determine distance away. Since the majority of caves are developed in calcareous rocks their included sediments are also calcareous, inhibiting the preservation of pollen. Nevertheless, pollen has been extracted from cave sediments by 'triumphs of preparation technique' (Barker 1977), but often in such small numbers from

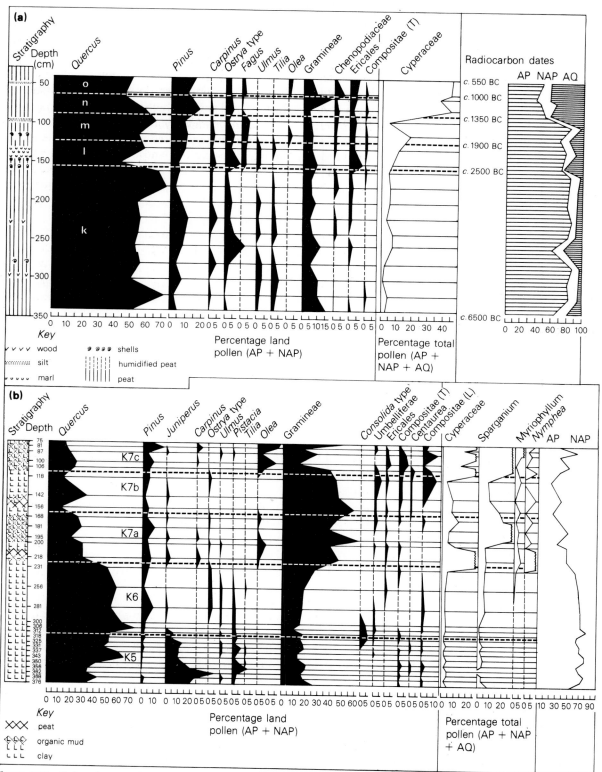

Figure 4.11 Pollen diagrams from Greece. (a) Phillipi 3; (b) Lake Kopais (from Greig & Turner 1974).

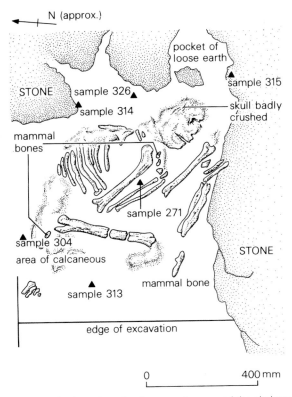

Figure 4.12 Location of pollen samples around the skeleton of Neanderthal burial Shanidar IV (from Solecki 1971).

such large quantities of sediment that the interpretation of vegetation changes is very difficult indeed (Campbell 1978, Horowitz 1979). Small-scale specific investigations have often provided more valid and reliable interpretation, a good example of which may be seen at the great Shanidar cave, northern Iraq (Solecki 1972). Here the famous Neanderthal burial Shanidar IV was proved by palynological work carried out by Mme A. Leroi-Gourhan (1968) to have been buried in a flower-lined grave sometime between late May and early July. Small, brightly coloured wild flowers, such as the grape hyacinth (*Muscari* sp.), hollyhock (*Althaea* sp.) and groundsel (*Senecio* sp.), had been worked into the branches of a pine-like shrub, *Ephedra altissima*. (The implications of this burial have been discussed more fully elsewhere (Shackley 1980)). Sediment samples taken from the grave contained sporadic air-borne pollen grains, but in the samples associated with the burial (Fig. 4.12) pollen from these species appeared in clusters of tens and

thousands, sometimes still resting inside the anther. The pollen, preserved by the rather humus-rich sediment, included at least seven species of flower, all to be found in the area today and most having medicinal properties. The precise dating of the burial to the early summer was achieved by noting the flowering periods of the species present, and the work is a magnificent example of painstaking analysis and thoughtful planning, illustrating both the diligence of the excavator and the humanity of Neanderthal man.

Examples of palaeoclimatic reconstructions for cave sediments are more common, for example those of Josette Renault-Miskorsky at the Mousterian cave site of Hortus (Provence) (de Lumley 1972).

A further Pleistocene example of palynology is seen at the open-air site of Terra Amata excavated near Nice, where early Acheulean hut emplacements were revealed with associated environmental evidence to establish a detailed stratigraphy for part of the Mindel glaciation (de Lumley 1972). Twenty-one separate occupation horizons were found corresponding to seasonal hunting camps where coprolite pollen showed that the hunters had visited the site briefly in spring, staying only a few days. Palynological analysis also permitted the reconstruction of the surrounding environments for the huts with seaside plants such as *Crithmum maritimum*, *Thymelaea* and *Plantago* being found, while further away, on the foothills of the nearby hills, pine and fir forest abounded.

Much work has been done on pollen analysis from coprolites at North American sites, for example the studies of Fry (1976) and Martin and Sharrock (1964). In general, the coprolite pollen included not only species which could have been deliberately eaten (such as *Zea* (corn), *Cucumbita* (squash) and *Opuntia* (prickly pear)) but also general wind-blown pollen seed. Pollen analysis of coprolites does not necessarily agree, as in the coprolite from Glen Canyon (Martin & Sharrock 1964) where at least one of the major pollen types, *Cleome* (beeweed), was not represented in the macrofossil record and was probably ingested without plant tissues. The suggested reason is that it was prepared for consumption by boiling the young plants, which, in conjunction with the processes of digestion, would destroy the plant tissues and leave the pollen unharmed.

4.10 Spores

Spores of non-vascular plants often occur with pollen samples and some species are readily identifiable (Fig. 4.3). An often-quoted example is the species *Puccinia graminis*, the wheat rust, found in a coffin at Great Barrow, Bishop's Waltham, which had presumably been lined with wheat straw to receive the cremation (Ashbee 1957). Bracken and common polypody (*Polypodium vulgare*, Section 4.3) are especially common and Dimbleby (1978) also lists the royal fern (*Osmunda regalis*), the moonwort (*Botrychium lunaria*) and the adder's tongue fern (*Ophioglossum vulgatum*) as being readily identifiable.

4.11 The elm decline

The elm decline was defined by Groenman-van Waateringe (1963, p. 292) as 'the relative decline of elms in the pollen diagrams at about 3000 BC, which occurred throughout Western and Northern Europe and which has therefore been accepted as the boundary between the Atlantic and the Subboreal'. Several reasons have been advanced for this phenomenon (Dimbleby 1961), particularly natural climatic cause (Iversen 1941) and the advent of Neolithic man (Faegri 1944, Troels-Smith 1953, 1955, 1960). The latter author suggested that stock was fed on elm branches which were thus prevented from blossoming and produced less pollen. Iversen (1941) was the first to note the appearance of *Plantago lanceolata* at this time, creating a hypothesis involving the burning-off of forest and grain cultivation followed by the grazing of livestock. This sequence was tested by Iversen in 1956 at Draved Skor in South Jutland to check the approximation to the pollen diagram and this so-called *landnam* theory was accepted, although the idea of Troels-Smith was rejected. Smith (1961) suggested the possibility of plant disease but this was opposed by Heybroek (1963). Radiocarbon dates for the elm decline cluster around 3000 BC (Godwin 1960, van Zeist 1964). An interesting factor is that, if it was of anthropogenic origin, it is difficult to explain this simultaneity, and to explain why it should occur in relatively sparsely populated regions such as

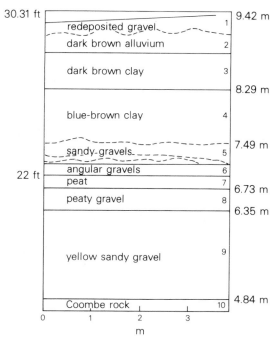

Figure 4.13 Section through the deposits at New Shide Bridge, Isle of Wight.

Ireland. Frenzel (1966) suggested a cold phase of short duration between 3400 and 3000 BC, but van Zeist (1959) and Troels-Smith (1960) had already dismissed the possibility of a temperature decline accounting for the sudden reduction in elm pollen, and even the dry period postulated for 3000–2000 BC by Tauber (1965) does not explain the simultaneous appearance of the elm decline and the first appearance of *Plantago maior* and *Plantago lanceolata*. It is very difficult to distinguish between climatic, environmental and anthropogenic influences, and this applies equally to forest clearance (Evans 1971). Unless Neolithic artefacts or cereal pollen accompany the elm decline and appearance of *Plantago*, Neolithic man was not necessarily present (Groenman-van Waateringe 1963). In unstable boundary zones such as river valleys or sea coasts, the natural pasture of wild grazing animals is found together with a vegetation community different from either of the meeting extremes. Soil is enriched by dung and affected by grazing. The number and variety of plant species is reduced and a similar phenomenon can result from grazing by man and livestock; and even before the Neolithic a vegetation occurred in naturally unstable areas where certain *Plantaginaceae* and other weeds of cultivation occurred. The elm decline is therefore a phenomenon for which there is no certain explanation, but it seems likely to be both anthropogenic and environmental. Both Godwin (1975) and Iversen (1941) showed the map of the vegetation changes of the Flandrian to be anthropogenic in origin, and the decline of elm and simultaneous appearance of herbaceous species such as *Plantago* in the mid-Flandrian is surely not coincidental.

4.12 Phytoliths

Phytoliths (or plant opals) are microscopic particles of silica which occur within the cells of certain species of plants, especially the grasses. Their shape and size is quite varied and in recent years several workers have attempted to identify them in archaeological deposits. The matter is complicated as the phytoliths of one species may be varied in size and shape and it seems unlikely that accurate identification to species level will ever be possible with complete confidence. Anderson (1980) noted the presence of plant phytoliths on prehistoric stone tools whose microwear was being studied using a scanning electron microscope, and identified the species using keys provided, for example, in the work of Taugordeau-Lantz *et al.* (1976).

References

Anderson, P. C. 1980. A testimony of prehistoric tasks: diagnostic residues at stone tool working edges. *Wld Arch.* **12**, 181–95.

Ashbee, P. 1957. The Great Barrow at Bishop's Waltham, Hampshire. *Proc. Prehist. Soc.* **23**, 137–66.

Barker, P. 1977. *Techniques of archaeological excavation.* London: Batsford.

Barkley, F. A. 1934. The statistical theory of pollen analysis. *Ecology* **15**, 283.

Beug, H. J. 1961. Beiträge zur Postglazialen Floren- und Vegetationsgeschichte in Süddalmatien; der See 'Malo Jezero' auf Ulyet. Parts 1 and 2. *Flora* **150**, 600–56.

Birks, H. J. B. 1974. Numerical zonation of Flandrian pollen count. *New Phytol.* **73**, 351–8.

Bonny, A. P. 1972. A method for determining absolute pollen frequencies in lake sediments. *New Phytol.* **71**, 393–405.

Bradley, D. E. 1958. The study of pollen grain surfaces in the electron microscope. *New Phytol.* **57**, 226–9.

Brown, C. A. 1960. *Palynological techniques.* Baton Rouge, Louisiana: privately published.

Buzas, M. A. 1970. On the quantification of biofacies. *Proc. North Am. Paleont. Convention* Chicago 1969. Proceedings B 101.

Campbell, J. B. 1978. *The Upper Palaeolithic period in Britain.* London: Cambridge University Press.

Clark, J. G. D. 1972. *Star Carr: a case study in bioarchaeology.* Boston, Mass.: Addison-Wesley Modular Publications in Anthropology No. 10.

Clymo, R. S. 1964. Apparatus for recovery of lost peat borers. *New Phytol.* **63**, 426–7.

Davis, M. B. and J. C. Goodlet 1960. Comparison of the present vegetation with pollen spectra from Brownington Pond, Vermont. *Ecology* **41**, 804–25.

Deacon, J. 1972. A data bank of Quaternary plant fossil records. *New Phytol.* **71**, 1227–32.

Dimbleby, G. W. 1957. Pollen analysis of terrestrial soils. *New Phytol.* **56**, 12–28.

Dimbleby, G. W. 1961. Soil pollen analysis. *J. Soil Sci.* **12**, 1–12.

Dimbleby, G. W. 1978. *Plants and archaeology*, 2nd edn. London: Granada.

Dimbleby, G. W. and J. G. Evans 1974. Pollen and land-snail analysis of calcareous soils. *J. Arch. Sci.* **1**, 117–33.

Echlin, P. 1968. The use of the scanning reflection electron microscope in the study of plant and microbial material. *Jl R. Microsc. Soc.* **88**, 407–18.

Erdtman, G. 1969. *Handbook of palynology.* Copenhagen: Munksgaard.

Erdtman, G., B. Berglund and J. Praglowski 1961. *An introduction to a Scandinavian pollen flora.* Stockholm: Almquist and Wiksell.

Erdtman, G., J. Praglowski and S. Nilsson 1963. *An introduction to a Scandinavian pollen flora*, vol. 2. Stockholm: Almquist and Wiksell.

Evans, J. G. 1971. Notes on the environment of early farming communities in Britain. In *Economy and settlement in Neolithic and Early Bronze Age Britain and Europe*, D. D. A. Simpson (ed.), 11–26. Leicester: Leicester University Press.

Faegri, K. 1944. On the introduction of agriculture in Western Norway. *Geol. Stockh. Förhand.* **66**, 449–62.

Faegri, K. and J. Iversen 1975. *Textbook of pollen analysis*, 2nd edn. Oxford: Blackwell Scientific.

Frenzel, B. 1966. Climatic change in the Atlantic/sub-boreal transition in the Northern hemisphere: botanical evidence. In *World climate from 8000 to 0 BC*, J. S. Sawyer (ed.), 99–123. London: Royal Meteorological Society.

Fry, G. F. 1976. *Analysis of prehistoric coprolites from Utah.* Univ. Utah Anthrop. Pap. no. 97.

Godwin, H. 1956. *History of the British flora.* Cambridge: Cambridge University Press.

Godwin, H. 1960. Prehistoric wooden trackways of the

Somerset levels: their construction, age and relation to climatic change. *Proc. Prehist. Soc.* **26**, 1–36.

Gordon, A. D. and H. J. B. Birks 1972. Numerical methods in Quaternary Palaeoecology: 1. Zonation of pollen diagrams. *New Phytol.* **71**, 961–79.

Greig, J. R. A. and J. Turner 1974. Some pollen diagrams from Greece and their archaeological significance. *J. Arch. Sci.* **1**, 177–94.

Groenman-van Waateringe, W. 1963. The elm decline and the first appearance of *Plantago maior*. *Vegetatio* **15**, 292–6.

Guillet, B. and N. Planchais 1969. Note sur une technique d'extraction des pollens des sols par une solution dense. *Pollen Spores* **11**, 141–5.

Handa, S. and P. D. Moore 1976. Studies in the vegetational history of mid Wales, IV. Pollen analysis of some pingo basins. *New Phytol.* **75**, 205–25.

Heslop-Harrison, J. 1968. Pollen wall development. *Science* **161**, 230–7.

Heybroek, H. M. 1963. Diseases and lopping for fodder as possible causes of a prehistoric decline of *Ulmus*. *Acta Bot. Neerl.* **12**, 1–11.

Horowitz, A. 1979. *The Quaternary of Israel.* London: Academic Press.

Hyde, H. A. and K. F. Adams 1958. *An atlas of airborne pollen grains.* London: Macmillan.

Iversen, J. 1941. The influence of prehistoric man on vegetation. *Dan. Geol. Unders.* Series 2, **6**, 1–25.

Iversen, J. 1960. Problems of the early Postglacial forest development in Denmark. *Dan. Geol. Unders.* **4**(3), 1–32.

Jarman, M. R. 1972. European deer economies and the advent of the Neolithic. In *Papers in economic prehistory*, E. S. Higgs (ed.), 125–47. London: Cambridge University Press.

Jewell, P. A. and G. W. Dimbleby 1966. The experimental earthwork on Overton Down: the first four years. *Proc. Prehist. Soc.* **32**, 313–42.

Jones, R. L. and P. Cundhill 1978. *Introduction to pollen analysis.* Br. Geomorph. Res. Group Tech. Bull. 22.

Kummell, B. and D. Raup (eds) 1965. *Handbook of paleontological techniques.* San Francisco: W. H. Freeman.

Leroi-Gourhan, A. 1968. Le Néanderthalen IV de Shanidar. *Bull. Soc. Préhist. Franc. C. R. Séanc. mensuelles* **65**(3), 79–83.

Lumley, H. de 1972. *La grotte de l'Hortus.* Marseille: Université de Provence.

Mackereth, F. J. H. 1958. A portable core sampler for lake deposits. *Limnol. Oceanogr.* **3**, 181–91.

Martin, P. and F. W. Sharrock 1964. Pollen analysis of prehistoric human feces: a new approach to ethnobotany. *Am. Antiquity* **30**, 168–80.

Muhlethaler, K. 1955. Die Strucktur einiger Pollenmembranen. *Planta* **46**, 1–13.

Olsen, E. C. 1970. Current and projected impacts of computers upon concepts and research in paleontology. *Proc. N. Am. Paleont. Convention*, Chicago, 1969, B 135.

Peck, R. M. 1973. Pollen budget studies in a small Yorkshire catchment. In *Quaternary plant ecology*, H. J. B. Birks and R. G. West (eds). Oxford: Blackwell Scientific.

Pennington, W. 1964. Pollen analysis from the deposits of six upland farms in the Lake District. *Phil. Trans R. Soc. B.* **248**, 205–44.

Pennington, W. and A. P. Bonny 1970. An absolute pollen diagram from the British Late-glacial. *Nature* **226**, 871–3.

Pilcher, J. R. 1968. Some applications of scanning electron microscopy to the study of modern and fossil pollen. *Ulster J. Arch.* **31**, 87–91.

Rankine, W. F., W. M. Rankine and G. W. Dimbleby 1960. Further excavations at a Mesolithic site at Oakhanger, Selborne, Hants. Part II: Report on pollen and charcoal. *Proc. Prehist. Soc.* **26**, 255–62.

Shackley, M. L. 1975. *Archaeological sediments: a survey of analytical methods.* London: Butterworth.

Shackley, M. L. 1980. *Neanderthal man.* London: Duckworth.

Simmons, I. G. 1969. Pollen diagrams from the North York Moors. *New Phytol.* **68**, 807–27.

Simmons, I. G. and G. W. Dimbleby 1974. The possible role of ivy *Hedera helix* L. in the Mesolithic economy of Western Europe. *J. Arch. Sci.* **1**, 291–6.

Smith, A. G. 1961. The Atlantic sub-boreal transition. *Proc. Linn. Soc. Lond.* **172**, 38–49.

Sokal, R. R. and P. H. A. Sneath 1963. *Numerical taxonomy: the principles and practice of numerical classification.* San Francisco: W. H. Freeman.

Solecki, R. S. 1972. *Shanidar: the humanity of Neanderthal man.* London: Allen Lane.

Sparks, B. W. and R. G. West 1972. *The Ice Age in Britain.* London: Methuen.

Tauber, H. 1965. Differential pollen dispersion and the interpretation of pollen diagrams with a contribution to the interpretation of the elm fall. *Danm. Geol. Unders.* II RK. 89.

Taugordeau-Lantz, J., J. Laroche, G. Lachkar and D. Pons 1976. La silice chez les végétaux: problème des phytolithaires. *Trav. Lab. Micropaleont.* **5**, 254–303.

Thompson, M. W., P. Ashbee and G. W. Dimbleby 1957. Excavation of a barrow near the Hardy Monument, Black Down, Portesham, Dorset. *Proc. Prehist. Soc.* **23**, 124–36.

Thornhill, J. W., R. K. Matta and W. H. Wood 1965. Examining 3-D microstructures with the scanning electron microscope. *Grana Palynol.* **6**, 4–6.

Tinsley, H. M. and R. T. Smith 1974. Surface pollen studies across a woodland/heath transition and the application to the interpretation of pollen diagrams. *New Phytol.* **73**, 547–65.

Troels-Smith, J. 1953. Ertebøllekultur-Bondekultur. *Aarbøger for Nordisk Oldkyndighid og Historie* 5–62.

Troels-Smith, J. 1955. Pollenanalystische Untersuchungen zu einigen schweizerischen Pfahlbauproblemen. In *Das Pfahlbauproblem*, W. U. Guyan (ed.), 9–58. Basel.

Troels-Smith, J. 1960. Ivy, mistletoe and elm, climate indicators – fodder plants. *Danm. Geol. Unders.* IV RK Bd4 4.

Tsukada, M. 1967. Chenopod and Amaranth pollen: electron-microscopic identification. *Science, N.Y.* **157**, 80–2.

Waterbolk, H. T. 1954. *De Praehistorische Mens en Zijn Milieu.* Groningen: Rijksuniversiteit.

Walker, M. J. C. and J. J. Lowe 1976. The Abbey piston cover. *Quatern. Newsletter* **19**, 1–3.

West, R. G. 1968. *Pleistocene biology geology and biology.* Harlow: Longman.

West, R. G. 1971. *Studying the past by pollen analysis.* Oxford: Oxford University Press.

Wijmstra, T. A. 1964. Palynology of the first 30 m of a 100 m deep section in Philippi, northern Greece. *Acta Bot. Neerl.* **18**, 511–27.

Wilson, G. J. 1971. A chemical method for the palynological processing of chalk. *Mercian Geol.* **4**, 29–33.

van Zeist, W. 1959. Studies on the post-Boreal vegetation history of south-eastern Drenthe (Netherlands). *Acta Bot. Neerl.* **8**, 156–84.

van Zeist, W. 1964. A palaeobotanical study of some bogs in Western Brittany (Finistere) France. *Palaeohistoria* 157–80.

5 Wood and charcoal

> 'Of all the trees that grow so fair,
> Old England to adorn,
> Greater are none beneath the Sun,
> Than Oak, and Ash, and Thorn.'

(Rudyard Kipling, *A tree song*)

5.1 Introduction

The identification of wood and charcoal samples forms one of the most important branches (*sic*) of environmental archaeology. On British sites the number of potential species present is not great and good reference collections and identification keys are readily available. Moreover, the making of a wood reference collection is not difficult and the preparation of archaeological samples for identification is relatively straightforward and not very time-consuming. Nevertheless, archaeological literature is 'rich in incorrect identifications' (Dimbleby 1978, p. 103), showing that the subject is not as simple as it seems. The basic structure of wood has been described with admirable succinctness by the same author and many standard reference works are available (p. 105). The morphology of plant tissues in general is treated in all basic botanical textbooks, for example that of Vines and Rees (1965) who divide them into three categories: (a) mechanical and supporting tissue; (b) water-conducting or vascular tissue; (c) outer epidermal layers. In addition there are the parenchymatous tissues (the word means 'found in beside'), a name invented by early histologists who saw them as filling matter for gaps left by the more solid components of the plant. The term **parenchyma** is usually applied to mature but undifferentiated cells, which compose almost the entire mass of pith and cortex of stems and roots. The vascular tissues, divided into **xylem** and **phloem** (Fig. 5.1), are the most important in describing the structure of wood, and in its strictest sense the term 'wood' should only be applied to the xylem of the secondarily thickened plant. A young twig has a pith of parenchymatous

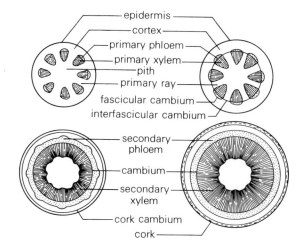

Figure 5.1 Diagram showing the development of a twig as it ages.

cells divided by radial strips of cells called medullary rays (Fig. 5.1). The pith will gradually die as the twig grows but the original medullary rays can still be seen, and many new rays of cells connecting the centre of the branch to the ring tissues of the epidermis will be formed. These parenchymatous rays store starch and are important when identifying a species since they have diagnostic patterns. The outer zone (sapwood) of a branch also contains some living parenchymatous cells which probably store food, but in the inner zone (heartwood) such cells are dead and probably function as containers of the polyphenols (tannins), gums, resins and various coloured substances produced as a result of the tree's photosynthesis. These give the characteristic dark colour to the heartwood and also act as a preservative. The growth of a branch is a result of growth of the vascular **cambium** tissues, an internal cambium and an external cork cambium. As the branch grows the individual bunches of xylem and phloem cells become linked together into fascicular cambium (Fig. 5.1), forming a complete ring of vascular tissue. Each cambial cell differentiates itself into secondary outer (phloem) elements and secondary inner (xylem) ones; as the tree grows, increasingly wide bands of xylem and phloem are developed, transversed by secondary medullary rays; seasonal activity is marked by annual rings which are the result of the death of some of the central xylem cells, producing a constantly widening band of the dark colour heartwood. The rings of secondary xylem (annual rings) consist of two elements in a mature plant, alternating wide bands of **tracheids** (dead and empty water-conducting cells with large cavities), and narrow bands of thick-walled tracheids with small cavities, marking the beginning and end of secondary growth each year.

The ray pattern forms the basis for identification, together with the type of distribution of the vessels; if the tree possesses vessels then it is **deciduous** and if it does not then it is a **conifer**. The vessel may either be arranged in rings (ring-porous) or scattered through the wood (diffuse-porous). Such elements as the shape of the cells, the distribution of the parenchymatous tissue and the pattern of pits on the vessel walls are also diagnostic. Wood samples should be identified with the aid of a good reference collection (Section 5.4) and the relevant source books, for example Maby (1932), Biek (1963), Salisbury and Jane (1940), Godwin and Tansley (1941), Blokhina (1964) or especially Schweingruber (1978) or the atlas of wood photomicrographs by Miles (1978). If wood is burnt in a reducing atmosphere it becomes charcoal, chemically inert and not subject to microbial attack. Charcoals usually preserve the structure of the plant with minimal distortion and may therefore be equally useful for identification. Further works useful in identification are those of Panshin and de Zeeuw (1970), Phillips (1949) – for conifers, and Brazier and Franklin (1961) – for hardwoods. A charcoal reference collection may be easily made by heating wood to a suitable temperature in the absence of air, full details being given by Koeppen (1972).

5.2 Field methods and sampling

5.2.1 Charcoal samples

Sampling methods for charcoal are simple, the main requirement being careful packing in kitchen roll within a rigid container. Large samples are not required (unless for dendrochronology or radiocarbon dating, p. 105) and it is unnecessary to retrieve all the fragments if they clearly belong to the same piece of wood. Smith and Gannon (1973) draw attention to the comparative problems of sampling charcoal and dry ancient wood from arid sites, recommending the use of a diamond saw to split large pieces, if required. Great care should be taken to ensure that all the different woods present have been sampled, and if the sampler is unable to distinguish between different woods everything should be sampled to be safe rather than sorry. It must be remembered that the preservation of charcoal is very variable; it may be solid but it may also be so friable that it will disintegrate when touched. Not all experts are agreed that any selective sampling on site is to be recommended; Dimbleby (1978) suggests that everything should be retrieved. All must be carefully packed and labelled in such a way that it is obvious to whoever is doing the identification whether samples come from the same specimen or were found in close proximity. No attempt should be made to separate charcoal from attached sediment as this will frequently cause the charcoal sample to break, nor should the material be washed.

5.2.2 Wood sampling

The term 'wood' may refer to anything from a sizeable chunk of tree to small fragments of twigs and leaves (Raftery 1970), varying in preservation from the near-perfect preservation achieved in acid peat to perilous friability in conditions of extreme aridity. If the wood is waterlogged it must never be allowed to dry out; this will result in gross distortion and probably mean that the sample is rendered useless (McKerrell & Oddy 1971–2). Such wood should be kept wet and packed in plastic bags or sheeting, with a small quantity of an appropriate fungicide added (Shackley 1975) as long as there is no question of the wood being later required for radiocarbon assay. Wood samples should also be carefully packed to avoid breakage and care should be taken to provide the laboratory with all relevant detail (as for charcoal, see above). It is especially important to know which woods were found in association, and this may involve sending a complete drawing of the feature to the laboratory, with the position of the wood samples carefully marked. Morgan (1975) recommends that a 50 mm cube be taken from an area showing least signs of decay and that unless the sample is composed of many small twigs (perhaps from wattle) it should be given an individual finds number since great confusion can arise if many samples (of different timbers) are taken from some complex feature, such as the lining of a well (Section 5.8).

5.3 Sample preparation (charcoal)

5.3.1 Dry sections
Methods for preparing charcoal samples for identification may be divided into two categories, those which require the charcoal to be impregnated with some medium (usually wax) and those which do not. The latter have the advantage of being relatively non-destructive and requiring the minimum of apparatus (a sharp single-edge razor). Three sections must be cut (transverse, radial and tangential to the grain) and the more accurately these are prepared the simpler the identification (Western 1969, Panshin & de Zeeuw 1970). Leney and Casteel (1975) recommend the following simple procedure:

(1) Determine the longitudinal (axial) grain direction and break the specimen perpendicular to this to obtain a transverse section. The breaking should be done by the same method employed for glass tubing, choosing a piece at least 25 mm long and less than 25 mm thick, making a small cut at right angles to the surface of the grain and about 0.5 mm in depth and holding the specimen over a rod with the cut side facing upwards. Pushing down and outwards makes a clean break.
(2) Determine the radial and tangential directions (Fig. 5.3) and split or cut accurate sections. A stiff single-edge razor is quite adequate. Dimbleby (1978) recommends that the faces of

the sections be ground on emery paper and then cleaned with a blast of compressed air to show all the features of the wood, but this is not necessary if a clean break has been obtained. In addition, if the specimen is very fragile, such grinding will destroy it.

5.3.2 Embedding
The literature of charcoal identification yields information on several early methods of embedding techniques, commented on by Leney and Casteel (1975) and including the identification of wood charcoals from microscopic examination of colloidon impression by Naumann (1917), sections taken from liquid wax (Fietz 1926), examination of ashed charcoal (Neuweiler 1910, Wittmack & Buckwald 1902) and of crushed charcoal using transmitted light (Tanner 1926). Maby (1932) used celloidin (cellulose nitrate) as an embedding medium and experimented with paraffin wax and various resins. The latter were used to make standard petrological-type thin sections (Section 1.3) by impregnation, grinding one face of the sample, cementing it to a microscope slide and grinding the other face to a uniform thickness of 50 μm, but this is very time-consuming and difficult to carry out with longitudinal sections. It is doubtful whether such complicated methods are necessary for charcoals, but they have been mentioned recently by Smith and Gannon (1973) and deplored by Western (1969). Leney and Casteel (1975) conclude that hand-sectioning is definitely preferable, using a microtome instead of a razor blade if the sample requires it. They recommend the use of ground sections if the charcoal is very sandy or full of minerals, or if sectioning requires the use of a heavy sliding microtome and none is available.

5.3.3 Epoxy resin sections
Celloidin sections (p. 96) are difficult as the finished blocks must be immersed in liquid. A more practical method is the use of epoxy resins (Smith & Gannon 1973), which has the advantage of enabling the final product to be sectioned using either a sliding microtome or to be ground for a thin section if required. Epoxy resin impregnation was used with success for the identification of exceptionally friable charcoals from sites in central and northern Oregon

(Gannon 1971). The method (Smith & Gannon 1973) involves the following stages (of which *stages 1–6 must be carried out in a fume cupboard*):

(1) Mix the ingredients for the resin (Epon 812, nadic methyl anhydride, dodecyl succinic anhydride, benzyldimethylamine).
(2) Select the charcoal samples, cutting the large pieces with a razor blade or diamond saw.
(3) Embedding in shell vials of 100% acetone with the sample number clearly marked in a partial vacuum for 24 h.
(4) Remove the acetone and replace with a 1:1 mixture of acetone and resin, also in a partial vacuum. Leave for 24 h.
(5) Replace with a 1:3 mixture of acetone and resin, leave over silica gel for 24 h and replace with enough pure resin to cover the sample. Leave for 24 h.
(6) Prepare a series of small embedding trays by cutting off the ends of polythene vials. Fill with enough resin to cover charcoal samples and leave a sufficiently thick surplus to be clamped in a sliding microtome.
(7) Transfer the charcoal samples together with their labels into the prepared vials, using forceps; place in a desiccator in an oven at 65 °C for 48–60 h.
(8) Cool. Strip off the vials from the blocks of resin using a small jig saw.

The resulting blocks may be stored indefinitely. If a microtome is being used to cut sections, both the block and the microtome knife should be lubricated using a 2:1 mixture of 95% ethyl alcohol and glycerine and sections cut at 8–10 μm before being dried, transferred to a slide, washed with alcohol and then covered with Canada Balsam or resin (Shackley 1975). The method is equally successful for partially carbonized wood samples, and since the resin is soft it may be cut with a microtome and does not require the diamond lap wheel necessary for petrological-type thin sections. The resulting block should be trimmed up and the three sections cut and then polished *without* using carborundum (silicon carbide) since particles easily become embedded in the resin. Carborundum-impregnated papers of different particle sizes may be used with water as a lubricant ('wet and dry papers'). A final drying in air and cleaning with alcohol before being mounted is recommended.

5.3.4 Dry sections (wood)
Dry fresh wood may be sectioned (also along three planes) with a razor blade, or with a microtome if necessary. If the material is friable it should be impregnated.

5.3.5 Impregnated sections (wood)
The method of Smith and Gannon (1973), outlined above, may also be used for wood, especially if the sample is dry. The authors recommend that wood samples be flooded with a little 1% aqueous solution of safranine stain before impregnation, and after about 5 min the slide is rinsed with 95% and then 100% alcohol for dehydration. It should then be rinsed once more with xylene (*these procedures must be undertaken in a fume cupboard*) and covered as described for charcoal. Waterlogged wood should be impregnated with Carbowax (polyethylene glycol), although this is very slow and a hand-cut section is preferable. Dimbleby (1978) notes that before identification the brown organic deposit frequently found on samples may be removed using sodium hypochlorite. In some cases the cell walls will have disintegrated and a section (and identification) be rendered impossible.

5.4 Sample identification

5.4.1 Charcoal
The identification of charcoals is a relatively straightforward business requiring a good reference collection, supplemented by books on wood structure. A hand lens and a microscope with magnifications of ×10, ×20 to ×100 and dark-field incident light is also necessary. Dimbleby (1978) notes that with especially good sections magnifications of ×400 may be useful, but in some cases the transverse section of a charcoal sample may be so definitive that a hand lens at very low magnification (×10 or ×15) is sufficient, or low power microscopy. However, most conifers and many hardwoods will require examination of all three planes at ×100 or higher, although a hand lens may be sufficient for

ring-porous species or where the potential number of species present is limited. Incident light is required, provided by a simple light source attached to the microscope or as an annular fluorescent illuminator (Rackham 1972).

5.4.2 Wood

Wood samples are examined in exactly the same way as that already described for charcoals and at the same magnifications. One problem is presented by what Dimbleby (1978, p. 101) called the 'inevitable variability' of wood, which does not alter basic structure but its more subtle manifestations, increasing the difficulty in matching the sample under examination with reference material. Even wood samples taken from different parts of the same tree may show marked differences which will produce difficulties when twigs rather than pieces of trunk are being examined, since the appearance of the twig may be superficially very different (Schweingruber 1978). Dimbleby (1978) also discusses the problems in distinguishing root and stem wood, the former having, for example, large thick fibre cells which are adapted to withstand tension. Variation within species caused by differences in growth rates may be especially confusing in the case of conifers, but also causes problems with other trees. Williams (1975) notes that a slow growth in ash will result in close proximity of the vessels from the earlywood and the latewood, and since the latter are small and few in number they are easily overlooked.

A first question to be asked is whether or not the tree is ring-porous or diffuse-porous; if it is the former and the sample is from a prehistoric context, then there are only four possible species. The most common tree found on English excavations is oak (*Quercus* sp.) and several specialists (e.g. Morgan 1975) have commented that much valuable (and expensive) laboratory time would be saved if excavators could learn to recognize it. Oak may be distinguished from ash and elm (also quite common) by the very wide rays and small vessels in the latewood which make a characteristic 'flame' pattern not seen in the scattered single or paired vessels from ash or the lines of small vessels parallel to the early wood in elm. Godwin (1956, p. 204) refers to the '. . . medieval encouragement of oak as the staple of swine-pannage, leather-tanning, ship-building and miscellaneous building and farm industry' which, since oak survives better than other species and was in frequent use for all purposes, accounts for the great preponderance of oak remains on medieval sites (Morris & Perring 1974). Williams (1975) claims that it is possible to identify oak on external features alone without sections, but still advises sectioning for confirmation.

Only three conifers are native to Britain, rendering identification quite easy, but the hardwoods (including oak, see above) may give more problems. The ring-porous species native to Britain include only oak, ash (*Fraxinus*) and elm (*Ulmus*), readily identifiable by two distinct growth zones in each annual ring formed by the production of a line of very large vessels (earlywood) in spring, separated by a zone of small dark cells (latewood) produced in summer. If these lines of clear annual rings are observed in transverse section, the choice is limited to one of these three species if the sample is medieval or earlier, although more species were introduced after the medieval period. Transverse sections of birch (*Betula*), hazel (*Corylus*) and alder (*Alnus*) show an overall scatter of small vessels surrounded by denser material with only a very faint line separating each annual growth. The identification of these species may be very difficult and will need minute observations of all the small details of structure together with a most comprehensive reference collection. The most useful keys are those of Clifford (1956), Miles (1978), Schweingruber (1978), Greguss (1959), the Forestry Research Board (1953, 1960, 1961), Jane (1970) and notes by Dimbleby (1978). Punch-card keys are available for assistance with the identification of commercial timbers, but these are not often applicable to archaeological problems. Each consists of photographs of the three sections of the wood, which should have been taken from different places on the tree, and a description of the ring and ray patterns and characteristics of the pores. Up-to-date varieties are now commercially available.

The colour of wood may be a supplementary guide to identification; for example, waterlogged oak is very black but elm is brown and ash varies from grey-brown to orange-brown. Oak is a sapwood tree and in a living example the sapwood is cream in colour, turning grey on weathering. The

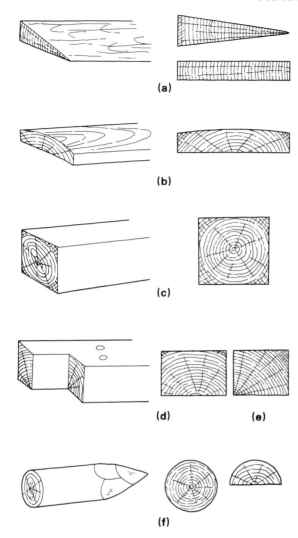

Figure 5.2 The most common cuts of timber found on archaeological sites. (a) Radially split and quarter-sawn planks; (b) flat sawn planks cut across the edge of the tree; (c) beam consisting of the entire trunk, slightly trimmed; (d) beam consisting of half the trunk with edges trimmed (sapwood may be preserved at the corners of both (c) (d)); (e) beam consisting of one quarter of the trunk; (f) stakes, either a complete or a split stem with the bark or bark edge remaining (after Morgan 1978).

heartwood, brown in the living tree, turns black. The sapwood may, of course, be absent if the archaeological sample comes from beams or planks (Fig. 5.2). Elm also has pale sapwood but in ash there is no colour differentiation between sapwood and heartwood (Morgan 1975).

5.5 Scanning electron microscopy

Keepax (1975) illustrates an application of scanning electron microscopy techniques to wood-like remains which occur as corroded iron objects. The scanning electron microscope showed that the iron had been deposited within the cell spaces of the decomposed wood, leaving internal casts fossilizing the original structure. The identification of such materials is difficult with the light microscope but easy using the scanning electron microscope, even when the wood is very soft. Fresh breaks are required, but the condition of the wood does not seem to affect the identification. Twenty-five examples were identified from the Saxon site of Mucking in Essex (Jones 1972) and seven from a waterlogged Roman well at Rudston in Yorkshire. The wood was stained or replaced to different degrees (Fig. 5.3) the degree of replacement varying even within small samples. The wood is not preserved by the iron, as happens with leather for more complex reasons, but replaced by it, and copper deposits have been found filling some wood cells (Hosking 1965), which suggests that a similar process might take place with that metal.

5.6 Charcoal and plaster impressions from Myrtos

Rackham (1972) describes the identification of eighteen collections of charcoal from the Early Bronze Age site of Myrtos (Crete), using simple examination under incident light combined with the use of a scanning electron microscope to compare the finer details of the charcoals and modern olive wood. A problem was presented by the nature of the material since the large numbers of trees and shrubs comprising the modern Cretan vegetation have not been adequately described and the structure of variations within modern Cretan wood is unstudied. Fortunately the archaeological material was one of three species (olive, oak and pine), but it was not possible to distinguish wild from cultivated olive (*Olea europaea* L.). Plots of the relative percentages of the three types showed an overwhelming preponderance of olive wood in collections 16 and 18 and forming the whole of collection 13. The timber

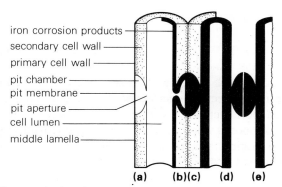

iron corrosion products
secondary cell wall
primary cell wall
pit chamber
pit membrane
pit aperture
cell lumen
middle lamella

(a) (b)(c) (d) (e)

Figure 5.3 Longitudinal and cross-sections of wood cells showing progressive replacement by iron corrosion products. (a) Bordered pit in cell wall of normal wood; (b) thin layer of iron corrosion products on inside of pit cavity and cell lumen; (c) pit cavity filled with iron corrosion products but cell wall still present; (d) and (e) cell wall decayed away leaving pit-pair cast and internal cell cast (from Keepax 1978).

seemed to be local, although the small amount of pine could be the result of a single driftwood tree. The presence of oak suggests a climate slightly less arid than the present day, although the narrow rings indicate that the tree was nearing its climatic tolerance limit. Most of the charcoal appeared to be from roof timber, wooden joints with bracken and scrapwood laid across them to provide a level surface for reeds or plaster. Impressions of the leaf-sheaths and blades of reeds were visible; the species represented were either *Arundo donax* L. or *Phragmites communis* Trin., which are both very variable and could not be separated on the available evidence. Bark impressions of part of a large *Quercus ilex* log were also seen.

5.7 Charcoals as palaeoenvironmental evidence

There are many examples of appendices to excavation reports which include an identification of charcoals; for example, Fox (1963) presents a note on the Neolithic charcoals from Hembury in eastern Devon which are used just as dating evidence associated with pottery. A more common trend in recent years is the use of charcoals as fragments of information helpful in the reconstruction of a palaeoenvironment. This trend really started many years ago with an interesting pair of papers which

appeared in the 1940s and serve to illustrate some of the pitfalls inherent in ecological interpretation from charcoals. Salisbury and Jane (1940) published a study of charcoals from Neolithic and Iron Age contexts at Maiden Castle, Dorset, comparing them with Roman charcoals from Verulamium (St Albans) and modern hazel charcoals growing on the Dorset chalklands and Hertfordshire clay-with-flints. A number of conclusions were drawn from this analysis, not all of which appear to have been valid when the underlying assumptions are subjected to a critical review, as was done by Godwin and Tansley (1941). Points at issue were the former authors' interpretation of the archaeological charcoals as wood collected in the immediate vicinity of the site (since the charcoals represented were mainly from small twigs, local collection seemed more likely). Godwin and Tansley rightly pointed out that to assume that the charcoals could therefore be taken as representative of the local flora was unjustifiable; one might expect some anthropogenic selection factor to have been working in the collection of twigs for firewood. Not all woods, after all, burn equally well. Moreover, the occurrence of twigs rather than large branches does not warrant the assumption made in the original report that branches were not used as fuel; indeed the twigs are likely to be the remains of such branches. The reconstruction of a vegetation of closed oak–hazel woodland on the downlands in Neolithic times on this evidence is questionable, but the authors used it as a basis for comment on the Neolithic geomorphology of the area. It is clear from work of this nature that the presence of charcoals in such contexts can prove but one thing: that the occupants of Maiden Castle had access to the variety of woods represented and made some economic use of them. In order to make large-scale hypotheses concerning the relationship of the charcoals to local vegetation and palaeoenvironment, comparative data is required.

5.8 Wood remains from York

Wood may be exceptionally well preserved in archaeological deposits with the requisite characteristics of dampness, as is exemplified by the important series of wood remains from York. These

Figure 5.4 12th century latrine seat from Coppergate, York.

include not only structural timbers but also the lining of wells and, perhaps most interesting of all, a complete latrine seat dated to the twelfth century from the Coppergate site. The seat (Fig. 5.4) was preserved by groundwater conditions that also enabled the survival of a wide range of organic debris including wooden box-lids (one decorated with domed bronze nails and originally with marquetry inlay) and another of closely woven rushes with a plaited rush handle. The latrine seat, a plank of wood with a round hole, was found on the site of the latrine to which it had originally belonged. Similarly, good preservation of wood was seen at the Skeldergate site in the south-west of the walled city, which yielded twelfth century rubbish and cess pits found behind a large town house. They ranged from 1 to 3 m in diameter and up to 2 m in depth, some-

times having been re-dug and re-lined, one with timber and a group of three with a wicker lining (York Archaeological Trust 1978). Equally good wood preservation was found in the remains of medieval town houses, where a typological series of cess-pit construction could be made. Just as the medieval citizen was obliged to dispose of his own rubbish, he was also obliged to organize his own water supply, and this resulted in a proliferation of wells. At the Bedern foundry site an elaborate thirteenth century well had been lined with at least three wooden barrels, placed in a large pit and based on a strong timber foundation. The barrels, each about 1.5 m high and 0.9 m in diameter, had been placed on top of one another and were constructed of curved oak staves each about 150 mm wide (Fig. 5.5). Unlike modern barrels, the hoops securing the

Figure 5.5 Barrel lining for a medieval well (York).

Figure 5.6 Medieval timber lined pit (York).

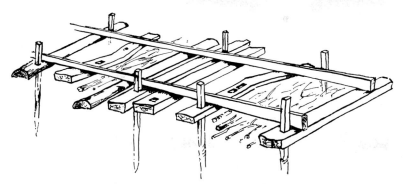

Figure 5.7 Reconstruction of the Meare Heath trackway, Somerset levels (after Godwin 1960).

staves were of withy, not metal. One even had a bung hole and the cooper's mark. A similar well was found at the Aldwark site but not in such a good state of preservation. It had been replaced at some later date by a timber-lined well also set on a square frame made of stout timbers tongued and jointed together. The upper lining in this case was of strong planks cut to size and slotted in between four large upright corner posts. The structure, perhaps 200 years later in date than the Bedern well, survived to a height of 2 m (Fig. 5.6).

5.9   Trackways in the Somerset Levels

Some of the most exciting constructions of very early date have been found in the Somerset Levels (Section 8.7.2) trackways, extensively recorded and studied by the Somerset Levels Committee and published in their reports (Coles 1975–80). An earlier report by Godwin (1960) describes the construction of the Meare Heath track, baulks of timber (mostly of oak but with some birch and alder) laid transversely and at irregular intervals. Godwin suggested a direct relationship between the lengths of timber and the nature of the ground to be covered, some tracks with very large main timbers being made in response to a need for bridging pools or channels in raised bog. This type of timber construction would have made travelling a slippery business but would have had the advantage of requiring a relatively small labour force for construction. The problem of slipping was overcome by the alternative constructional method of a transverse corduroy road used for the Meare Heath and also for the Neolithic Abbott's Way track (p. 106) or by covering a longitudinal track with brushwood and twigs (as in the Honeygore track). Some of the tracks must have bridged the boggy areas by floating like rafts on their surfaces, tied together with stakes or piles set either vertically or obliquely. Figure 5.7 shows the construction of the Meare Heath track, transverse timber baulks at irregular intervals varying from contact to a distance of 1.5 m, and consisting either of timbers split in half or of thick planks. Vertical piles were used to pin the timbers to the bog, projecting about 300 mm above the track to hold long wooden stringers, suggesting that the track might have been designed for the use of wheeled traffic. A final covering of brushwood completed the road, which crossed a highly humified *Sphagnum–Calluna* peat bog with pools of standing water. The total observed length of the track is some 1200 m, and parallels have been drawn between the Somerset Levels trackways and those found in the Netherlands, which are of similar construction. Abbott's Way, for example, resembles the Nieuwe Dordrecht track dated to 3840 ± 55 BP (GRO 1085) which was found in association with a large broken oak cartwheel some 645 mm in diameter (van Zeist 1956).

5.10   The organization of Roman military timber supply

An interesting paper by Hanson (1979) deals with the problem faced by the Romans in obtaining sufficient suitable timber for their military constructions, often in countryside which did not support suitable forests at that period. The problem, however, was not simply one of *quantity* (since both classical authors and pollen analysts agree that Britain was still heavily forested at the time) but of *quality*. Seasoned timber which would not move or

Table 5.1 Wood identifications at Romano–British forts.

Fort site	Alder	Ash	Birch	Elm	Oak	Comments
Ambleside					×	
Bagington					×	
Bar Hill					×	
Birrens		×			×	
Burrow-in-Lonsdale					×	
Caerleon			×		×	
Caermote			×		×	
Carlisle		×			×	
Castledykes			×	×	×	
Castleshaw					×	
Cawthorn			×			
Ghesterholm					×	
Coelbren					×	
Elslack					×	
Gloucester					×	
High Rochester					×	
Old Burrow					×	
Manchester					×	
Martinhoe					×	
Melandra					×	
Newstead					×	
Oakwood	×		×		×	
Pen Llystyn	×	×	×		×	the alder from a post-hole was assumed to be intrusive, but only on grounds of its unsuitability as a building-timber
Red House, Corbridge		×	×		×	
Slack					×	
Valkenburg	×	×		×	×	of a total of almost 200 samples, over 50 per cent were alder
York					×	

warp was required, the process of seasoning aiming to reduce the moisture content of timber to a percentage midway between the extremes it is likely to experience in use. Furniture wood will therefore require a far lower percentage than timber used for external construction purposes (Blake 1924). Within 40 years of the Roman conquest the south of England was pacified and nearly all forts were located in highland areas, undoubtedly partly forested, although pollen analysis on sediments from the Roman fort at Fendoch with a marked absence of pollen from the rampart section suggested to the excavator that timber for construction must have been brought from elsewhere (Richmond & McIntyre 1938–9). Later work on the vegetational history of the area showed that this would, in fact, have been unnecessary (Steven & Carlisle 1959). At Brough-on-Humber, Wacher (1969) suggested that the Roman fort was either located in a clearing or at the extreme edge of a mixed forest, and at Pen Llystyn in Carmarthen the timber of the ramparts seems to have come from open areas near woodland

dominated by oak and birch. Other fort sites have produced wood remains, generally as charcoal, but the origins of the charcoal can never be established with absolute certainty without suitable corroborative evidence (Section 5.2). Table 5.1 shows the range of species represented at Romano-British forts. If air-dried wood had been used for construction, some shrinkage would be inevitable, but only sufficient to produce minor gaps between the timbers, relatively easy to fill (perhaps with moss, see Section 3.4). With seasoned timber this would not be necessary, and it has the additional advantage of being more resistant to decay since most wood-rotting fungi will not be active if the moisture content of the timber is less than 20% of the dry weight. Wood in direct contact with the ground will, however, decay in any case since water rises by capillary action, reducing the life span of posts and stakes (Clarke & Boswell 1976). It is interesting that there is so little evidence for Roman timber-seasoning, with the exception of the writings of classical authors who describe strange methods including smearing the timber with dung. Hanson (1979) calculated that the volume of timber required for the palisade gate and towers of a 4 acre (1.62 ha) fort could amount to 6500 cubic feet (184 m³) with at least another 10 000 cubic feet (283 m³) required for the roofs of buildings and a further 6000 cubic feet (170 m³) for their walls. It seems unlikely that the 22 000 cubic feet (623 m³) was available for each of the numerous forts which were occupied at the same time, or that such large quantities of timber would be transported any further than necessary due to transport costs and manpower wastage. The minimum required area for felling would be between 16 and 30 acres (between 6.5 and 12.1 ha) in the case of fully mature stands of oak, but this figure can only be approximate. It does, though, give an idea of the problems faced by Roman military architects. Some evidence exists which supports the contention that certain timber constructions (for example gates) were dismantled and re-assembled at another site, but this is unlikely to have been a general practice. It seems likely that large stocks of timber for military purposes were kept, perhaps at centralized military store-yards, which might account for some strange archaeological features such as the apparently sterile walled enclosure at Thorpe-by-Newark (J. S. Wacher, personal communication). Such an assumption tells us a great deal about the efficiency of the Roman army, which would, if this was the case, be able to build substantial forts in unforested areas where local timber was not suitable either in quantity or quality. The question of whether or not the timber was seasoned remains open, but the problem of supply sources could perhaps be solved by some more pollen analyses from areas in close proximity to the forts.

5.11 Radiocarbon dating and dendrochronology

Details of these dating methods fall outside the scope of this book and the reader is referred to the works of Tite (1972) and Michels (1973) for the best summaries. It is, however, important to consider the sampling of wood and charcoal for these special purposes. For dendrochronological analysis (Bannister 1962, Ferguson et al. 1966) only oak is at present used in Britain, since it is the only tree which occurs with sufficient frequency in archaeological deposits and thus has enough annual growth rings available for a sequence to be constructed. Timbers with narrow growth rings (1–2 mm wide) but with a wide range of variation are preferred, a sample of fifty growth rings (c. 75 mm radius) being required for dating, which should be accurate to within ±5 years. Some timbers need to have the sapwood preserved, and as in oak this occurs at a uniform ring width of about 25 rings. This makes it possible to estimate the felling date of the tree even if the sapwood alone is recovered. Most wood samples will be radially split (Morgan 1975) or quarter sawn planks where the rings run at right angles to the width of the plank (the plank forms one segment of a circular trunk; Fig. 5.2). Stakes and posts are often made from oak but are of comparatively little value, although they can help the internal relative dating of the site and shed light on matters such as woodland management (coppicing or pollarding). Dendrochronological samples are taken with a cross-cut saw, avoiding knots or areas of decay, and 5 g is sufficient. They should be stored in wet plastic bags with a fungicide (if the timbers were waterlogged as is usually the case). Examples of the dendrochronological analysis of oak may be seen in the work of Berger (1970), Fletcher (1974a, b), Fletcher et al. (1974), Charles (1971) and Baillie (1974). Schove and Lowther (1957) discuss the applications of dendrochronology in medieval archaeology.

Samples for radiocarbon dating (Barker et al. 1969) must be larger, at least 100 g at present, although refinement of analytical techniques makes it probable that smaller samples will be necessary in the future, and collected with great care. No fungicide should be used and all possibility of contamination should be avoided. The tree-ring calibration of radiocarbon is described by Suess (1967), Renfrew (1970, 1973) and the correlation between radiocarbon dates and vegetation history by Smith and Pilcher (1973).

References

Baillie, M. G. L. 1974. A tree-ring chronology for the dating of Irish post-medieval timber. *Ir. Folklife* **20**, 1–23.

Bannister, B. 1962. Dendrochronology. In *Science in archaeology*, D. Brothwell and E. Higgs (eds), 191–205. London: Thames and Hudson.

Barker, H., R. Burleigh and N. Meeks 1969. British Museum natural radiocarbon measurements VI. *Radiocarbon* 11, 278–94.

Berger, R. (ed.) 1970. *Scientific methods in medieval archaeology*. Los Angeles: University College, Los Angeles.

Biek, L. 1963. *Archaeology and the microscope*. London: Lutterworth Press.

Blake, E. G. 1924. *The seasoning and preservation of timber*. New York: van Nostrand.

Blokhina, H. G. 1964. Analiz uglei iz paleoliticheskikh stoianok v kostenkakh. *Kratk. Soobshch. Inst. Arch.* 97, 64–5.

Brazier, J. D. and G. L. Franklin 1961. *Identification of hardwoods: a microscope key*. Forest Products Res. Bull. 46. London: HMSO.

Charles, F. W. B. 1971. The science of dating buildings by tree-rings. *Timb. Trades J.* Suppl. (30th Oct.), 14–19.

Clarke, J. C. and R. C. Boswell 1976. *Tests on round timber fence posts*. Forest Record 108. London: HMSO.

Clifford, M. 1956. Key for identification of British trees and shrubs by their wood anatomy. In *History of the British flora*, H. Godwin. Cambridge: Cambridge University Press.

Coles, J. (ed.) 1975–80. *Somerset Levels papers* nos. 1–6. Cambridge: Cambridge University Press.

Dimbleby, G. W. 1978. *Plants and archaeology*, 2nd edn. London: Baker.

Ferguson, C. W., B. Huber and H. E. Suess 1966. Determination of the age of Swiss lake dwellings as an example of dendrochronologically-calibrated radiocarbon dating, *Z. Naturf.* 21a, 1173–7.

Fietz, A. 1926. Prähistorische Holzkohlen aus der Umgebung Brünns I Theil. *Planta* 2, 414–23.

Fletcher, J. M., 1974a. Tree-ring dates for some panel paintings in England. *Burl. Ag.* 116, 250–8.

Fletcher, J. M. 1974b. Annual rings in modern and medieval times. In *The British oak*, M. G. Morris and F. H. Perring (eds), 80–97. Farringdon: Classey.

Fletcher, J. M., M. C. Tapper and F. S. Walker 1974. Dendrochronology – a reference curve for slow grown oaks AD 1230–1546. *Archaeometry* 16, 31–40.

Forest Products Research Board 1953. *An atlas of endgrain photomicrographs for the identification of hardwoods*, Forest Products Res. Bull. 26. London: HMSO.

Forest Products Research Board 1960. *Identification of hardwoods: A microscope key*. Forest Products Res. Bull. Bull. 25. London: HMSO.

Forest Products Research Board 1961. *Identification of hardwoods: A microscope key*. Forest Products Res. Bull. 46. London: HMSO.

Fox, A. 1963. Neolithic charcoal from Hembury. *Antiquity* 37, 228–9.

Gannon, B. L. 1971. Preliminary investigation of an archaeological site in the Clarno basin of North Central Oregon (abstract). *Oregon Acad. Sci. Proc.* 6 (6).

Godwin, H. 1956. *History of the British flora*. Cambridge: Cambridge University Press.

Godwin, H. 1960. Prehistoric wooden trackways of the Somerset Levels: their construction, age and relation to climatic change. *Proc. Prehist. Soc.* 26, 1–36.

Godwin, H. and Tansley, A. G. 1941. Prehistoric charcoals as evidence of former vegetation, soil and climate. *J. Ecol.* 29, 117–26.

Greguss, P. 1959. *Holzanatomie der Europäischen Laubholzer und Sträucher*. Budapest: Akademiai Kiado.

Hanson, W. S. 1979. The organisation of Roman military timber-supply. *Britannia* 9, 293–305.

Hosking, K. F. G. 1965. Cypriot copper-bearing wood. *Camborne Sch. Mines Mag.* 65, 68–82.

Jane, F. W. 1970. *The structure of wood*. London: Black.

Jones, M. U. 1972. The Mucking, Essex, cup mark sites. *Essex J.* 7 (3).

Keepax, C. 1975. Scanning electron microscopy of wood replaced by iron corrosion products. *J. Arch. Sci.* 2, 145–50.

Koeppen, R. C. 1972. *Charcoal identification*. US Forest Service Research Note FPL-D217.

Leney, L. and R. W. Casteel 1975. Simplified procedure for examining charcoal specimens for identification. *J. Arch. Sci.* 2, 153–9.

Maby, J. C. 1932. The identification of wood and wood charcoal fragments. *Analyst* 57, 2–8.

McKerrell, H. and A. Oddy 1971–2. The conservation of waterlogged wood using dewatering fluids: an evaluation. *Museums J.* 71, 165–7.

Michels, J. W. 1973. *Dating methods in archaeology*. New York: Seminar Press.

Miles, A. 1978. *Photomicrography of world woods*. London: HMSO.

Morgan, R. A. 1975. The selection and sampling of timber from archaeological sites for identification and tree-ring analysis. *J. Arch. Sci.* 2, 221–30.

Morris, M. G. and F. H. Perring (eds) 1974. *The British oak: its history and natural history*. Farringdon: Classey.

Naumann, E. 1917. Mikroreliefer i färgat kollodium. *Bot. Notiser*, 197–202.

Neuweiler, E., 1910. Untersuchungen über die Verbreitung prähistorischer Hölzer in der Schweiz. *Vierteljahrsschrift der Naturforschenden Gesellschaft in Zürich* 55, 156–202.

Panshin, A. J. and C. de Zeeuw 1970. *Textbook of wood technology*, Vol. 1. New York: McGraw-Hill.

Philips, E. W. S. 1949. *Identification of softwoods by their microscopic structure*. Forest Products Res. Bull. 22. London: HMSO.

Raftery, J. 1970. Prehistoric coiled basketry bags. *J. R. Soc. Antiq. Ir.* 100, 167–8.

Rackham, O. 1972. Charcoal and plaster impressions. In *Myrtos: an Early Bronze Age settlement in Crete*,

P. Warren (ed.), 299–304. London: Thames and Hudson.

Renfrew, C. 1970. The tree-ring calibration of radiocarbon: an archaeological evaluation. *Proc. Prehist. Soc.* **36**, 280–311.

Renfrew, C. 1973. *Before civilisation: the radiocarbon revolution and prehistoric Europe*. London: Cape.

Richmond, I. and J. McIntyre 1938–9. The Agricolan fort at Fendoch. *Proc. Soc. Antiq. Scot.* **73**, 110–54.

Salisbury, E. J. and F. W. Jane 1940. Charcoals from Maiden Castle and their significance in relation to the vegetation and climatic conditions in prehistoric times. *J. Ecol.* **28**, 310–25.

Schove, D. J. and A. W. G. Lowther 1957. Tree-rings and Medieval archaeology. *Medieval Arch.* **1**, 78–95.

Schweingruber, F. H. 1978. *Microscopic wood anatomy. Structural variability of stems and twigs in recent and subfossil woods from Central Europe*. Birmensdorf: Swiss Institute of Forestry Research.

Shackley, M. L. 1975. *Archaeological sediments*. London: Butterworth.

Smith, F. H. and B. L. Gannon 1973. Sectioning of charcoals and dry ancient woods. *Am. Antiquity* **38**, 468–72.

Smith, A. G. and J. R. Pilcher 1973. Radiocarbon dates and vegetational history of the British Isles. *New Phytol.* **72**, 903–14.

Steven, H. M. and A. Carlisle 1959. *The native pinewoods of Scotland*. Edinburgh: Oliver and Boyd.

Suess, H. E. 1967. Bristlecone pine calibration of the radiocarbon time scale from 4100 BC to 1500 BC. In *Proceedings of the Monaco symposium on radiocarbon dating and methods of low-level counting* 143–51.

Tanner, H. G. 1926. Identification of 'Norit' and other wood charcoals. *Analyst* **51**, 50.

Tite, M. S. 1972. *Methods of physical examination in archaeology*. London: Seminar Press.

Vines, A. E. and N. Rees 1965. *Plant and animal biology*, Vol. 1. London: Pitman.

Wacher, J. S. 1969. *Excavations at Brough-on-Humber 1958–61*. London: Society of Antiquaries of London.

Western, A. C. 1969. Wood and charcoal in archaeology. In *Science in archaeology*, D. Brothwell and E. Higgs (eds), 178–87. London: Thames and Hudson.

Williams, D. 1975. Identification of waterlogged wood by the archaeologist. *Sci. and Arch.* **14**, 3–4.

Wittmack, L. and J. Buchwald 1902. Pflanzenreste aus Hünenburg bei Rinteln an der Weser und verbesserte Methode zur Herstellung von Schnitten durch verkohlte Hölzer. *Ber. Dt. Bot. Ges.* **20**, 21–31.

Wymer, J. J. 1970. Radiocarbon date for the Lambourn Long Barrow. *Antiquity* **44**, 144.

York Archaeological Trust 1978. *2000 years of York: the archaeology story*. York: York Archaeological Trust.

van Zeist, W. 1956. De Veenbrug van Nieuwe-Dordrecht. *Nieuwe Drentse Volksalmanak* **74**, 314–8.

6 *Seeds, fruit and nuts*

*And he gave it for his opinion, that whoever could make
two ears of corn . . . to grow upon a spot of ground where
only one grew before, would . . . deserve better of mankind
than the whole race of politicians put together.*

(Jonathan Swift, *Gulliver's travels*)

6.1 Introduction

A **seed** is a reproductive structure basically composed of a protected embryo plant. The main class of seed-bearing plants (spermatophytes) is the angiosperms, where the seeds are enclosed within special structures (carpels) and the reproductive systems are generally flowers. Figure 6.1 shows in a simple diagrammatic way the component parts of an angiosperm flower which has male parts (stamens) and female parts (carpels with ovules), although there are endless variations on this basic theme. In order for the plant to reproduce itself the pollen grain (with its male gametes) develops and fertilizes the ovules of another plant which develop into seeds. The whole gynaecium, with the carpel walls which enclose the seeds, becomes a **fruit**. Sometimes the receptacle or even the calyx may develop as well as the gynaecium, resulting in a composite structure described as a **pseudocarp** (false fruit), found, for example, in the strawberry. When the fruit has ripened and matured the seeds must be dispersed over as wide a territory as possible to maximize

chances of reproduction of the species, accomplished by a variety of agencies, including animal vectors and the wind. An angiosperm seed (Fig. 6.2) consists of an **embryo** inside a **testa**. The former has one or two **cotyledons** (Fig. 6.2) which may contain stored food. Seeds are described and identified by details of their structure, the number of cotyledons and the presence or absence of an **endosperm** (food-storing tissue). The seed remains inactive until germination in a suitable environment initiates the series of complex physical and physiological changes producing seedlings followed by primary and secondary growth (p. 94). It is clear that the more resistant phases of this reproductive cycle, namely the fruit and seeds, are far more likely to survive than the structure of leaves or flowers and are equally useful in identifying the plant. A true fruit will include the pericarp (ovary wall) and the seeds, its form being decided by the structure of the young ovary from which it developed and the way in which the pericarp tissues are differentiated during ripening. The pericarp may become hard and dry (as in nuts) or soft and fleshy. In the former case classifications are made on the basis of whether or not the mature fruit opens to disperse its seeds and in the latter by the way in which the ovary wall differentiates. Seeds and fruit may be relatively easily identified using keys, which in fact may be almost as explicit as reference collections, although both should be taken together. Examples are found in the work of Vines and Rees (1964) or Renfrew (1973). It is reasonably easy to establish a reference collection of at least the most common species, which should be studied in conjunction with descriptions and drawings in order to make oneself familiar with structure and classification. Some commercial firms do produce collections of seeds for teaching

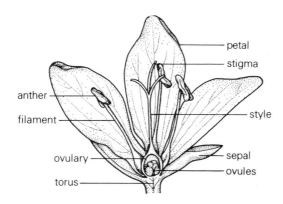

Figure 6.1 Structure of a flower.

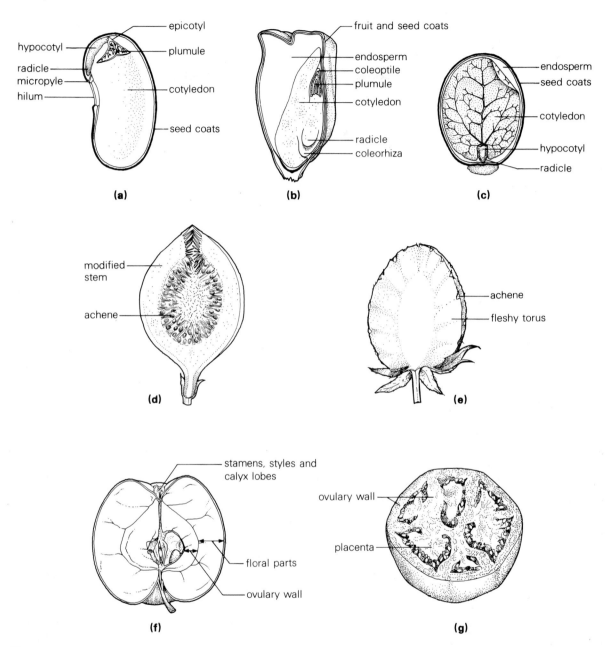

Figure 6.2 Structure of seeds, fruits and nuts.

purposes, although these tend to be expensive, but many museums have excellent herbarium collections which are useful for reference. Two main types of succulent fruit occur. The **drupe** is fleshy and contains one or more seeds, each enclosed by a hard stony portion of the pericarp (e.g. the cherry, almond or coconut, and the blackberry or raspberry which are collections of small drupes). The **berry** is a fleshy fruit also containing one or more seeds, but each will be surrounded by its own hardened seed coat at dispersal, not by portions of the hard pericarp. Examples of these include the tomato, grape, orange and date. False fruits (see above) include the strawberry and rose hip.

6.2 Preservation

Seeds may be preserved in archaeological deposits in one of three main ways: by anaerobic waterlogged conditions (which exclude decay bacteria), by carbonization and also by mineral replacement. They may occur as the result of a physical accident (such as a favourable burial environment) or by deliberate storage (as in Iron Age pits; see p. 14). Carbonized material is the most common, where the grains and seeds have retained their original form but were slowly heated (while being protected from direct contact with the flames), becoming reduced to carbon while retaining their original characteristics. Much seed material is also recovered from waterlogged deposits or environments such as ditches, wells and the fills of cess pits, using various methods and combinations of sieving and flotation. The occurrence of mineralized seeds has been described by Green (1979) and is of especial interest, since seeds preserved in this way may be recovered from such deposits as completely aerobic soils which would generally be thought unsuitable for seed preservation. In addition, the technique of froth flotation is not the most suitable for the recovery of such material since it will generally not float. A completely different picture of local flora may be obtained if mineralized material is examined. Green (1979) quotes an example from the site of Castle Acre Castle (Norfolk) where one sample (some 5000 ml in size) produced only 46 seeds of six species preserved by carbonization and 400 seeds of some 20

species preserved by mineralization. The preservation of plant material by the precipitation of metal corrosion products has already been recorded from wood by Keepax (1975). Helbaek (1969) reported finds of plant material preserved by calcareous and gypsumiferous replacement. Mineralized seeds are generally honey-brown in colour and with a poorly crystalline inorganic structure, often appearing to be fresh. In some cases even the surface ornaments of the seed epidermis may be preserved by mineral replacement, but the degree of preservation is variable, and sometimes the mineralizing agent acts selectively on compounds of different durability. Phosphate-mineralized seeds are common in faecal deposits and produce evidence of diet. However, as Green (1979) noted, the seeds which pass unharmed through the human digestive tract are woody and it is these that are likely to have become fossilized. An additional advantage of studying mineralized seeds was mentioned above – they are likely to occur in aerobic soils where other types of preservation do not occur. Oats (*Avena* sp.) are the cereal most commonly found mineralized, but other cereals such as *Triticum* sp. (wheat) and *Hordeum* sp. (barley) occur, together with legumes, and fruits such as *Prunus* spp. (plums, cherries, etc.), *Vitis vinifera* L. (grape), *Ficus* sp. (fig) and *Rubus* sp. (blackberry and raspberry).

Seeds may also be preserved by 'secondary' means, such as impressions on baked clay, which are common and form an important class of evidence. Impressions are most plentiful in the case of domestic pottery production, where the processes of food producing and 'cottage' industry went along side by side, so that stray grains could easily become incorporated into a pot, or into clay daub on the wall of a house (although matting and leaf impression are more common here). Hopf (1965) gives examples where grain was deliberately used to ornament a vessel, but often during the firing of the pot any grains accidentally incorporated will become burnt out, leaving an impression, often very detailed, of their form. Renfrew *et al.* (1976) remind us that just as clay shrinks up to 5% in firing (or even up to 10% in very fine ware) the grain impressions will also shrink. If grain impressions are used as a source of information about ancient cereals, the source of pottery production must be very accurately

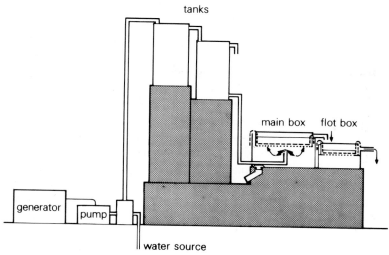

Figure 6.3 The water separator (after French 1971).

established, or else the information is interesting but meaningless.

Small fragments of the glumes or epidermis of grains and seeds may also survive as silica skeletons in mudbrick or coarse pottery, particularly in more arid areas where frost action is less likely to fragment the material. During its growth the epidermal cells of many grasses undergo a mineralization process whereby the minute spaces in the cellulose cell wall become filled with silica. When the plant is burnt or destroyed the silica survives, if not fragmented mechanically, and the cells of individual species may be recognized from their morphology.

6.3 Retrieval methods

The best introduction to the site sampling and processing of seed-bearing deposits is given in a very helpful booklet, *First aid for seeds* (Renfrew *et al.* 1976), published by Rescue. This also contains a good bibliography, list of suppliers of material and useful definitions.

6.3.1 Water separation

Water separation is the process in which the floating material is automatically carried off by moving water and deposited in a separate tray, which contrasts with 'flotation', where the floating material is generally skimmed off manually. The former is much quicker. Much confusion exists over the terminology. Various techniques are available, related to

different sets of site circumstances, which may be combined with flotation to give the best results, the entire sample being washed through with a jet of water and each sieve contents dried and examined. Numerous variations on these methods exist, often related both to the ingenuity of the excavator and the type of available water supply. The simplest type of water separation is carried out by washing the sample through a sieve and drying the residue, or frequently by using an entire series of sieves. The device for water separation most frequently described was invented at the British School of Archaeology at Ankara by French (1971) and uses continuous water flow to produce the necessary agitation but no flocculating agent. Both this and the Cambridge Flotation Cell (Section 6.3.3) were initially developed for light, easily processed sands and soils in the Near East but have been adapted with varying degrees of success for heavier soils of Europe. The Ankara machine (Fig. 6.3) is filled with water from a storage tank by means of a small pump or gravity and forced into a main tank (the Siraf version of this apparatus used a 50 gallon (227 litre) oildrum (Williams 1973)). The necessary agitation is produced by a tin or plastic deflector forcing the jet of water on to the main body of water in the tank, so that the light plant material will rise to the top of the tank (the sediment is poured into a large sieve of *c.* 1–2 mm mesh suspended just below the water surface) and be carried via the overflow into the flot tank to be caught by a 300 μm sieve. The water which carries the plant remains over then passes through the sieve and back into the storage tank, leaving clean residue on the coarse sieve which may be searched. It is quite cheap to build but requires a lot of water. Sediment is fed into the main box, where the water flow carries off the 'flot', leaving the heavy particles <1.5 mm² ('sludge' which runs to the bottom of the tank) and the heavy particles >1.5 mm² which are retained on the 1.5 mm mesh nylon sieve. The lighter fraction (flot) is carried over the weir into the flot box and passes through a 1.5 mm mesh or 250 μm mesh nylon sieve. The residue is washed, dried and manually sorted. The Siraf machine described by Williams (1973) incorporated two units supplied from a single water source. Its total cost was £26.20, using local labour and materials in South Iran. Williams (1973) gives details on sorting speeds, recovery and much comparative data.

6.3.2 Water separator devices, 'tub' flotation, etc.

Limp (1974) used a manual water separator device analogous in many ways to the 'tub flotation' beloved of American archaeologists but two to three times as efficient. The tub flotation method was very slow and laborious, resulting in the fact that only a relatively small amount of the site could be processed. At the Apple Creek site, Illinois (Parmalee et al. 1972), less than 1% of the total excavated sediment could be processed (2.76 out of 280 m³), producing inevitable sampling errors and the inevitable question of how reliable the sample was. Such water-sieving methods were developed over a number of years, and are catalogued in the work of French (1971). Tub flotation consists of placing the sample in a large tub which has its bottom replaced with appropriately sized mesh and raising and lowering it into water. As the tub is lowered a small hand sieve (mesh size 0.5 mm) is dipped just below the surface and used to 'skim' off the floating organic materials. French's apparatus involved a pump to force water into storage tanks, developing pressure, the water flowing into the main box lined with mesh, and a valve used to regulate inflowing water through the sample, carrying with it floating material. The sample is then agitated, washed and dried and the screen (1 mm) replaced (Fig. 6.3). Limp (1974) described a modified apparatus which could be

made for $250 (excluding cost of pump), a cross between tub flotation and the French machine. Tests were undertaken on its efficiency by separating samples taken from the same unit of excavation processed by 'tub' and separator methods. The latter was two to three times as efficient (measured by volume of soil processed).

The so-called Izum water separator device (Davis & Weslowsky 1975) was similar in construction and used at Hellenistic and a site of Stobi in Yugoslavian Macedonia to process 1.7 litres of sediment per person per hour (three times the rate of tub flotation and with greatly increased efficiency) using a mesh size of 1 mm.

6.3.3 Froth flotation

One of the most commonly used sets of techniques for recovering plant remains is called flotation, which may be manual flotation in a bowl, froth flotation using a seed machine or paraffin flotation, the last-mentioned being described on p. 142. Flotation depends on the relative specific gravities of the floating medium and the material to be recovered, and the surface tension of the liquid. Inorganic material with a relative density of around 2.5 will sink in a water suspension, while the lighter, carbonized materials (relative density between 0.3 and 0.6 (Renfrew et al. 1976, Jarman et al. 1972)) will float and may be decanted. The simplest flotation method only involves mixing the sample with a bowlful of water and pouring the result through a 1000 μm (1 mm) sieve after allowing it to stand. The light, carbonized, organic material with the finest parts of the sediments will be held in suspension and should be caught on the sieve, leaving the heavier fraction behind in the bowl. This has the disadvantage of leaving the heavier fruits and nuts together with the more porous ones behind, but it is very cheap.

Flotation should be carried out on dry sediment except where drying will cause the carbonized material to fracture. In such cases (e.g. damp clay) pretreatment involving acid or some other defloculant is preferred. Machine flotation is particularly suitable for soils but should not be used for organic deposits such as waterlogged ditch fills, when manual or paraffin flotation is preferable. Organic deposits should be sampled using the procedures outlined by Shackley (1975) and wet sieving is used, followed by flotation if necessary. Deflocculants such as sodium hexametaphosphate may be used for clays. Such hand flotation is very slow but machine flotation requires a great deal of water; both have their advantages. The Cambridge Froth Flotation Cell (Jarman *et al.* 1972) was an important development, many modifications of which are now used. Figure 6.4 shows the original apparatus, consisting of a circular tank with a butterfly valve at the base, the top of the tank being fitted with a weir and a series of test sieves (1 mm, 0.3 mm) suspended over the edge to catch the flot. Air is bubbled into the tank and the sample tipped in, a flocculating agent (e.g. terpineol) and a collector (paraffin or kerosene) having been added to the water in the tank which produces a froth, carrying the light plant remains over the weir into the sieves. After this operation has been completed the butterfly valve is opened and the residue let out into large sieves (2 mm mesh), to be checked in a settling tank for any material that sank during flotation. A 180 litre drum was used for water storage, but much of the water used was recycled from the settling tank. A preliminary coarse sieving of the deposit is required to remove the coarsest fraction. Froth flotation has been in use for some time in industrial contexts, for example, the removal of coal from shale, a fact which suggested its application to the retrieval of carbonized plant remains. The Cambridge cell was constructed of polypropylene sheeting (6 mm thick), which is tough and cheap, but other materials have been used, including metal. Power for the compressed air is obtained from a two horsepower petrol-driven engine. The mesh sizes of the collecting sieves can be varied according to the needs of the deposit. Approximately 20 litres (two small buckets) may be processed at any one time and under optimum conditions 1–2 m^3 of sediment may be processed by three people in an 8 h working day. Little comparative work has been done between the Cambridge and Ankara machines, but Williams (1973) noted that the Siraf version of the Ankara machine processed less material but also required less labour. The use of dispersants could help in heavy soils (Schreider & Noales 1980), important in Britain where processing at Southwark, London (for example) was greatly hindered by the hard water which made the bubbler in the Cambridge Flotation Cell difficult to operate. Of the two the Cambridge method is probably the most efficient. Both have the disadvantage of the possibility of losing heavy or dense material (unless

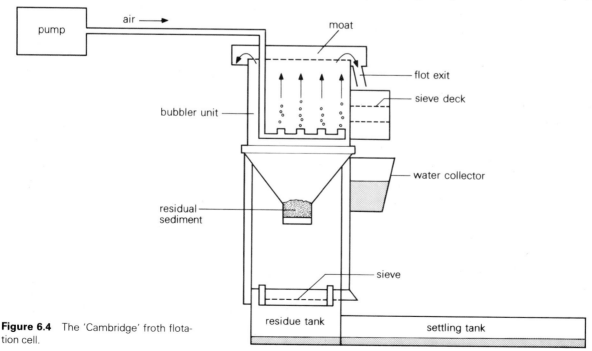

Figure 6.4 The 'Cambridge' froth flotation cell.

the residue is sampled) and very small seeds which may get trapped in soil agglomerates. Dennell (1972) noted the interesting fact that although in theory prolonged flotation should increase recovery, in practice the opposite is true.

6.3.4 Other flotation methods

A flotation medium of higher specific gravity than water may be used to offset the problems of sinkage of heavy debris (p. 112) but it may create its own difficulties. However, Struever (1968) devised a method to separate materials by their different settling rates in water or the denser zinc chloride solution and claimed 100% recovery. A simple salt flotation method designed for site use was described by Nunez and Aalto (1978), but it has the dis-advantage of requiring a copious water source nearby. A more complex salt-water flotation tank was described by Lange and Carty (1975) who worked on a pre-Columbian site on the north-western Pacific coast of Guanacaste province, Costa Rica. They had problems with obtaining sufficient fresh water since there was only one well for the local community, and as they observe (Lange & Carty 1975, p. 120): 'Rural persons in Latin America (to say nothing of North America) are sufficiently un-nerved by the archaeologist gathering and washing small broken bits of pottery and stone, without straining credulity by using scarce water resources for washing dirt. In reality, considerably more than credulity would be strained.' Alternative methods of removing large quantities of sediment to a suitable water source or waiting until the rainy season, were discarded, and it was decided to utilize the abundant water supply offered by the Pacific Ocean. In fact the wave motion in the sea assisted with the process and the greater salinity effectively combined the concepts of fresh water and chemical flotation. Initial sieving through a ½ in (12.7 mm) mesh screen was carried out and the sediments dried in the sun. A preliminary wet separation was carried out by placing the sample into boxes of timber and 1/16 in (1.6 mm) mesh and washing them in the sea. The light fraction was obtained by submerging the box deeply in water and scooping off the floating debris using either sieves of 420 μm (0.165 in) mesh or tea strainers (Struever 1968). Both light and heavy fractions were dried and stored, the silt residue

seemingly having no effect on preservation. Small land snails dominated the light material fraction, interesting but difficult to deal with since little com-parative material exists. Baerreis (1973) showed the value of land snails in climatic/seasonality recon-struction in North American archaeology, and this work provided samples of sufficient size for quanti-tative determination. Seeds, small bones, charcoal and large numbers of insects were also recovered. The method was simple and inexpensive and has led to the conclusion that microfauna and vegetative remains can now be successfully recovered in acid coastal areas.

Mineralized seeds may also be recovered. Sedi-ment samples should be disaggregated in water, with hydrogen peroxide added if necessary (p. 127), and washed through a 250 μm (2 φ) sieve.

6.3.5 Storage

Care should be taken in storing seed samples to avoid crushing or any distortion, by packing them in kitchen roll inside rigid cardboard or plastic con-tainers, preferably in polythene bags or storage tubes inside boxes for maximum protection. The usual care in labelling and record-keeping (Shackley 1975) should be observed, and after flotation samples may be preserved in methanol until identi-fication.

6.4 Sampling and identification

It is, of course, a truism that every site is unique and presents its own sampling problems. Dennell (1972, 1974) classified sampling contexts, and a simplified version of his classification was produced by Ren-frew et al. (1976) in a discussion of sampling prob-lems. In storage contexts such as pits, for example, the seeds obtained may be heavily biased towards one crop, and this may have only been of minor importance. However, detailed information about such matters as crop purity, disease and efficiency of processing may be obtained. The flora from domestic hearths, ovens and corn driers may include crops at different stages of preparation, drying and consumption, while seeds obtained from floor de-posits will be much more varied in nature. Rubbish contexts, such as the sewers, middens, rubbish pits, cess pits and ditches which might be found in a medieval town, may contain seeds from many different sources to give an idea of vegetation environment and economy. The information obtainable from impressions (p. 110) or coprolite (p. 156) is usually limited by its context and sample bias.

When large deposits are found all must be sampled, leaving the botanist to make his own subsamples. Column sampling (p. 127) is a recommended procedure, or the taking of a fixed volume of sediment from each layer within randomly selected features. Renfrew *et al.* (1976) recommend the division of site features into the types of contexts described above and then the selection of features for sampling on the basis of a random number table. Large seed deposits occurring outside these chosen features must obviously be sampled, but a separate interpretation will be necessary. As for all biological samples, too much is better than too little. Contamination must be avoided as far as possible by taking precautions regarding cleanliness, and the specialist may be given a sample of the modern topsoil so that he can check it for an idea of what to expect from the natural contamination. The retrieval of seed and grain impressions from pottery should take place as the ceramics are recorded by the small finds specialist, and caution is therefore indicated in the sorting and marking of pottery on site. The problem of potential contamination is one accurately recognized by modern bioarchaeologists. Careless sample collection is one obvious source, together with aerial contamination or, more avoidably, contamination with other samples or modern material if sieving or flotation techniques are being used. Increased care can obviously reduce the possibility of sample contamination but will not eliminate it entirely; there will always be 'natural' factors such as earthworm activity and movement of organic material through the soil by gravity or rainwash which will result in contamination. The problem is to recognize contamination when it occurs and one solution (the examination of a 'background' flora from topsoil) has already been given. Keepax (1977), in a paper dealing with this problem, suggests that there are really only two reliable ways to distinguish contaminants: firstly, if the species present are quite different from modern vegetation; secondly, by different preservation (charred seeds

will probably be ancient) – but that does not necessarily mean that all uncarbonized material is modern (p. 108).

Keeley (1978) made a survey of the cost effectiveness of the main methods of recovering macroscopic organic remains from archaeological deposits, noting the wide range of methods employed and that the sample type, recovery method and experience of the workers influenced the time needed. Choice of sampling size was variable, some people preferring whole deposits and some samples of 1–25 kg, collected either from selected deposits or on a systematic basis. Large sample sizes (5–10 kg) were really required since work undertaken by the York Unit suggests a very wide range of variability in intersample results when a 10 kg sample was divided into 1 kg subsamples. Keeley recommends random sampling during excavation to establish the limits of variation (material common to all deposits), the comparison of material recovered from whole deposits with that recovered by samples of different sizes to establish optimum sampling size, and experimental work on the way in which biological material is incorporated into deposits (such as that being done in taphonomic studies, p. 164) and on decay. The paper included tables of the times taken for these various sampling methods in sediments of different types. Variations are great; for example one operator estimated that in machine flotation 10 min would be required for sample-taking and recording on site, using an average sample size of 6.37 dm³ and processing fifteen samples per day. Output is 95.61 dm³ per day involving 12.75 manhours, although heavy clay-loams increase this figure. Further time must be allowed for boxing and listing (*c.* 1 h per 20 or 30 samples). A figure of £100 for one sample is not unrealistic, and between one and three weeks might be required for each category of organic material. This must be allowed for in the pre-excavation planning. It is interesting to compare this figure of £90 for a flotation machine with the work of Williams (1973) who built one for £26.60 at Siraf, and current (1980) commercial prices start at £200 for the pumps alone. Inflation hits flotation?

Context, type of sampling method, sampling and processing efficiency are clearly the basic factors which will influence interpretation. The questions raised by a consideration of the provenance of the floral material together with its original depositional environment and depositional medium must also be considered. In certain cases 'artificial' deposits may include large quantities of preserved plant material, but in such contexts it will invalidate any palaeoecological interpretation since provenance cannot be accurately established. In such cases, frequently waterlogged ditches, all that can be said with certainty is that a particular species is present at a particular time, and that is almost the limit of inference. However, such groupings, although not autonomous, may provide interesting pieces of

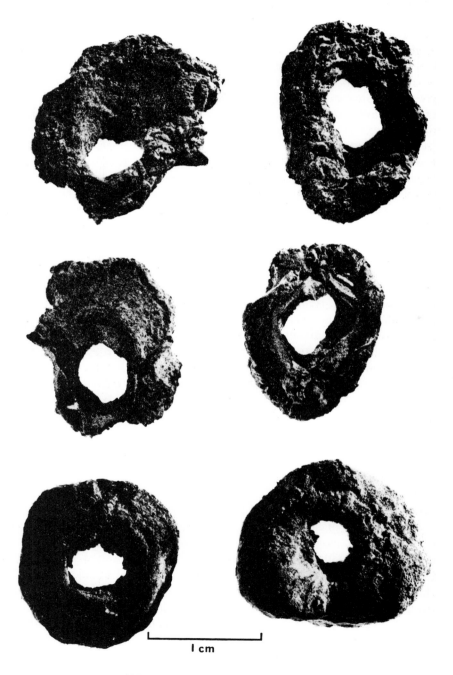

Figure 6.5 Crab apple rings from Ur, context PG/1054.

1 cm

116

information. Willcox (1977) studied exotic plant remains from Roman waterlogged sites in London showing a number of species (e.g. peach, *Prunus persica*; olive, *Olea europaea*; cucumber, *Cucumis sativa*) which had not been previously recorded from Romano–British sites. Their status and economic importance is, of course, impossible to gauge simply from a presence/absence report, but it does suggest that a wider range of imported economic plants might have been available to Roman Britain than had been previously thought. Comparable material is known from York, Caerwent and Silchester and gives weight to the classical writers who speak of the extensive food trade in the Roman world at this time. Spices such as dill, coriander and fennel (*Anethum graveolens* L., *Coriandrum sativum* L., *Foeniculum vulgare* Miller) enter the British archaeological record for the first time and cucumber (a native of Africa but common in the Roman world and occurring at two London sites) seems to have arrived from a secondary area of diversity in India. It is not impossible that the plants were being grown for seed stock, as were the peas and lentils. It is likely that much of the foodstuffs were imported in amphorae (for example the first century 'carrot' amphorae, found at Colchester and known to have been used for the importation of dates from the Near East). However dubious the socio-economic factors which have governed the preservation of such remains, their presence provides the grounds for speculation into potential available food resources.

6.5 Applications

6.5.1 Carbonized material at Ur

Ellison *et al.* (1978) investigated some preserved food remains from the important urban site of Ur in Mesopotamia, excavated by Sir Leonard Wooley nearly 50 years ago. The food remains, which had been placed on saucers or in other pottery vessels, accompanied the mid-third millenium 'Royal Cemetery' graves. For example, an impression of chickpeas (*Cicer arietinum*) in fine dust was recovered from inside a silver water-pot, and a small sample of carbonized wheat, barley and pea seeds (the residue of crop-processing rather than a collection of seeds for food, see p. 110) from a deep trench

grave. Further material included carbonized datestones and some broken grains of six-row barley. Perhaps the most interesting find came from saucers placed as foundation deposits, each of which consisted of small crab apples which had been cut in half transversely and threaded on a string before being carbonized (Fig. 6.5). The method of carbonization is rather puzzling, and although crab apple halves have previously been noted from European sites they have not been identified before in the Near East. As stated above, in order to become carbonized slow heating without direct exposure to flame is required (p. 110). It is difficult to imagine how this could have happened to this material; perhaps deliberate exposure rather than accidental burning is the answer, since the latter seems more likely to have destroyed the data.

6.5.2 Seeds and fruit from burials

There are a number of cases where quite extensive deposits of seeds and fruit have been recovered either from intestinal contents of mummified remains (for example, Helbaek 1950, 1958) or from sediment recovered from the area occupied by the intestines, although only the skeletal remains and no fleshy tissue have survived (e.g. Warren 1911). Three basic sets of conditions exist which permit the preservation of soft tissue, and all are equally likely to preserve associated plant remains. Deep-freeze, as in the Pazyryk burials (p. 155), is, of course, quite rare, but this series of tombs did produce an appreciable amount of vegetable material, including hemp seeds.

Extreme aridity also preserves tissue (p. 159). It has been noted, for example, that the intestines of salt-mummified bodies in Nubia contained melon and grape seeds and barley husks. It is, however, the Danish bog burials which have produced truly remarkable amounts of seeds and grain, 66 species in the case of Grauballe man (Helbaek 1950, 1951), all but 11 being wild. The reason for the ingestion of such large quantities of comparatively unpalatable material was thought by Glob (1971) to be ritual, since the intestinal contents recovered represent a 'last meal' taken less than 24 h before death, probably to ensure propagation and fertility of all the plant species represented by a ritual human sacrifice. In both the Tollund and Grauballe men the alimentary canals were intact, preserving the last meal. Table 6.1 lists the contents, three crosses indicating the presence of more than 15 specimens, two indicating 5–15 and one less than five specimens. A problem is met with here since the estimation of the original proportions of the meal rest upon the subjective judgement of the botanist concerned, who was obliged to investigate material from the different degrees of disintegration. The excellent preservation in the Graubelle example of the seeds of cereals such as wheat and rye enabled precise identification of species such as emmer wheat (*Triticum dicoccum*) and spelt (*T. spelta*). Plant diseases such as ergot of rye (p. 52) were identified, together with several intestinal parasites (Section 9.3). Eleven species of weed or wild grasses were found from different habitat requirements. Vegetable fats were contributed by large amounts of linseed and animal fat from a few bone fragments, probably of piglet. The last meal is certainly not representative of the diet of Iron Age men in Denmark, although carbonized deposits and imprints on pottery indicate that weed seeds were a regular dietary component. The appearance, structure and significance of the various species of cereals are given in detail by Helbaek (1958). It is interesting that no seasonal vegetables such as fruit or berries were found; nothing had been eaten that would not keep well below ground, but Helbaek suggests that sacrifice at the midwinter festival to ensure fertility in the New Year must be considered.

Hazeldine Warren (1911) noted the occurrence of various species of plants in association with a prehistoric burial of undetermined date at Walton on the Naze, Essex. The body had been wrapped in the tough roots of the sand grass, probably to keep it in a contracted position. The collection of seeds in the position of the former viscera was removed with care. They included blackberry seeds together with a small number of rose seeds and *Atriplex* (orache). The precise form of rose present is uncertain, probably not *Rosa arvens* or *R. spinossisma*. Both *Rosa* and *Atriplex* were eaten, although the latter is not a particularly popular vegetable today. The seed report concludes with an amusing note. The excavator (Warren) suggested that the volume of seeds represented (at least a pint) indicated the ingestion of such a large quantity of berries that he specu-

lated if the man could have died as a result: '. . . I wondered if the man might have died from the effects of dining well, rather than wisely, upon the enticing fruit' (Warren 1911, p. 202), but the palaeopathologist did not agree with him, noting prosaically: 'It needs a lot of haws and blackberries to keep even a little man going for twenty-four hours' (Warren 1911, p. 206).

Fruit seeds from early burials are, in fact, quite common. Troels-Smith (1959) describes the find of clusters of strawberry (p. 110) and raspberry (p. 110) seeds from the Neolithic site of Muldbjerg in Denmark, interpreted as the remains of human coprolite. The larger raspberry seeds were crushed as a result of chewing and the find gives an idea of the season of occupation of the site, since these fruits are available only in early July. This seasonal dating agreed well with other pieces of floral and faunal evidence. A compendium of human food plants was produced by Brouk (1975) and includes details about cereals, vegetables and fruit, beverages, smoking and chewing and fermentative microorganisms, making an important reference work.

6.5.3 Coprolite as evidence of diet

Vast amounts of evidence concerning dietary patterns have been obtained from the analysis of coprolite, particularly in the USA, developing from the work of Harshberger (1896), who suggested that the examination of human faecal material could give information on diet. Early studies include that of Netolitzky (1906), who analysed prehistoric Egyptian faeces and made comparative observations with contemporary material. Heizer and Napton (1969) produced a summary of much of the early work on coprolite analysis and the development of various analytical procedures. Bryant (1974) has produced a summary of methods and applications of coprolite analysis. Systematic studies such as those of Callen (1965) consider very large-scale questions, including the development of agriculture in the New World deduced from coprolite evidence. Details of the techniques used for extracting such information are given in Section 9.2.2. Large sample sizes are necessary; Napton and Heizer (1970), for example, processed over 300 coprolites from three cave sites, producing a detailed analysis of dietary patterns and utilization of available habitat and food resources.

Table 6.1 The stomach contents of the Tollund and Grauballe men (from Helbaek 1958).

Species	Common name	Grauballe	Tollund
Triticum dicoccum Schübl.	wheat	+++	
Triticum spelta L.	spelt		
Secale cereale L.	rye	+	
Hordeum testrastichum Kcke.f. nudum	barley	++++	++++
Hordeum testrastichum Kcke.	barley		
Avena sativa L.	oats	+++	
Avena fatua L.	wild oats		
Setaria viridis L.Beauv.	green panicum	+	
Echinochloa crus-galli L.Beauv.	cockspur panicum	++	+
Phleum sp.	cat's tail grass	+	
Holcus lanatus L.	Yorkshire fog	+++	
Deschampsia caespitosa L.Beauv.	tufted aira	++	
Phragmites communis Trin.	common reed	+	
Sieglingia decumbens L.Bernh.	decumbent triodia	+	
Poa nemoralis L.	wood poa	+	
Poa sp.	poa	+	
Promus mollis L.	brome grass	++++	
Lolium perenne L.	ryegrass	+++	
Lolium remotum Schrank	darnel		
Agropyron caninum L.R.et.S.	fibrous couch-grass	++	
Carex leporina L.	hare sedge	+	
Luzula campestris L.DC.	field woodrush	+	
Rumex crispus L.	curled dock	+	+
Rumex acetosella L.	sheep's sorrel	+++	+
Polygonum lapathifolium agg.	pale polygonum	++++	++++
Polygonum persicaria L.	persicaria		
Polygonum aviculare L.	knotweed	+	
Polygonum convulvis L.	black bindweed	+++	+++
Chenopodium album L.	fat hen	+++	+++
Chenopodium sp.	goosefoot	+	
Cerastium caespitosum Gilib.	mouse-ear chickweed	+	
Stellaria graminea L.	lesser stitchwort	+	
Stellaria media L.	chickweed	++	+
Scleranthus annulus L.	annual knawel	+	
Spergula arvensis L.	corn spurney	+++	+++
Ranunculus acer L.	buttercup	+	
Ranunculus repens L.	creeping buttercup	++	
Fumaria officinalis L.	fumitory	+	
Camelina linicola Sch.et.Sp.	gold of pleasure	+	+++
Thlaspi arvense L.	penny cress	+	+
Capsella bursa-pastoris L. (Moench)	shepherd's purse	++	+
Erysimum cheiranthoides L.	treacle mustard	+	+
Brassica campestris L.	field cabbage		+
Aphanes avensis L.	parsley piert	+	
Potentilla argentea L.	hoary potentilla	+	
Potentilla erecta L.Hampe	tormantil	+	
Trifolium campestre Schreb.	hop trefoil	+	
Trifolium dubium Sibth.	lesser clover	+	
Linum usitatissimum L.	linseed	++	++++
Viola arvensis Murr.	field pansy	++	+++
Myosotis arvensis L.Hill	field forget-me-not	+	
Brunella vulgaris L.	self-heal	++	
Galeopsis tetrahit agg.	common hemp nettle	++	++
Solanum nigrum L.	black nightshade	++	
Veronica serpyllifolia L.	thyme-leaved speedwell	+	
Phinanthus cf. minor L.	yellow rattle	+	
Plantago major L.	greater plantain	+++	
Plantago lanceolata L.	ribwort	+++	+
Campanula glomerata L.	clustered campanula	+	
Achillea millefolium L.	milfoil	+	

Table 6.1 (continued)

Species	Common name	Grauballe	Tollund
Matricaria inodora L.	scentless matricaria	+	
Lapsana communis L.	nipplewort	+	
Leontodon autumnalis L.	autumnal hawkbit	+	
Sonchus asper L.Hill	sowthistle	+ +	
Crepis tectorum L.	hawk's beard	+ +	
Crepis capillaris L.Wallr.	smooth hawk's beard	+	

+ + + + = principal components of the meal.   + + = 5–15 specimens of the species found.
+ + + = over 15 specimens of the species found.   + = less than five specimens of the species found.

At one of the sites, Lovelock Cave (Napton 1969, 1971), analysis of the coprolite showed markedly lacustrine-orientated subsistence, over 95% of the plant species being aquatic forms and protein having been obtained from fish and waterfowl. The work is summarized by Napton (1969) together with an analysis of the hair, bird bones and pollen recovered from the coprolite. Many excellent reviews are available (for example Heizer 1960, 1969, 1970). Callen (1968) described the dietary evidence from human coprolites, documenting the transition from hunter–gatherer to agriculturalist in Mexico. The work of Fry and Hall (1973, 1975) integrates the study of seed remains from coprolite with sparse faunal debris and evidence of disease. Callen (see above) was a major figure in coprolite research and left a very extensive collection of slides, comparative specimens, photo-micrographs, line drawings and a card index which is housed in the Laboratory of Anthropology, Texas A. and M. University, and is available for use by scholars.

It is sometimes difficult to distinguish human from animal coprolite; for example, of the six coprolites recovered from the Acheulean site of Lazaret (France) only one was considered by Callen (1969a,b) to be definitely human, although another might be. Two others are definitely carnivore. A test case occurred at Juke Box Cave (West Utah, USA), where coprolites were found which were initially thought to be non-human. However, analysis of the seed content (Jennings 1953) showed that the seeds in them had been parched and milled, indicating the human origins of the coprolites. This study was, surprisingly, the first serious attempt to analyse coprolite from archaeological sites in the Great Basin of the USA, but a great deal of important work has been done since then. Using the presence of milled seeds to infer that the coprolite is human is a common technique but not one without drawbacks. For example, Fonner (1957) investigated coprolites from Danger Cave originally identified as bear faeces, but showing evidence of omnivorous diet including seeds of *Allenrolfea occidentalis*. In three of the samples the seeds appear to have been lightly milled, only 50% being intact. This indicates the possibility that the coprolite might, after all, be of human origin. Byrne (1972) includes a section which discusses methods of distinguishing dog coprolite from those of humans (Fry 1975) and Häntzschel *et al.* (1968) have produced a bibliography of non-human coprolite in older geological deposits. Statistical processing of dietary data is another relatively recent trend. Marquardt (1974) expressed the dietary data from 27 human coprolites from Mammoth Cave, Kentucky, as weights of dietary components per specimen, and then subjected them to contingency, correlation and factor analysis. The results of each technique were compared with the other two, and with a contingency analysis of coprolites from Salts Cave. A further example of statistical analysis is provided in the work of Fry and Adorasio (1970), who analysed coprolite data from two Archaic Indian sites and then subjected them to factor analysis, stepwise discrimination and mean-linkage cluster analysis, combining the results with an analysis of intestinal parasites. Results showed that, despite geographical proximity, contemporaneous occupation and cultural and ecological similarities, the sites were inhabited by sociopolitical groups that seldom, if ever, inhabited the other.

6.5.4 *The problem of 'mummy' wheat*

Fresh-looking seeds may be preserved in Egypt (e.g. the so-called 'mummy wheat') which look like freshly harvested material and occur complete with all details of hairs on kernels. It does not, however, contain any protein and thus is unable to germinate. Zeven *et al.* (1975) studied the residual proteins in *Triticum* spp. and suggested that the maximum age at which albumin- and globulin-like proteins still survive is between 125 and 175 years. They considered that the presence of extractable proteins could help with rough dating of cereal grains of unknown ages and in discovering frauds. Comparative analysis showed that wheat grains from Thirtieth Dynasty tombs (*c.* 300 BC) at Saqquara, Egypt, had no protein remaining. Neither did samples from a layer dated between 110 BC and AD 73 at Masada, Israel, suggesting that the reported incidences of germination of Egyptian wheat of great antiquity are untrue.

6.5.5 *The origins of British brewing*

Plant remains were recovered from the 14 m long tenth century boat found at Graveney, Kent, a merchant ship which had a capacity of about 7 tons and probably traded across the North Sea. At least 100 plant taxa were identified by pollen analysis and plant macrofossils obtained by wet sieving, producing a picture of the vegetation of the estuarine clays in which the boat was lying and the local upstream vegetation. The samples taken from within the boat were of particular interest since they included plentiful remains of hops (*Humulus lupulus* L.) and it is suggested that the boat was, in fact, carrying a cargo of hops. They were not found in undisturbed samples beneath the keel nor from samples outside the hull. No hop-pollen was found; this is very surprising, since the male hop plant produces abundant wind-blown pollen. Wild hops have been part of the British flora since before agriculture (Godwin 1956), living in wet alder and oak woods. Their domestic and industrial uses include the production of beer, and of a fibre from the stems. The young shoots can also be eaten. No fibre traces were found at Graveney. Since the fossil hop remains were nuts (Fig. 6.6) the shoots would not

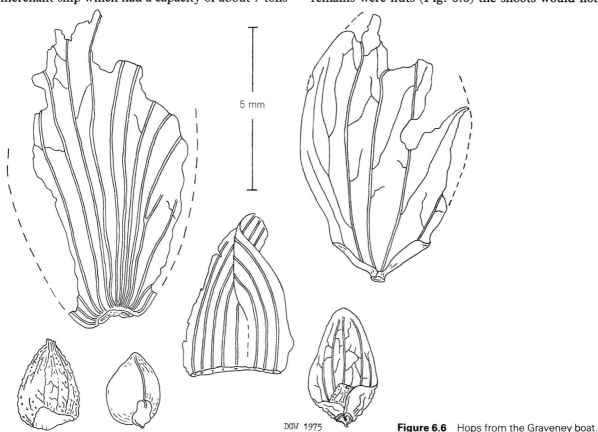

5 mm

DGW 1975

Figure 6.6 Hops from the Graveney boat.

have been in season. Other uses for hops include dye production and medicine, but the large numbers of fossils here (nearly 4500 fruit remains) suggest that they were more probably being traded for brewing. From the ninth century onwards French monasteries brewed beer with hops, at first using wild plants and then planting hop-gardens. By AD 859–875 there are references to hop-gardens of the abbey of Freisingen (Bitterauf 1967: 1, 666–715). In Kent there is pre-Conquest evidence of hop cultivation, for example in documents belonging to the abbey of St Augustine at Canterbury, which at the time of Domesday had a brewery renowned for its excellence and monks renowned for their indulgence (Brewer 1861, p. 51). The monks at Canterbury would certainly have been in contact with their European colleagues and it is possible that hops were traded across the Channel. There is no evidence to suggest that the hops were actually grown at Graveney, but they do provide the first evidence for the early use of hops in British brewing (Wilson & Connolly 1978).

6.5.6 Crops – their interpretation

There is a vast volume of literature concerning the domestication of plants, for example general works such as those of Schwanitz (1966), Renfrew (1973), Bender (1975), Helbaek (1969), Wilkes (1972), Ucko and Dimbleby (1969), and more specialized papers on individual crops such as that of van Zeist and Bakker-Heeres (1975) who reviewed the evidence for linseed cultivation before 6000 BC. It is important to know whether plant remains are those of crops, residues from crops, etc., and which stage of preparation is represented. Plants may be associated with numerous prehistoric activities, of which food production is only one, and may have many different uses even on the same site. It is, after all, impossible to conclude that a plant was cultivated just from the fact that it could have been eaten or was represented in the archaeological evidence. Dennell (1976) suggested that the economic value of a particular crop could be gauged by considering it within a general framework of crop-processing activities, distinguishing between actual and potential plant resources and evaluating their relative importance. The neglect of the study of the economic status of plant resources seems to be a result of

the questions asked by archaeologists, who are more interested qualitatively about diet (e.g. the range and type of plants eaten) rather than quantitatively about the ways and proportions in which the different available plants were exploited. Botanists tend to take the opposite view – hence the large numbers of papers dealing with the origins and dispersal of domesticated plants. However, a change in emphasis towards a more botanical view has resulted from progressively sophisticated retrieval techniques (Section 6.3), increasing the range and type of plant remains preserved and enabling studies of the relative economic importance of plant foods to be made. Carbonized plant material (p. 110) can never be random and is therefore not representative of the relevant economy. The processes of plant recovery bias results towards certain categories; leaves, roots and stalks are rare and therefore little is known of the early history of leaf and root crops. Crop processing may also affect the nature of the sample. Helbaek (1952) noted that some cereals (einkorn, emmer, spelt) need to be parched to free the grains, meaning that they are more likely to become accidentally carbonized. Fruit preservation depends on the numbers of seeds per fruit which may on occasion be plentiful, as (p. 118) is the case with raspberries, strawberries and figs. Large seeds such as plumstones or nutshells are much less likely to be preserved except in isolated localities, for example the acorn cache at Sesklo (Renfrew 1973, p. 28) or the almonds from a shipwreck off Cyprus (Renfrew 1973, p. 17). Economic uses also affect interpretation; dried fruits may be found, but plants used for dyeing or crushing for juice may be poorly represented. The greater the amount of preparation needed the greater the chances that a particular food crop will be preserved, meaning that fodder crops will seldom survive except by luck (p. 110) and pulse foods which need little preparation suffer the same fate. These and other factors result in the widely differing representation of plants from different places in the same archaeological layer and mean that the economic significance of a plant must not be judged by its numerical superiority, although lentils from Nea Nicomedia (van Zeist & Bottema 1971, p. 535) and emmer in Neolithic Thessaly (Renfrew 1973, p. 25) were regarded as important food plants simply on these grounds. At Sitagroi, Jane Renfrew tried to get round this problem, while working with carbonized material, by counting the number of samples in which a species was most common rather than the number of seeds or grains of a species in one sample. However, a plant would not be considered as a resource unless it was the most common plant in at least one sample, meaning that minor resources would be left out. Nor are crop-processing activities taken into consideration. Dennell (1976) produced two case studies of crop-processing at the early Neolithic settlements at Chevdar and Kazanluk in Bulgaria, dating to between 5300 and 4700 BC. He considered each plant represented in relation to specified domestic activities concerned with the production or preparation of plant foods, concluding that at the former site the occupants had utilized a far smaller range of plants than those at their disposal. The same author drew analogies between the metrical aspects of certain carbonized seed samples and the effect of sieving crops for the removal of weed seeds. Dennell (1972, 1974) also suggested that prehistoric crop-processing could be recognized from certain metrical parameters of the samples, reflecting their composition. However, the statistical assumptions involved were critically examined by Hubbard (1976), who suggests that simple statistical tests are unlikely ever to yield unambiguous evidence concerning the existence or extent of crop-processing and emphasizes the need for detailed considerations of archaeobotanical contexts.

References

Baerreis, D. A. 1973. Gastropods and archaeology. In *Variations in anthropology: essays in honor of John C. McGregor*, D. W. Lathrap and J. Douglas (eds). Springfield, Ill.: Illinois Archaeological Survey no. 44.

Bender, B. 1975. *Farming in prehistory*. London: Baker.

Bitterauf, T. 1967. *Die Traditionen des Hochstifts Freising Quellen und Erörterungen zur bayerischen und deutscher Geschichte*, N.F. 4 I AD 744–926,

Brewer, J. S. 1861. *Giraldi cambrensis opera*, Rerum Britannicum Medii Aeri Scriptores XXI.

Brouk, B. 1975. *Plants consumed by man*. New York: Academic Press.

Bryant, V. M., Jr 1974. The role of coprolite analysis in archaeology. *Bull. Texas Arch. Palaeont. Soc.* 45, 1–28.

Byrne, D. R. 1972. *Prehistoric coprolites*. MA thesis, Department of Anthropology, University of Auckland.

Callen, E. O. 1965. Food habits of some Pre-Columbian Mexican indians. *Econ. Bot.* 19, 335–43.

Callen, E. O. 1968. Plants, diet, and early agriculture of some cave-dwelling Pre-Columbian indians. *Actas Mems XXXVII Congr. Int. Americanis tas* 2, 641–56.

Callen, E. O. 1969a. Diet as revealed by coprolites. In *Science in archaeology*, 2nd edn, D. Brothwell and E. Higgs (eds), 235–43. London: Thames and Hudson.

Callen, E. O. 1969b. Les coprolites de la cabane Acheuleene du Lazaret, II: Analyse diagnostic. In *Une cabane Acheuleene dans la Grotte du Lazaret*, by H. de Lumley, 123–4. *Mém. Soc. préhist. fr.*

Davis, E. M. and A. I. B. Weslowsky 1975. The Izum: a simple water-separation device. *J. Fld Arch.* 2, 271–3.

Dennell, R. W. 1972. The interpretation of plant remains: Bulgaria. In *Papers in economic prehistory*. E. S. Higgs (ed.), 149–59. Cambridge: Cambridge University Press.

Dennell, R. W. 1974. The purity of prehistoric crop. *Proc. Prehist. Soc.* 40, 132–5.

Dennell, R. W. 1976. The economic importance of plant resources represented on archaeological sites. *J. Arch. Sci.* 3, 229–47.

Ellison, R., J. Renfrew, D. Brothwell and N. Seeley 1978. Some food offerings from Ur excavated by Sir Leonard Woolley and previously unpublished. *J. Arch. Sci.* 5, 167–79.

Fonner, R. L. 1957. Mammal feces from Danger Cave. In *Danger Cave 303*, by J. D. Jennings. Univ. Utah Anthrop. Pap. no. 27.

French, D. H. 1971. An experiment in water-sieving. *Anatolian Stud.* 21, 59–64.

Fry, G. F. 1976. Prehistoric diet. In *Handbook of North American Indians*, vol. IX, *The Great Basin*, W. L. D'Azeuedo (ed.). Washington: Smithsonian Institution.

Fry, G. F. and J. M. Adorasio 1970. *Population differentiation in Hagup and Danger caves: two archaic sites in the eastern Great Basin*. Nevada State University Anthropology Paper 15.

Fry, G. F. and H. J. Hall 1973. *The analysis of human coprolites from Inscription House: preliminary report*.

Fry, G. F. and H. J. Hall 1975. Human coprolites from Antelope House: preliminary analysis. *Kiva* 41, 87–96.

Glob, P. V. 1971. *The bog people*. London: Paladin.

Godwin, H. 1956. *History of the British flora*. Cambridge: Cambridge University Press.

Green, F. J. 1979. Phosphatic mineralization of seeds from archaeological sites. *J. Arch. Sci.* 6, 279–85.

Häntzschel, W., F. El-Bax and G. C. Amstutz 1968. *Coprolites: an annotated bibliography*. Mem. Geol Soc. Am. no. 108.

Harshberger, J. W. 1896. The purposes of ethno-botany. *Bot. Gaz.* 21, 146–54.

Heizer, R. F. 1960. Physical analysis of habitation residues. *Viking Fund Publ. in Anthropology* 68, 93–157.

Heizer, R. F. 1969. The anthropology of prehistoric Great Basin human coprolites. In *Science in archaeology*, D. Brothwell and E. Higgs (eds), 244–50. London: Thames and Hudson.

Heizer, R. F. 1967. *Analysis of human coprolites from a dry Nevada cave.* Berkeley: Univ. Calif. Arch. Survey Rep. 70, 1–20.

Heizer, R. F. and L. K. Napton 1969. Biological and cultural evidence from prehistoric human coprolites. *Science* 165, 563–8.

Helbaek, H. 1950. Tollund mandens didste maaltid. *Aarbøger for Nordisk Oldkyndighed og Historie* 311–41.

Helbaek, H. 1952. Early crops in southern England. *Proc. Prehist. Soc.* 18, 194–233.

Helbaek, H. 1958. Grauballe mandens sidste maaltid. *Kuml Aarhus*, 83–116.

Helbaek, H. 1969. Plant collecting, dry-farming and irrigation agriculture in prehistoric Deh Luran. In *Prehistory and human ecology of the Deh Luran plain*, F. Hole, K. V. Flannery and J. A. Neely. Mem. Mich. Mus. Anthrop. no. 1.

Helbaek, H. 1969. Palaeo-ethnobotany. In *Science in archaeology*, 2nd edn, D. Brothwell and E. Higgs (eds), 206–14. London: Thames and Hudson.

Hopf, M. 1969. Plant remains and early farming in Jericho. In *The domestication and exploitation of plants and animals*, P. J. Ucko and G. W. Dimbleby (eds), 355–9. London: Duckworth.

Hubbard, R. N. L. B. 1976. Crops and climate in prehistoric Europe. *Wld Arch.* 8, 159–68.

Jarman, H. N., A. J. Legge and J. A. Charles 1972. Retrieval of plant remains from archaeological sites by froth flotation. In *Papers in economic prehistory*, E. S. Higgs (ed.), 39–48. London: Cambridge University Press.

Jennings, J. D. 1953. Danger Cave: a progress summary. *El Palacio* 69, 179–213.

Keeley, H. C. M. 1978. The cost-effectiveness of certain methods of recovering macroscopic organic remains from archaeological deposits. *J. Arch. Sci.* 5, 179–85.

Keepax, C. 1975. Scanning electron microscopy of wood replaced by iron corrosion products. *J. Arch. Sci.* 2, 145–50.

Keepax, C. 1977. Contamination of archaeological deposits by seeds of modern origin with particular reference to the use of flotation machinery. *J. Arch. Sci.* 4, 221–9.

Lange, F. W. and F. W. Carty 1975. Salt water application of the flotation technique. *J. Fld Arch.* 2, 119–23.

Limp, W. F. 1974. Water separation and flotation processes. *J. Fld Arch.* 1, 337–42.

Marquarat, W. H. 1974. A statistical analysis of constituents in human paleofecal specimens from Mammoth Cave. In *Archaeology of the Mammoth Cave area*, P. J. Watson (ed.), 193–202. New York: Academic Press.

Napton, L. K. 1969. *Archaeological and paleobiological investigations in Lovelock Cave, Nevada.* Kroeber Anthrop. Soc. Special Pub. no. 2.

Napton, L. K. 1971. *Archaeological investigations in Lovelock Cave, Nevada.* Ph.D. dissertation, Department of Anthropology, University of California.

Napton, L. K. and R. F. Heizer 1970. Analysis of human coprolites from archaeological contexts, with primary reference to Lovelock Cave, Nevada. In *Archaeology and the prehistoric Great Basin lacustrine subsistence regime as seen from Lovelock Cave*, R. F. Heizer and L. K. Napton (eds), 87–129. Univ. Calif. Archaeol. Res. Fac. Contr. no. 10.

Netolitzky, F. 1906. *Die Vegetabilien in den Fäces: eine Mikroskopische-Forensische Studie.* Vienna: Moritz Perles.

Nunez, M. G. and M. Aalto 1978. A simple economical method for the recovery of plant remains from archaeological deposits. *Arch. baltica* 3, 149–53.

Parmalee, P., A. Paloumpis and N. Wilson 1972. Animals utilized by woodland peoples occupying the Apple Creek site, Illinois. *Illinois State Museum Reports of Investigations* 23, 13.

Renfrew, J. M. 1973. *Palaeoethnobotany: the prehistoric food plants of the Near East and Europe.* London: Methuen.

Renfrew, J. M., M. Monk and P. Murphy 1976. *First aid for seeds*, Hertford: Rescue Publications 6.

Schwanitz, F. 1966. *The origin of cultivated plants.* Cambridge, Mass.: Harvard University Press.

Shackley, M. L. 1975. *Archaeological sediments: a survey of analytical methods.* London: Butterworth.

Struever, S. 1968. Flotation techniques for the recovery of small-scale archaeological remains. *Am. Antiquity* 33, 353–62.

Troels–Smith, J. 1959. The Muldbjerg dwelling-place: an early Neolithic archaeological site in the Aamosen Bog, West-Zealand, Denmark. *Smithson. Instn a. Rep.*, 577–601.

Ucko, P. J. and G. W. Dimbleby 1969. *The domestication and exploitation of plants and animals.* London: Duckworth.

Vines, A. E. and N. Rees 1964. *Plant and animal biology*, vol. 1, 2nd edn. London: Pitman.

Warren, S. H. 1911. On a prehistoric interment near Walton on the Naze. *Essex Nat.* 16, 198–208.

Wilkes, H. G. 1972. Maize and its wild relatives. *Science* 177, 1071–7.

Willcox, G. H. 1977. Exotic plants from Roman waterlogged sites in London. *J. Arch. Sci.* 4, 269–82.

Williams, D. 1973. Flotation at Siraf. *Antiquity* 47, 288–92.

Wilson, D. G. and A. P. Connolly 1978. Plant remains including the evidence for hops. In *The Graveney boat: a tenth century find from Kent*, V. Fenwick (ed.), 133–51. British Archaeological Report no. 53.

van Zeist, W. and J. A. H. Bakker-Heeres 1975. Evidence for linseed cultivation before 6000 BC. *J. Arch. Sci.* 2, 215–21.

van Zeist, W. and S. Bottema 1971. Plant husbandry in Early Neolithic Nea Nikomedia, Greece. *Acta Bot. Neerl.* 20, 524–38.

Zeven, A. C., G. J. Doekes and M. Kislev 1975. Protein in old grains of *Triticum* sp. *J. Arch. Sci.* 2, 209–13.

7 *Molluscs*

The further off from England the nearer is to France.
Then turn not pale, beloved snail, but come and join the dance.

(Lewis Carroll, *Alice in Wonderland*)

7.1 Introduction

There are three main applications of the study of molluscan faunas in archaeology: the reconstruction of palaeoclimatic and palaeoenvironmental data, the study of food sources, and the use of molluscs as artefacts, including tools, ornaments, jewellery, dye sources, etc. This third category has not generally been the subject of much quantitative attention since the molluscs investigated are seldom obtained by systematic sampling, but the same cannot be said for the first category, which has been thoroughly investigated by Dr J. G. Evans, Senior Lecturer in Archaeology at the University of Cardiff. His many pioneering publications in this field are listed at the end of the chapter (Evans 1966, 1967, 1968, 1968–69, 1969, Evans & Jones 1973) and the present writer is greatly indebted to his book *Land snails in archaeology*, which will no doubt remain the classic text on the subject for some considerable time. An early paper (Evans 1968) summarizes the history of both subfossil and freshwater molluscan analysis for the interpretation of ancient environments, a subject which has developed since the time of Lane-Fox (1872). Major workers in this field are Kennard, Birkell and Sparks, the first-mentioned having over some 50 years produced a number of regional studies (Kennard 1897, 1923, 1943). These included a classic paper on the Grimes Graves flint mines in Norfolk (Kennard & Woodward 1914), where the snails were used not only as indicators of local environments but as evidence for the Holocene date of the mines in relation to the (then) current controversy (Clarke & Piggott 1933). After Kennard's death in 1948, Birkell made a synthesis of Holocene land snails in south-east England and suggested that it was possible to characterize the successive stages of the period through the composition of the assemblages. Little work was done with direct relationship to archaeological sites until the papers of Sparks (1960), Kerney (1967) and Evans (1966), which are appendices to excavation reports, with the exception of a few small papers, such as Connah and McMillan (1964). The full potential of molluscan analysis in archaeology had not been realized due to the lack of systematic sampling procedures and methods of processing. Collection of material would often be random and on a partial basis, resulting in an emphasis on the larger species (Castell 1963), with little attention paid to the study and description of the deposits from which the faunas were extracted and a great reliance on the use of molluscan faunas without any form of corroborative evidence (such as pollen, p. 85).

B. W. Sparks was the first British scientist to apply correct sampling procedures to molluscan analysis, plotting groups of ecologically related species and percentage frequency histograms and interpreting vertical changes as a result of changes in local environment (Sparks 1957). More recently these methods have been applied by Kerney (1963) to Devensian and Postglacial deposits on the chalk of southern England in a series of studies designed to illustrate the effect of man on the landscape.

Early efforts to analyse the molluscs from archaeological deposits tended to place too much emphasis on climate, or to use the snails as dating evidence for the deposits. More recent papers have concentrated on the reconstruction of local palaeo-environmental conditions, due to the extreme sensitivity of molluscs to local ecology.

Molluscs are small invertebrates whose soft parts are enclosed within a hard shell (forming an exoskeleton) largely composed of calcium carbonate (present in the crystal form aragonite) and are thus best preserved in calcareous conditions (Fig. 7.1). Methods of snail analysis rely on good sampling and correct identifications, comparing the ancient faunas with existing modern analogues to interpret palaeoenvironments. The term 'snail' is used for both land and freshwater molluscs, but not usually for marine species (Section 7.5). The preservation of a snail shell is a function of its thin proteinaceous coat (called the periostracum) which is usually destroyed within one year of the death of its owner in aerobic conditions but which may survive well in the anaerobic conditions of wells, ditches and deposits of peat. Acidity or abrasion are the destroying factors. Thin-shelled species such as *Oxychilus* are more easily destroyed than robust species such as *Cepea*, but few species are so fragile as never to appear in the subfossil record at all. The abundance of each species within a community is usually partially controlled by environmental factors and partially by heredity, although some species (e.g. *Vertigo pygmaea*) will be common whatever the conditions. The ratio of different species is obviously related to their different powers of survival and

reproduction, but the natural environment remains the main controlling factor. One might generalize in amplification of this statement and comment that this is the main contribution of invertebrates to archaeozoological studies, unlike vertebrates which provide primarily economic information. The regional distribution and abundance of certain species may be controlled by soil alkalinity or by temperature, for example the species *Pomatias elegans* which is found exclusively on chalk downland and limestone, with a few occurrences in the west of England on local outcrops of Devonian limestone or wind-blown shell sand.

Snails live both within and above soils, some very close to the soil surface in leaf litter at the base of grass. Others will frequent the stalks of herbaceous plants or specific habitats such as the bark of fallen trees and some species will live far above ground level in trees or walls. Each species has its favoured habitat but may be able to live in a series of others, producing both synchronic and diachronic distribution patterns related to changes in local ecology. Species which habitually live on vegetation may hibernate within the soil or die there in severe

(a)

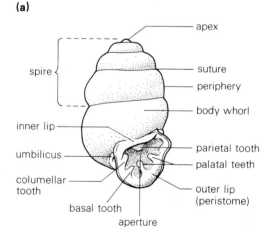

(b)

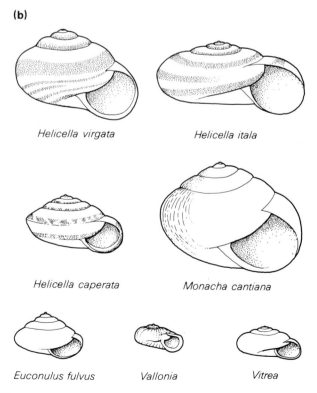

Figure 7.1 (a) Shell of *Vertigo pygmaea* showing main features; (b) comparative appearances of mollusc shells.

conditions. This introduces two very important concepts, that of the **death assemblage** and the **subfossil assemblage** (Evans 1972). At death all snails, irrespective of their preferred vertical habitat during life, are concentrated at the ground surface, with the exception of those which lived below the soil surface and remain there. This alters the structure of the resulting population since the snails may not be fossilized in the position or preferred habitat which they occupied when alive. This difference between the structure of the original living population and extant available assemblage will clearly be greater in forest than grassland. The subfossil assemblage is produced by the various natural taphonomic processes (p. 163) which act on the death assemblage to produce the actual collection of snails which we see, and is even further removed from the living population. Destructive processes are both biochemical and physical, including differential destruction related to the shells' resistance to weathering, and the segregation of shells of different sizes and species by worm action. Thus in an archaeological context the molluscan assemblage being examined is a subfossil assemblage, but it is necessary to understand the processes which produced it in order to see what relation it bears to the original death assemblage.

7.2 Field methods and sampling

A most important prerequisite in any work with land snails is correct sampling and detailed recording of the snail-bearing deposits. This must be done not only for the stratification of the archaeological site but also for the surrounding geomorphology. As usual, detailed drawings and a photographic record of the sections must be made, together with the sampling locations. Evans (1972, p. 41) states a fundamental principle: 'Sampling is done at a point where the stratigraphy is most complete and most representative of the deposits as a whole, remembering at the same time that the exact location will be reflected in the composition of the snail fauna'. Samples (of about 1 kg in size) are taken with a pointing trowel from a cleaned vertical section, starting at the base. The interval between samples is usually 100 mm, but closer intervals are necessary for deposits which have accumulated very slowly or which are very fine grained. An alternative method is the monolith tin, hammered into the section, which has the advantage of allowing a unit of deposit to be removed intact. Boring is not generally to be recommended unless the deposits are too deep for a pit to be dug, although Sparks (1961) concludes that the amount of sample contamination induced by sampling Pleistocene deposits in this manner is minimal. Large shells such as the adults of the species of *Cepea* and *Succinia* should be removed by hand-picking during the excavation (and kept in bags with an accurate record of their exact stratigraphic position) since they are rarely present in most soil samples and identification of some of the larger species is difficult if the material is fragmentary or only represents juveniles.

7.2.1 Sample preparation

Air-dried material (0.5–2 kg) should be used in order to facilitate comparative counts, the snails being extracted by mixing the sediment with water (when many will float) and sieving through a graded sieve nest of mesh diameters 2.0 mm (-1φ), 1.0 mm (0φ) and 0.5 mm (1φ). The resulting shells are oven-dried and the fine material which passes the finest sieve is deflocculated with hydrogen peroxide or sodium hexametaphosphate and the small shells

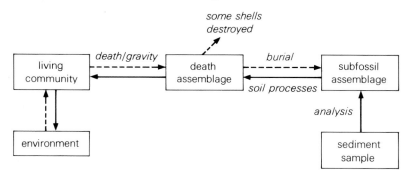

Figure 7.2 (1) Stages in the formation of a sub-fossil assemblage (after Evans 1972); (2) stages in analysis and interpretation; (3) factors controlling the composition of snail communities.

extracted from it with a fine paint-brush and a hand lens or low power stereomicroscope. Only the shell apices are counted, in order to obviate the possibility of counting numerous fragments of the same shell, but a careful record must be kept of the presence of species not represented, for some reason, by their apices. In cases where the apertural fragments are more diagnostic than the apices (as with the genera *Cochliopa*, *Clausila*, *Vertigo* and *Cepea*) these are counted instead.

7.2.2 Identification

A problem with identification is the lack of one standard reference work on British land and fresh-water mollusca, but notwithstanding this it would be true to say that the availability of reference texts and collections is greater for molluscan analysis than for almost any other branch of environmental archaeology, with the possible exception of palynology. The available textbooks tend to deal mainly with adult individuals and often concentrate on features of the living snail which are lost in the sub-fossil state. Major reference works include Ellis (1964, 1969), Adams (1896), Taylor (1894–1921), Turton (1859), Quick (1949, 1960) and Evans (1972). Continental works such as Adams (1960) on Belgian snails and Lozek (1964) on the molluscs of Czechoslovakia are also useful. Kerney and Cameron (1979) have just published a very useful field guide to land snails of north-west Europe. Only 50 species of land snails are common on British archaeological sites, from a potential 200 living and extinct species. The problems of identification are therefore not insuperable, but the process is very tedious, and it is necessary to have a good reference collection of specimens of different ages and in different stages of preservation. The common terms used in shell identification are shown in Figure 7.1, which shows a shell of *Vertigo pygmaea* with five denticles (to distinguish it from *V. geyeri* and *V. alpestris* which have only four), and a strong callus (the thickening behind the aperture where the palatal denticles are inserted).

7.2.3 Presentation of results

A mollusc diagram (Fig. 7.4) is constructed in a manner very similar to that already described for a pollen diagram, with the vertical axis representing

the depth below the modern soil surface or any other chosen datum point. A schematized representation of the stratigraphy is given at the left, and on the far right a brief summary of the general environment of each horizon. The horizontal axis is the relative abundance of the species plotted, the arrangement of groups or groups of species depending on the patterns of change which the diagram is illustrating. Most of the faunas described by Evans (1972) are terrestrial and are divided into three groups: (a) woodland or shade lovers, (b) intermediate (catholic) species, and (c) open country species, which are arranged from left to right. In Kerney's treatment of the late Devensian fauna of south-east England (Kerney 1963), the arrangement of the diagram is done on a climatic basis, with climatically

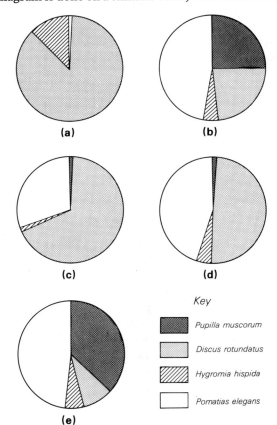

Figure 7.3 Pie diagram of shell assemblages from British Neolithic and Bronze Age sites. (a) Peaty alluvium, Ebbsfleet; (b) sub-aerial loam, Bean valley; (c) Bronze Age alluvium, Ebbsfleet; (d) Bronze Age peaty silt, Brook Vale; (e) Turf line beneath the long barrow Juliberries Grave (after Burchell & Piggott 1939).

tolerant species on the left and relatively thermophilous species on the right, irrespective of their habitat preferences. Sparks (1961, 1964) illustrates the point that freshwater species may be classified on either an ecological or a climatic basis. The percentages shown are generally based on the total number of shells in each sample, although there are exceptions (for example *Ceciloides acicula*, which is a burrowing species, found at depths of up to 2 m, which is either represented as a percentage separate from the rest or as an open graph, like hazel pollen (Fig. 4.8) or excluded altogether). Values less than 1.5% are plotted simply as a + sign in the histogram, but a + sign in tables indicates a non-apical fragment not included in the percentage calculations. Alternative methods of presenting results include the simple histograms and sector (pie) diagrams. The former is especially useful in comparing individual faunas at different sites, plotting the percentages present along the vertical axis and the species or groups of species along the horizontal.

7.3 Factors affecting the composition of an assemblage

It is sometimes necessary to check statistically significant differences between faunal composition on different levels at the same site or between different sites. Tests such as chi-squared to show significant differences must then be supported by a consideration of the ecological implications of these differences. Where the faunal succession in a single deposit shows marked changes in relative abundance of the different species, this is generally either the result of environmental change, stratigraphical and pedological processes or some other non-environmental factor such as a statistical bias introduced by the possibility that one value may be worked out on a lower initial count, making the figures insignificant. It follows, therefore, that in order to assess the significance of an assemblage (and of the conclusions which are being drawn from it) one must know the total number of shells which form the basis for the percentage calculations, the number of species or groups plotted, the maintenance of constant values over two or more samples and any other corroborative environmental data.

Factors controlling the distribution of snails include temperature, humidity, available food and shelter, the presence of predators or parasites and the degree of competition and changes in a population will be the result of a complex interaction of such environmental factors. In his book Evans (1972) gives a detailed analysis of the distribution, habitats and history of British non-marine mollusca, later dividing them into their ecological groups. He relates this to the soils and sediments in which they are found and quotes a series of representative modern soils with their associated faunas. One can distinguish the type of snails which might be found, for example, in colluvial deposits, caves, dry valleys and ditches, but much of the work has been done on the well-documented habitat changes in the calcareous regions of southern England. The changes in snail populations with time, if not related directly to an environmental factor, may also be a social response to the introduction of a new species, an evolutionary change or a change in ecological tolerance. Variations may also be related to life cycles, for example in the relative abundance of juveniles and adults, or to short-term fluctuations of a non-environmental origin.

7.4 Land molluscs

7.4.1 Vegetation cover and change

Spencer (1975) considered habitat change in sand dune areas, examining the snail faunas of coastal shell sand deposits in North Cornwall and the Orkneys. These extensive tracts of calcareous sand blown inland by on-shore winds encouraged the establishment of snail populations, the shells being preserved by incorporation into the sands which are all Postglacial and overlie well-defined buried soils. Results of the analysis were shown as histograms of relative abundance, with each species or group as a percentage of the total fauna and also given in the form of a table. In the histograms the snail species were arranged ecologically with shade-loving species on the left; intermediate (catholic habitat) in centre; and open country on the right. The project demonstrated the former presence of woodland in these now open territories and suggested that, in some instances, deforestation took place *before* the accumulation of sand, and in others the two processes were coeval. The areas studied were occupied during the early settlement of Britain by farming communities, and it is possible that deforestation was directly brought about by man. The reverse of this hypothesis is equally feasible, inundation of woodland by sand *causing* the deforestation with the subsequent open country landscape and calcareous soils becoming attractive to agriculturists.

7.4.2 The comparative use of pollen and snail analyses

Pollen analysis has been used in the past to work out the palaeoenvironment mainly in peat and lake sediments. These act as catchments for pollen derived from wide areas, but archaeological sites are seldom found in direct association. Although the pollen analysis of mineral soils has improved during the last 15 years (Section 4.6), the technique is still most effective in highly acid environments, with the result that much of the land (for example the chalk downlands) which was very important to early farmers has remained unstudied. On chalk land snail analysis has been conspicuously successful, but major difficulties exist in the interpretation of fine structure and composition of vegetation. The conjunction of pollen and snail analysis was attempted to remedy this. Dimbleby and Evans (1974) discussed the relative uses of pollen and molluscan analyses from nine soils with high pH values in southern England, all preserved beneath Neolithic earthworks (Fig. 7.4). Of these nine, eight were on chalk and one on Jurassic limestone. Very interesting results were obtained from the study of the profiles. It is suggested on the basis of stony profile and the presence of open-country land snails that cultivation took place at Waylands Smithy and Horselip at one stage in the history of these profiles, but at Beckhampton Road there were no cultivation marks and the snail fauna in main profile thickness was woodland. Open-country faunas only occurred in the surface turf-lines. At Windmill Hill and Knapp Hill the faunas were of woodland or possibly scrub type with no marks of cultivation. At five sites the faunas indicated dramatic environmental changes in the upper profile level, deforestation and open country as a result of the activity of early farmers in tree-felling and stock-rearing. There

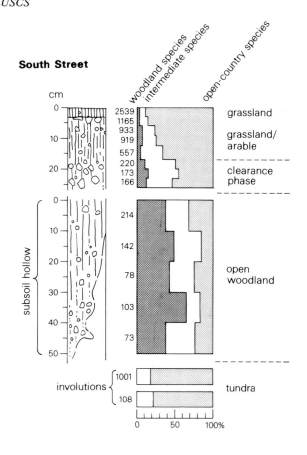

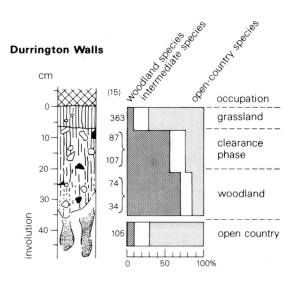

Figure 7.4 Comparison of snail diagrams from South Street and Durrington Walls (after Dimbleby & Evans 1974).

were two distinct types of land use. At Ascot and Beckhampton the profile had remained undisturbed and contained a woodland fauna, whereas at South Street, Waylands Smithy and Horselip the profile had been disturbed to its base and snails were of open-country type throughout. Durrington and Avebury remained intermediate between these two extremes.

Not surprisingly, the pollen analyses did not always lead to the same conclusion as the molluscs. Snail shells are comparatively large and found in calcareous soils which contain worms which can disturb the vertical distribution of pollen. Plant communities react quickly to change and even short episodes may give a characteristic spectrum. If a forest is cleared, a cover of flowers and grasses may replace it next or the same year, but the reverse process is slower since shrubs and trees do not flower until ten years or more in age. Snails take longer to adjust to change and it is therefore difficult to compare the results of two such different forms of analysis, as pollen reflects the latest changes in ecology, to which the snails have not had time to adjust. The general absence of pollen evidence of past ecology which is indicated from snails may be due to the fact that no pollen from earlier periods survives except as very resistant types which are difficult to interpret. Each site probably has biological peculiarities which make blanket forms of comparison and interpretation impossible.

7.4.3 Early fields

Fowler and Evans (1967) discussed the application of excavation techniques and subsequent molluscan analysis to the study of early field systems. The recognition of such fields relies heavily on the identification of plough marks beneath barrows. Studies were also made on the use of archaeological finds and stratification of fields for dating purposes and the recognition of early field boundaries. The Fowler and Evans (1967) project was concerned with crisscross plough marks, not strip lynchets, at sites in Yorkshire and under the South Street long barrow at Avebury (Wiltshire) where the plough marks had been protected by the buried soil under the barrow mound. At this latter site the ploughmarks were very clear grooves in the chalky substrate filled with dark soil. Two main sets appeared, crossing more or

less at right angles, with a number of subsidiary diversions possibly related to further land clearance. The profile from the buried soil produced a snail fauna enforcing a picture of the initial clearance of a shaded environment followed by intermittent agriculture, at least two periods of cultivation separated by a fallow stage. The later history of the barrow was reconstructed from the ditch fill, where a second series of plough marks could be traced across at the same level where the molluscan fauna shows clearance from woodland. Thus, the South Street barrow has produced archaeological evidence for initial land clearance in the Neolithic followed by a Beaker second period clearance and ploughsoil, each phase being associated with deep cross-ploughing and followed by intermittent agriculture (Fig. 7.5).

7.5   Marine molluscs

7.5.1   Molluscs as a food source

Abundant shell deposits (or middens) are quite common on archaeological sites near a lake, estuary or the sea, and their contents are of great potential value. The most frequently cited shell-midden cultures are the southern African Strandloopers and the European Mesolithic Ertebølle culture, but very large middens are also found lining the coasts of South America, Australia and eastern Russia (Shackleton 1969). The majority of these remains are of food debris and it is possible to evaluate the food value and meat weight represented by molluscs with greater accuracy than in the case of animal bones. Variations in patterning might represent variations in culture or time, and temporary fluctuations may indicate changes in diet or in population concentration. Some sites exhibit marked seasonality, while others seem to have been occupied on a year-round basis.

Estimating the meat volume from a mollusc shell may be done easily by filling it with water and then measuring the volume of the water, an accurate method except in the case of the cockle, whose body does not fill the whole volume of its shell. Shackleton (1969) quotes an example from the Neolithic site of Saliagos in the Aegean where the size range of limpets (Patella sp.) was determined, one particular accumulation of significantly smaller size shells

Figure 7.5 Plough marks under South Street longbarrow (after Fowler & Evans 1967).

suggesting a period of scarcity. Detecting the precise function of a solitary mollusc shell, whether it genuinely represents food debris or was used as a tool, may be difficult, especially as food shells may be re-used for tools or jewellery. The majority of the food molluscs are bivalves (oyster, cockle and mussel), together with marine snails (gastropods) such as the whelk, periwinkle and abelone, certain cephalopods (cuttlefish, octopus and squid) and a very few land snails. The eating of shellfish is known from very early times onwards. In some cases it is associated with an island economy without large mammals, or with a change in coastal formation. There is, for example, a marked correlation between the rise in sea levels during the Postglacial, in-creasing coastline length per surface area of the land, the Mesolithic Ertebølle shell-midden sites and the ancient shores of the Littorina Sea (Clark 1952).

Shellfish may also be an important item in the diet of cultures whose economy is not successful and who are unable to compete for the best hunting grounds, which may have been the case with the Mousterian inhabitants of Devil's Tower (Gibraltar). It is interesting that such a concentration of shellfish eating should be found amongst Mesolithic peoples, where man was engendering a change of life style associated with the spread of forest at the end of the Pleistocene, and a consequent economic change from big game hunting to a more mixed economy. Indeed, some Mesolithic cultures seem to have exploited molluscs to the exclusion of almost all other animal foods, which does not imply a drop in nutritional standards, since shellfish (if eaten with vegetable food) are just as nourishing as meat. However, it has been pointed out, that much effort is wasted in their collection since the amount of inedible debris is considerable, although the actual food source may occur in very large concentrations. Shellfish may often be a dietary supplement rather than a food base, and are often found with cultures which practised domestication (as in the Sipontiano culture of Italy, in which domestic cattle were raised). Changes in a prehistoric economy from shellfish to meat eating, or vice versa, or to different varieties of shellfish, are generally related to an environmental or cultural change. Treganza and Cook (1950) showed the relationship between the edible flesh available from the different mollusc species compared with that from birds. One gram of bird bone in a midden represents the same amount of meat weight as 100 g of clam shells. At the Little Harbour site on Catalina Island of southern California the midden samples consisted of up to 58% shell, but analysis of the other components of the mound showed that molluscs could not have been more than one half of the flesh foods utilized (Meighan 1959). Unfortunately, accurate shell to flesh ratios are not always available and regional variations may cause discrepancies in such calculations. A large quantity of mussel shells may mean very little meat, while a little fish bone may have been a feast. At a Californian site of the Canilino culture a change of emphasis from concentration on the abelone to the murex was observed, simply a case of over-exploitation of a resource which necessitated its replacement by another. The availability of a particular species of shellfish may depend on the local environment, for example *Patella* (limpet) is more common on a rock bottom while *Cardium* (cockle) likes muddy estuaries. Over-exploitation of shellfish may lead to extinction of a particular species but this in turn may enable another to build up numbers and act as a replacement food supply. This may be caused by some natural enemy of the shellfish or by a microclimatic change, perhaps in the temperature of the sea. A good example of the latter phenomenon may be seen today in southern England where oysters are cultivated in the water of the Solent, artificially warmed as a result of by-products from the vast Fawley oil refinery near Southampton.

No evidence has yet been produced for the successful domestication of shellfish, since exploitation leads away from domestication rather than towards it. Their method of reproduction does not lend itself to human interference and even with the culturing of oysters only growth is affected, to get a maximum yield per minimum area of the sea bed. Greater possibilities for domestication are seen in the land snails, an important food resource for certain prehistoric cultures such as the Capsian of north Africa.

7.5.2 Midden analysis

Not only are shell middens found at the coast but they are common (and composed of freshwater molluscs) along some major rivers. The name is confusing since it is applied both to archaeological deposits almost entirely composed of shell as well as to sites where the shell content may fall below 1%. If a midden deposit contains more than 30% shell (by weight), the rest of the material will be very inconspicuous since the accompanying rock and soil are more dense and of smaller volume. Meighan (1969) recognized three principal types of sites:

(a) Shell middens of hunter–gatherers. In such cases molluscs were an important food staple, often used to ballast a meat diet, and as a resource available all year round to assist the growth and maintenance of a relatively dense population. This last point has been explored by Kroeber (1939), who showed that hunter–gatherers in northern America could maintain about twice the density of population along the coasts as they did inland due to the fact that shellfish are a very predictable resource.

(b) Shell middens representing a protein supplement in a mixed economy.

(c) Shell middens in market towns or commercial centres connected with trading. Examples of the latter would be the Mexican site Barra da Navidad, where there is evidence of commerce involving salt and shellfish dating back to considerable antiquity, and Arrica (Chile) where an Inca fishing community exported fish and shellfish in exchange for agricultural products.

The quantitative analysis of shell middens should give evidence of diet, local ecology, and population density, and a broad range of quantitative methods has been used (Heizer & Cook 1960). It is usual to take a series of small samples from a midden (15–20 samples, each 2–3 kg in size), sampling from the trench wall and avoiding obvious concentrations. Greenwood (1961) experimented with sieve meshes from ½ to ¹⁄₁₆ in (12.7–1.6 mm), but experiments showed little variation in sample constitution with mesh size, a conclusion directly opposite to that drawn by those concerned with the processing of archaeological deposits for small bones (p. 182). Meighan (1969) suggests ¼ in (6.4 mm) as the most practicable size for site work, due to the 500% increase in sorting time for a sample from the finer ¹⁄₁₆ in (1.6 mm) mesh. After washing the material, identification and sorting must be carried out with even very small shell fragments (¼ in, 6.4 mm) being collected. Individual species are identified on the basis of shape, lustre, colour and texture (p. 128) but it is generally found that an entire midden deposit will consist of two or three species.

A paper by Cook and Treganza (1947) analysed the constituents of nineteen Californian mound sites to obtain an idea of the interrelationships between the materials as part of a larger project examining the physical components of archaeological sites. They took the bone and shell content as an index of the quantity of animal food available to the inhabitants, although the greater part of the diet no doubt consisted of plant foods of which no evidence survives. Their calculations of total available meat weight are interesting but outmoded, obtained by multiplying the weight of bone by forty and using ratios of mollusc shells to flesh weight which had already been calculated for modern examples (Cook 1947). After complicated calculations they arrived at population densities, concluding that the presence of huge inexhaustible mussel beds in the San Francisco Bay area was a major reason for intensive occupation of the area from very early times.

Work on European middens includes that of Spencer (1975) and Mellars and Payne (1971) who investigated two Mesolithic shell middens on the Isle of Oronsay (Inner Hebrides), important since they preserved evidence for the economy and subsistence of the human groups in the area in the late pre-agricultural phase. Data was collected by water-sieving material through 2 mm and 1 mm mesh sieves, and, although the sites yielded a large proportion of fish bone, many mollusc shells were also extracted. Most were the common limpet, *Patella vulgata*, with smaller numbers of the common periwinkle, *Littorina littorea*, the dog whelk, *Nucella lapillus*, the oyster, *Ostrea edulis*, cockle, *Cardium edule*, scallop, *Pecten maximum*, and razor shells (*Ensis* sp.). 'Limpet scoops' made from stone or deer antlers were also found, together with several flattened pebbles possibly used as hammers or anvil stones. Another Mesolithic site, this time in the south of England, at Portland Bill, was described by Palmer (1967). A spread of shells on top of stones, mostly of *Littorina littorea* and *Patella* sp., were identified, but in some cases the identification to species level was difficult. The list of species present was almost the same as that found on Orkney, with a few additional intertidal species where the natural habitat ranged from the supralittoral to sublittoral fringes. It would seem that such shellfish formed a major item of diet, pebbles with one edge abraded or deliberately bevelled by a single blow being plentiful and again identified as 'limpet scoops'. No doubt in both cases such a boring diet was supplemented by edible plants and roots which have left no trace, but it is interesting that no animal bones were found.

7.5.3 Snails as food

Salin (1959) reports the occurrence of fossil shells in Merovingian burials (for example the gastropods *Leriticum lapidi*, *Trocha* and *Lymnaea* at Armentières (Aisne)). Non-fossil shells, either pierced or unpierced, are also present, for example *Patella vulgaris* at Enrermen (Seine Maritime) and *Murex*. Snails are found which seem to have been used as food (*Helix pomalis* at Parfonderal in Normandy). Two to three dozen Gallo-Roman shells of *Helix nemoralis* are reported from an association with skeleton no. 9 at Maison-Blanche (Auvergne) and fossil shells in association with burials are also very numerous, for example those detailed by Meaney (1964). Reed (1962), in a classic paper on the molluscs of Iran, has demonstrated selective exploitation of *Helix salomonica* at the expense of the equally abundant *Levantina diolfensis*. *Helix* (the edible snail of southern Europe) also occurs on

Figure 7.6 A snail pick (from Reed 1962) comprised of a microlith mounted in a wooden handle.

archaeological sites of 6000–8000 BP in the Near East, Iraq and Iran. It is definitely puzzling that the somewhat larger and equally palatable *Levantina* was not eaten. Reed prepared a banquet in the best French tradition with microlithic bladelets as snail-picks (Fig. 7.6) and some 500 of the snails were cooked. A second experiment, tried without herbs in a more Spartan fashion (presumably closer to the eating habits of the sixth millenium local inhabitants) showed both types to be equally tasty and there seems no reason why *Levantina* should not have been equally popular. The Romans bred a variety of large snail in *vivaria* for size and colour, but the species (probably *Helix homateia*) has not been properly identified and it is suggested that the experiment was merely academic. Synanthropic snails which live in close association with man and which are to a certain extent dependent on him for cleared ground were also eaten, for example *Helix aspersa* and *Helix pomatia*.

7.5.4 Other applications

The data obtained by Mellars and Payne (1971) from Orkney shell-mounds were also used for $^{18}O/^{16}O$ studies of sea temperature, a topic discussed by Shackleton (1969). It is possible to calculate water temperatures by analysing the calcium carbonate of a mollusc shell, even taking samples of seasonal layers in a single shell. Only 0.5 mg of material is required and the error is less than 1%, major problems being firstly that ocean temperatures fluctuate widely over quite short periods (requiring a large number of measurements for long term mean values) and secondly that the isotopic components of the water itself vary. Shells may be used for radiocarbon and amino acid racemization dating.

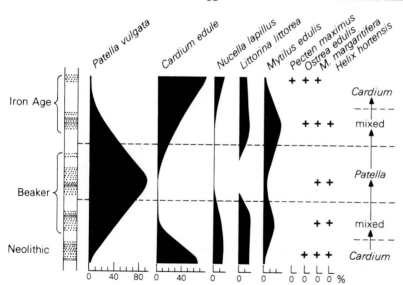

Figure 7.7 Changes in the relative abundance of various food molluscs in a prehistoric midden at Northton, Isle of Harris, Scotland (Spencer 1975).

References

Adams, L. E. 1896. *The collector's manual of British land and freshwater snails.* Leeds: Taylor Bros.

Adams, W. 1960. *Faune de Belgique: mollusques,* Tome 1: *Mollusques terrestres et dulcicole.* Brussels: L'Institute Royal des Sciences Naturelles de Belgique.

Castell, C. P. 1963. Appendix V: land molluscs. In The excavation of the Willerby Wold Long Barrow, East Riding of Yorkshire, England, T. G. Manby. *Proc. Prehist. Soc.* **29**, 173–205.

Clarke, J. G. D. and S. Piggott 1933. The age of the British flint mines. *Antiquity* **7**, 166–83.

Connah, G. and N. F. McMillan 1964. Snails and archaeology. *Antiquity* **38**, 62–4.

Cook, S. F. 1947. A reconsideration of shellmounds with respect to population and nutrition. *Am. Antiquity* **12**, 50–3.

Cook, S. F. and A. E. Treganza 1947. The quantitative investigation of aboriginal sites: comparative physical and chemical analyses of two Californian Indian mounds. *Am. Antiquity* **13**, 135–41.

Dimbleby, G. W. and J. G. Evans 1974. Pollen and land-snail analysis of calcareous soils. *J. Arch. Sci.* **1**, 117–33.

Ellis, A. E. 1964. *Key to the land shells of Great Britain*. Conchological Society of Great Britain and Ireland, papers for students no. 3.

Ellis, A. E. 1969. *British snails*. Oxford: Oxford University Press.

Evans, J. G. 1966. Land Mollusca from the Neolithic enclosure on Windmill Hill, *Wilts Arch. Nat. Hist. Mag.* **61**, 91–2.

Evans, J. G. 1967. *The stratification of mollusca in chalk soils and their relevance to archaeology*. Ph.D. thesis, University of London.

Evans, J. G. 1968. Periglacial deposits on the chalk of Wiltshire. *Wilts Arch. Nat. Hist. Mag.* **63**, 12–26.

Evans, J. G. 1968–69. Interpretation of land snail faunas. *Univ. Lond. Inst. Arch. Bull.* **8–9**, 109–16.

Evans, J. G. 1969. Land and freshwater Mollusca in archaeology: chronological aspects, *Wld Arch.* **1**, 170–83.

Evans, J. G. 1972. *Land snails in archaeology, with special reference to the British Isles*. London: Seminar Press.

Evans, J. G. and H. Jones 1973. Subfossil and modern land-snail faunas from rock-rubble habitats. *J. Conch.* **28**, 103–29.

Fowler, P. J. and J. G. Evans 1967. Plough-marks, lynchets and early fields. *Antiquity* **41**, 289–301.

Heizer, R. F. and S. F. Cook 1960. *The application of quantitative methods in archaeology*. Chicago: Quadrangle Books.

Kennard, A. S. 1897. The post-Pliocene non-marine Mollusca of Essex. *Essex Nat.* **10**, 87–109.

Kennard, A. S. 1923. The Holocene non-marine Mollusca of England. *Proc. Palaeont. Soc. Lond.* **15**, 241–59.

Kennard, A. S. 1943. The post-Pliocene non-marine Mollusca of Hertfordshire. *Trans Herts Nat. Hist. Soc. Fld Club* **22**, 1–18.

Kennard, A. S. and B. B. Woodward 1914. The molluscs. In *Report on the excavation of Grimes Graves, Weeting, Norfolk*, W. G. Clarke (ed.), 220–31. London.

Kerney, M. P. 1963. Late-glacial deposits on the Chalk of South-East England. *Phil. Trans R. Soc. B* **246**, 203–54.

Kerney, M. P. 1967. Distribution and mapping of land and freshwater Mollusca in the British Isles. *J. Conch.* **26**, 152–60.

Kerney, M. P. and R. A. D. Cameron 1979. *A field guide to the land snails of Britain and north-west Europe*. London: Collins.

Kroeber, A. L. 1939. *Cultural and natural areas in native North America*. Berkeley: Univ. Calif. Publ. Am. Arch. Ethnol. 38.

Lane-Fox, A. H. 1869. Further remarks on the hillforts of Sussex: being an account of excavations in the forts at Cissbury and Highdown. *Archaeologia* **42**, 53–76.

Lozek, V. 1964. QuartärMollusken der Tschechoslowakei. *Rozpr. ústred. úst. geol.* **31**, 311–74.

Meaney, A. 1964. *A gazetteer of early Anglo-Saxon burial sites*. London: Allen and Unwin.

Meighan, C. W. 1959. The Little Harbor site, Catalina Island: an example of ecological interpretation in archaeology. *Am. Antiquity* **24**, 383–405.

Meighan, C. W. 1969. Molluscs as food remains in archaeological sites. In *Science in archaeology*, 2nd edn, D. Brothwell and E. Higgs (eds), 415–22. London: Thames and Hudson.

Mellars, P. A. and S. Payne 1971. Excavation of two Mesolithic shell middens on the island of Oronsay (Inner Hebrides). *Nature* **231**, 397–8.

Palmer, S. 1967. The second report on excavations at Portland site 1: 1967 to 1968. *Proc. Dorset. Nat. Hist. Arch. Soc.* **92**, 168–80.

Quick, H. E. 1949. *Slugs, Synopsis of the British Fauna no. 8*. London: Linnean Society.

Quick, H. E. 1960. British slugs (Pulmonata, Testacellidae, Amorsidae, Limacidae). *Bull. Br. Mus. Nat. Hist. Zool.* **6**, 103–226.

Reed, C. A. 1962. *Snails on a Persian hillside: ecology, prehistory – gastronomy*. Yale Peabody Museum Publication no. 66.

Salin, E. 1959. *La civilization Mérovingienne*. Paris: Picard et Cie.

Shackleton, N. J. 1969. Marine mollusca in archaeology. In *Science in archaeology*, 2nd edn, D. Brothwell and E. Higgs (eds), 407–14. London: Thames and Hudson.

Sparks, B. W. 1957. The non-marine Mollusca of the interglacial deposits at Bobbits Hole, Ipswich. *Phil. Trans R. Soc. B* **241**, 33–44.

Sparks, B. W. 1960. Appendix II: Land Mollusca. In Report on the investigation of a round barrow on Arreton Down, Isle of Wight, J. Alexander, P. C. Ozanne and A. Ozanne. *Proc. Prehist. Soc.* **26**, 263–302.

Sparks, B. W. 1961. The ecological interpretation of Quaternary non-marine mollusca. *Proc. Linn. Soc., Lond.* **172**, 71–80.

Sparks, B. W. 1964. Non-marine mollusca and Quaternary ecology. *J. Anim. Ecol.* **33**, 87–98.

Spencer, P. J. 1975. Habitat change in coastal sand-dune areas: the molluscan evidence. In *The effect of man on the landscape: the Highland Zone*, 96–103. London: Council for British Archaeology.

Taylor, J. W. 1894–1921. *Nomograph of the land and freshwater Mollusca of the British Isles*, 3 vols and 3 parts, unfinished. Leeds: Taylor Bros.

Treganza, A. E. and S. F. Cook 1950. The Topanga culture: first season's excavation of the Tank Site, 1947. *Univ. Calif. Anthrop. Record* **12** (4).

Turton, W. 1857. *Manual of the land and freshwater shells of the British Islands*. London: Longman.

8 *Insects*

And the poor beetle, that we tread upon,
In corporal sufferance finds a pang as great
As when a giant dies.

(William Shakespeare, *Measure for Measure*)

8.1 Introduction

The phylum Arthropoda is undoubtedly the most diverse and successful within the Animal Kingdom. Within it the class Insecta has colonized every available habitat since the early Devonian (at least 390 Ma ago) and nearly a million species have been described. Fossil records of insects are, however, rather sparse, except in the peats and muds of the Pleistocene and in more recent deposits. Since the study of the mid-Devensian fauna from Upton Warren (Worcestershire) (Coope *et al.* 1961) the importance of insect remains for reconstructing palaeoclimatic changes has been fully realized, and much work has been done in more recent years by Coope and his colleagues on the Pleistocene sequence of environmental and climatic change (Coope 1959, 1967, 1970, Coope & Angus 1975, Coope & Brophy 1972, Coope & Osborne 1967, Coope *et al.* 1971). As early as 1911 a few identifications of insect remains were made from Roman Caerwent (Lyell 1911) and further projects carried out by Henriksen (1933) and Bell (1922). Workers such as Osborne (1969, 1971, 1972, 1973, 1974, 1976), Buckland (1974, 1975, 1976a,b) and Kenward (1974, 1975a,b,c, 1976a,b,c) have pioneered the use of insect remains in British archaeology, although important work on archaeological faunas on the Continent has been confined to Finland (Koponen and Nuorteva 1973) and Germany (Kock 1971).

The remains of insects in archaeological deposits are usually found dissociated into individual plates (sclerites) of the external chitinous armour (exoskeleton) (Fig. 8.1). A **fauna** is a term used to mean a group of insects found together in a deposit and defined by the numerical composition of the species,

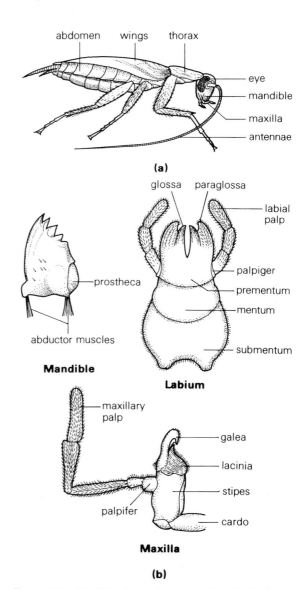

Figure 8.1 (a) Side view of male cockroach *Periplaneta americana* to show parts of the body; (b) cockroach mouth parts.

137

but a better term would be **thanatocoenosis** (death assemblage). The chitinous exoskeleton (cuticle) of many insects, especially the Coleoptera (beetles) is remarkably resistant to decay, and even the head, thoraces and elytra (Fig. 8.2) of beetles eaten by owls or foxes are still clearly recognizable in the animals droppings. Insect remains do not survive well in damp aerobic conditions but good insect assemblages may often be recovered from anaerobic (especially permanently waterlogged) deposits, often in conjunction with other types of palaeo-environmental information such as pollen grains (Section 4.1). Carbonized insect remains are also identifiable, in much the same manner as that already described for carbonized grain (Section 6.2) and dry, arid conditions will preserve both faunal and floral material (Zacher 1937, Burleigh & South-gate 1975). Occasionally, superficial calcification may also preserve insect remains from an unfavourable environment, as in the case from a 17th century drain at York (Buckland 1976a). By far the largest amount of archaeological work has been done in waterlogged deposits from wells, drains, gulleys, etc., although there is a growing body of data from totally waterlogged prehistoric sites in districts close to sea level, for example on the east coast where aggregation from a late-glacial low sea level has resulted in the widespread preservation of organic deposits over large areas.

The systematic collection and interpretation of insect faunas is, however, only a product of the last few years, and relatively little advantage has been taken of the many rich opportunities for multi-facetted interdisciplinary environmental reconstructions which have presented themselves in the past. However, the steadily increasing number of publications on the subject has tempted a few entomologists to work on archaeological material and some archaeologists to train themselves as entomologists, a state of affairs which augurs well for the future.

By far the commonest class of Arthropoda preserved are the beetles (Coleoptera), although flies (Diptera), Hymenoptera (ants and wasps) and Hemiptera (bugs) also occur. Spiders and mites are much less common (Koponen & Nuorteva 1973, Karppinen & Koponen 1974, Girling 1977), as are freshwater Crustacea such as *Daphnia* (Table 8.1). Three other important classes of arthropods which are common today but are rarely preserved are the woodlice (Isopoda), millipedes (Diplopoda) and centipedes (Chilopoda), because their exoskeletons are fragile. However, Girling (1979) has shown that although the exoskeletons do not survive unaltered they may be replaced by calcium carbonate, resulting in the identification of five species of woodlice together with three millipedes and a centipede from 11 different sites. The sites vary from Roman ditch

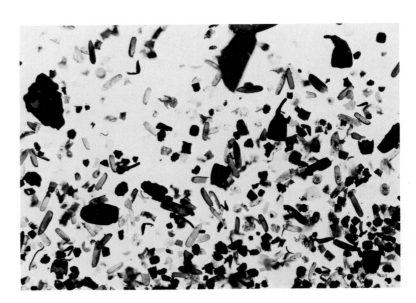

Figure 8.2 Appearance of an insect assemblage after paraffin flotation.

fills to the infall of Iron Age pits at the Chalk hillfort site of Winklebury, Hampshire (Smith 1977), and the author concludes that the examination of calcareous subsoils or calcified deposits on archaeological sites is an important potential source of information.

8.2 Field methods and sampling

As with all the other topics covered so far, a systematic and meticulous sampling procedure must be undertaken before any reliance may be placed on the interpretation of an assemblage. In peat and silt, sampling units separated by 50 mm are sufficient as at lesser intervals minor sedimentary structures and the reworking effects of any basal fauna act as contaminants. Since waterlogged deposits are notoriously difficult fields for archaeological interpretation, great care must be taken to avoid contamination, perhaps by unidentified intrusive features or minor chanelling. Modern insect contamination can also occur, and Buckland (1976b) quotes the example of the introduction of the species *Aridius bifasciatus* from Australasia, which arrived in Britain through trade.

Sample sizes vary with the nature of the deposit, but a good general policy is to let the analyst take his own samples or, if this is really not possible, for as much material as is practicable to be removed in well-sealed plastic bags. A late Bronze Age trackway on Thorne Moor (Yorkshire) produced several thousand individuals, whereas a 20 kg block of coarse fluviatile silt of the same age from the river Don yielded less than 100. At the other end of the scale, Hall and Kenward (1976) obtained very large samples of grain beetles from sediment samples only 5 g in size (p. 149). A sample size of around 5 kg is a reasonable general minimum. It need not be stated that the procedure already outlined for the sampling, labelling and storage of organic material must be followed with great care, bearing in mind that many of the insect parts are very small and extremely fragile.

Organically rich clays and silts vary considerably in the quantity of insect remains, depending on the rate and mode of deposition. Wells, cess pits and rubbish pits frequently produce very large quantities of material, the former being especially important in the interpretation of both regional and local conditions. Peats, if they have not dried, tend to be rich in insect remains, although they are often difficult to disaggregate. Fen peats tend to preserve insects better than acid peats as a result of the greater diversity of habitats offered.

The possibility that the deposits have been contaminated must always be borne in mind. Kenward (1975b, 1976c) suggests in a study of the blind colidiid beetle *Aglenus brunneus* (Gyllenhal) which occurs in Roman and medieval sites in York that specimens of the insect might enter deposits predating their lifetime by burrowing. One uniform layer on the Lloyds Bank site (Kenward 1976c), whose composition made it unsuitable for the breeding of *A. brunneus*, was cut into locally by a deposit of leather off-cuts in which the beetle was extremely abundant (32 individuals per kilogram of sample). A sample from below this intrusion still contained more than 10 times as many *A. brunneus* (13 individuals per kilogram) as a sample from another part of the layer (1 individual per kilogram). This indicates contamination.

8.3 Sample preparation

In biogenic sediments such as felted peat the material may be carefully split along the bedding planes and the insect remains picked out by hand using a low power lens and forceps. This is particularly useful as it enables associated remains of the same individual to be extracted, but there is a subjective bias towards the largest and most obvious insects. Buckland (1976b) recommends the following procedure for inorganic silts and sands as well as peats. It must, of course, be carried out under strict supervisory control.

(1) About 5 kg of sample is placed in a bowl and disaggregated by warm water or gently working the material with the fingers, splitting it along the bedding. Silts and clays often need soaking overnight in hot water and harder deposits need a deflocculant. Fairly dry sediments may be boiled in caustic soda, but very gently and using dilute solutions.

(2) The sample is then washed through a 300 μm (1.75 φ) sieve, which should retain all the insect remains together with plant debris.

(3) Larger objects, pottery, bones, stone and wood are removed, the latter being examined for evidence of insect borings.

(4) The residue on the sieve is drained of excess water and returned to the bowl. Paraffin (kerosene) is added, preferably with the bowl inside a fume cupboard and with all appropriate precautions (see Section 4.3) being taken. The paraffin is gently worked into the material.

(5) Surplus paraffin is drained off and warm water added so that large numbers of air bubbles are included. The paraffin, which is adsorbed on the insect fragments, assists them to float to the surface and separate off from inorganic and plant debris.

(6) After the sample has stood long enough for this separation to take place the flotant is tipped off into the sieve and washed, first with hot water and detergent and then with alcohol.

(7) Insect remains are stored in alcohol until they can be sorted under a binocular microscope.

Afterwards the float part of the sunken residue must be searched to check efficiency, since especially with fibrous peats it is not possible to obtain a good separation; sometimes the whole sample must be sorted. Great care is needed to recover all fragments lest the sample become seriously biased: the elytra of the larger beetles which are rather heavy tend to sink and this can result in a significant bias in the fauna recovered. After sorting the insect fragments (Fig. 8.2) are mounted with a water-soluble glue on card mounts, covered by microscope slides and sealed by thin metal frames. Some beetles will tend to 'curl', especially dung beetles which, with insect genitalia, wings and other fragile parts, have to be mounted in a more viscous medium which will maintain the shape of the object. Dimethylhydrantoin formaldehyde resin (DMHF) is the most effective, but Euparal is also suitable. Kenward (1974) elaborates and discusses this and alternative methods for removing and concentrating the fossils, avoiding contamination in sampling and processing and the storage and mounting of fossils using the card slides developed by Shotton (1970).

8.4 Identification

Insect identification cannot be learnt from books and one hour of tuition is worth many hours studying drawings. There are, however, a series of standard works on the subject, although the keys provided for use with the complete insects so lovingly collected by Victorian clergymen are often less efficacious with fragmentary material from archaeological deposits. Joy (1932) and the Handbooks for the Identification of British Insects (published by the Royal Entomological Society 1950 *et seq.*) are the most useful.

During the last 100 years insects such as butterflies and moths and also beetles have been intensively collected and studied by both amateur and professional entomologists and it is this information which enables palaeoenvironmental interpretation. Beetles are very specific in their requirements and many plant-feeding (phytophagous) beetles are frequently restricted to a single host, which may provide a very detailed picture of the background vegetation of an area. Many *Carabid* ground beetles are sensitive to the amount of shade at ground level and certain species will only be found on open ground exposed to the sun while others are typical of a woodland habitat. The dung beetles of the family *Scarabaeidae* are usually found in the droppings of large mammals and the presence of many of these suggests open grazing land (p. 151), especially when they are accompanied by beetles such as the *Elaterids*, whose larvae ('wireworms') are pests in pasture land today. Insect fossils may only be identified by comparison with reliably named collections of modern insects, and in Britain such a collection only occurs in the Department of Entomology, British Museum (Natural History). Even this collection is short of some rare and recently recognized species, so that their full range of variation cannot be appreciated. Determination is a matter for experts and some groups can be only named by someone specially well qualified to deal with them, as the differences separating the species are very subtle. Mounted insect remains are compared with named fragments until the closest match is found. The specimen is then compared with a long series of those species closest to it so that the ranges of variation of the parameters do not overlap. Some or all parts of many species are not diagnostic at the present stage of knowledge and can only be named to genus, subfamily or even family (p. 42). Often Diptera and Hymenoptera can be named only to superfamily, although further work will improve this state of affairs. A good binocular microscope giving magnification at ×100 is sufficient, although a transmitted light microscope at higher magnification of up to ×500 is sometimes needed for examination of genitalia.

Many insects hitherto quite common may now be very rare and not figure in modern collections, and at the Late Bronze Age site of Thorne Moor nearly 20% of the forest insects consisted of species with a very limited distribution in the present day. Some species may no longer be native to this country and others may have been introduced by trade since the Roman period. The majority of fragments recovered tend to be from Coleoptera. Wings of some Diptera (two winged flies), Trichoptera (caddis flies) and some Hymenoptera (bees, ichneumons, etc.) can be identified using the relevant keys, but there are many groups where wing venation is not diagnostic.

8.5 Processing of results

After identification the Coleoptera and Hemiptera are listed on standard sheets, tabulating for each species the number of sclerites of each kind (heads, thoraces, right and left elytra, other parts) or the presence of small fragments of particular sclerites. Other groups are listed under appropriate headings. Examples of data presentation and interpretation may be seen in Figure 8.4 and Table 8.1.

8.6 Factors affecting the composition of an insect assemblage

8.6.1 Influence of climate on insect distributions
Insect remains are probably the greatest potential source of information concerning minor climatic fluctuations. A large number of species have their northern or southern limits in the British Isles, in many cases around the level of Lincolnshire or Yorkshire. Many other species become very much rarer in northern England (Addyman *et al.* 1976).

The difference in mean July temperature between the areas where a species can be seen to be well established and its northern limits is often as little as one degree Celsius, so that relatively small climatic changes may cause comparatively great extensions or contractions of insect range. Coope *et al.* (1971) make a strong case for the argument that insects respond more rapidly to climatic events than plants.

8.6.2 Habitat changes in the interpretation of assemblages
About a dozen species of beetle whose northern limits are now south of Yorkshire have been found in early medieval deposits from York. At first sight this suggests that present day temperatures are lower than those in the 10th and 11th centuries, but this evidence needs scrutinizing with the greatest care. Several of the species are now rare and have scattered populations in southern England. These insects may be limited in the north by problems of colonization or be present as outliers of the main distribution which have been overlooked by collectors. Little is known of the exact distribution of most species and nothing at all of the pattern of distributional changes during the 'Little Ice Age'. It is suggested that many insects may not have recolonized the northern parts of their potential habitat ranges following this cold episode due to fragmentation and isolation.

Some other beetles recorded from medieval York, like the fen-dwelling *Dromius longiceps* (Dej.) now present only as far north as Lincolnshire (Lindroth 1974, Moore 1957) may have become extinct in Yorkshire as a result of the destruction of their habitats. Forest species may also be limited by ecological as well as climatic events (Buckland & Kenward 1973). Archaeological records based on single specimens may be of stray individuals, since insects may fly or be carried over considerable distances.

8.6.3 Influence of artificial habitats on insect distributions
The artificial habitats of the medieval urban environment may have permitted the occurrence of northern populations of species otherwise limited to warmer climates. The abundance of the beetle *Aglenus brunneus* (Gyll.) in medieval York and

Durham may have been due at least in part to deposits of rotting vegetation which are now absent. Since this is a wingless species, rare in the present day, it is probable that the vegetation assisted with problems of colonization, and that the beetle was accidentally transported by man from town to town. Decaying organic matter would have contributed to a higher temperature regime in the towns which favoured this and other species.

There is also an essential consistency in the insect groups which are found together, although there have been great changes in insect distributions. Even since the Bronze Age 11 species of beetle have been lost from British faunas (Osborne 1969, 1972, Buckland & Kenward 1973), although one species lasted until Roman times before it disappears from the record (Osborne 1974). The actual figure for Postglacial extinctions is probably much higher since so few sites have been studied, but species have been gained at a greater rate during the last two millenia, largely due to human importations (Hammond 1973).

8.6.4 Effect of local ecology on distributions

Many insect species are dependent on locally available ecological conditions which limit their ranges ecologically rather than climatically, examples already having been quoted by the factors involved in the changing distributions of *Aglenus brunneus* and *Xestobium rufivillosum*. Ecological information must be derived not from single species but from groups of species which are characteristic of a particular habitat. It may eventually be possible to distinguish these by their specific and numerical composition but currently this presents problems due to overlap of different habitats and lack of data.

Kenward (1975c) has shown that a test of the accuracy of reconstructions based on modern death assemblages may be misleading, if a direct proportional relationship of the abundance of a species to that of its habitat in the immediate surroundings is assumed. Some of the habitats indicated by the insect remains from a modern drain sump in an alleyway were absent from the surroundings, while the relative importance of some others was not accurately represented by the assemblage (Table 8.1). The abundance of Coleoptera and Heteroptera of various habitats in an assemblage from a modern drain sump, and the availability of the habitats in the immediate surroundings was also assumed.

8.6.5 Insects as a source of climatic information

Certain insects, which are of little interest to man and therefore not deliberately imported, probably present the best source of straight palaeoclimatic information. However, accidental transportation may occur, especially of stored-product insects or those associated with artefacts, such as the southern European longhorn beetle, *Hesperophanes fasciculatus*, recorded by Osborne (1971) from Alcester in Warwickshire, but this can normally be detected from the associated imported materials.

Insects are also sensitive indicators of climatic change even over a short period of time and may be used successfully to determine past climatic regimes. This is especially successful with pre-Neolithic faunas, but after the arrival of farming cultures many forest-dwelling species disappear due to man's interference with their habitat rather than a climatic change. Even minor subsequent variations of summer temperatures are indicated by the insect faunas.

The basic assumption for all reconstructions of past climates from insect remains is that the physiology and behaviour of any insect species has remained constant. Physiology leaves no easily investigated method of testing this hypothesis, and behaviour can be reconstructed only through such matters as larval borings in artefacts. There is good evidence for specific stability during the past few hundred millenia, and all the species examined by Kenward (1976b) appeared to have remained morphologically constant during that period. Such constancy extends to the male genitalia (a highly characteristic structure in many species), exemplified by those of the Hoxnian insects described by Shotton and Osborne (1965), and work on Tertiary insects has shown that some species remain morphologically constant for much longer (Matthews 1970, Gersdorff 1971).

The bug *Heterogaster urticae* (F.) provides good evidence for the existence of temperatures above those of the present day during Norman and early medieval times, since it is free of human influence. It is a phytophage (plant eater) using the stinging nettle *Urtica dioica* (L.) as its principal host (Southwood

Table 8.1 Number of species and specimens of insect in each of several habitat classes. Data from Kenward (1975c).

Ecological group	Number of species	specimens	Implications	Actual ecology
aquatic				
true aquatics	4	8	presence of this group suggests a deposit formed in quiet water, e.g. ditch, pond, water-filled pit	not a water body of this kind – sump water would not support or attract these species
at water margin	1	1		
on open ground	7	12	surrounding of open or sparsely vegetated ground; probably fairly dry, sunny, damper and shaded in places	small patches of habitat for some of these in yards but not in alleyway
at roots of low plants (i.e. often found amongst the matted stems and detritus at the base of herbs)	24	34	it is not feasible to divide this group into 'mainly' and 'sometimes' found in this situation; none are confined to it, but this group, with the following one, suggests a good cover of low plants in places	no extensive short plant community, only isolated plants
phytophagous				
true phytophages	15	28	indicate Ranunculaceae, Urticaceae, Cruciferae, Papilionaceae (probably disturbed ground weed flora) and Rosaceous shrubs	plants of these groups not at all abundant; very small numbers of *Capsella* (Cruciferae) in yards but no other members of these families recorded; some rose bushes
secondarily tied to plants by predation	5	12	indicate only the presence of living plants	a few suitable plants for these in yards
in rotting plant matter				
mostly in this habitat	8	38	abundance of species of decaying plant matter and those facultative to it indicates the presence of masses of compost-like material; possibly the deposit included some of this matter; such habitats are man-made	although small amounts of dead plant matter present, it is not abundant and none is close to the sump
able to exploit the habitat	27	58		
able to exploit this habitat, generically named	6	14		
in dung				
primarily in (herbivore) dung	4	4	all have been recorded in wet rotting vegetation (one only very exceptionally) but as a group suggest presence of herbivore dung	no dung of herbivores (or suitable wet rotting vegetable matter) present
able to exploit dung	8	21	lend weight to the above evidence but all also found in rotten plant matter	
in dead wood exclusively	4	22	strong indication of dry seasoned and slightly damp rotten wood near-by	moderate amounts of dry timber and mouldering wood within a few metres
able to exploit rotten wood	2	8	mouldering dead wood but both also able to utilize compost	
with man				
strongly synanthropic	2	6	taken as a group strongly suggest the area to be greatly influenced by the activities of man, and that buildings may be present; all the species have, however, been found in the wild in some circumstances; the whole fauna falls in this category, even the aquatics being characteristic of garden ponds	no natural habitats present in the entirely man-made landscape
often in direct association with man, in buildings	18	57		
often in direct association with man, in buildings, generically named	8	29		
often found in areas disturbed by man	whole fauna			

& Leston 1959) and is occasionally found on other related plants (Davies & Lawrence 1974). It prefers to live in open sunny nettlebeds, especially towards the northern limits of its range (Davies 1973). Nettle is very abundant in Britain (Greig-Smith 1948) and its seeds are also very commonly found in archaeological deposits (Godwin 1975). The bug is, however, only commonly found now in southern England, with just a few records from north of East Anglia and Lincolnshire and old, unconfirmed ones from Yorkshire and Cheshire (Southwood & Leston 1959, Massee 1955), being extremely rare north of Huntingdonshire where it is local and abundant when found (Davies 1973, 1975). *H. urticae* is common in medieval deposits which lie outside the modern range of the species, for example those from the Lloyd's Bank and Coppergate sites at York (Buckland *et al.* 1974) and must have been a common insect at that time. This suggests a change in distribution and abundance which can only be attributed to a climatic deterioration since early medieval times. This change cannot be a result of problems of colonization since the 'Little Ice Age' as the bug flies easily and its host plant is very common, and one can but conclude that early medieval temperatures were higher than those of the present day. Since the bug is fond of sunshine and in the present day is confined to a southern and eastern distribution, Addyman *et al.* (1976) suggest that the medieval climate may have been more continental.

Studies of urban insect assemblages provide much evidence about past climates but reliable data is only to be obtained from a systematic study of faunas from long time-spans and wide geographical areas. Such work is, of course, limited by the conditions necessary for the preservation of insect remains in the past and must include studies of natural assemblages, but it could provide a precise picture of gross climatic changes as well as smaller fluctuations such as annual weather patterns. Buckland (1975) discusses in detail the evidence for climatic change which can be adduced from the death watch beetle *Xestobium rufivillosum* (Deg.) and concludes that it was severely curtailed in the 16th and 17th centuries. He suggests that the modern infestations may have originated from natural relict populations but that it is possible that early medieval tempera-

tures were high enough for the beetle to disperse by flight; its existence in the northern parts of its range is now mainly due to man since it probably succumbed to the effect of the medieval 'Little Ice Age' in the wild.

8.6.6 *The detection of ancient habitats*

Climate is fundamentally uniform over large areas which grade into one another, so that a sample taken from a deposit which represents a short time-span will enclose insects subject to a single climatic regime but from many different habitats. To gain information of use to the archaeologist each of these habitats should be recognized and approximately quantified. The main problems are to determine the ecological requirements of the recorded species and to distinguish the insects from different habitats in the same assemblage, then to estimate the relative abundance and extent of each of the implied habitats and their distances from the deposit.

The actual depositional site will be portrayed in the fauna. Water-lain deposits will contain aquatic species which may identify the water as still or fast-flowing and also indicate the presence or absence of vegetation. Wells function as pit-fall traps while in use and contain fauna which live on the ground and wander in search of food. Middens and refuse heaps contain insect assemblages whose preference they are, but they also contain household materials attacked by insects, such as infested grain or skins which would have been thrown on the rubbish dump. Small items of furniture damaged by wood-boring species may also be present (Osborne 1971). This can give a good indication of the state of the premises and it may be possible to say whether the house was damp, whether the timbers were infested with fungus, what activity was being carried on and whether it was generally dark and dirty.

A species may not adequately define the place where it may be found as suitable microhabitats may occur in unexpected circumstances. This is illustrated by a consideration of the Colydiid beetle *Aglenus brunneus* (Gyllenhal) which is abundant in some archaeological deposits and has been discussed by Kenward (1975b, 1976c). An extensive literature exists, yet all that is surmised of the ecological requirements is that it likes damp organic matter and may be a fungus-feeder, probably needing

(a)

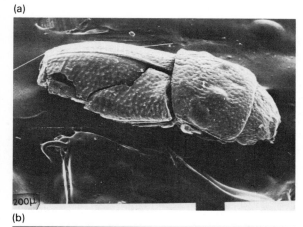

(b)

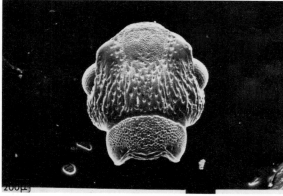

Figure 8.3 Scanning electron photomicrographs of (a) charred pronutra of *Aglenus brunneus* and (b) waterlogged preservation of *Anotylus rugosus*.

temperatures above those found in the open throughout the year in Britain. A similar state of ignorance may be found for the vast majority of insects occurring in archaeological assemblages.

8.6.7 The 'background' fauna

The analysis of insect 'death assemblages' is a well established but under-utilized technique. Coope (1970) reviews work on Pleistocene assemblages up to 1969, but subsequent research (e.g. Gaunt *et al*. 1972, Kenward 1976a) has given clearer indications of changing environmental conditions during the last and penultimate interglacials and the intensity of two ameliorations during the last (Devensian) glaciation (Morgan 1973, Girling 1974, Coope & Angus 1975). Although insect 'death assemblages' are a valuable source of evidence for past ecological

conditions, there are some serious potential sources of error. Often only a very limited amount of information can come from archaeological sites, particularly when isolated samples are being considered, instead of systematically collected samples related in space and time.

Kenward (1976b) suggests that each insect 'death assemblage' includes a transported component (which he calls 'background fauna') as well as the remains of insects derived from the immediate surroundings of the sampling locality. This 'background fauna' is principally derived from bird droppings and from airborne insects and may detract from the accuracy of the reconstruction of past ecological conditions. It may also be biased in favour of species from temporary habitats. The presence of a 'background fauna' may be indicated by such clues as a high proportion of a particular species or ecological group, suggesting that its habitat existed near to the deposit enclosing the fauna, although there may be exceptions. Attempts to recognize and compensate for the relative importance of a background fauna must take into account factors such as the alteration in the composition of such faunas with human changes in town and countryside.

The recognition and identification of the background assemblage is of the greatest importance in archaeology. Any exposed area receives a rain of insects, dead or alive, which may be exaggerated by the presence of some concentrating mechanism, for example a sediment receiving run-off water. The contribution from live insects will be larger if the sampling point was near upright objects (fences, buildings, etc.) which enhance settling to leeward (Lewis 1966). The relative tendency of the species to resume flight (or to avoid drowning if the deposit is aquatic) is also important. More insect corpses will be introduced by birds if there are suitable perches and sometimes where the local fauna is sparse the background fauna may totally alter the reconstructed character of an area (Table 8.1).

The frequency with which a species occurs in the background fauna will be determined by its abundance within the geographical region and by the number and distance from the deposit of suitable habitats, as well as by its flight activity and the behaviour of its predators. The background will be dominated by the local rather than the regional component and so controlled primarily by local ecological conditions. In Roman or Viking York, for example, the background insect rain would be different from that of the present day due to changes in the town and regional land use. How different the background fauna was can only be determined by the gradual accumulation of data on species behaviour, relative abundance in the past and perhaps by the examination of ancient deposits strategically chosen for their probable high background influence.

8.7 Palaeoecological reconstruction and the evidence for climatic change

8.7.1 Thorne Moor

At Thorne Moor (Buckland & Kenward 1973) the study of the palaeoecology of an area in southern Yorkshire revealed an exotic element in the Bronze Age insect fauna (c. 1100 BC) together with evidence for southerly restriction in the distribution of some British species. Thorne Moor is a remnant of a once extensive blanket bog where one site revealed on excavation part of a trackway constructed in the peat. This and an associated area of burnt trees represented a small temporary clearance in the mixed oak forest at 3090 ± 90 BP (Birm 336), preceding the main period of peat formation on the moor. The construction of the trackway was a response to the increasingly wet conditions which curtailed all previous agricultural activities in the area, and, like the early post-Roman flooding at York (p. 149), is likely to be a result of changes in the configuration of the mouth of the Humber, which increased the access of tides to the estuary, backed up the river outflow and caused flooding. The insect fauna includes non-British and southern English beetles such as Prostomis mandibularis (F.) (Table 8.1), which was associated with oak and is recorded as living in the extreme south of Sweden and in Europe south of the Baltic. A single thorax of Rhysodes sulcatus (F.) was found in an accumulation of silt, and this is a species of southerly distribution in Europe, the Caucasus and Anatolia. It has been previously recorded from Neolithic deposits as Shustoke in Warwickshire (Kelly & Osborne 1964).

Other equally thermophilous species were recovered from the same deposit and many species (Colydium elongatum (F.), Dryophthorus corticalis (Payk.), Hypulus quercinus (Quens.), Mesosa nubulosa (F.), Microlomalus parallelopioedus (Hbst.) and Platypus cylindricus F.)) do not now live as far north as Yorkshire and have clearly been restricted in their ranges since Bronze Age times. Five of the species from Thorne have now disappeared from the British fauna, including the dung beetle Aphodius quadriguttatus (Hbst.), which is recorded in the fauna from the Wilsford shaft at 3390 ± 90 BP (NPL 74) (Osborne 1969). The range restriction is probably a result of anthropogenic rather than climatic factors. The total disappearance of the type of dense woodland which once housed this fauna from Thorne from the area is also related to geomorphological factors. Many species dependent on mature forest would have been reduced to populations whose small size would make them liable to extinction by any minor climatic change, the isolation of each community precluding re-immigration. A good example of this is the beetle Teredus cylindricus (Ol.), which was abundant at Thorne and is now very rare, found only in parts of Sherwood and Windsor forests. This species, and many others like the Thorne insects which are associated with rotting wood, are now seriously endangered in Europe by the forest clearance which has steadily progressed since Neolithic times.

8.7.2 The Somerset Levels

The archaeology of the peats of the Somerset Levels, a project directed by John Coles, has also provided some interesting opportunities for interdisciplinary correlation using insect remains. The nature of the peaty deposits provide excellent preservation for wood (Coles 1975–80). During 1975 insect remains from a late Neolithic trackway, Abbot's Way (dated to c. 4000 BP), were sampled. Marked differences in successive beetle assemblages provided evidence for changing local ecological conditions before the construction of the trackway, and the presence in the lower part of the monolith of two beetle species, Oodes gracilis and Anthicus gracilis, now extinct in Britain, suggested a slightly warmer than present climate. Samples for beetle analysis (2 kg) were collected vertically at 50 mm intervals from freshly exposed peat face. The technique of extracting the remains varied with the peat composition, but in reed-dominated peat the extraction was straight-forward and followed that already described by Buckland (1976b). Pretreatment of samples dominated by *Eriophorum* (Table 8.2) was difficult as strands of the plant floated, impeding the paraffin extraction. In *Sphagnum* peat insects were generally extracted by microscopic examination of untreated material. Girling (1976) recorded the sample numbers, minimum total numbers of individuals of each taxon and environmental interpretation. The

Table 8.2 Summary of the major environmental changes based upon terrestrial and aquatic habitat requirements and host–plant preferences of successive beetle assemblages from the Abbot's Way. Radiocarbon ages based upon: (1) Coles and Coles (1975) (approximate average of quoted trackway dates) and (2) Dewar and Godwin (1963). From Girling (1976).

Depth	Sample	Environment	Vegetation	Aquatic conditions
5	1			
25	5	diverse acid bog fauna some dry habitats	Carex/Juncus Erica Polygonacea Eriophorum	
50	10	restricted fauna	Eriophorum dominated flora	numerous small stagnant acid pools with fluctuating levels
75	15	decaying vegetation habitats trackway 2030 BC (1)		
100	20	restricted fauna	Eriophorum dominated flora	
		aquatic fauna		flooding/local high level
125	25	increasingly acid bog fauna	Calluna Erica some Eriophorum	small peaty stagnant pools
150	30			
		rich mossy fauna	moss Cruciferae some Carex	small pools
175	35			
		(dry habitat species)		? flooding from high ground
200	40	mossy fauna		eutrophic pools
		reedy habitats		thickly vegetated eutrophic pools with clear areas providing open-water habitats
225	45	large numbers of decaying vegetation habitats especially reed refuse	Carex Typha	
250	50	reed bed		standing eutrophic water
275	55	Some species tolerant of brackish conditions	Phragmites Typha Carex	
285	57	species of wet clay habitats 3550 BC (2)	aquatic Umbellifcrae	thickly vegetated with reeds and lemna

base of the monolith yielded a beetle assemblage composed almost entirely of the reed-bed species *Dyschirius aeneus* and other Carabidae dominantly associated with reed situations. Several of the species tolerate salty conditions and one (*Bembidion fumigatum*) prefers salty coastal marshes. The whole fauna seems indicative of a brackish estuarine deposit, and is similar in many ways to the fauna from an early Postglacial deposit at Le Havre. Above this level there is continuing but decreasing evidence for reeds, and more beetles which lived in rotting vegetation. The aquatic fauna indicates pools of eutrophic water with some clear stretches amongst the vegetation. A distinct change is seen after sample 40 (Table 8.2), where a number of new taxa occur, including two dry land species (*Phyllopertha horticola* and *P. hemipterus*), although these may have been washed from higher ground. The many phytophagous species suggest the presence of moss and *Carex* (sedge), but from this mossy layer to the trackway the peat fauna becomes an increasingly important component of the vegetation and few phytophages appear in the fauna. The aquatic fauna is dominated by species which live in stagnant, peaty water (for example *Ilybius guttiger*). The insect fauna from the actual trackway to the peat surface becomes more diverse but is still an acid bog assemblage. Throughout the monolith there is evidence of woodland near the site, confirming that the clearances indicated by pollen analysis did not remove all tree cover. The wood-associated species do, however, form only a small element of the Abbot's Way fauna and suggest that the individuals were casual arrivals from surrounding woodlands or the smaller islands, rather than beetles living *in situ*. Faunas from the actual trackway show that it was built across an uneven acid peat bog, dominated florally by *Eriophorum* with peat tussocks and stagnant acid pools of water with fluctuating levels. Large numbers of insects lived in the accumulation of decaying vegetation recovered from the trackway level, but it is not possible to say whether they were contemporary with the track usage or arrived after the timbers had been overwhelmed by peat. At the trackway level the insect fauna suggests a climate similar to the present day and the more thermophilous species present in the lower levels have disappeared.

Further work on the Somerset Levels was carried out on Rowland's Track, a brushwood construction dated to 4210 ± 90 BP (HAR-1383), *c.* 2260 BC, in order to determine the environment at the time the trackway was in use and compare this with older peat levels from the site. Girling (1977) illustrates the peat stratigraphy of the beetle monolith taken through the trackway, together with scanning electron microscope photographs of some of the remains. The fauna resembled that from the raised bog deposits containing the Abbot's Way, although there is some evidence to suggest that Rowland's Track may have crossed a drier landscape. The proportion of water beetles (for example *Hyroporus tristis*, *H. melanarius* and *H. obscurus*) is lower and there is a decrease in the humification of the peat samples which probably reflects reduced water levels.

8.8 The identification of building use and food infestation

8.8.1 Alcester

This extensive Romano-British site contained habitation and industrial areas, including a pit full of leather scraps dated to the Antonine period (middle to late second century). One hundred and fifty pounds (68 kg) of highly organic mud were sampled from this pit, and leather, bone potsherds and large stones removed by sieving. The washed slurry yielded many insect remains which were tabulated by counting the number of the part that was most numerous, thus the figure represents the minimum number of individuals which must have been present (Fig. 8.4). Osborne (1971) gives a full species list which shows that the pit had contained refuse, almost all species present being found today in accumulations of decaying vegetable matter. A second component of the fauna does not come from refuse of the dung and/or compost habitat type, but these are often represented by one species only and are probably accidental occurences. However, the phytophagous families *Chrysomelidae* and *Curculionidae*, whose members are frequently attached to some specific host plant, give some clue to local vegetation. The surrounding vegetation seems to have consisted chiefly of open meadow land, which

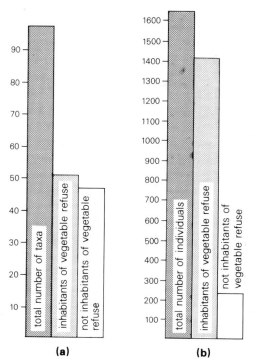

Figure 8.4 Insect fauna from the Roman well at Alcester (after Osborne 1971).

is confirmed by the insect remains. Several species (*Amphicyllus globus, Pediacus dermestoides, Endophloeus markovichianus, Cerylon histeroides*) all live in rotten wood but could have been brought to the site in a single log. The fauna also included wood-boring beetles such as *Anobium punctatum* (the furniture beetle) and the powder-post beetle *Lyctus fuscus*. Both species will attack dead wood and were found together at the Bronze Age site of Wilsford, Wiltshire (Osborne 1969). Near the refuse pit the remains of a large building with timber floor and joists and walls and roof supported on beams was contemporary with the leather-working factory and would have provided a habitat for these beetles. With a heavy infestation many of the dead beetles are to be found lying on the floor, where they would have been swept up with the leather off-cuts and other debris and thrown into the refuse pit. Osborne considers that one of the most interesting aspects of the fauna from this site was the number of species that were the pests of stored food, such as *Oryzaephilus surinamensis, Stegobium paniceum, Palorus subdepressus, Tenebrio obscurus* and *Sitophilus*

granarius (altogether 28 individuals). The most important numerically was *O. surinamensis*, the saw-toothed grain beetle, of which heads, pronota and elytra were found representing at least 20 individuals. This is a pest of starchy foods, especially cereal grains, and its modern habitat suggests that the Roman grain had been damaged to some extent by crude threshing methods and was probably stored without being thoroughly dried. The storage places were in all probability not kept scrupulously clean and need not have been heated during the winter months. Hitherto, in the absence of any definite evidence, it had been supposed that insect pests of stored deposits were spread round the world by modern commercial traffic, but those which favour stored cereal crops (apart from rice) were widespread even in Roman times.

8.8.2 *Egyptian lentil infestation*

Food offered in Egyptian funerary rites also suffered from insect depredations (Chadwick & Leeds 1972, Solomon 1965, Burleigh & Southgate 1975). During a recent search through samples of ancient food materials in the Department of Egyptian Antiquities at the British Museum, a quantity of lentils (*Lens culinaris*) showed evidence of infestation by Bruchidae (which today are well established in association with leguminous food material). The well-preserved remains of several adults were found, which proved to belong to a previously unknown species, together with egg cases attached to lentil testas, larvae preserved within seeds and fragments of tests with exit holes. There is no doubt that infestation by the Bruchidae took place either just prior to or very soon after the lentils were harvested, since only fresh undesiccated seed is prone to attack. The radiocarbon date for the sample (about whose provenance there was some doubt) was 2112 ± 48 BP (*c.* 162 BC) or a calendar date of 215 BC, thus assigning it to the early Ptolemaic period (BM-1139).

8.8.3 *Roman riverside warehouses at York*

In their study of the biological evidence for the usage of Roman riverside warehouses at York, Hall and Kenward (1976) noted one particular humic silt layer sealing a lower building, probably a warehouse. The silt deposit was remarkable for the high concentration of insect remains, contrasting markedly with grain-bearing samples from a later structure which seemed to have been a grain warehouse. It was necessary to examine the silt in small subsamples only 5 g in size, since the normal archaeological samples of 5–10 kg produced insects in impracticably large numbers. As the authors point out, this is not normally a problem encountered by those working on insects from archaeological deposits, indeed the reverse is generally true, but here each subsample contained the remains of approximately 500 beetles, a number comparable to that which might be expected from a full size sample and equivalent to a population of about 100 000 individuals per kilogram of deposit. The beetle fauna consisted almost entirely (over 99%) of grain pests, with *Oryzaephilus surinamensis* (L.), *Cryptolestes ferrugineus* (St.), *Palorus ratzeburgi* (Wiss.) and *Sitophilus granarius* (L.) the most abundant species. Some other insects, as well as false scorpions and mites, were also present, but such a community could only be found in an old grain residue. The lower structure in question, which had no function that was obvious from its archaeology, clearly served as a grain warehouse like its successor, and is dated to within the period AD 90–110. The insects must have destroyed a large quantity of grain and the existence of such a huge beetle population at a grain unloading point would have provided a source of infestation for all grain passing through. The excavators estimate that at least 10 million grain beetles occurred in extremely high densities throughout the excavation, and every granary or store receiving grain from this point would have become heavily infested. This high level of insect infestation would obviously have been evident to contemporaries, and the dumping of a layer of clay 400 mm thick over the remains of the lower warehouse seems to have been a deliberate attempt to ensure that no pests survived the dismantling to jeopardize the new structure. It was obviously successful since the level of infestation in the upper warehouse is low.

8.8.4 Insects as human food

Insects may occasionally be used as human food, but finding such information depends on human coprolites which are not well preserved in temperate climates. However, studies of coprolites from Peru and Mexico show that various insects and invertebrates had been eaten (Callen 1969). Macneish (1958) found the presence of plentiful remains of grasshoppers (wings and legs) in 11 prehistoric coprolites from the Sierra Madre in Mexico, together with the presence of *Drosophila* larvae and the pupae of at least three species indicating the consumption of overripe fruit. Parts of various bees, wasps, ants, spiders, beetles, mites and termites were also present, although the undamaged nature of the remains of the spiders and tenebrionid beetles suggests that they colonized the faeces after their deposition. The other insects and beetles which were in small fragments have almost certainly been eaten, and indeed the consumption of grasshoppers and locusts as a delicacy is by far from being confined to South America and is widely recorded from other parts of the world.

8.8.5 Insect fauna used as corroborative data

There are some sites where, although an insect assemblage may be recovered, the possibility of using it for detailed palaeoenvironmental reconstruction is precluded by small sample size. Such a case occurred in a late third millenium BC peat bed near the river Medina at New Shide Bridge (Isle of Wight), where a small collection of beetle and arthropod remains (Table 8.3) was recovered in addition to macroscopic floral remains, a pollen spectra and animal skeletal material (Shackley 1976). Mutually corroborative palaeoenvironmental information enabled a detailed profile of the ecology of the area to be assembled. The pollen spectra indicated pastoral activity and the animal bones included the remains of a domestic form of *Bos primigenius*, at a date of 4200 BP (225 BC) (Birm-360a and b). The peat had accumulated in an area of stagnant water, probably a small 'oxbow' lake separated from the main river channel, which accounts for the conflicting presence in the insect assemblages of the larvae of *Sialis* and species of *Daphnia* (which prefer very slow flowing or actually stagnant water) together with *Limnius*, which is usually found in running water. Members of the species *Aphodius* and *Megasternum* are usually associated with the dung of large herbivorous mammals (whose bones, including an early record of *Equus*

Table 8.3a Pollen analysis of segment W3, layer 7.

Species	No. of grains	Percentage of sample (%)
Alnus	535	62.57
Quercus	26	3.09
Salix	9	1.07
Rhamnus	4	0.47
Corylus	21	2.50
Ilex	14	1.66
Rumex	10	1.19
Artemisia	11	1.31
Plantago	16	1.90
Caryophyllaceae	12	1.43
Compositae lig	13	1.54
Umbelliferae	6	0.71
Ranunculaceae	6	0.71
Hedera helix	7	0.83
Gramineae	120	14.30
Athyrium type	16	1.90
Polypodium vulgare	3	0.35
Bryophyta	8	—
Varia	10	1.19

Total number of grains counted (excluding moss spores) = 839.

Table 8.3b Insect remains from the peat bed (layer 7), Newport, Isle of Wight.

Species	Preferred habitat
Coleoptera	
Dyschirius globosus (Hbst.)	—
Megasternum boletophagum (Marsh)	dung of large herbivorous mammals
Syntomium aeneum (Muell.)	open woodland
Phyllodrepa ioptera (Steph.)	—
Lathrobium sp.	—
Aleocharinae sp.	—
Amauronyx maerkeli (Aubé)	associated with ants
Bryaxis sp.	—
Limnius sp.	running water
Anobium sp.	dead wood
Helodidae sp.	—
Aphodius sp.	dung of large herbivorous mammals
Megaloptera	
Sialis sp.	larva in slowly flowing or stagnant water
Trichoptera	
indeterminate	
other arthropods	
species of Daphnia	include still water forms
species of mites	

sp.) occur in the same deposit. These animals presumably grazed on the local patches of cleared ground which the pollen evidence suggests were present in a general landscape of open woodland. Thus, although the primary source of palaeo-environmental evidence in this case is not the insect remains, they may be used as corroborative evidence for a picture assembled from other sources.

8.8.6 Coffin faunas

Stafford (1972) discusses the remains of beetles belonging to the species *Rhizophagus parrelocollis* from a fifteenth century burial where a body had been wrapped in layers of linen (possibly waxed) within a lead coffin. The subsequent puncturing and corrosion of the coffin had resulted in decomposition of the corpse, but the beetles could have entered any time after the burial was first made. Most of the insect remains (mainly fragments of wing case, head and thorax) were found under the head of the corpse, some in the hair. The absence of ectoparasites (Section 9.1) was surprising in view of medieval standards of hygiene, and it seems possible that they had been eaten by other insects. At least several hundred individuals were represented, and they had probably fed upon corpse decomposition products. The beetle, which is quite small (3.5–4 mm long) is sometimes called the 'graveyard beetle' for this reason and has been recorded from many burials, including a group from Saxony (Reinhard 1882). Insect remains of different types have been recovered from many burials and an extensive study of coffin fauna made by Mégnin (1894). Species include the beetle *Cerylon histeroides* from medieval burials of a woman and her separately-embalmed foetus at Wymondham Abbey (Norfolk) and an extensive faunal study was carried out by Motter (Stafford 1972) on over 100 bodies from Washington, DC, exhumed between 1896 and 1897. A beetle belonging to the same family as *Rhizophagus parellocollis* was common in this sample in bodies that had been interred for between two and six years, and it is suggested that such beetles entered the coffin soon after it first became perforated but not at the time of burial.

References

Addyman, P. V., J. S. R. Hood, H. K. Kenward, A. Macgregor and D. Williams 1976. Palaeoclimate in urban environmental archaeology at York, England: problems and potential. *Wld Arch.* **8**, 220–34.

Bell, A. 1922. On the Pleistocene and Later Tertiary British insects. *A. Rep. Yorks. phil. Soc.* 41–51.

Buckland, P. C. 1974. Archaeology and environment in York. *J. Arch. Sci.* **1**, 303–16.

Buckland, P. C. 1975. Synanthropy and the death watch: a discussion. *Naturalist, Hull* **75**, 37–42.

Buckland, P. C. 1976a. The environmental evidence from the Church Street Roman sewer system. In *The archaeology of York*. London: Council for British Archaeology.

Buckland, P. C. 1976b. The use of insect remains in the interpretation of archaeological environments. In *Geoarchaeology*, D. A. Davidson and M. L. Shackley (eds), 369–97. London: Duckworth.

Buckland, P. C. and H. K. Kenward 1973. Thorne Moor: a palaeoecological study of a Bronze-Age site. *Nature* **241**, 405–6.

Buckland, P. C., J. R. A. Greig and H. K. Kenward 1974. York: an early medieval site. *Antiquity* **48**, 25–33.

Burleigh, R. and B. J. Southgate 1975. Insect infestation of stored Egyptian lentils in antiquity. *J. Arch. Sci.* **2**, 391–2.

Callen, E. O. 1969. Diet as revealed by coprolites. In *Science in archaeology*, 2nd edn, D. Brothwell and E. Higgs (eds), 235–43. London: Thames and Hudson.

Chadwick, P. R. and F. F. Leeds 1972. Further specimens of stored products insects found in ancient Egyptian tombs. *J. Stored Prod. Res.* **8**, 83–6.

Coles, J. (ed.) 1975–80. *Somerset Levels papers 1–6*. Cambridge: Cambridge University Press.

Coles, J. M. and M. M. Coles 1975. Checklist of radiocarbon dates. In *Somerset Levels paper 1*, J. Coles (ed.), 54–5. Cambridge: Cambridge University Press.

Coope, G. R. 1959. A late Pleistocene insect fauna from Chelford, Cheshire. *Proc. R. Soc. B* **151**, 70–86.

Coope, G. R. 1967. The value of Quaternary insect faunas in the interpretation of ancient ecology and climate. In *Quaternary palaeoecology*, E. J. Cushing and H. E. Wright (eds), 359–80. New Haven: Yale University Press.

Coope, G. R. 1970. Interpretations of Quaternary insect fossils. *Ann. Rev. Ent.* **15**, 97–120.

Coope, G. R. and R. B. Angus 1975. An ecological study of a temperate interlude in the middle of the last glaciation, based on fossil Coleoptera from Isleworth, Middlesex. *J. Anim. Ecol.* **44**, 365–91.

Coope, G. R. and J. A. Brophy 1972. Late-glacial environmental changes indicated by a coleopteran succession from North Wales. *Boreas* **1**, 97–142.

Coope, G. R. and P. J. Osborne 1967. Report on coleopterous fauna of the Roman well at Barnsley Park, Gloucestershire. *Trans Bristol Gloucs Arch. Soc.* **86**, 84–7.

Coope, G. R., A. Morgan and P. J. Osborne 1971. Fossil Coleoptera as indicators of climatic fluctuations during the last glaciation in Britain. *Palaeogeogr. Palaeoclimatol. Palaeoecol.* **10**, 87–101.

Coope, G. R., F. W. Shotton and I. Strachen 1961. A late Pleistocene fauna and flora from Upton Warren, Worcestershire. *Phil. Trans R. Soc. B* **244**, 379–420.

Davis, B. N. K. 1973. The Hemiptera and Coleoptera of stinging nettle (*Urtica dioica* L.) in East Anglia. *J. Appl. Ecol.* **10**, 213–46.

Davis, B. N. K. 1975. The colonisation of isolated patches of nettles (*Urtica dioica* L.) by insects. *J. Appl. Ecol.* **12**, 1–14.

Davis, B. N. K. and C. E. Lawrence 1974. Insects collected from *Parietaria diffusa* Mert. and Koch and *Urtica urens* L. in Huntingdonshire, *Ent. Mon. Mag.* **109**, 252–4.

Dewar, H. S. L. and H. Godwin 1963. Archaeological discoveries in the raised bogs of the Somerset Levels, England. *Proc. Prehist. Soc.* **29**, 17–49.

Gaunt, G. D., G. R. Coope, P. J. Osborne and J. W. Frank 1972. *An interglacial deposit near Austerfield, southern Yorkshire*. Rep. no. 7214, Inst. Geol. Sci. London.

Gersdorff, E. 1971. Weitere Käfer (Coleoptera) aus dem Jungterhär Norddeutschlands. *Geol. Jb.* **88**, 629–70.

Girling, M. A. 1974. Evidence from Lincolnshire of the age and intensity of the Mid-Devensian temperate episode, *Nature* **250**, 270.

Girling, M. A. 1975. Fossil Coleoptera from the Somerset Levels: the Abbot's Way. In *Somerset Levels Papers 2*, by J. Coles *et al.*, 28–33. Cambridge: Cambridge University Press.

Girling, M. A. 1977. Fossil insect assemblages from Rowland's Track. In *Somerset Levels Papers 3*, by J. Coles *et al.*, 51–60. Cambridge: Cambridge University Press.

Girling, M. A. 1979. Calcium carbonate-replaced arthropods from archaeological deposits. *J. Arch. Sci.* **6**, 309–20.

Godwin, H. 1975. *History of the British flora: a basis for phytogeography*, 2nd edn. Cambridge: Cambridge University Press.

Greig-Smith, P., 1948. Biological flora of the British Isles: *Urtica dioica* L. *J. Ecol.* **36**, 343–55.

Hall, R. A. and H. K. Kenward 1976. Biological evidence for the usage of Roman riverside warehouses at York. *Britannia* **7**, 274–6.

Hammond, P. M. 1973. Changes in the British Coleopterous fauna. In *The changing flora and fauna of Britain*, Systematics Association Special Vol. 6, D. L. Hawksworth (ed.), 323–69. London: Academic Press.

Henriksen, K. L. 1933. Undersøgelser over Denmark-skånes Kvartaere Insektfauna. *Vidensk Meddr. dansk. naturh. Foren* **96**, 73–355.

Joy, N. H. 1932. *A practical handbook of British beetles.* London: Witherby.

Karppinen, E. and M. Koponen 1974. Further observations on subfossil remains of oribatids (Acar. Oribates) and insects in Piilonsno, a bog in southern Finland. *Acta ent. fen.* **40**, 172–5.

Kelly, M. and R. J. Osborne 1964. Two faunas from the alluvium at Shustoke, Warwickshire. *Proc. Linn. Soc. Lond.* **176**, 37–65.

Kenward, H. K. 1974. Methods for palaeoentomology on site and in the laboratory, *Sci. Arch.* **13**, 16–24.

Kenward, H. K. 1975a. Where there's muck, there's beetles. *Bull. York Arch. Trust* **2** (3), 25–31.

Kenward, H. K. 1975b. The biological and archaeological implications of the beetle *Aglenus brunneus* (Gyll.) in ancient faunas. *J. Arch. Sci.* **2**, 63–9.

Kenward, H. K. 1975c. Pitfalls in the environmental interpretation of insect death assemblages. *J. Arch. Sci.* **2**, 85–94.

Kenward, H. K. 1976a. The insect fauna of the interglacial deposits at Quinton, Birmingham. *Bull. Inst. Geol. Sci.*

Kenward, H. K. 1976b. Reconstructing ancient ecological conditions from insect remains; some problems and an experimental approach. *Ecol. Ent.* **1**, 7–17.

Kenward, H. K. 1976c. Further archaeological records of *Aglenus brunneus* (Gyll.) in Britain and Ireland including confirmation of its presence in the Roman period. *J. Arch. Sci.* **3**, 275–7.

Kock, K. 1971. Zur Untersuchung subfossiler Käferreste aus Römanzeitlichen und mittelalterlichen Ausgrabungen im Rheinland. In *Beiträge zur Archaeologie des Römischen Rheinlands II*, 373–448. Dusseldorf: Rheinland-Verlag.

Koponen, M. and M. Nuorteva 1973. Uber subfossile Waldinsekten aus dem Moor Piilonsno in Südfinnland. *Acta ent. fen.* **29**, 3–84.

Lewis, T. 1966. An analysis of components of wind affecting the accumulation of flying insects near artificial windbreaks. *Ann. Appl. Biol.* **58**, 365–70.

Lindroth, C. H. 1974. *Handbook for the identification of British insects*, Vol. IV (2), *Coleoptera, Carabidae*. London: Royal Entomological Society.

Lyell, A. H. 1911. Appendix on the insect remains. In Excavations at Caerwent, Monmouthshire on the site of a Romano-British city of Venta Silurum, in the years 1909 and 1910, T. Ashby, A. E. Hudd and F. King. *Archaeologia* **62**, 445–7.

Macneish, R. S. 1958. Preliminary archaeological investigations in the Sierra Leone Sierra de Tampaulipas, Mexico. *Trans Am. Phil. Soc.* **48** (6), 1–210.

Massee, A. M. 1955. The county distribution of the British Hemiptera – Heteroptera. *Ent. Mon. Mag.* **91**, 7–27.

Matthews, J. V. 1970. Two species of *Micropeplus* from the Pliocene of western Alaska with remarks on the evolution of Micropeplinae (Coleoptera: Staphylinidae). *Can. J. Zool.* **48**, 779–88.

Mégnin, P. 1894. *La faune des cadavres. Applications de l'entomologie à la médecine légale.* Paris.

Moore, B. P. 1957. The British Carabidae (Coleoptera). Part II. The county distribution of the species. *Ent. Gaz.* **8**, 171–80.

Morgan, A. 1973. Late Pleistocene environmental changes indicated by fossil insect faunas of the English Midlands. *Boreas* **2**, 173–212.

Osborne, P. J. 1965. The effect of forest clearance on the distribution of the British insect fauna. *Proc. XII int. Congr. Ent. London 1964*, 456–7.

Osborne, P. J. 1969. An insect fauna of late Bronze Age date from Wilsford, Wiltshire. *J. Anim. Ecol.* **38**, 555–66.

Osborne, P. J. 1971. An insect fauna from the Roman site at Alcester, Warwickshire. *Britannia* **2**, 156–65.

Osborne, P. J. 1972. Insect faunas of late Devensian and Flandrian age from Church Stretton, Shropshire. *Phil. Trans R. Soc. B* **263**, 327–67.

Osborne, P. J. 1973. Insects in archaeological deposits. *Sci. Arch.* **10**, 4–6.

Osborne, P. J. 1974. An insect assemblage of early Flandrian age from Lea Marston, Warwickshire, and its bearing on the contemporary climate and ecology. *Quatern. Res.* **4**, 471–86.

Osborne, P. J. 1976. Evidence from the insects of climatic variation during the Flandrian period: a preliminary note. *Wld Arch.* **8**, 150–8.

Reinhard, H. 1882. Beiträge zur Gräber-Fauna. *Verh. zool.-bot. Ges. Wien* **31**, 207–10.

Shackley, M. L. 1976. Palaeoenvironmental evidence from a late third millenium BC peat bed at New Shide Bridge, Isle of Wight. *J. Arch. Sci.* **3**, 385–9.

Shotton, F. W. 1970. Quaternary entomology. *Proc. Coventry Dist. Nat. Hist. Scient. Soc.* **4**, 101–9.

Shotton, F. W. and P. J. Osborne 1965. The fauna of the Hoxnian interglacial deposits of Necheus, Birmingham. *Phil. Trans R. Soc. B* **248**, 353–78.

Smith, K. 1977. The excavation of Winklebury Camp, Basingstoke, Hampshire. *Proc. Prehist. Soc.* **43**, 31–129.

Solomon, M. E. 1965. Archaeological records of stored pests: *Sitophilus granarius* L. (Coleoptera: Curculionidae) from an Egyptian pyramid tomb. *J. Stored Prod. Res.* **1**, 105–7.

Southwood, T. R. E. and D. Leston 1959. *Land and water bugs of the British Isles.* London: Warne.

Stafford, F., 1972. Insects of a medieval burial. *Sci. Archaeol.* **7**, 6–10.

Zacher, F. 1937. Verratsschädlinge und Vorratschutz, ihre Bedeutung für Volkersnährung und Weltwirtschaft. *Z. Hyg. Zool.* **29**, 1–11.

9 *Parasites*

So naturalists observe, a flea
Hath smaller fleas on him that prey;
And these have smaller fleas to bit'em;
And so proceed ad infinitum.

(Jonathan Swift, *On Poetry*)

9.1 Introduction

A parasite has been defined above as an organism which lives in or on another, from which it obtains its food. Unlike the previous chapters, which have concentrated on different classes of biological material, this chapter is concerned with a particular mode of existence, particularly important since so many parasites are pathogens (Section 2.1), whose effect on human and animal communities may be adverse, if not lethal. Plant parasites have already been described above (Section 2.3) and a full discussion of parasitic micro-organisms may be found in Chapter 2. Parasitism may be defined as a relationship between two organisms, generally of different species, in which one (the parasite) obtains advantages from its association with the other (the host) which as a result suffers some ill effects (Vines & Rees 1964). The condition of parasitism may take many forms and may be between one animal and another, one plant and another, a parasitic animal and a plant host, or between a bacterium or virus and either a plant or animal host. In many cases it is difficult to distinguish the parasite from an organism living in symbiosis, and a parasite does not necessarily live all its life in that condition. In many types of parasitic animal a free-living larval stage precedes the parasitic mode of life which the organism adopts as an adult (for example the hookworm in man). A poorly preserved trichurid or capillarid (whipworm) ova has recently been reported from a Roman burial at Poundsbury, Dorset, emphasizing the need for the closer examination of the gut areas of inhumations (Jones 1980).

Both internal (*endo*) parasites and external (*ecto*) parasites are of great interest in archaeological contexts, since they yield information concerning the range and antiquity of various pests and diseases in both animals and man. In many cases this is directly related to palaeoenvironmental conditions, extrapolation from present day parasites, hosts or vectors (carriers) being used to deduce past conditions. Many varieties of parasitic organism affect both animals and man, and some (for example *Moniliformis clarki*, the thorny-headed worm) are confined to a specific host. Some human viruses (Section 2.5) also have relatives which produce a specific disease in animals, and in any case the link between animals and man is often a very close one due to the endomorphic parasite requiring an animal vector.

Parasitic organisms may adapt to different animal hosts, such as the plague bacillus (Section 2.6) which is transmitted via the black rat (*Rattus rattus*) to man. Examples of more complex cycles may be seen in the development of malaria or yellow fever, the latter being passed to man from *Haemogogus* mosquitoes, which have collected it from certain species of monkey. The liver fluke (*Fasciola hepatica*) is another example, with a complex life cycle involving several hosts and vectors. It is clear that apart from their intrinsic use as indicators of past environments the identification of parasitic organisms is going to be of the greatest interest to the palaeopathologist. Unlike diseases such as leprosy, arthritis or tuberculosis, which leave traces on the skeletal material (Section 10.7.3), parasites are only identified if soft tissue or decayed tissue is present, or if they can be recovered from coprolite (fossil faeces). For the latter to be possible the faeces must have been buried in an environment which will preserve the contents, and generally this is one of extreme aridity. The faecal remains must then be rehydrated and their contents examined and identified, a laborious and odorous process. The examination of ancient faeces has, however, produced a splendid series of human parasites, particularly from various American sites.

The comparatively rare occasions when soft tissue has been preserved have given examples of human ectoparasites such as the head louse (*Pediculus humanus*) in mummified tissues or in tissues preserved in acid anaerobic groundwaters (Helbaek 1958). The volume of accumulated data is, however, relatively small. Wakefield and Dellinger (1936) reported on the diet of the Bluff Indians of the Ozark mountains of Arkansas and Missouri, working on the remains of mummies buried in flexed position in crude feather-down bags (the first duvets?) or under pieces of baskets. The commonest food remains were vegetable, especially the fruit of the sumac (*Rhus capallina*) and the remains of ground acorns from the black oak (*Quercus velutina*). Various small beetles had been ingested along with this food, together with some ants, lice and mites. Attempts were made to culture faecal material for micro-organisms, but none appeared.

The phylum *Nematoda* contains serious parasites of both domestic animals and man, including *Trichinella spiralis* (a small cylindrical worm) which infects the host when he eats meat containing viable cysts, the walls of which are digested in the intestine to release the young worms. Infected pork may contain as many as 80000 cysts per ounce of meat (~ 3000 cysts per gram), but since each female will produce over 1000 young, a mass infection of over 40000000 worms could occur from that amount of meat. Other nematode parasites of man which cause serious conditions are the hookworms (e.g. *Acyclostoma duodenale*) and threadworms (e.g. *Ascaris lumbricoides*). The liver fluke of the sheep, *Fasciola hepatica*, is also found in other mammals and occasionally in man (p. 158) and has a complex life cycle involving the water snail as an intermediate host, although man may be directly affected by drinking infected water. Other varieties of flukes may have very serious consequences, for example the blood flukes of the genus *Schistosoma* and the Chinese liver flukes *Clonorchis* (*Opisthorchis*) *sinensis*. Perhaps the most common of the parasites recognized in archaeological contexts are the tapeworms,

Taenia solium, the pork tapeworm, and *T. saginata*, the commoner beef tapeworm. The life history of the tapeworm is, inevitably, complex and involves intermediate hosts, but the physiological adaptation of the organism to a parasitic existence is particularly interesting. In a healthy human being the effect of a single tapeworm is never fatal, but will lower the resistance to other diseases and produces severe weight loss. The majority of mammalian species also harbour tapeworms, one of the commonest being *Dipylidium caninum* in which the primary host is the dog and the secondary host the dog flea. *Diphyllobothrium latum*, another tapeworm found in man, has two secondary hosts, the first a water flea and the second a freshwater fish.

9.2 Sample preparation

9.2.1 Mummified tissues

The term 'mummy', although theoretically limited to the products of Egyptian embalming mortuary practices, is also used for bodies preserved by other kinds of dehydration, either by intent or by chance circumstance. Sandison (1969) has provided a useful summary of the areas where mummified tissue is most common, and discussed the efficiency of the various techniques. Pioneering studies in the palaeopathology of mummified tissues were carried out by Ruffer (1921) using naked-eye and microscopic examination of various tissues softened by alcohol and sodium carbonate, and sectioned in paraffin wax. Studies of Basket-Maker Indians and Cliff-Dweller Indians have been undertaken using similar techniques, and also using weak solutions of formalin as a softening agent. The basic techniques became more elaborate involving softening of tissues by rehydration followed by conventional dehydration, then double-embedding in celloidin and paraffin for sectioning by microtome. Automatic tissue-processing machines speed up the process, and may also be used to cut large sections from bone. Routine staining methods, such as van Gieson, Mallory, Masson phosphotungstic acid haematoxylin, Heidenhain's iron haematoxylin, orcein, Verhoeff's and Weigert's elastica stains, are often valuable. The preparation of tissue slides involving rehydration followed by double embedding, outlined above and described in detail by Sandison (1969), must include decalcification if the material contains any bone. The blocks obtained are then embedded in paraffin and cut by any conventional microtome, resulting tissue sections being stained with a reagent which will differentiate between collagen and epithelia. Sections of tissue can show bacteria which have been present since the onset of putrefaction but which are checked by embalming. Ectoparasites such as larvae may sometimes be observed (p. 159), no doubt derived from eggs laid between the time of death and the wrapping of the body and which may continue to develop for some time after wrapping.

9.2.2 Coprolite

Analysis of faecal matter has a long history in medicine, admirably summarized by Fry (1976). The analysis of human and animal coprolite from archaeological sites offers a unique opportunity to study the remains of actual meals, giving information about diet, resource utilization, ecological adaptation, seasonality, palaeoclimate and behaviour patterns (p. 118) as well as about parasites. The disadvantage of coprolite study is primarily their restricted geographical distribution, confined to relatively arid conditions. Some difficulty is occasionally experienced in distinguishing animal from human coprolites. Specimen selection is the most arbitrary aspect of coprolite analysis, making conclusions about parasites one degree less reliable than studies made of mummified or dried tissues. Classification of coprolite is made from an examination of morphology, colour and visible contents, and human coprolite may be distinguished by its diverse contents and the fact that on rehydration it will turn the immersing fluid dark brown or black (Fry 1968, Callen & Cameron 1960). Control tests have shown that only human coprolite has this property. Most of the papers dealing with coprolite analysis seek to reconstruct diet as well as palaeoecology, treating any parasitic remains as part of a total ecosystem. Lists of relevant papers are given by Fry (1976) and Wilke and Hall (1975), but work on parasites in faeces must be traced back to the early papers of Jones (1910) on Egyptian coprolite and Young (1910), who examined archaeological coprolite from Salts Cave, Kentucky. Some of the most important parasitological analyses are described in the work of Callen and Cameron (1960), Samuels (1965), Pike (1967), Moore *et al.* (1969), Fry (1970a) and Fry and Moore (1969).

The earliest workers in the field of coprolite analysis examined their specimens dry, but Callen and Cameron (1955) used rehydration techniques involving an aqueous solution of trisodium phosphate, separating out wet components to make wet mounts on glass microscope slides. Heizer (1969) also used this method to separate the faecal components, which were then dried and separated using graded sieves, before identification and weighing. A variation on this method is the technique of Colyer and Osborne (1965) where graded sieves were combined with a lye solution for hydration, but the methods of Fry (1970a) are the most detailed. Before analysis Fry removes extraneous material such as rock fragments from the surface of the coprolite, which is then weighed, measured and described. For dietary analysis between 2.5–5.0 g of coprolite must be separated, weighed and rehydrated, the sieved components being weighed. For parasite analysis two methods of rehydration are used: that described by Samuels (1965), which involves a 2% solution of sodium hydroxide plus 0.5% EDTA, and that of Van Cleave and Ross (1947) (also used by Callen & Cameron (1960)), consisting of a 0.5% aqueous solution of trisodium phosphate (Fry & Hall 1969). The first method was observed to lead to the distortion of parasite eggs after 12 h and their disintegration after three days, but the second method reconstituted the parasite ova to their original shape and form with only slight distortion in a few eggs and no deterioration. Fry (1976) tested two concentration techniques: a modified zinc sulphate method and a modified formalin-ether technique which concentrated without distortion. He gives the following 'recipes'.

Trisodium phosphate rehydration of coprolite
(1) Place a small sample (the size of a pea) in a 15 ml tube.
(2) Add approx. 5 ml of a 0.5% solution of trisodium phosphate.
(3) Leave it for 24 h, covering to prevent contamination.
(4) Prepare a microslide.

Modified formalin–ether technique for rehydration

(1) Crush a small sample with a mortar and pestle and place it in a thick-bottomed 12 ml conical centrifuge tube.
(2) Add 10 ml of trisodium phosphate solution and leave it for 24 h.
(3) Centrifuge for 1 min at 2000–2500 rev min^{-1} and decant fluid.
(4) Add 10 ml of trisodium phosphate solution.
(5) Repeat (3).
(6) Add 10 ml of formalin, mix thoroughly and let it stand for 5 min.
(7) Add 3 ml of ether. Close the tube and shake vigorously, removing the stopper with care since pressure will build up during shaking.
(8) Centrifuge at 1500 rev min^{-1} for 1 min. Four layers should result.
(9) Free debris from tube sides and decant top three layers including plug of debris.
(10) Mix sediments with fluid that drains down the sides and prepare a microslide.

Preparation of slides

(1) Place one or two drops of sample on a 3 in × 1 in (76.2 mm × 25.4 mm) microslide.
(2) Add one drop of Lugal's iodine solution and stir until stain and sample are mixed.
(3) Add the coverslip. Examine the slide under microscope using the standard transverse scan. After examination those slides which are positive for parasite eggs should be sealed with Permount, although this is not effective for periods longer than 10 months. ×10 and ×40 lenses will be required, on a binocular microscope with a phototube.

9.3 Parasitic infections

9.3.1 Endoparasites

The work of Ruffer (1921) on Egyptian mummies laid the foundation stone for much of the later palaeopathological work on tissue with his identification of a case of schistosomiasis leading to later searches which identified *Entamoeba* (Szidat 1944), *Trichiuris trichiura* (Pizzi & Schenone 1954) and *Ascaris* in association with human remains. An identification of hookworm (*Ancylostoma duodenale*) in the small intestine of a pre-Columbian mummy from coastal southern Peru was made by Allison *et al.* (1974), the first recorded cases of this infection in the Americas prior to the advent of Europeans. Egg casings and casings with decaying larvae were also seen, and although the cause of death of the individual was not determined it was certainly not due to the hookworm, which would have produced illness but not death. Ruffer's (1921) method for histological examination of mummified tissues identified diseases such as pneumonia, renal abscesses and cirrhosis of the liver. He also recognized two cases which had clearly suffered from bilharzia, demonstrated by the presence of large numbers of calcified eggs of the fluke *Bilharzia haemotobia* among the straight tubules of the kidneys of two Twentieth Dynasty mummies.

Pizzi and Schenone (1954) and Pizzi (1957) studied the mummified frozen body of a young boy found in a stone structure at 18 000 ft (5500 m) in the Andes near Santiago, Chile. This seemed to be a human sacrifice, dating to just after the Spanish Conquest. The intestine contained ova of the whipworm *Trichiuris trichiura* and possible cysts of the *Entamoeba coli*. It had been thought that the whipworm was spread to America from the Old World, but recent studies suggest it was well established there in pre-Columbian times. Witenberg (1961) reports it in 1800-year-old coprolites from a Dead Sea cave, together with cysts of *Entamoeba histolytica*, *E. coli*, *Giardia lambila* and *Chilomastix mesnili* – all parasites found in modern Israeli populations.

Szidat (1944) studied the Dröbnitz girl (600 BC) and the Karwinden man (AD 500), bog bodies from East Prussia. Both contained eggs of the intestinal roundworm *Ascaris lumbricoides*, and the whipworm. The latter also contained possible eggs of the fish tapeworm *Bothriocephalus latus* (*Diphyllobothrium latum*) and a well-preserved body from Ch'angsha (China), described by Hall (1974), contained whipworms, pinworms and schistosomes.

Jansen and Over (1962) reported a long list of parasites in human faecal material from northwestern Germany from 100 BC to AD 500, including the common intestinal roundworm, whipworm, other *Trichuri*, either *T. ovis* or *T. globulosa*, *F. hepatica*, *T. solium* or *T. saginata*, and fish tapeworm. Other parasites found at the site included *Toxocara canis* and *Oxyuris equi*. They also investigated material from the first century Roman fort at Valkenbury-on-Rhine, Netherlands (Jansen & Over 1966), which also yielded whipworm ova, intestinal roundworm and *O. equi*. From this it would seem that human populations of north-western Europe in the first century AD were host to a wide variety of endoparasites. Medieval samples have yielded similar parasites, a bibliography of which is given by Gooch (1972).

An interesting discovery was made by Taylor (1955) on the site of a medieval pit at Winchester, Hants. The timber-lined pit (or tank) contained a greenish-grey peaty sediment some 8 ft (2.4 m) below ground surface, and an examination of the material (which proved to be faecal in origin) was made using techniques first developed for veterinary medicine. This revealed a quantity of nematode eggs, no less than 5700 per gram of *Trichuris trichura*, 600 of *Ascaris lumbricoides* and the presence of *Dicrocoelium dendriticum*. The eggs were exceptionally well preserved (a fact also noted by Szidat (1944)), showing the clear outlines of larval integuments with little indication of degenerative change. Both *Ascaris* and *Trichuris* are parasites of swine in the present day, suggesting that the deposit is of porcine origin. The presence of *Dicrocoelium dendriticum* in the pig is less likely, although it does occur in pigs in countries where they are very common. It was suggested that it was not impossible that the material was human in origin, and that the high concentration of parasite eggs could be explained by a latrine in use for many years, when the nonfermentable material had been destroyed in time. The large size and solid construction suggests a public building, and, moreover, one where food hygiene standards could best be described as lax. It is possible that the eggs of *Dicrocoelium* could be a result of pseudoparasitism, through man having eaten the livers of highly infected animals.

Pike and Biddle (1966) describe the sampling and analysis of another of the Winchester sites, a similar pit on Lower Brook Street and dating to the 11th century. The dark green-brown organic cess deposit examined was sampled and small subsamples washed, centrifuged and mixed with zinc sulphate solution so that the parasite eggs could be removed from the surface film and transferred to microscope slides. Very large numbers of eggs of the abovenamed species were found, an estimated concentration of 1400–3200 eggs per gram of deposit in the case of *Trichuris*, in association with seeds, pollen, spores and parts of arthropods. The pollen included the remains of the cornflower (*Centaura cyanus*), which is quite rare today, a point paralleled by the occurrence of *D. dendriticum* eggs, which are at present restricted to rather isolated parts of the British Isles.

A similar study was undertaken by Grzywiński (1961), who examined material from an 11th–13th century Slavic settlement at Opole Ostrówek, in Poland. Coprolites had been discovered in and around the cottages, some from ruminants and some that might have been produced either by pigs or dogs. Disintegration of the specimens was carried out with saline and potassium carbonate and the results showed high percentages of vegetable tissues together with pollen and fruits of *Setaria* and *Galium* sp. More interesting is the occurrence in four of the samples of the badly preserved eggs of *Fasciola hepatica* (liver fluke) but none of the other parasite eggs which were found so abundantly by Taylor (1955) or Pike and Biddle (1966).

The eggs of *Trichuris* were also identified by Helbaek (1969) in the intestinal duct of the Grauballe man. They would have caused an almost continuous stomach-ache, a condition which one cannot but suspect had been aggravated by his diet, seen to consist of sixty-six different plant species, only seven of which were cultivated, and many suffering from plant diseases such as ergot and smut (Section 2.3).

The analysis of 100 coprolites from Antelope House Pueblo site (Fry & Hall 1975) provides a splendid example of palaeoparasitology. Seven specimens were positive for *Enterobius vermicularis* (pinworm) which is a ubiquitous, exclusively human intestinal worm reported from various New World populations. It is one of the oldest of human parasites and essentially benign, causing nervousness and perianal itching. A 15% infection rate deduced from the coprolite indicates a probably higher actual rate of infection since in modern populations, with a 50–100% actual infection rate, direct faecal examination shows only a 5% infection.

Most of the inhabitants of Antelope House were infected, by person-to-person contact as eggs can be ingested or inhaled. Other small organisms present in the coprolite included nematodes and mites in egg, nymph and adult stages, but these were living as coprophageous species and would not have affected individual or community health.

A fluke egg was identified in a probably human coprolite recovered from a Glen Canyon (Utah, USA) site. Only one egg was identified in the 20 microscope slides from the coprolite, and it was not possible to determine its species. It most closely resembles an egg of the *Opisthorchis*, *Clonorchis* and *Heterophyes* genera, which requires two intermediate hosts, usually snails and fish. Humans will become infected by eating the intermediate host and the flukes may invade the biliary and pancreatic ducts or intestinal wall, becoming fatal in heavy infections. However, it is possible that this may be another case of false parasitism in which a man had ingested the raw viscera of the mammalian hosts, so that the infection passed harmlessly through his gut in a manner similar to that suggested for the Winchester site (p. 158).

At the Hogup cave, also in Utah, a broad parasitological study was made of 75 coprolites. Positive identification was made of the eggs of a thorny-headed worm from coprolites ranging in date from 6400 to 2000 BC. The life cycle of the species of *Acanthocephala* (thorny-headed worms) found in the area today (*Moniliformis clarki*) involves an insect host and a definitive rodent host (Fry 1970b), but the definitive host is not specific and may include man, who could have ingested the infected insects or possibly become a victim of false parasitism by eating the rodent host. The worm burrows into the intestinal wall and causes diarrhoea, weight loss, anaemia and often death. Of American children in major cities, 30–50% suffer from this worm today.

A much higher concentration of eggs occurred in coprolite from Danger Cave (Utah) where 11 ft (3.3 m) of cultural debris span 10 000 years with coprolite obtained from each level. Moore *et al.* (1969) describe the iodine and saline preparations of reconstituted coprolite which was examined for parasites like veterinary specimens, with a result that *Acanthocephala* eggs were also discovered. It is suggested that the intermediate host was the camel cricket, *Ceuthophilus utahensis*, and that the definitive host was mainly rodents, which are known to have been eaten whole (Steward 1933); it is certain that the intermediate host formed part of human diet. No record of infection with *Moniliformis clarki* exists, although there is a recorded experimental infection of a related species, *Moniliformis dubius*, which was cured by extracts of the male fern *Aspidium filixma*. Unlike parasitism by the more common helminths such as *Ascaris lumbricoides*, *Enterobius vermicularis* or *Trichuris trichuria*, infection by this worm probably greatly affected health and could sometimes be fatal.

The above examples illustrate the value of routine analysis for parasite ova, which will greatly enhance our knowledge of the disease patterns of early populations.

9.3.2 Ectoparasites

Ectoparasites are much less common than endoparasites but include the flea (*Pulex irritans*) and the louse (*Pediculus humanus*). The former is the commonest ectoparasite of birds and mammals and 1000 species are known, although beyond a certain amount of skin irritation it has little effect on health. The common flea of the black rat (*Rattus rattus*), *Xenopsylla cheopis*, transmits plague whose causative organism is a bacterium *Pasteurella pestis* (Section 2.6).

The exoskeleton of a louse (*P. humanus*) was reported by Fry (1976) from coprolite at a Palaeoindian site of Davis Kiva and a louse egg came attached to human hair from Danger Cave. Numerous other insects and ectoparasites from New World coprolites have been described by Samuels (1965), Callen (1969), Fry (1968) and Heizer and Napton (1969).

References

Allison, M. J., A. Pezzia, H. Ichiro and A. J. Gerszten 1974. A case of hookworm infestation in a Precolumbian American. *Am. J. Phys. Anthrop.* **41**, 103–6.

Callen, E. O. 1969. Diet as revealed by coprolites. In *Science in archaeology*, D. Brothwell and E. Higgs (eds), 235–44. London: Thames and Hudson.

Callen, E. O. and T. W. M. Cameron 1955. The diet and parasites of prehistoric Huaca Prieta Indians as determined by dried coprolites. *Proc. Trans R. Soc. Can.* **5**, 51–2.

Callen, E. O. and T. W. M. Cameron 1960. A prehistoric diet revealed in coprolites. *New Scient.* **8**, 35–40.

Colyer, M. and D. Osborne 1956. Screening soil and fecal samples for recovery of small specimens. *Soc. Am. Arch. Mem.* **19**, 186–92.

Fry, G. F. 1968. *Prehistoric diet at Danger Cave, Utah: as determined by the analysis of coprolites.* MA thesis, Department of Anthropology, University of Utah.

Fry, G. F. 1970a. *Prehistoric human ecology in Utah, based on the analysis of coprolites.* Ph.D. dissertation, Department of Anthropology, University of Utah.

Fry, G. F. 1970b. Appendix III: Preliminary analysis of the Hogup Cave coprolites. In *Hogup Cave*, by C. M. Aikens. Univ. Utah Anthrop. Pap. no. 93.

Fry, G. F. 1976. *Analysis of prehistoric coprolites from Utah.* Univ. Utah Anthrop. Pap. no. 97.

Fry, G. F. and H. J. Hall 1969. Parasitological examination of prehistoric human coprolites from Utah. *Proc. Utah Acad. Sci. Art Letters* **46**, 102–5.

Fry, G. F. and H. J. Hall 1975. Human coprolites from Antelope House: preliminary analysis. *Kiva* **41**, 87–96.

Fry, G. F. and J. G. Moore 1969. *Enterobius vermicularis:* 10,000-year-old human infection. *Science* **166**, 1620.

Gooch, P. S. 1972. *Helminths in archaeological and prehistoric deposits*, Annotated Bibliography no. 9. St Albans: Commonwealth Institute of Helminthology.

Grzywiński, L. 1961. Analysis of faeces from the Middle Age period, *Zool. Pol.* **10**, 195–9.

Hall, A. J. 1974. A lady from China's past. *Nat. Geog. Mag.* **145**, 660–8.

Heizer, R. F. 1969. The anthropology of prehistoric Great Basin human coprolites. In *Science in archaeology*, 2nd edn, D. Brothwell and E. Higgs (eds), 244–51. London: Thames and Hudson.

Heizer, R. F. and L. K. Napton 1969. Biological and cultural evidence from prehistoric human coprolites. *Science* **165**, 563–8.

Helbaek, H. 1958. The last meal of Grauballe Man, *Kuml* 83–116.

Helbaek, H. 1969. Palaeo-ethnobotany. In *Science in Archaeology*, 2nd edn, D. Brothwell and E. Higgs (eds), 206–14. London: Thames and Hudson.

Jansen, J. Jr and H. J. Over 1962. Het voorkomen van Parasieten in Terpmateriaal uit Noordwest Duitsland. *Tijds. Diergeneesk* **87**, 1377–9.

Jansen, J. Jr and H. J. Over 1966. Observations on helminth infections in a Roman army camp. *Proc. int. Congr. Parasitol.* **II**, 791.

Jones, F. W. 1910. Mode of burial and treatment of the body. In *Report on the human remains*, G. E. Smith and F. W. Jones, 181–220. Cairo: National Printing Department.

Jones, A. 1980. Palaeoethnoparasitology. *Assoc. Environ. Arch. Newsletter* **3**, 5.

Moore, J. G., G. F. Fry and E. Englert Jr 1969. Thorny-headed worm infection in North American prehistoric man. *Science* **163**, 1324–5.

Pike, A. W. 1967. The recovery of parasite eggs from ancient cesspit and latrine deposits: an approach to the study of early parasite infections. In *Diseases in antiquity*, D. Brothwell and A. T. Sandison (eds), 184–8. Springfield, Ill.: Charles C. Thomas.

Pike, A. W. and M. Biddle 1966. Parasite eggs in medieval Winchester. *Antiquity* **40**, 293–6.

Pizzi, T. 1957. Estudio parasitologica. In *La mia del cerro el plomo*, G. Mostny (ed.), 22–3. Boln Mus. Nac. Hist. Nat. Chile **27** (1).

Pizzi, T. and H. Schenone 1954. Hallazho de Huevos de *Trichuris trichiura* en contenido intestinal de un Cuerpo Arqueológico incaico, *Boln Chil. Parasit.* **9** (3), 73–5.

Ruffer, M. A. 1921. *Studies in the paleopathology of Egypt.* Chicago.

Samuels, R. 1965. Parasitological studies of long-dried fecal samples. *Soc. Am. Archeol. Mem.* **19**, 175–9.

Sandison, A. T. 1969. The study of mummified and dried human tissues. In *Science in archaeology*, 2nd edn, D. Brothwell and E. Higgs (eds), 490–502. London: Thames and Hudson.

Steward, J. H. 1933. *Ethnography of the Owen's Valley Paiute.* Univ. Calif. Publs Am. Arch. Ethnol. **33** (3).

Szidat, L. 1944. Uber die Erhaltungsfähigkeit von Helmintheneiern in Vor- und Frühgeschichtlicken Moorleichen. *Z. Parasit Kde.* **13**, 265–74.

Taylor, E. L. 1955. Parasitic helminths in mediaeval remains, *Vet. Rec.* **67** (12), 216–8.

Van Cleave, H. J. and J. A. Ross 1947. A method for reclaiming dried zoological specimens. *Science* **105**, 318.

Vines, A. E. and N. Rees 1964. *Plant and animal biology*, Vol. I 2nd edn. London: Pitman.

Wakefield, E. G. and S. C. Dellinger 1936. Diet of the bluff dwellers of the Ozark Mountains and its skeletal effects. *Ann. Internal Med.* **9**, 1412–18.

Wilke, P. J. and H. J. Hall 1975. *Analysis of ancient faeces: a discussion and annotated bibliography.* Berkeley: University of California Department of Anthropology.

Witenberg, G. 1961. Human parasites in archaeological findings. *Bull. Israel Explor. Soc.* **25**, 86.

Young, B. H. 1910. *The prehistoric men of Kentucky.* Filson Club Publication no. 25.

10 *Animal bones*

*All animals are equal but some
animals are more equal than others.*

(George Orwell, *Animal Farm*)

10.1 Introduction

Archaeozoology is now the best-known branch of
environmental archaeology for several reasons; it is
the oldest, bones are a comparatively easily seen
component of excavated material and their value is
more readily apparent to the excavator than that, for
example, of insect remains. General Pitt Rivers was
one of the earliest excavators to appreciate the value
of animal bones and, as in many other things, his
achievements remained unsurpassed for some time.
The majority of archaeozoologists are zoologists
attached to university departments or to museums
who are unlikely to be available for fieldwork at all
seasons and whose research times will in most cases
be severely limited. Frequently several zoologists
specializing in different fields will be required for
the material from one site, presenting occasional
difficulties in correlating results and problems in
integrating work programmes. Bone studies are
expensive because the amount of material involved
is often very great, but the statistical probability of
finding bone at any site is much higher than for any
other category of organic material. An international
committee on archaeozoology was set up in 1971 and
some of its work may be seen in the collection of
papers edited by Clason (1975). Much of the
pioneering work on archaeozoology was done in
Germany and various detailed reports were produced, including the classic study of fauna from the
Iron Age *oppidum* of Manching (Boessneck *et al*.
1971). After a period of 'appendix' faunal reports,
attention is now being directed to the important
Roman and post-Roman sites which have previously
been neglected on the premise that historical sites
should be able to provide the answers to such
questions as matters of diet from documentary
sources. Platt (1974) expressed this widely held

delusion when he said, 'Bones and other environmental evidence will seldom have the same value on
a medieval or an early modern site as they might
have if found in a prehistoric context'. The growth
of interest in archaeozoology coincided with the
development of intensive rescue excavation and just
preceded the various financial crises. The recovery
and processing of bones is, unfortunately, a slow and
expensive process.

Two kinds of reports tend to appear, the specialized studies of particular aspects of the fauna and the
site reports on small samples. The lack of complete
faunal reports on major British sites is quite striking
and directly related to the sheer quantity of material
available and the time needed to process it. A few
exceptions to this do occur, for example, the
Porchester Castle report on some 20 000 bone fragments (Grant 1975, 1976) and the Melbourne Street
(Southampton) report (Bourdillon & Coy 1980).
Reports shortly to be published from other important urban centres include London and Winchester but at present the Exeter report (75 000 fragments) from 1971–75 excavations at a major pro-
vincial centre, is the largest British archaeozoological report available. One difficulty in dealing
with such quantities of material is the mode of
publication. The Exeter faunal report is a monograph in its own right, separated from the archaeological reports, and other innovations in publishing
include the listing of 'specialist' environmental and
other data on microfiche which accompanies a main
report, conforming to the recommendations of the
Frere Committee (e.g. Williams 1979).

The rapid growth of faunal studies has resulted in
the development of a large number of (frequently
conflicting) methodologies but little standardization. There is no established way of completing a
bone report, just some general trends. A good intro-

duction is provided by Coy (1978), and Cornwall (1956), Chaplin (1971), Payne (1972b), and Ryder (1968) give the best reviews. The collection of papers edited by Clason (1975), ranging from sampling problems to specific case studies, provides a good overview of the field. Bone studies require pre-excavation consultation supplemented (ideally) by a full-time on-site specialist to deal with problems of sampling and difficult interpretations (for example animal burials) and to compile the raw data for the bone report at the same time as the excavation. This is especially desirable since such work is time-consuming and expensive if carried out as part of a post-excavation project; moreover, the specialist is faced with the material out of context. Each specialist will have different requirements for site collection and sampling and each site will produce its own set of difficulties concerning preservation and interpretation, in addition to the usual ones of sampling and recording. If, for example, work is being carried out at some exotic location in Asia or Central Africa, the acquisition of the necessary reference material for the identification of the bones may be difficult. Archaeozoological work requires thoughtful sampling and identification, necessitating reference specimens, keys, comparative data and perhaps statistical assistance. The most usual topics on which bones may provide information can be divided into two main groups: economic and environmental. In the former group the raw data of bone types and animal species present may be used to estimate relative proportions of the major species, the number of animals present, their heights, and their age and sex ratios. These in turn provide information on ancient husbandry practices, hunting and herding. Butchery techniques, the history of domestication and the investigation of animal palaeopathology may also fall within the frame of reference, together with general information on diet and other economic uses of animals.

10.2 Bone growth and classification

The majority of archaeozoological studies are concerned with the analysis of bone shape and size, and it is therefore necessary to understand both the way in which a bone grows and the type of processes which may affect this growth. The skeleton of a vertebrate is on the inside (an *endo*skeleton), acting as a frame and a support for all the soft tissues, in contrast to the exterior (*exo*skeleton) of molluscs. Some simple vertebrates possess both kinds. The different bones of the skeleton have numerous functions which can be placed in four main groups: to *support* the soft tissue, to provide *attachments* for muscles, ligaments and tendons, to *protect* the internal organs and to *store and release minerals* such as calcium and phosphate (Chaplin 1971).

Bones may be divided into four broad shape classes which are also related to these functions, firstly *long* bones (Fig. 10.1) found in the limbs and primarily supportive in function. There are two different processes of ossification (bone growth): from fibrous tissue (intramembranous) and from cartilage (endochondral). A long bone grows by the latter method with three primary centres of ossification at the shaft (diaphysis) and the two ends of the bone (epiphyses, Fig. 10.2). During growth the shaft is separated from the ends by unossified growing cartilage and the epiphyses fuse at a known age in each species – important when estimating age of death. Growth is completed soon after both epiphyses are joined to the shaft, but as the animal grows older the bones may be modified by, for example, a fracture, when the break is repaired by very rapid but irregular bone growth in wild animals where the break is not set. Changes in the metabolism of the animal as a result of illness, diet or pregnancy also affect the bone composition but less information is available on them. *Flat* bones (such as the cranium, ribs and pelvis (Fig. 10.1)) are primarily protective but are also important for muscle attachments. *Compact* bones are usually small and sub-rectangular, such as the metacarpals and metapoidals and other bones of the wrist and ankle joints (Fig. 10.1), which provide attachments for tendons and also dissipate stresses. They are quite similar in composition to the long bones, made internally of spongy tissue covered by more compact bone. In flat bones this form is varied according to their location and function. The fourth category comprises the *vertebrae* which combine elements from all the other groups. The central neural canal of the vertebrae contains the spinal cord and is protected by a neural arch (Fig. 10.3). The centrum is

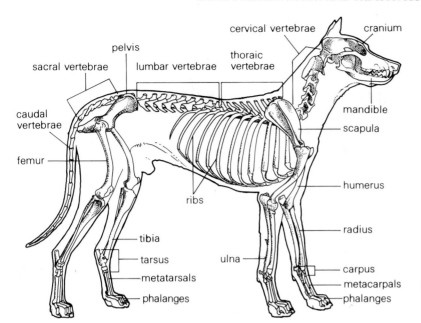

Figure 10.1   Skeleton of a dog (*Canis familiaris*).

solid to resist compression, and the spines and wings provide attachments for the myriad muscles and tendons of the back. The central (medullary) cavity and the interstices of the spongy network of bone at the ends are filled by marrow or fat in adult bones, and the marrow cavity is lined by an osteogenic (bone-forming) membrane called the *endosteum*. Externally the bone is covered by a similar membrane, the *periosteum*, except over the joint surfaces which are covered in cartilage.

The composition and morphology of bones does, of course, vary during the life of the animal in relation to external factors. American experiments with weightlessness related to space travel provided an extreme example of this, the beginning of bone resorption, together with partial atrophy of the cartilage and ligaments. The greatest changes take place during the initial development of bone and teeth and are especially important for archaeologists since they may be used to answer one of the most commonly posed archaeozoological questions, that of the age distribution of a fauna. This may be of the greatest importance when estimating, for example, the available meat weight and its consequent implications for economy and dietary patterning. Teeth are especially useful in calculating animal ages and they are very resistant to decay.

10.3   Bone preservation and taphonomy

The remarks made on p. 127 concerning the difference between death and subfossil assemblages have equal relevance when considering bone material. Bones are perhaps easier to deal with since they are on the whole larger and more resistant to chemical and physical decay than, for example, invertebrates. On the other hand, assemblages of mollusc shells are subject to different kinds of bias; the structure of the assemblage is not affected by the possibility that the animal may have functioned as an important food source but is more influenced by microenvironmental and sampling errors.

After a bone has been buried various processes will affect its composition and appearance. These include burning and decalcification, the latter leaving the shape unchanged but altering the consistency. Fresh bone has an active inorganic mineral component, a passive inorganic component and an organic fraction. The collagen of the organic fraction is quite resistant to decay and even after all the bone shape has vanished may remain in the sediment matrix as residual proteins, detectable by amino acid analysis (Garlick 1969). It is sometimes possible to get cases where the bone collagen is preserved but no minerals, and if these are dried out they will split and crack. The inorganic fraction of the bone decays in different ways related to bone composition and the characteristics of the surrounding matrix (Section 1.2) and bones may pass through many stages before vanishing completely under the action of various weathering agents, perhaps with an intervening stage of a soil silhouette representing concentrations of various mineral components of the bone marking the original position of a skeleton (Fig. 1.20). The decay of bone material has recently been discussed by Binford and Bertram (1977) with especial reference to attrition, erosion and weathering, and Isaac (1967) undertook experiments to observe the differential weathering of parts of the same skeleton which varies even under identical conditions. Survival also depends on the physical and chemical properties of the bone and of the depositional environment. It may be related to anthropogenic factors, such as cooking which makes the bone more friable. The bones of different species are treated differently by man, producing bias in samples. For example, sheep and pig joints are usually bought today on the bone, whereas beef is bought without. This is related both to the size of the household and the price of the meat. The uncooked long bones of large animals buried in alkaline sediments have, therefore, optimum chances of survival and retrieval. The corollary to this statement would be to say that minimum chances must be the lot of fragile bird bones or rib fragments of small mammals in acid sediments. They will be under-represented, producing a misleading idea of diet as a result of differential preservation.

Taphonomy is the systematic study of death assemblages. Since there may be considerable differences between the animals represented in a subfossil assemblage, a death assemblage and the original living parent community, it is important to

Figure 10.2 Stages in the epiphyseal fusion of long bones.

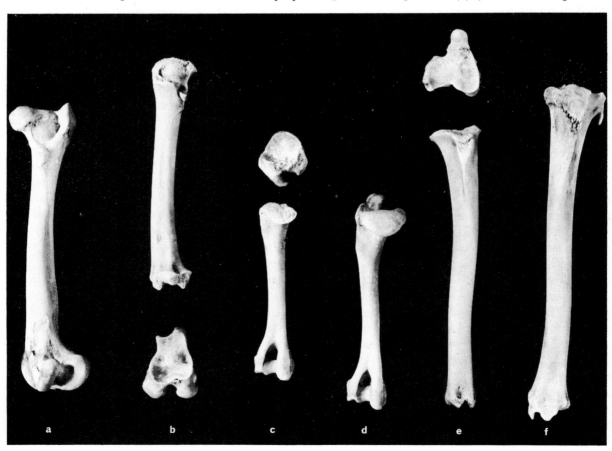

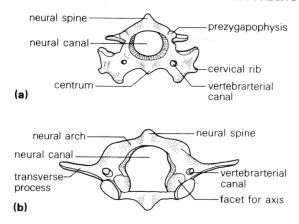

neural spine

neural canal

centrum

prezygapophysis

cervical rib

vertebrarterial canal

(a)

neural arch

neural canal

transverse process

neural spine

vertebrarterial canal

facet for axis

(b)

Figure 10.3 Cervical vertebrae of rabbit: (a) dorsal view of atlas; (b) posterior view of atlas.

know what processes operated to produce the extant available assemblage – the distortion which occurs during the passage of remains 'from the biosphere to the lithosphere'. What processes resulted in the available assemblage? How did each bone reach the find spot? It is clearly impossible to answer such questions for each individual bone, but it is necessary to study the processes which produced the assemblage, the nature of the animal communities which have contributed and the kinds of environment in which those communities lived. Most taphonomic work has been done on Pleistocene deposits, summarized by Behrensmayer (1975, Behrensmayer & Hill 1980), but very recently interest has turned towards later sites, although little is yet published. In most cases it is possible to recognize the various bone collecting agencies, but these become more complex with more advanced societies and as the number of introduced variables also increases.

A very early piece of taphonomic work was undertaken by Lubbock (1865) who reported disparities in the relative representation of skeletal parts on Danish kitchen-midden sites, related to gnawing by dogs and with a correlation between durable bones and bone parts with early ossification during growth. Brain (1969) undertook a detailed analysis of Hottentot bone refuse to assist in cultural interpretation and Lee (1965) discussed the contents and features of abandoned bushmen camps with the object of relating cultural debris to known life patterns. Isaac (1967), in a paper looking at

Acheulean sites in Kenya, reconstructed the processes which disperse bone debris from an initial area of concentration, and the proportional representation of skeletal parts in bone assemblages which have accumulated under known and monitored sets of conditions. The 'classic' paper dealing with the problems presented by bone taphonomy in Pleistocene caves is that of Brain (1976), which also includes an extensive bibliography. The number of bone accumulating agents in such contexts is formidable: the activities of early man, carnivores and porcupine accumulations, together with death by falling into the cave system and the arrival of bones via gravity or hillwash. The contribution of the hyaena to bone assemblages is an especially controversial matter, discussed, for example, by Sutcliffe (1970).

A first step in the analysis of a bone assemblage is therefore to distinguish those species which may act as environmental indicators from those whose representation is primarily biased by anthropogenic and/or economic considerations. One must determine, in the case of environmental indicators, what kinds of environments they suggest (using modern analogy). Unfortunately, however, the proportion of palaeoenvironmental indicator species will have been biased by preferential inclusion or survival caused by many factors (species death rate, mode of death, type and rate of sedimentation, geomorphology of the area, etc.) and the estimates can be corrected for this where necessary, working from control data obtained from taphonomic studies. The necessary weightings are extremely difficult to calculate (and for this reason very seldom undertaken) due to the complexity of factors operating on any death assemblage. It is, however, important to allow for them as if this is not done the zoologist runs the risk of misinterpretation.

10.4 Recording and sampling

The value of any analysis depends on the quality of the sample on which it was based. Normal excavation provides a misleading and biased sample of ecofacts which will already have been affected by differential preservation and other taphonomic factors. Payne (1972a, 1975) considers unsieved faunal samples and points out their bias in favour of large mammals, although of course this varies with the standards of preservation and excavation. At Dorestad a wet sieving experiment was carried out by Clason and Prummel (1971) which produced large quantities of fish, bird and small mammal bone, whereas unsieved material from the same site had a very strong bias towards the larger mammals, favouring cattle and horse bones at the expense of those of pigs, sheep and goats. In urban conditions it is frequently impossible to sieve all (if any) of the sediments and a flexible approach with an intelligent sampling strategy and selective sieving is required. Sampling problems in towns include the need to allow for different occupation areas (industry, markets, dwellings, public buildings, etc.), each of which will provide different types of assemblage with considerable synchronic variations.

Dry sieving for bone can yield 100% retrieval if the sediment characteristics and sieve mesh size are suitable, and this can be checked by re-sieving. Dry, sandy, rather fine-grained sediments are best, in an arid environment, with additional provisos concerning the nature of the operation. In contrast to the flotation or wet-sieving methods already described (Section 6.3), dry sieving can be carried out quite efficiently using relatively untrained local labour, but it is essential to avoid the piling-up of material waiting to be sieved. The best dry sieving strategies are very labour intensive. The writer has found that using untrained labourers with two-man 'tray' sieves (Fig. 10.4) of 2 mm mesh, it is possible to sieve all the sediment from an excavation at a rate of 1–2 m³ per day using a team of three workmen (two sieve men and a bucket-carrier) together with a supervisor. Not more than two dry sieves can conveniently be operated at the same time and a ratio of one troweller to the team mentioned above is about right to prevent a backlog. The boredom rate of locally recruited workmen on non-European sites (where most dry sieving takes place) is relatively low; not inconsequential as boredom produces errors.

Water separation and sieving (Section 6.3) is suitable for a much wider range of sedimentary conditions and provides good samples of small bones which are more affected than larger ones by sampling errors. With the larger mammals (over 25 kg in weight) remains are more easily seen in the field and Thomas (1969) has studied the relationship between mammal size and sieve mesh, noting that as the size of the mammal increases so does the efficiency of the various meshes of sieve, assuming that a ¹/₁₆ in (1.6 mm) mesh (-0.5φ) will recover 100% of each sample. With very small material sieving is absolutely essential, although samples can be biased by other recovery procedures. Sparks (1961) presented data concerning the biasing of terrestrial mollusc samples by hand-sorting in the field, which favours large specimens or those which contrast in colour with their backgrounds. A similar study was made by Fitch (1966) on the otoliths of marine fish (p. 183) and Casteel (1976) noted a 100% loss of all fish remains from some units unsieved in the field and later compared with samples from the same units which had been washed, screened and examined in the laboratory with a low power microscope. Comparative sieving techniques are discussed by Payne (1975), Cherry (1975) and Clason and Prummel (1971, 1976). It is important, though, not to get carried away, as various experiments in total sieving have produced unworkable residues. For example the residues from the Franchthi cave (Jacobsen 1976) comprise (after total sieving) four separate size fractions of which the two largest (greater than 5 mm sieve mesh) have been sorted and identified, but it took eight people one year. The two smaller fractions (less than 2.8 mm and 2.8–5 mm) still remain to be done, some 400–500 bags of them. At the risk of sounding like a school mathematics problem, let it be stated that a one litre subsample from 120 bags takes 250 man-days to sort and identify, and to do the entire contents of those same bags would take one person 21 years. The entire sample would take one worker between 40 and 50 years to complete. Watson (1972) suggests a method for using data from water-sieved sites to estimate and correct the effect of preferential recovery on the figures for the relative proportion of different species at unsieved sites. A *sampling strategy* is clearly needed, and different sampling strategies for different problems are discussed by Gamble (1978). If the total range of species is required, then each bone needs to be examined, but the relative proportions of the principal taxa can be calculated from a small fraction of the sampled population. The

Figure 10.4 Dry sieving at the *Equus* cave excavations.

solution to many of the problems in sampling is to sample spatial, not faunal, units, using cluster sampling where the frame consists of spatial units and bones are only one population recovered from the clusters (i.e. the spatial units) that are sampled. Payne (1972b, p. 67) reiterates three questions which are fundamental to the interpretation of bone samples: To what extent is the *sample* submitted for analysis representative of what was actually present in the sediment? To what extent is the *area* excavated representative of the whole site? Is there a *significant change* within the series of successive units which have been grouped together to make the sample? The question of context sampling has already been discussed for seeds (Section 6.3) and is equally relevant for bone.

Whole skeletons, complete skulls, articulated joints or large collections of mixed bones *in situ* require specialist attention on the site, and may indeed need to be consolidated *in situ* for them to be removed *en bloc*. In many cases a site record form may require the excavator to distinguish between animal and human bone, not always possible as a training in elementary zoology is far from being a prerequisite for excavation direction. Site cleaning of material which is to be lifted *en bloc* should be kept to the minimum as it will obliterate the less obvious categories of evidence, including parasite eggs which might be present, and *in situ* consolidation with poly(vinyl acetate) (PVA) or other liquids should be avoided unless absolutely necessary since, among other things, it will render the bone useless for radio-carbon dating. The author has been experimenting with various plastics of the type generally used as floor sealers and found them to be quite effective but to be avoided unless absolutely essential. Slow drying of bones is the best policy and it is necessary to follow the specialists' advice as to whether or not the material is to be washed. Brothwell (1965) points out that the addition of chemicals, even those in washing-up liquid, restricts the chance of recovering blood groups, etc.

Chaplin (1971) gives much useful advice on the lifting of whole skeletons. Fragile bones should be wrapped in padding, tied with string and a label attached before being packed in rigid cardboard boxes (the standard-size Department of the Environment variety are the best). If the material is not to be used for radiocarbon dating, small bones may be packed in paper towels inside plastic tubes and large bones such as skulls in foam or polystyrene chips inside a box, great care being taken with labelling.

10.5 Analytical methods

It is impossible to provide here a reference work on bone recognition and identification. Various classic textbooks are available (Sisson 1953, Schmid 1972, McFadyean 1953) but, as usual, books do not replace personal tuition, experience and reference material. In any work with animal bones the first thing to be determined is the *identity of the bone*. This is easier than it sounds and requires a good reference collection. Perhaps the most useful single skeleton for teaching oneself elementary bone identification is that of a dog (Fig. 10.1), which is relatively easily obtained and has bones of reasonable size. A horse would be nice, but impractical. Other reference skeletons must either be bought (expensive) or obtained by devious means and initiative (p. 169). The second stage in the work is the *identification of the species* from which the bone came. Useful criteria are size and specific features of bones from different species, and the bone must be matched with known material. The number and weight of bone fragments are also calculated and each bone aged (if possible) and features such as butchery marks or any palaeopathology noted. Each archaeozoologist has his own preferred recording method, usually some type of standard record card or sheet, which may or may not be suitable for computerization. It is usual to note and separate bones which are likely to be the source of further detailed information, for example the calculation of sex or stature. This stage of qualitative description and sample counting and weighing is of the utmost importance. It is also extremely tedious and time-consuming. The next step is the calculation of the all-important 'minimum number of individuals' (MNI) present for each species. Some zoologists do not use an MNI calculation but work by quantifying either the frequencies of the different bones or their fragment weight, but both these methods are becoming less fashionable. The theoretical basis of calculating an MNI is obvious and simple (no animal can have more than one left tibia and if there are six left tibia then a minimum number of six animals was present), but in practice the MNI is calculated on a total of all the bones present. After initial identification, the bones are divided into groups comprising the fragments or complete bones of one particular bone from one species (e.g. cow humeri). The left and right side bones are then distinguished and the MNI represented for each side is counted. After the bones from both sides have been counted, results are amalgamated and a maximum and minimum value can be obtained. The sides must be checked against each other as the bones from the left-hand side will often be from the same animal. This is checked using specific ageing criteria and measurement of selected bones done

using a set of Vernier callipers and an osteometric board. The whole process is described in detail by Chaplin (1971). However, an MNI can be obtained in different ways which, applied to the same material, will give different results. Each method is subject to sample size variation (Casteel 1977) and at Exeter (Maltby 1979) the MNI for each bone element and each species and each feature was obtained by separating left from right and counting shaft fragments as well as fragments where the articular surface was preserved. Payne (1972b) gives examples of MNI calculations, but the MNI is only a device to quantify data and should not be taken literally: 'The statement that a minimum number of 60 cattle and 30 pigs were represented on a site does not mean that cattle were twice as numerous as pigs. It merely states that the method of calculation used in the analysis produced these results' (Maltby 1979, p. 6). Clason (1972) discusses various methods for the use and presentation of archaeozoological data, emphasizing the difference between primary data (identified parts of species and their measurements) and secondary data (inferences drawn and estimates made). There is, however, a general lack of agreement or unified methodology. Methods of work vary considerably. At Exeter the ribs and vertebrae (other than the atlas, axis and sacrum) were counted but not identified to species, which saved time. The rest of the material was divided into large, medium and small mammals and a fragment count done, but this favours larger mammals and those with the most bones (a horse has 12 phalanges, cattle have 24, pig 48 and a dog 52–58). Various features of the individual skeleton influence its survival, such as the different robustness of bones (teeth, distal humeri and calcanii survive well and proximal humeri, and caudal vertebrae do not).

Metrical analysis may in theory be used to differentiate between species and in the calculation of sex. It may also assist in assessing the size and quality of stock animals and note any improvements. Von den Driesch (1976) discusses the question of measurements with specific reference to instruments and techniques and the object of making such measurements internationally usable. Sex determination can be made and is useful if there is marked sexual dimorphism, differences in the form of the pelvis or other anatomical features. Unique secondary sexual characteristics such as the baculum (penis bone) of male carnivores (Fig. 10.1) or the antlers of deer are also useful. Kiszely (1974) describes the chemical sexing of bones by a modified chromatographic method which works on the theory that females accumulate more citrate in their bone tissues than males. This hypothesis is not generally accepted. In domestic stock all kinds of variables affect sex determination, including the presence of castrated males and sex differences between breeds. The most usual method used is the calculation of statistical distributions of bone dimensions, especially the metapodials (which are probably the most commonly found, intact bone). Howard (1963) looked at modern cattle metapodials and Zalkin (1961) worked on sheep. In order to calculate sexual groups and breeds of animals, accurate measurements must be supported by experimental work. It is theoretically possible to convert bone dimensions of cattle into animal weight and height, but this varies greatly between breeds and between sexes in the same breed. Height estimates are made using several bones to eliminate potential error. A classic paper is that of Higham (1969) who compiled the limb bone measurements of Aberdeen Angus and Danish Red cattle, producing figures which correlate dimensions and weight with information about sexual dimorphism. A definitive work on measurement is that of Duerst (1926), but various zoologists have reservations about the amount of valid information which can be obtained from metrical data.

The age of an animal is determined separately from several bones, and in the interpretation of the age structure of a sample either the data from one particular bone is chosen, or else the summary of calculations from several bones. One method for ageing animals has already been mentioned – the fusion of the epiphyses of a limb bone. The age of fusion has been worked out for most domestic species (Silver 1969) and the sequence of fusion in any one species is regular, although there is much interspecies variation. The age of fusion will be affected by domestication and selective breeding and it is necessary to be cautious when applying modern data to an ancient population. The fusion of the skull bones is used as a guide to age, especially with animals which have a short life span. Tooth eruption and replacement is useful for the opposite

reasons, as it can only be used on young animals before the last tooth in a series appears. Happily (for us) animals used as major food sources generally tend to be killed rather young and the method, which relies on modern data for tooth eruption ages in different species, is extremely useful but not uncontroversial. Ewbank *et al.* (1964) found a wide variety of eruption ages in the teeth of Iron Age sheep but Grant (1975) produced six tooth-eruption stages in cattle and pig based on the wear patterns on selected samples of mandibles. Other, less important means of ageing animals are the development of structures such as calcified tissue, general growth and size of bone, and antler development in the deer family. Standardization of analytical techniques in ageing is discussed by Grant (1975), Payne (1973) and Noddle (1974), and of techniques for estimating height and size by Noddle (1975).

Bone palaeopathology has received less attention than estimations of age, sex or height, and is perhaps of more intrinsic zoological rather than archaeological value. Jubb and Kennedy (1963) classify bone lesions and their diseases and many archaeological bone reports include short notes on palaeopathology (p. 174). Biddick and Tomenchuk (1975) describe a system for specifying the locations of pathological features and butchery marks on bones, designed for computer storage of such information with a view to more accurate comparability studies.

10.6 Reference collections

One difficulty is that it may be hard to obtain comparative material or, indeed, to trace specimens in museums. Clutton-Brock (1975) comments on the assistance provided by computerized data-retrieval systems. A catalogue of animal remains from British archaeological sites is kept at the British Museum (Natural History), together with a separate record of bone material from Department of the Environment excavations not stored at the museum, both designed for computer retrieval (substantial collections are also to be found in Veterinary Schools). Acquiring reference specimens becomes a minor obsession with many archaeozoologists. The writer has a friend who recently made university history by dragging a large sack of decaying badgers across campus before boiling them down and another (working in Australia) who retrieves and buries any kangaroos that are the unfortunate victims of road accidents and exhumes them after the decay of the fleshy tissue has been completed. Chaplin (1977) lists procedures for preparing skeletal material and arrived at a total of 104 species of British Recent mammals which might turn up on an archaeological site. The larger animals form the bulk of post-Neolithic food protein but the small mammals may yield important palaeoenvironmental information. In Neolithic sites a mixture of wild and domestic species is likely, just as today. This figure of 104 species must be greatly increased if one is working with Palaeolithic material and may differ for other countries and vary with the type of site and of the natural or artificial environment represented. However, in practice the range of animals present on any one archaeological site, although potentially large, is actually quite small, and the bulk of the bones usually belong to a very small number of species indeed. Chaplin elaborates his total by dividing the number into three size classes (Table 10.1) to which one might add a further category including all other type of bones which might turn up (shrews, bats, mice, voles and the young of the mammals listed which would appear in a different size category from that of their parents). On British Neolithic sites onwards the greatest number of bones will come from horse, cattle, sheep/goat (p. 175) and pig, with lesser quantities of the different deer, domestic and wild cats and dogs and a few small mammals and birds. The minimum number of reference skeletons necessary is therefore horse, cattle, red deer, sheep, goat, fallow deer and roe deer (which together will have supplied some 90% of the available meat), together with dog and any small mammals. Rabbit might be added to this list because, although it is not an important food source until medieval times, odd rabbit bones frequently turn up in earlier assemblages as a result of disturbance. The remaining 10% of animals not included in the list might be contributed by 20–30 species of bird, fish and mammal and will be likely to require the attention of a different zoologist, as will the bones of any aquatic mammals (p. 188). The problems encountered by the archaeozoologist who specializes in mammalian remains are of a different order of magnitude from those of the archaeoornithologist, who might have a potential 500 species.

Table 10.1 British mammals: size classes. After Chaplin (1971).

large	cattle (*Bos.* sp.)
	horse (*Equus* sp.)
	red deer (*Cervus elaphus*)
	elk (*Alces alces*)
	fallow deer (*Dama dama*)
	reindeer (*Rangifer tarandus*)
	pig (*Sus* sp.)
	man (*Homo sapiens sapiens*)
	brown bear (*Ursus arctos*)
	walrus (*Odobenus rosmarus*)
	(together with most Cetacea)
medium	sheep (*Ovis* sp.)
	goat (*Capra* sp.)
	roe deer (*Capreolus capreolus*)
	wolf/dog (*Canis* sp.)
	fox (*Vulpes* sp. and *Alopex* sp.)
	badger (*Meles meles*)
	otter (*Lutra lutra*)
	cat (*Felis* sp.)
	hare (*Lepus* sp.)
	rabbit (*Oryctolagus cuniculus*)
	beaver (*Castor fiber*)
	(together with some Cetacea and seals)
small	hedgehog (*Erinaceus europaeus*)
	pine marten (*Martes martes*)
	stoat (*Mustela erminea*)
	weasel (*Mustela nivalis*)
	polecat (*Mustela putorius*)
	red squirrel (*Sciurus vulgaris*)
	black rat (*Rattus rattus*)
	brown rat (*Rattus norwegicus*)
	(together with the larger bats)

10.7 Interpretation

Archaeozoological evidence obtained from any one collection may be divided into two broad groups: what the archaeologist asked for, and what the zoologist is able to tell him. The latter will generally be the larger category of information unless the excavator has set up an unusually sophisticated series of hypotheses. It is up to the zoologist to test the limits of the available evidence and make inferences and conclusions. The days of a routine appendix labelled 'animal bones' with little attempt to integrate it into the text are nearly over. Archaeologists realized some time ago that since men are what they eat the study of the actual food debris is as important as a consideration of the artefacts used in its preparation and consumption. Of course, animal bones can give information on much more than diet and on many sites a large proportion of the species represented will not have been used for food at all. On such sites, in the absence of other data, bland faunal lists may be a research tool if one makes the assumption (not always warranted) that preferred habitats have not changed. Pioneering studies of this kind were carried out as early as the 1930s in, for example, the work of Garrod and Bate (1937), analysing the change in proportional representation of deer and gazelle in the Mount Carmel Cave (Israel).

The bones which are retrieved from archaeological sites could be classified in the following way:

(a) bones representing animals killed by man for meat or some other economic/technological reason

(b) bones representing the kill of other animals living on or near the site

(c) bones of animals which died *in situ*

(d) bones of animals which died nearby and were transported to the site by a non-biological agency (e.g. water, hillwash, gravity)

(e) bones which are contaminants and represent animals which entered the sediments after their deposition (e.g. rabbit burrows).

In any population there will be a wide variety in size and other features due to a range of factors including sexual dimorphism. Secondly, the environment in which the animals lived in antiquity may differ from that in which they live in the present day. Not only may this cause one to make false palaeoenvironmental correlations, but it means that modern and ancient species of, say, cattle have very different physical characteristics. Since bone work relies on the ability to relate an ancient bone assemblage to known characteristics of modern fauna, the range of variation within modern populations is of the greatest importance, and there are, unfortunately, large gaps in our knowledge. Similarly, one cannot assume that the range of variations existing in a modern population will necessarily be the same as that in an ancient one.

The question of context interpretation is clearly most important. It is necessary to estimate how fast a particular layer accumulated, what were the agents of accumulation and disturbance, and whether the characteristics of the sediment could have modified the bone assemblage. In the case of a rubbish pit, for example, one would like to know (among other things) whether it was filled in a single glorious event or by a slow trickle of debris over a period of many years. Slow accumulation increases the potential interpretations that may be put on the bone assemblage by compounding the possibility of disturbance. If a series of pits can be associated with one particular building phase (or even with each other by the use of other forms of relative dating evidence such as pottery) then this information is useful in making an interpretation of the fauna. Parts of the same animal could, for example, have found their way into more than one pit if a number of pits were open at any one time. If the deposit being examined is a midden or general refuse tip, then the slow accumulation and open context may mean the dispersal of parts of the skeleton. Closed context analysis may be of particular value (for example the detailed study of rubbish or cess pits, or even of the rare complete room (Schmid 1967) like those at Pompeii). Such studies have been undertaken on a wide variety of sites from single-occupation kill/butchery sites of Palaeolithic date to well-documented medieval rubbish pits.

A major area of archaeozoological research is the recognition of husbandry practices and economy; hundreds of papers are published on this every year. Examples are the work of Perkins and Daly (1968) at the Neolithic site of Suberde in Turkey who analysed the relative frequencies of forelimb and hindlimb bones and reconstructed hunting and butchery practices. Chaplin (1971) studied sheep remains from Roman sites, noting the very low percentage of pelvae and femurs, suggesting that these parts were shared or traded away from the site. Guilday *et al.* (1962) wrote a seminal paper on butchery marks and much work has now been done on the debris of modern hunting communities such as the !Kung bushmen. Yellen (1977) looked at bushman material, evaluating the 'worthless parts' of animals left behind at camp sites, the consumption of parts of the kill away from the camp, the method of primary butchery for retrieving the meat and the means of preparing it.

The whole question of definitions of domestication occupies a very large slice of the archaeozoological literature. Various collections of papers and the results of symposia have been published (e.g. Brothwell & Higgs 1969, Ucko & Dimbleby 1969, Matolcsi 1973), together with specialist papers on, for example, the effect of domestication on bone structure (Drew *et al.* 1971, Watson 1975), age and sex structures of populations (Collier & White 1976, Saxon & Higham 1968, 1969, Grigson 1976). No single book is available to present the current state of the art, and the reader is referred to the above works, which contain extensive bibliographies.

10.7.1 Human bones

Human bones present, in many ways, similar problems to those of animals, but the questions asked are often different. The interpretation of human bone assemblages is worth a book in its own right, and the reader is referred to the classic work of Brothwell (1965) and to textbooks of human palaeopathology. Human bones, whether formally buried or not, require special treatment on site since they are going to provide material for behavioural reconstruction.

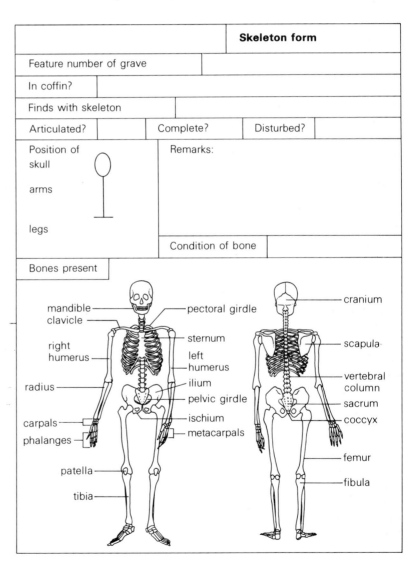

Figure 10.5 Standard record card for burials (after Hirst 1976).

Figure 10.5 shows the burial record *pro forma* recommended by Hirst (1976) for human burials. The idea is that in the absence of an archaeozoologist the bones present on site can be shaded or coloured on the diagram. Information recorded here must not be taken as absolute; if the skeleton is buried in a contracted position or has collapsed, or if there are multiple burials present, most excavators would need help to disentangle precisely what they have got. The form is, however, very useful as a general guide. In dealing with supposedly human material there are various questions to ask. First, whether the bone is indeed human or just animal (and in some cases it may be difficult to tell if preservation is poor). Secondly, one must calculate the MNI, together with absolute and relative ages and lifespans. Thirdly come the estimates of sex. Fourthly is what might be termed ethnic markers (height, skull form, familial abnormalities and blood groups). Last is the presence of any palaeopathological evidence. Absolute ages may be obtained by radiocarbon dating and relative age by some means such as fluorine/nitrogen/uranium context (Michels 1976) or amino acid degradation and racemization (Krueger 1965, Bada & Helfman 1975). Details may be found in any good textbook of dating (e.g. Michels 1976). The estimation of lifespan is helped by microscopic and X-ray analyses. In a subadult, age can be estimated from tooth eruption, epiphyseal closure and the length of long bones, as it can for animals. In a child, by the end of its first year all 24 deciduous teeth will have erupted, between age 2 to 6 the ossification of the roots takes place and between 6 and 11 the deciduous teeth are replaced by permanent ones. This is completed by the addition of the second molars at any time after the age of 12. The age of an adult can also be estimated from molar wear, 'lipping' of vertebrae, the wear and tear of the large joints, changes in the pubic symphesis and the morphology and microscopy of the long bones, especially the heads of the femur and humerus. Sex is determined principally by an examination of the skull and pelvis. The range of palaeopathological features detectable in bone ranges from the obvious (dental disease, trauma) to the results of infection, arthritis, congenital and metabolic diseases, blood disorders and tumours. Clearly a large sample is best as it increases the chances of obtaining such information and reduces the quality of statistical error. That is why the calculation of, for example, average adult height for the human burials of the Anglo-Saxon period is reasonable because the potential sample is very large, whereas a similar calculation made for *Australopithecus* would be subject to a very wide range of error.

10.7.2 Dog bones

Harcourt (1974) described the development and changes in size and shape of dog skulls from British contexts dating from the Mesolithic to the end of the 11th century AD. He also noted changes in the size of the animals, using for this purpose an estimation of shoulder heights from a modification of the original calculation derived from the total length of the long bones first published by Koudelka (1885). Sample sizes were variable, four specimens from the Mesolithic, 37 long bones and six skulls from the Neolithic (including two complete skeletons – one from Windmill Hill and one from Easton Down), and a few fragments from ten Bronze Age sites. In the Iron Age dog remains become more common, 453 specimens from 28 sites, and from Romano-British contexts another 1156 bones were added. Dog bones were much less common in the early post-Roman, 189 specimens being obtained. The Mesolithic material is interesting since it includes the controversial skull from Star Carr, thought by Degerbøl (1961) to be a dog, not, as had at first been supposed, a wolf. Clutton-Brock (1969) agrees that the Star Carr dog was indeed a dog and not a wolf but the matter is far from straightforward. Many of the earliest dogs were no doubt similar to local wolf groups and the attachment to man was doubtless not very strong, although certain morphological changes had occurred, probably as a result of a complex of factors including restricted mating possibilities and micro-environmental change (Brothwell 1975). In a proposed eight-point system to evaluate the degree of domestication, Brothwell (1975) puts the Star Carr dog at DZ ('camp-following'). The man–animal relationship was probably less close than that of the dingo in recent times, where there has been some selective breeding for particular qualities beyond the range of variation seen in a wild population. Degerbøl (1961) suggested that this and other early dogs were used as food, bred for the purpose as an insurance policy in times of famine, a suggestion supported by cut marks on the bones from Star Carr, Highfield (Jackson 1932) and Owslebury (Collis 1968). In the Iron Age specimens a slight general reduction in height was observed but small dogs were in the minority, perhaps suggesting use as hunting dogs as well as food. The large Roman sample permitted even more interesting conclusions and revealed the appearance of a new phenomenon – the lap dog. The height range of Norman dogs was very wide, and the sample from both Roman and Anglo-Saxon sites included some huge guard-dogs, whose existence is supported by documentary evidence such as the well-known remarks of Strabo: '. . . these things accordingly are exported from the island as also hides and slaves and dogs that are by nature suited to the purposes of the chase'. In Anglo-Saxon times two distinct populations of dog can be distinguished from the available samples, but the sample size is small, not always from domestic sites, and would seem to contradict literary evidence for many different varieties of dog. Harcourt (1974) makes the suggestion that dogs were commonly exploited in a variety of different ways when alive and used as food when dead. Dog meat is, after all, eaten in parts of the world today (Herre 1969) and formed part of Amerindian diet (White 1955).

The Neolithic dog skeletons mentioned above were compared with the more recent find of a dog from flint mines at Grimes Graves, Norfolk (Burleigh et al. 1977). This specimen, which either died in the mine shaft or was intentionally buried there, closely resembled the Easton Down Dog (Jackson 1935) and was of comparable (less than one year) age at its death. Neolithic dogs from Orkney (Clutton-Brock 1979) and Ireland (van Wijngaarden-Bakker 1974) support Harcourt's view that the small degree of variability in Neolithic dogs suggests a single homogeneous population, probably approximating to the description of the Grimes Graves dog (Burleigh et al. 1977, p. 365): 'We only know that it stood about 52 cm at the shoulder, that it had a rather short, wide head and that it was young, healthy and probably thin'. The description of early dogs as resembling one or other of the modern breeds is thought to be anachronistic since these are the end products of a highly selective

breeding programme for characters that are not necessarily reflected in the skeleton.

Work has also been undertaken on domestic dogs from Peru (Burleigh & Brothwell 1978, Brothwell et al. 1979), both on morphological changes and evidence for diet. One of the questions being investigated was whether dogs were being deliberately fattened for food in early Peru, a practice supported by documentary evidence and pottery figurines for other parts of the Americas. Dogs were very important in Peruvian life and were even ceremonially buried (Allen 1920). Studies of the $^{13}C:^{12}C$ ratios of hair samples from ten Peruvian dogs showed that maize sometimes formed over 60% of their diet, either as a result of intentional feeding or of scavenging human food remains (Burleigh & Brothwell 1978). A later paper on the remains of 42 dogs from Peru including ritual burials (Brothwell et al. 1979) suggests that dogs were kept for both food and ritual purposes, as well as for human protection and to guard flocks.

10.7.3 Animal palaeopathology

Siegel (1976) reviewed some of the possibilities and problems of animal palaeopathology, a topic also discussed by von den Driesch (1975) and Wäsle (1976). Palaeopathological features on specimens have been noted since the 18th century but systematic examination of bones as part of regular archaeozoological work is a comparatively recent innovation (Brothwell 1965). Only the reaction of a *bone* to an illness can generally be considered, since the surrounding soft tissue, cartilage and ligaments are no longer present. Palaeopathological studies technically include the work on parasites described in Chapter 9 and some of the pathogenic microorganisms of Chapter 2. Animal disease may be of great importance to human communities and one obvious example is the transmission of disease (Section 2.4). A growing literature is being accumulated on disease in early human populations, but comparatively little has yet been published on animals. A further problem is caused by imprecise description. Siegel (1976) presents a long table citing literature within the field of veterinary pathology which is relevant in archaeological work and then considers the pathology of eighteen selected British sites, Neolithic to medieval in date. Features of note included a high incidence of lesion in dog bones from one Roman site (Godmanchester), possibly related to maltreatment. High instances of dental disease and arthritic disorders were also observed, the latter being grouped under 'arthropathy' to include non-infective degenerative diseases, a term proposed by Olsson (1971). Many of these were to be found in elderly animals, the result of 'overwork', especially in horses. The statistics were not corrected for possible under-representation of certain species, with the result that red deer and fowl appeared relatively free of disease because of their scarcity in the sample. This pinpoints one of the major problems of palaeopathological work: how meaningful the incidence or lack of incidence of a particular disease actually is. Van Wijngaarden-Bakker and Krauwer (1979) produced an interesting study of animal palaeopathology from various Dutch sites of Late Bronze Age–medieval date. Their total of 49 pathologically afflicted bone fragments corresponding to a MNI of 30 animals came from 15 sites, not a very high total of the animal bones found. The most common features were again the results of trauma, dental disease and arthritis with rare congenital disorders. The incidence of fractures in dog and poultry bones was high, while cattle and horse showed a higher percentage of arthritic disease. No pathological pig remains were found, attributable, perhaps, to the extensive pig herding methods common in the Netherlands, but some comparison with the pathology of modern pig populations would have been useful here. A general *increase* in pathological changes was observed with time, related either to new economic circumstances or types of husbandry. The authors also commented on the lack of standardized pathological nomenclature and the distressing (and confusing) tendency to use different names for the same disease.

Quite a different type of palaeopathological emphasis may be seen in a paper by Clutton-Brock (1974) on the earliest true horse from Egypt, found at the fortress of Buhen. The specimen, a nineteen year old male, showed uneven tooth wear, with excessive abrasion of the lower left second premolar and absence of the lower right second premolar. Clutton-Brock considers that the animal was ridden or driven with a bit (the earliest evidence for this in antiquity), which would have caused the excessive wear on these premolars without wear on the upper teeth unless the bit was chewed or the mouth held closed with a tight noseband. Horse burials at the Iron Age cemetery of Magdalenska (Bökönyi 1968) included two specimens with abraded premolars, one actually found with the bit. Such confirmatory evidence is rare in archaeological palaeopathology and closer collaboration with veterinary science seems indicated.

10.7.4 Sheep and goats

The problem of separating the sheep from the goats in archaeozoology is legendary. This has hampered studies of the parts played by wild populations of these animals in, for example, the early Postglacial of the Near East. The recent studies of Boessneck *et al.* (1964), Boessneck (1969) and Schramm (1967) have made it possible to separate at least the majority of bones in modern animals. The many variables found in ancient populations present a different problem, and great experience and familiarity with the material is necessary. The particular value of the work of Boessneck *et al.* (1964) is the large number of breeds and whole range of variation that they studied, variations reflecting selection pressure as a result of domestication. Although only a small number of sheep bones were recovered from this very early level, the discovery is important since it refutes the suggestion of Payne (1969) that sheep and goats had a common wild ancestor and diverged in the early stages of domestication. The two genera are seen by Clutton-Brock and Uerpmann (1974) to be quite distinct and the early date of the material indicates that an original wild form of sheep did exist. Harrison (1968) mentions a wild sheep population in Oman, perhaps the sole relict of a widespread pre-Neolithic population. The goat bones from pre-pottery A layers at Jericho could not be distinguished from those of the wild *Capra aegagnus*, and the large size of the bones suggest that the latter was present, although domestication had taken place by pre-pottery B times. Noddle (1974) examined the bones of 53 modern goats of known age, sex and breed to establish the age of epiphyseal closure and tooth eruption. It was found that the former varied greatly with sex and breed, feral goats being about a year behind domestic goats and

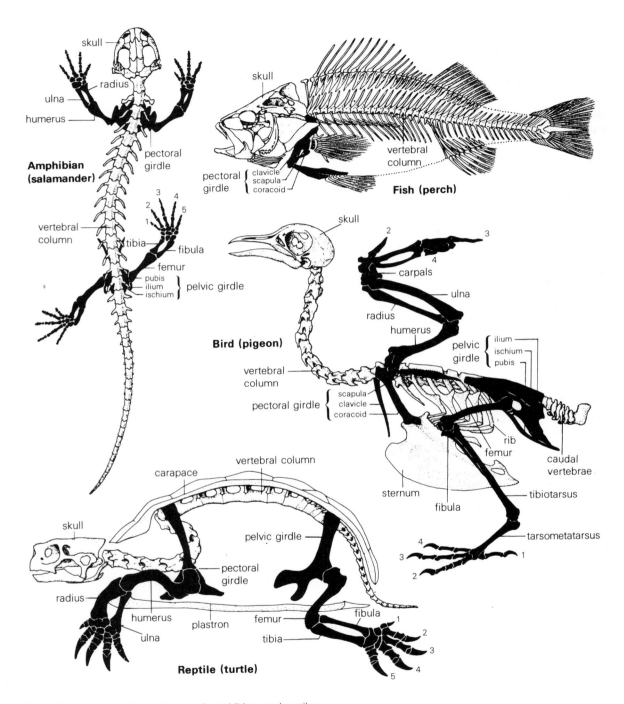

Figure 10.6 Comparative skeletons of amphibians and reptiles.

castrated males anything up to four years behind females. Goats mature later than sheep (at least in modern samples). The feral goats used by Noddle were obtained from culling activities in northern Scotland, and could be aged by their annual horn rings. This information concerning castrates is of especial interest to the archaeozoologist since large numbers of male goat horns are often found and sometimes (as at medieval King's Lynn) it has been suggested that the animal was a castrate. Male castrates, domestic and feral goats mature at different rates, but this does not seem to influence the final proportions of the bones. Clutton-Brock and Uerpmann (1974) discussed criteria for distinguishing sheep from goat at Jericho, showing that sheep were present in both pre-pottery Neolithic A levels (c. 8000 BC) and pre-pottery Neolithic B (c. 7000 BC).

10.7.5 Small mammals

The bones of small mammals and amphibians are often found in the fill of rubbish pits or ditches, where the animals have fallen and been unable to climb out. Mice and voles can sometimes survive inside storage pits (Fertig & Edmonds 1969) on a very dry diet, but their presence is of little importance except as a contaminant. Advances in the use of small mammals are considered in a publication by the Institute of Archaeology, London, as part of a larger synthesis of archaeozoology (Brothwell *et al.* 1981).

Rodents may be either a source of palaeoclimatic information or (more commonly) indicators of disease or pollution. The role of the black rat (*Rattus rattus*) in the spread of plague has already been discussed. The congested living conditions of prehistoric and early historic settlements often favoured the growth of large populations of rodent pests. Petrie (1891) excavated a Twelfth Dynasty workers' town at Kahun, Egypt, and found that in nearly every room rodent tunnels had been dug, the inhabitants making frantic efforts to keep them out by blocking the holes with stones and rubble. The fortress-town of Buhen near the Second Cataract, already mentioned as the finding of the Buhen horse (p. 175), also produced abundant rodent remains in its brickwork. Egypt is important for the veneration of some species of small mammals, especially the cat

and mongoose, one useful for killing rodents and the other for killing snakes.

10.7.6 Amphibians and reptiles

There is very little preserved evidence of amphibians or reptiles from archaeological sites and if such remains are listed they are frequently not catalogued or are lumped together as 'turtle' or 'snake' (Bullen & Sleight 1959), which is the result both of a lack of available expertise in identification and the often fragmentary condition of the bones (Harris & Eddy 1963). Excavators are often unfamiliar with the skeletal elements of reptiles and amphibians and isolated cranial elements can easily be mistaken for flakes or chips of bone from larger animals (Olsen 1968).

Taxonomists distinguish the living reptile species by scale arrangement, colour pattern and size, but the published keys are confusing even to herpatologists. Carr and Goin (1955) quote the characters stated for identifying the common five-lined skink (*Eumeces fasciatus*) as 'the combination of a body either with five lines or without lines'. Frequently such keys make no mention of skeletal characteristics. Olsen (1968), to counter this difficulty, produced a simple field and laboratory manual for archaeological use, but this is unfortunately geared towards the reptiles and amphibia from the southern United States. It includes a useful series of drawings and distribution maps and some splendid illustrations of rarities such as the natural mummies of lizards which occurred on several sites. A major problem is to distinguish between species that were a food source and those which were not. The contribution of reptiles and amphibians to the diet of various Amerindian groups was discussed by Bourke (1884).

References

Allen, G. M. 1920. Dogs of the American aborigines. *Bull. Mus. comp. Zool. Harv.* **63**, 431–517.

Bada, J. L. and P. M. Helfman 1975. Amino acid racemisation dating of fossil bones. *Wld Arch.* **7**, 160–73.

Behrensmayer, A. K. 1975. The taphonomy and paleoecology of Plio-Pleistocene vertebrate assemblages east of Lake Rudolf, Kenya. *Bull. Mus. comp. Zool. Harv.* colln. **146**, 473–578.

Behrensmayer, A. K. and A. P. Hill 1980. *Fossils in the making*. Chicago: Chicago University Press.

Biddick, K. A. and J. Tomenchuk 1975. Quantifying continuous lesions and fractures on long bones. *J. Fld Arch.* 2, 239–49.

Binford, L. R. and J. B. Bertram, 1977. Bone frequencies and attritional processes. In *For theory building in archaeology*, L. R. Binford (ed.), 77–153. New York: Academic Press.

Boussneck, I. 1969. Osteological differences between sheep and goats. In *Science in archaeology*, 2nd edn, D. Brothwell and E. Higgs (eds), 331–68. London: Thames and Hudson.

Boessneck, J., H. H. Müller and M. Teichert 1964. Osteologische Unterscheidungsmerkmale zwischen Schaf (*Ovis aries* L.) und Ziege (*Capra hircus* L.). *Kuhn. Arch.* 78, 1–129.

Boessneck, J. A., A. von den Driesch, U. Mayer-Lemppenau and E. Wechsler-von Ohlen 1971. Die Tierknochen-funde aus dem Oppidum von Mancking. *Die Ausgrabungen in Mancking* 6. Wiesbaden: Franz Steiner.

Bökönyi, S. 1968. Mecklenburg collection, Part 1. Data on Iron Age horses of central and eastern Europe. In *Am. Sch. prehist. Res. (Peabody Mus. Harv.) Bull.* no. 25, H. Henken (ed.).

Bourke, J. G. 1884. *The snake-dance of the Moquis of Arizona*. New York.

Bourdillon, J. and J. Coy 1980. The animal bones. In *Saxon Southampton: excavations in Melbourne Street*, P. Holdsworth (ed.). London: Council for British Archaeology.

Brain, C. K. 1969. The contribution of Namib Desert Hottentots to an understanding of australopithecine bone accumulations. *Scientific Papers of the Namib Desert Research Station* no. 39, 13–22.

Brain, C. K. 1976. Some criteria for the recognition of bone collecting agencies in African caves. In *Berg. Wartenstein Symposium 69*. New York: Wenner-Gren Foundation.

Brothwell, D. R. 1965. *Digging up bones*. London: British Museum (Natural History).

Brothwell, D. and E. Higgs 1969. *Science in archaeology*. London: Thames and Hudson.

Brothwell, D. R. 1975. Salvaging the term 'domestication' for certain types of man–animal relationship: the possible value of an eight-point scoring system. *J. Arch. Sci.* 2, 397–401.

Brothwell, D., A. Malaga and R. Burleigh 1979. Studies on Amerindian dogs, 2: Variations in early Peruvian dogs. *J. Arch. Sci.* 6, 139–63.

Brothwell. D., K. Thomas and J. Clutton-Brock (eds) 1981. *Research problems in zooarchaeology*. London: Institute of Archaeology (in press).

Bullen, R. P. and F. W. Sleight 1959. *Archaeological investigations of the Castle Windy Midden, Florida*. Orlando, Fla: William L. Bryant Foundation.

Burleigh, R. and D. Brothwell 1978. Studies on Amerindian dogs, 1: Carbon isotopes in relation to maize in the diet of domestic dogs from early Peru and Ecuador. *J. Arch. Sci.* 5, 355–63.

Burleigh, R., J. Clutton-Brock, P. J. Felder and G. de G. Sieveking 1977. A further consideration of Neolithic dogs with special reference to a skeleton from Grimes Graves (Norfolk), England. *J. Arch. Sci.* 4, 353–67.

Carr, A. and C. J. Goin 1955. *Guide to the reptiles, amphibians and freshwater fishes of Florida*. Gainsville: University of Florida Press.

Casteel, R. W. 1976. *Fish remains in archaeology*. London: Academic Press.

Casteel, R. W. 1977. Characterization of faunal assemblages and the minimum number of individuals determined from paired elements: continuing problems in archaeology. *J. Arch. Sci.* 4, 125–34.

Chaplin, R. E. 1971. *The study of animal bones from archaeological sites*. London: Seminar Press.

Cherry, J. F. 1975. Efficient soil searching: some comments. *Antiquity* 49, 217–9.

Clason, A. T. 1972. Some remarks on the use and presentation of archaeozoological data. *Helinium* 12, 139–53.

Clason, A. T. (ed.) 1975. *Archaeozoological studies*. Elsevier: Amsterdam.

Clason, A. T. and W. Prummel 1971. Collecting, sieving and archaeological research. *J. Arch. Sci.* 1, 171–5.

Clason, A. T. and W. Prummel 1976. Collecting, sieving and archaeozoological research. In *Thème spécialise B: Problèmes ethnographiques des vestiges osseux*, F. Poplin (ed.), 75–6. Nice: IX Congrès UISPP.

Clutton-Brock, J. 1969. The origins of the dog. In *Science in archaeology*, 2nd edn, D. R. Brothwell and E. Higgs (eds), 303–9. London: Thames and Hudson.

Clutton-Brock, J. 1974. The Buhen horse. *J. Arch. Sci.* 1, 89–100.

Clutton-Brock, J. 1975. A system for the retrieval of data relating to animal remains from archaeological sites. In *Archaeozoological studies*, A. T. Clason (ed.), 21–34. Elsevier: Amsterdam.

Clutton-Brock, J. and H.-P. Uerpman 1974. The sheep of early Jericho. *J. Arch. Sci.* 1, 261–75.

Collier, S. and J. P. White 1976. Get them young? Age and sex inferences on animal domestication in archaeology. *Am. Antiquity* 41, 96–102.

Collis, J. R. 1968. Excavations at Owslebury, Hants.: an interim report. *Antiquaries J.* 48, 18.

Cornwall, I. W. 1956. *Bones for the archaeologist*. London: Phoenix.

Coy, J. 1978. *First aid for animal bones*. Hertford: Rescue.

Degerbøl, M. 1961. On a find of a preboreal domestic dog (*Canis familiaris* L.) from Star Carr, Yorkshire, with remarks on other Mesolithic dogs. *Proc. Prehist. Soc.* 27, 35–55.

von den Driesch, A. 1975. Die Bewertung pathologisch-anatomischer Veränderungen an vor- und frühgeschichtlichen Tierknochen. In *Archaeozoological studies*, A. T. Clason (ed.), 413–25. Amsterdam: Elsevier.

von den Driesch, A. 1976. *Das Vermessen von Tierknochen aus vor- und frühgeschichtlichen Siedlungen*. München: Universität München Institut für Paläoanatomie.

Duerst, J. 1926. Untersuchungmethoden am Skelett bei Sangern. In *Handbuch der biologischen Arbeitsmethoden*, Abt. VII, *Methoden der vergleichenden morphologischen Forschung*, Heft 2, S. Abderhalden (ed.). Univ. Berlin.

Ewbank, M., D. N. Phillipson, R. D. Whitehouse and E. S. Higgs 1964. Sheep in the Iron Age: a method of study. *Proc. Prehist. Soc.* **30**, 423–6.

Fertig, D. S. and V. W. Edmonds 1969. The physiology of the House Mouse. *Scient. Am.* **221** (4) 103–110.

Fitch, J. G. 1966. *Additional fish remains, mostly otoliths, from a Pleistocene deposit at Playa del Rey, California*. Los Angeles Museum Contrib. Sci. no. 119.

Gamble, C. 1978. Optimizing information from studies of faunal remains. In *Sampling in contemporary British archaeology*, J. F. Cherry, C. Gamble and S. Shennan (eds), 321–55. B.A.R. Brit. Series no. 50.

Garlick, J. D. 1969. Buried bone: the experimental approach in the study of nitrogen content and blood group activity. In *Science in archaeology*, 2nd edn, D. Brothwell and E. Higgs (eds), 503–12. London: Thames and Hudson.

Garrod, D. A. E. and D. M. A. Bate 1937. *The Stone Age of Mount Carmel*, 2 vols. London: Oxford University Press.

Grant, A. 1975. The animal bones. In *Excavations at Porchester Castle*, Vol. I, *Roman*, B. W. Cunliffe (ed.), 378–408 and 437–50. Rep. Res. Com. Soc. Ant. Lond. no. 33.

Grant, A. 1976. Animal bones. In *Excavations at Porchester Castle*, Vol. II, *Saxon*, B. W. Cunliffe (ed.), 262–87. Rep. Res. Com. Soc. Ant. Lond. no. 33.

Grigson, C. J. 1976. The craniology and relationships of four species of *Bos*. 3. Basic craniology; *Bos taurus* L., sagittal profiles and other non-measurable characteristics. *J. Arch. Sci.* **3**, 115–36.

Guilday, J. E., P. W. Parmalee and D. P. Tanner 1962. Aboriginal butchering techniques at the Eschelman Site (36 La 12), Lancaster County, Pennsylvania. *Penn. Arch.* **32**, 59–83.

Harcourt, R. A. 1974. The dog in prehistoric and early historic Britain. *J. Arch. Sci.* **1**, 151–75.

Harris, A. H. and F. W. Eddy 1963. *Vertebrate remains and past environmental reconstructions in the Navajo Reservoir district*, Papers in Anthropology 11. Santa Fe: Museum of New Mexico Press.

Harrison, D. L. 1968. On three mammals new to the fauna of Oman, Arabia, with the description of a new subspecies of bat. *Mammalia* **32**, 317–25.

Herre, W. 1969. The science and history of domestic animals. In *Science in archaeology*, 2nd edn, D. R. Brothwell and E. Higgs (eds), 257–72. London: Thames and Hudson.

Higham, C. F. W. 1969. The metrical attributes of two samples of bovine limb bones. *J. Zool., Lond.* **157**, 63–74.

Hurst, S. 1976. *Recording on excavations, I: The written record*. Hertford: Rescue.

Howard, M. M. 1963. The metrical attributes of two samples of bovine limb bones. In *Man and cattle*, A. Mourant and F. Zeuner (eds), 91–100. Royal Anthrop. Inst. Occ. Pap. no. 18.

Isaac, G. L. 1967. Towards the interpretation of occupation debris: some experiments and observations. *Kroeber Anthrop. Soc. Papers* **37**, 31–57.

Jackson, J. W. 1932. Report on the animal bones. In The Highfield pit dwellings, Fisherton, Salisbury, Wilts., F. Stevens (ed.). *Wilts. Arch. Nat. Hist. Mag.* **46**, 579–621.

Jackson, J. W. 1935. Report on the skeleton of the dog from ash pit C. Excavations at Easton Down, Winterslow, 1933–4, J. F. S. Stone (ed.), 76–8. *Wilts. Arch. Nat. Hist. Mag.* **47**, 76–8.

Jacobsen, T. W. 1976. 17000 years of Greek prehistory. *Scient. Am.* **234** (6), 76–81.

Jubb, K. U. F. and P. C. Kennedy 1963. *Pathology of domestic animals*, vol. 1. London: Academic Press.

Kiszely, I. 1974. On the possibilities and methods of the chemical determination of sex from bones. *Ossa* **1**, 51–62.

Koudelka, F. 1885, cited by Muller, R. 1967. *Die Tierknochenfunde aus den spätrömischen Siedlungsschichten von Lauriacum*. Dissertation, Munich University.

Krueger, H. W. 1965. The preservation and dating of collagen in ancient bones. *Proc. Sixth. int. Conf. Radiocarbon and Tritium Dating, Washington, 1965* 332–7.

Lee, R. B. 1965. *Subsistence ecology of !Kung bushmen*. Doctoral dissertation, University of California, Berkeley.

Lubbock, J. 1865. *Prehistoric times*. London: Williams and Norgate.

McFadyean, J. 1953. *The comparative anatomy of the domesticated animals*, Part 1, *Osteology and arthrology*, 4th edn. London: Ballière, Tindall and Cox.

Michels, J. M. 1976. *Dating methods in archaeology*. London: Seminar Press.

Noddle, B. A. 1974. Ages of epiphyseal closure in feral sheep and domestic goats and ages of dental eruption. *J. Arch. Sci.* **1**, 195–204.

Olsen, S. J. 1968. *Fish, amphibian and reptile remains from archaeological sites. Part 1. South east and south west United States of America*. Papers of the Peabody Museum of Archaeology and Ethnography, Harvard, no. VI (2).

Olsson, S. 1971. Degenerative joint disease (osteoarthrosis): a review with special reference to the dog. *J. Small Anim. Pract.* **12**, 333–42.

Østergard, M. 1980. X-ray diffractometer investigations of bones from domestic and wild animals. *Am. Antiquity* **48**, 59–63.

Payne, S. 1969. A metrical distinction between sheep and goat metacarpals. *The domestication and exploitation of plants and animals*, P. J. Ucko and G. W. Dimbleby (eds), 295–305. London: Duckworth.

Payne, S. 1972a. Partial recovery and sample bias: the results of some sieving experiments. In *Papers in economic prehistory*, E. Higgs (ed.), 49–64, London: Cambridge University Press.

Payne, S. 1972b. On the interpretation of bone samples from archaeological sites. In *Papers in economic prehistory*, E. Higgs (ed.), 65–81. London: Cambridge University Press.

Payne, S. 1973. Kill off patterns in sheep and goats: the mandibles from Asvan Käle. *Anatolian Stud.* **23**, 281–303.

Payne, S. 1975. Partial recovery and sample bias. In *Archaeozoological studies*, A. T. Clason (ed.), 7–17. Amsterdam: Elsevier.

Perkins, D. Jr and P. Daly 1968. A hunters' village in Neolithic Turkey. *Scient. Am.* **219** (5), 96–106.

Petrie, W. M. F. 1891. *Illahun, Kahun and Gurob*. London: Royal Anthropological Institute.

Platt, C. P. S. 1974. Priorities in publication. *Rescue News* 8.

Reed, C. A. 1963. Osteo-archaeology. In *Science in archaeology*, 2nd edn, D. Brothwell and E. Higgs (eds), 204–16. London: Thames and Hudson.

Ryder, M. L. 1968. *Animal bones in archaeology*. Oxford: Basil Blackwell.

Saxon, A. and C. F. W. Higham 1968. Identification and interpretation of growth rings in the secondary dental cementum of *Ovis aries* L. *Nature* **219**, 634–5.

Saxon, A. and C. Higham 1969. A new research method for economic prehistorians. *Am. Antiquity* **34**, 303–11.

Schmid, E. 1967. Tierreste aus einer Grossküche von Augusta Raurica. *Basler Stadtbuch*, 177–86.

Schmid, E. 1972. *Atlas of animal bones for prehistorians, archaeologists and quaternary geologists*. Amsterdam, London and New York: Elsevier.

Schramm, Z. 1967. Morphological differences of some sheep and goat bones (translated title). *Roczniki Wyszsei Rolniezey w Poznanin* **36**, 107–33.

Siegel, J. 1976. Animal palaeopathology: possibilities and problems. *J. Arch. Sci.* **3**, 349–84.

Silver, I. A. 1969. The ageing of domestic animals. *Science in archaeology*, 2nd edn, D. Brothwell and E. Higgs, 283–303. London: Thames and Hudson.

Sisson, S. 1953. *The anatomy of domesticated animals*, 4th edn. London: Saunders.

Sparks, B. W. 1961. The ecological interpretation of Quarternary non-marine Mollusca. *Proc. Linn. Soc. Lond.* **172**, 71–80.

Sutcliffe, A. J. 1970. Spotted hyaena, crusher, gnawer, digester and collector of bone. *Nature* **227**, 1110–3.

Thomas, D. H. 1969. Great Basin hunting patterns: a quantitative method for treating faunal remains. *Am. Antiquity* **34** (4), 392–401.

Ucko, P. and G. W. Dimbleby (eds) 1969. *The domestication and exploitation of plants and animals*. London: Duckworth.

Wäsle, R. 1976. *Gebissanomalien und pathologisch-anatomische Veränderungen an Knochenfunden aus archäeologischen Ausgrabungen*. München: Duss.

Watson, J. P. N. 1972. Fragmentation analysis of animal bone samples from archaeological sites. *Archaeometry* **14**, 221–8.

Watson, J. P. N. 1975. Domestication and bone structure in sheep and goats. *J. Arch. Sci.* **2**, 375–83.

White, T. E. 1955. The dog bones from Buffalo Pasture site. *Am. Antiquity* **21**, 170–8.

van Wijngaarden-Bakker, L. H. 1974. The animal remains from the Beaker Settlement at Newgrange, Co. Meath – first report. *Proc. R. Ir. Acad. C* **74**, 313–83.

van Wijngaarden-Bakker, L. H. and M. Krauwer 1979. Animal paleopathology. Some examples from the Netherlands. *Helinium* **19**, 37–53.

Williams, F. 1979. Excavations on Marefair, Northampton, 1977. *Northamptonshire Arch.* **14**, 38–79.

Yalden, D. 1977. Small mammals and the archaeologist. *Bull. Peakland Arch. Soc.* **30**, 1–25.

Yellen, J. E. 1977. Cultural patterning in faunal remains. In *Experimental archaeology*, Ingerson, J. E. Yellen and W. MacDonald (eds), 271–331. New York: Guildford.

Zalkin, V. I. 1961. The variability of metapodialia in sheep. *Byull. Mosk. Obsh. Isp. Prir. Otd. Biol.* **66**, 115–32.

11 Fish remains (and marine mammals)

Alive without breath,
As cold as death;
Never thirsty, ever drinking,
All in mail never clinking.

(J. R. R. Tolkien, *The Hobbit*)

11.1 Introduction

Fish, with their wide range of habitats, may be used as a guide to ancient hydrology, including the environment of deposition of the matrix sediments (Section 1.8), the range of aquatic environments exploited by man and the season of occupation of some sites. For example, if salmon is present the season of occupation may be gauged with some accuracy since the fish is anadromous, living part of its life cycle in freshwater and part in the sea. The presence of marine mammals such as the dolphin, seal or whale when combined with deep sea fish remains suggests skill in fishing and catching, involving the use of boats (Clark 1947).

The first work specifically concerned with fishbones is that of Sauvage (1875) dealing with material from the Upper Palaeolithic sites of Lartet and Christy. Kishinouye (1911), in a study of prehistoric fishing in Japan, produced another important paper which utilized the evidence of fish bones, scales and otoliths (p. 183) from a series of shell mounds, employing retrieval techniques including water separation and microscopic analysis for the extraction and identification of the faunas. However, it is true to say that fish remains have been less studied than any other form of vertebrate remains in archaeology (with the exception of birds) as a direct result of the paucity of reference collections and the inadequacy of much on-site retrieval. (Ryder 1969).

Fish may be divided into marine, estuarine and freshwater types. Marine fish occupy a series of habitats including rock pools, rocky coast, sandy coast and the deep sea; and freshwater fish fall into two separate categories depending on whether they live habitually in well oxygenated water (large lakes or rivers) or poorly oxygenated water such as ponds, backwaters or sluggish rivers. The types of fish remains include all the elements of the complex skeleton, which breaks up into a number of separate units, the most easily identifiable being the jaw bones and teeth. Vertebrae and other parts are more difficult but may be identified if a good reference collection is available. Otoliths (ear stones) are especially useful since they are easily identifiable to species and have the peculiar characteristic of growing in annual rings (as do the scales and vertebrae). It is therefore possible to use them to obtain an age for the fish, and hence some approximate estimate of size, and also to test for seasonality. They are, unfortunately, comparatively rarely recorded on archaeological sites, with the exception of North American coastal sites. Fish scales form the third category of information but are also quite rare.

It is important to remember that the fishbones identified from any site only represent a small percentage of the fish actually consumed at the site. Much care must be taken, both in excavation and identification, and there is still likely to be an unquantifiable element of fish species which are not represented by any remains. This is especially true of the shark and ray family (elasmobranchs) where the skeleton is cartilaginous and in which the only hard parts likely to survive are the skin denticles, jaw teeth and occasional fin spines. The first two categories are usually small and apt to be overlooked; the third is not present in all species. It is therefore quite possible that large quantities of the smaller sharks could have been captured but have left no archaeological trace. Such errors of sampling bias and interpretation may be important in the evaluation of an assemblage and it seems likely that the interpretation of fish remains is more error-prone than almost any other branch of environmental archaeology.

11.2   Field methods and sampling

The study of animal remains of any kind from an excavation has always been complicated by heavy bias in the method of retrieving the evidence. The implications of this bias are frequently skipped over in the report if, indeed, they are mentioned at all. With fish remains the bias is greater than for any other group since the fish are smaller and have more fragile hard parts than any other group of edible animals. Consequently, not only is their survival less likely, but additional bias is added from failure to remove the bones excavated (Wheeler & Jones 1976, Casteel 1972). This is mainly due to two factors: a failure to recognize fragments of fish (otoliths and certain skin structures may be mistaken, for example, for seeds), and secondly by the inability of the excavator to extract the smaller remains from their matrix sediment. The work of Payne (1972) demonstrated the importance of sieving in the recovery of small bones and illustrated the fact that only by sieving could a representative assessment of the fauna be reached. Payne produced a list of nine species of fish obtained from the spoil heaps of the Sitagroi excavation, where no fish remains had been obtained by conventional hand picking. Mellars and Payne (1971), reporting on shell middens from Orkney, stressed the need for a very fine sieve mesh (1 mm and 2 mm) to collect fish bones. They noted one species (the saithe, *Pollachius virens*) from a Mesolithic site whose presence was revealed by fine sieving and which is also found in the area today. It had, however, been omitted from earlier fish lists on similar sites (Bishop 1913), presumably because the bones were missed in excavation. The Great Yarmouth excavations (Wheeler & Jones 1976) showed the large amount of information which could be obtained from fish remains by a combi-

nation of hand picking and flotation. The excavated sediment was first hand sorted for pottery, mammal and fish bones and small finds. This was followed by flotation, using a version of the Siraf flotation tank (Williams 1973) modified by fitting a recycling centrifugal water pump and settlement tank. This latter was fitted with 1 mm mesh, found to be an optimum size since anything coarser let through too many bones and very fine meshes clogged too quickly. A total of 2130 kg of sediment passed through this apparatus and the problem of the initial tedious sorting of the residue was overcome by using inexperienced schoolchildren under the supervision of professional archaeologists. As a direct consequence of these methods of retrieval, Wheeler and Jones obtaincd a far more complete record of the fish caught by the early medieval inhabitants of Great Yarmouth than was previously available for any site in England. Nineteen species of marine fish were identified from their various remains, providing a useful comparison with a nearby site at East Lynn where only hand picking was carried out and thus produced only eight species. The Great Yarmouth sample represented not only a broader spectrum of available food resources but also the remains of several smaller species which were no doubt of great importance both to the fishing industry and to the diet of the inhabitants. Follett (1969a,b, 1970) discusses the recovery of fish remains from coprolite.

11.3   Sample identification

Although illustrated textbooks such as those of Olsen (1968, 1971) have been used to show basic osteological differences, it is still essential to have a reference collection. Since, on the last count, there were only two large comprehensive collections available in the UK for consultation in this country, many people prefer to make their own. Fish, unlike the larger mammals, are reasonably easy to clean, deflesh and prepare. Standard works on fish anatomy such as Starks (1901), Lagler *et al.* (1962) and Gregory (1933) are the most useful, together with the works cited by Casteel (1976b) describing the detailed characteristics of particular families of fish.

11.4 Otoliths

These occur widely among the different groups of vertebrates but are most distinctive with fish. They consist of small concretions of calcium carbonate (derived from food and the immersing water) within the fish inner ear, which is filled with a fluid (endolymph) forming part of the system which controls balance and hearing and (possibly) the analysis of sounds (Fig. 11.2). Two main groups of otoliths may be distinguished. *Statoconia* are the smaller of the two, 1–50 mm in diameter, not characteristic to species and occurring in such Orders as Chondrostei (sturgeons) and Cyclostomata. *Statoliths* are larger and are found in all higher bony fishes with the exception of the sturgeon family, which has both types. They are made of calcium carbonate in the crystal form of aragonite and occur in three pairs, called after their shapes the sagitta (arrow), lapilla (small stone) and astericus (small star). The inner face of the otolith (Fig. 11.2) is flat or convex and highly sculptured, its features enabling the fish to be identified to species level. The otolith identification system was used well back in the nineteenth century but is comparatively limited in its archaeological applications. Von Ihering (1891) wrote a pioneer study in this field concerning archaeological sites in Brazil whose fish remains he identified by making a reference collection of species from the local market. Later papers such as those of Fitch (1967), Witt (1960) and Priegel (1963) used otolith remains to

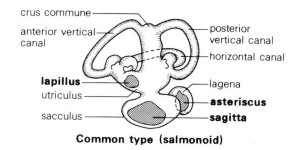

Common type (salmonoid)

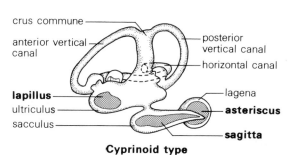

Cyprinoid type

Figure 11.2 Location of otolith types in the fish inner ear (after Lagler *et al.* 1962).

study the fish from palaeo-Indian sites. Other important papers are those of Shumway *et al.* (1961), Morse (1963) and Follett (1965, 1967b) but no work of this type has been done outside North America.

11.4.1 Extraction and identification

Otoliths are best extracted by wet sieving using a mesh size of 10–30 (3 φ), and identified with a low power microscope (Frizzell 1965, Fitch 1966, Fitch & Reimer 1967).

11.4.2 Estimation of live weight

There is a direct relationship between the size of the fish and the size of the otoliths, demonstrated by Templeton and Squires (1965) who worked on haddock, and Trout (1954) who worked on cod. Two statistical techniques have been employed, single and double regression, using a linear measure of otolith size rather than otolith weight since this latter may change on fossilization or burial. The length, rather than the breadth, of the otolith is used (Irie 1960). An example of this single regression method may be seen in the work of Casteel (1974a) on the asterisci of the family Catostomidae (suckers) using the formula

$$\log Y + 0.8845 + 3.4288 \log X,$$

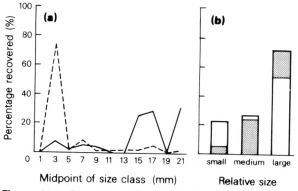

Figure 11.1 Bias in sampling fish otoliths and terrestrial molluscs. The solid line represents samples collected by eye and the dotted line bulk samples collected after fine screening and examination under the microscope. (a) Mollusc samples (after Sparks 1961 and Casteel 1972); (b) fish otoliths (after Fitch 1966 and Casteel 1972).

where X is the live weight of the fish (in grams) and Y is the length of the otolith (in millimetres). The resultant variables correlated to $r > 0.97$. Witt (1960) used the double regression method to estimate the size of freshwater drum (*Aplodinotus grunniens*) from the archaeological site of Lee Mill Lane (Mississippi River, Minnesota).

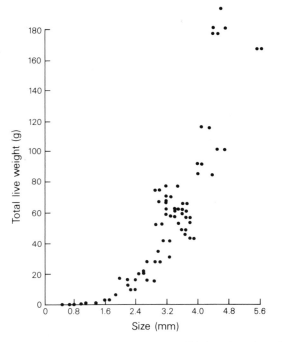

Figure 11.3 Relationship between otolith length and total live weight in 89 samples of the asterisci of Catostomodae (from Casteel 1974).

11.4.3 Other applications

Other applications include the calculation of the minimum number of individual fish present which was done, for example, by White (1953) for paired skeletal elements. It is quite easy to distinguish the right and left of a pair of otoliths but necessary to allow for animals of different sizes within the same species. Otoliths may also be used for seasonal dating, as was first done by Reibisch (1899), using their annual growth rings, a method at least as effective as similar calculations done from scales. The high carbonate content of the otoliths also makes them suitable for $^{18}O/^{17}O$ palaeotemperature analysis, an example being the work of Devereux (1967) on Pliocene and Miocene fish.

11.5 Scales

There are four different types of scale, distinguished by their shape: *placoid* (platelike) with each plate bearing a small cusp – this type is common among sharks and related fishes; *rhombic* (ganoid), diamond-shaped scales characteristic of the gars; *cycloid* (thin, smooth discs), roughly circular in shape and characteristic of many of the freshwater fishes especially the minnows; *ctenoid* scales which carry small pointed projections (ctenii) along the poterior margin and are especially common among the perches. In addition to these groups of scales some species possess spines, which may be identifiable, as in the sturgeon or stickleback. Cycloid or ctenoid scales may identify the fish to species by showing different characteristics on their surface. These must be compared with keys produced by Lagler (1947), Peabody (1928), and Cockerell (1910, 1911, 1913). However, despite the claims of Casteel (1976a) that all fish scales are identifiable to species, various workers are still of the opinion that the precise identification of all material recovered from excavations is, and always will be, impossible.

11.5.1 Archaeological applications

Fish scales are quite common on excavations and a long list of examples is given by Casteel (1976b). The size of the fish may be estimated from careful measurement of the scales (Fig. 11.4) to compare the data obtained with information from modern species. Dietary patterning, seasonal variations, minimum numbers of individuals present and estimates of population are then possible. Examples of different site applications may be found in the work of Bishop (1913) on a Mesolithic shell mound in Orkney, Heizer and Krieger (1956) on cave deposits, Napton and Heizer (1970) and Bryant (1974) on coprolite, Gehlbach and Miller (1961) on North American fish and Goodwin (1946) on South African prehistoric fishing methods.

11.6 Skeletal elements

Of all the fish skeletal elements occasionally represented on archaeological sites vertebrae are by far the most common and in some cases may be the only bones recovered (Cheynier 1965). Each vertebra consists of a centrum and attached spines, although the latter will sometimes be missing and often broken. Identification to family and perhaps to species level should be possible from the surface features of the centrum, but since archaeological material is generally dislocated and fragmentary such studies rely upon an almost extra-sensory ability to recognize key features on a specimen seen out of context. A good reference collection is essential. The anterior and posterior faces of vertebrae also have annular rings which may be used for age assessment, and weight estimates are made using ratios and formulae similar to that already described for otoliths (p. 183). Casteel (1976b) lists some of the more important archaeological examples, including recent Russian work.

Wheeler and Jones (1976) took the measurements of cod, whiting and haddock bones using a conventional dial calliper reading to 0.1 mm. The bones used were the upper jaw (premaxilla), using the width across the base of the ascending process and the articular process (P, Fig. 11.5) and the dentary

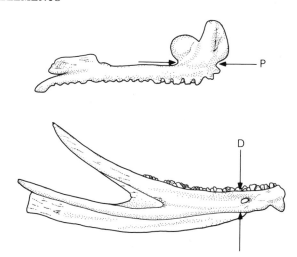

Figure 11.5 Good jaw bones showing points of measurement across the premaxilla (P) and dentary (D) (after Wheeler & Jones 1976).

(D, Fig. 11.5), measuring the depth of the bone across the proximal edge of the foramen from the base of the tooth row to the angle of the bone. These two bones were selected since they were strong, heavy and survived well. The other head bones are not usually so distinctive except in specific instances such as the gurnard (characteristic sculptured cranial bones), the halibut (maxilla), bass (strongly toothed subercles), ling (vomer) and haddock (posttemporals), which were also used as they were diagnostic.

11.6.1 The Fullers Hill excavation, Great Yarmouth

This excavation (Wheeler & Jones 1976) was located at the highest point of the medieval town and revealed an 11th and 12th century occupation stratified between layers of sand, divided into 12 phases. Fishing formed the basis of the economy (Rogerson 1976) and information obtained from the fish bones included the comparative importance of different species to the fishing industry, and of the sizes and meat weights of the more important species. Examination of the list of species present (Table 11.1) suggests that herring, cod, whiting and mackerel were dominant in all phases. It seems, therefore, to be a fair inference that they were the most important species captured. Plaice also occur in most samples, as do haddock and conger eel

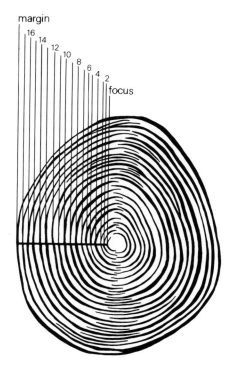

Figure 11.4 Diagram of a fish scale showing the annual rings, thus the sunfish scale is enlarged × 175.

Table 11.1 Fish remains from Fullers Hill, Great Yarmouth (data from Wheeler & Jones 1976).

Phase	Approximate weight of recovered bone (g)	Spur dog	Thorn-back ray	Cartilaginous fishes	Eel	Conger eel	Garfish	Herring	Whiting	Cod	Haddock	Ling	Bass	Horse mackerel	Mackerel	Tub gurnard	Turbot	Flounder	Plaice	Halibut	Dover sole	Other flatfish
I	85		××			×		×××	××	××××	×			××	××							
II	280		××			×		×××	×××	×××	×			××	××	×			××			×
III	40		×			×		×××	×××	×××				××	××				×			
IV	60					×		×××	××	××				×	×××							
V	140			×	×	×	×	×××	×××	×××				××	××				×××			×
VI	200		×		×	×		×××	××	×××	×			××	××				×××	×		×
VII	1080	××	×		×			×××	×××	×××××	×	×		××	××		×		××			×
VIII	2270		×		×	××		×××	××	×××××	×	×	×	×	×		×	×	××		××	×
IX	250		×		×	×		×××	××	×××××				×	×					×	××	×
X	120				×	×		×××	××	×××××		×		××	×				×			×
XI	100		×	×	×			×××	××	×××××					××				×			
XII	2200			×	×	×		×××	××	×××××	××	×		××	×				×××	×		×

×, species present; ××, fairly frequent; ×××, most abundant species.

(although less abundantly). The remaining fishes are represented by relatively few bones and are widely spread through the phases. They were probably less important food fish.

Estimate of live weight. One of the most important values calculated from the fish remains was the actual meat weight represented. The relationship of length to weight in normal width is logarithmic and within certain limits the weight of a specimen of known or estimated length can be found quite accurately by plotting a regression for these paramaters. This was done for cod by measuring the premaxilla width and dentary depth with the results being plotted graphically and showing a clear linear relationship. The length-to-weight relationship of North Sea cod has been calculated by Blackner (1969) in a set of data showing, for example, that a cod of length 500 mm weighs an average 1.09 kg after gutting. A fish twice this length gives an average gutted weight of 8.67 kg (Fig. 11.6). Thus, the gutted weight of the cod represented in the excavations could be calculated. The project was extended to give the maximum and minimum weights represented and the frequency of occurrence of cod of estimated weight expressed in the forms of histograms, based on data derived from the dentary and premaxilla bones of Phases 8 and 11 when cod is best represented (Fig. 11.6). In Phase 8, cod occurred in two well represented size classes,

0.5–2 kg and 4–8 kg by premaxilla measurements, 1–2 kg and 3.5–6 kg by dentary measurements. In Phase 12 there is only one broad peak of fish of 4–8 kg estimated weight (premaxilla measurements) and 2–7 kg dentary measurement, with a single smaller fish recorded of weight approximately 0.5 kg. The calculation based on the premaxilla probably gives a more accurate representation of the sample, as the size range of the measurement is larger, resulting in less measuring error.

Fishing methods. Of the 19 species represented (Table 11.1), five are classed as pelagic (surface-living), the herring (*Clupea harengus*), horse mackerel (*Trachurus trachurus*), mackerel (*Scomber scombrus*), garfish (*Belone bellone*) and bass (*Dicentrarchus labrax*). Although the bass, mackerel and garfish could be caught on hooks, the herring and horse mackerel are most likely to be caught by surface nets. The fishhooks from Phases 1–9 are all large and many have a distinct bar, effective only in the capture of the largest fish such as spur dog (*Squalus acanthias*), conger eel (*Conger conger*), ling (*Molva molva*), cod (*Gadus morhua*), large haddock (*Melanogrammus aeglefinus*), turbot (*Scophthalnus maximum*), and halibut (*Hippoglossus hippoglossus*). Many of the smaller fish could also be captured in a small shore sieve, for example whiting (*Merlangius merlangus*), plaice (*Pleuronectes platessa*), small cod (*Gadus morhua*) and sole (*Solea solea*). Two species, the eel (*Anguiia anguiia*) and the flounder (*Platichthys flesus*) were caught in rivers or tidal waters in Great Yarmouth on hooks, although both can be speared. The many-pronged leister (fish spear) was the traditional method of catching eels in East Anglia, as it was in the Netherlands and elsewhere. Most of the species identified could be caught off Great Yarmouth today, but three would be classified as rare or uncommon. The haddock was more common in the southern North Sea than it is today, a change due to climatic alteration or heavy fishing pressure. It could also be inferred that the cod bones which represented two divergent length groups might be the result of two different fisheries. Young cod are common today in winter in the southern North Sea but large ones are much less common. The histograms show two distinct groups of cod represented by the remains in Phase 8, and it is tempting to interpret this as evidence of local fisheries which produced the smaller fish as a result of winter fishing and importation from distant waters. The evidence is not clear cut and it is, of course, possible that larger cod were more common in the southern North Sea in medieval times than they are today. The authors conclude that fishing was undoubtedly practised by several methods, including nets and line and hook. It was probably carried out at all seasons of the year, depending on the availability of the various species. The nearness of the river would give fishing even when the weather was too rough to put out to sea and would also have been the location of the eel and flounder found in the deposits. This report is important as an example of careful, painstaking extraction techniques and reasoned interpretation, giving a vital perspective on the lives of the medieval inhabitants of the town.

11.6.2 Prehistoric coastal economy at Galatea Bay, New Zealand

This site consists of midden deposits on an island off North Island, New Zealand, overlooking a sheltered area of the sea from the mouth of a small and now dry valley (Shawcross 1967). An initially specialized cooking area was replaced by dumps of food waste and then abandoned, the fishbone being systematically recovered in excavation and examined for information concerning the size and type of fish being caught, relevant both to studies of meat weight availability and possible fishing methods. Density plots of bone show two areas of very high concentration where the finds consisted almost entirely of fishbone. Three jawbones (premaxilla, maxilla and dentary) were measured (Fig. 11.7), together with the vertebrae. Most of the jawbones belonged to a single fish species, the snapper

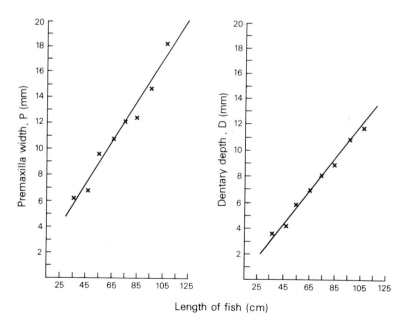

Length of fish (cm)

Figure 11.6 Relationship between premaxilla width and dentary depth with total length of cod (after Wheeler & Jones 1976).

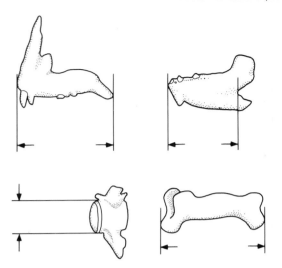

Figure 11.7 Measurements of the premaxilla, dentary, maxillary and vertebrae used by Shawcross (1967) at Galatea Bay.

(*Chrysophrys auratus* Forster). A reference collection of common local fish was made by recording weights and dimensions and then steaming the specimens to remove the flesh. Calculations based on this data showed a minimum number of 108 snapper at the site, as 'clearly there cannot have been less individuals than there were right-sided jaws' (Shawcross 1967, p. 112). The relative frequencies of the different parts of the snappers' bodies are shown in Figure 11.8, with the proportions shown as percentage calculations on the theory that the expected frequency of the bones should be a complete skeleton multiplied by the total number of fish. The best represented bones are clearly those of the head, with the trunk poorly represented and the extremities most poorly of all. This might be because the jaws are the strongest bones, but the vertebrae are at least as solid. The bones of the head do tend, of course, to hold together while the rest is dispersed. Ethnographic observations (Best 1925, p. 34) also suggest that the Maoris dried fish on site with the head already separated. Further ethnographic evidence suggests that Maori life was strongly influenced by the seasons and that there were regionally distinct activity cycles. It would seem that this site was occupied during the summer months since the dental state of the subfossil snapper jaws corresponds closely to a modern control sample of fish

caught locally and examined for the eruption, anchylosis and exfoliation of their teeth. The gross seasonal differences which become apparent in snapper dentition are a reflection of a change in diet from shellfish (eaten in winter) to 'jellyfish' (especially the salp, *Thallia democratica*) eaten in the summer. The summer teeth appear to be fragile but during the winter become firmly embedded in the jaws. The relationship between the percentage of exfoliated summer teeth in the summer-season contemporary sample and the two groups of the subfossil teeth may be seen in Table 11.2.

11.6.3 Marine mammals: whales as an economic factor in prehistoric Europe

Clark (1947), in a classic study, examined the evidence for the hunting and utilization of the flesh of various species of whale, porpoise and dolphin, collating prehistoric, Dark Age and medieval evidence. He concluded that while stranded whales certainly played as important a role in the prehistoric economy as they did in the medieval (especially in northern Scotland and the islands) there is evidence to suggest that various species of marine mammals were actively hunted, at any rate in Scandinavia. Eskimos hunt Greenland whale from skin-covered boats (umiaks) of a type certainly used as early as the Upper Palaeolithic, using harpoons with detachable heads and heavy lances. Various British sites, including Skara Brae, contain fairly numerous whale bones, but this may under-represent the importance of whales in the economy since bones would only have been retrieved if destined for toolmaking, due

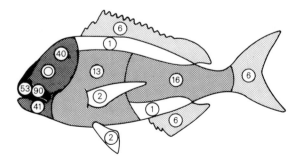

Figure 11.8 The relative frequencies of the different parts of the snappers' bodies found at Galatea Bay, New Zealand. The maxillary was used to estimate the total number of fish present but it still only has a value of 90% due to the unequal numbers from each side of the jaw (from Shawcross 1967).

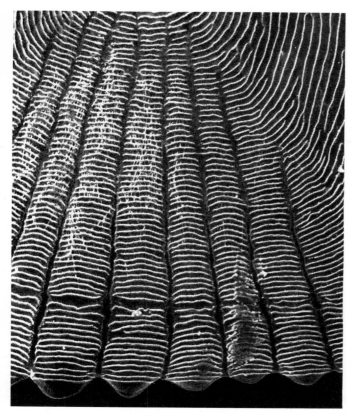

Figure 11.9 Scanning electron photomicrograph of fish scales × 175.

Table 11.2 Comparing subfossil snapper jaws with contemporary samples from winter and summer, and internally comparing the dental state of two separate dumps of subfossil jaws.

Season	Jaw	State	Contemporary sample (%)	A–D (%)	E–F (%)
winter	dentary	eruption	1.7	1.1	1.5
		anchylosis	98.1	0.1	0.1
		exfoliation	0.2	98.8	98.4
	premaxillary	eruption	1.4	1.0	1.2
		anchylosis	98.4	0.1	0.8
		exfoliation	0.2	98.9	98.0
summer	dentary	eruption	0.9	1.1	1.5
		anchylosis	3.1	0.1	0.1
		exfoliation	96.0	98.8	98.4
	premaxillary	eruption	1.4	1.0	1.2
		anchylosis	1.1	0.1	0.8
		exfoliation	97.5	98.9	98.0

to their weight and size. Table 11.3 lists the incidence of the different whale species on prehistoric sites and rock-engraving in Scandinavia, showing a marked emphasis on the smaller toothed whales (94.3%) at the expense of the larger Baleen whales (5.7%). The common porpoise is remarkably numerous, occurring in 69% of the representations of findings. This seems strange, but specialized porpoise fisheries were known from medieval and later Europe, the flesh being considered a delicacy although 'of very hard digestion, noysome to the stomack, and of a very grosse, excrementall and naughty juyce' (Venner 1620, p. 106). It is possible that the relatively small numbers of whale bones on early sites might also suggest that whales were not so fiercely pursued as seals, which were easier to hunt. The whale had numerous uses: its flesh and blubber as food, light and warmth, its leather for boots, ropes and shoelaces. Whalebone, too, was used as everything from fuel to house construction, so the effort involved in hunting these large mammals was clearly worthwhile.

Table 11.3 The incidence of different species of whale among remains from prehistoric sites and among representations on Stone Age rock-engravings of Scandinavia.

	Danish sites	Swedish sites*	Norwegian sites	Total from sites	Representations on rock-engravings
Balaenidae (right whales)					
Greenland	1	—	—	1	—
Biscay	—	—	—	—	—
Balaenopteridae (rorquals)					
humpback	—	—	—	—	—
sei-whale	—	—	—	—	—
lesser finwhale	—	—	—	—	—
blue whale	1	—	—	1	—
common rorqual	—	—	—	—	—
total baleen whales	2	—	—	2	—
Physeteridae					
sperm whale	1	—	—	1	—
bottle-nosed whale	—	—	—	—	1?
Delphinapteridae					
white whale	1	—	—	1	—
narwhale	—	—	—	—	—
Delphinidae (true dolphins)					
pilot whale	—	—	1	1	1
killer whale	3	1	2	6	3
common porpoise	10	3	3	16	20
Risso's dolphin	—	—	—	—	—
white-sided dolphin	—	—	1	1	—
white-beaked dolphin	1	2	—	3	—
common dolphin	1	1	—	2	—
bottle-nosed dolphin	1	—	—	1	—
dolphin sp. ?	1	—	—	1	4
total toothed whales	19	7	7	33	29
total whales	21	7	7	35	29

*In addition, *Mesoplodon bidens* occurred at a West Swedish site.

References

Best, E. 1925. *Maori agriculture. Dom. Mus. Bull.* no. 9.

Bishop, A. H. 1913. An Oronsay shell-mound – a Scottish pre-Neolithic site. *Proc. Soc. Antiq. Scot.* **48**, 52–108.

Blackner, R. W. 1969. Chemical composition of the zones in cod (*Gadus marhua* L.) otoliths. *J. Cons. Int. Explor. Mer.* **33**, 107–8.

Bryant, V. M. Jr 1974. Prehistoric diet in southwest Texas: the coprolite evidence. *Am. Antiquity* **39**, 407–20.

Casteel, R. W. 1972. Some biases in the recovery of archaeological remains. *Proc. Prehist. Soc.* **38**, 382–8.

Casteel, R. W. 1974. A method for the estimation of live weight of fish from the size of skeletal elements. *Am. Antiquity* **39**, 94–8.

Casteel, R. W. 1976a. Comparison of column and whole unit samples for recovering fish remains. *Wld Arch.* **8**, 192–6.

Casteel, R. W. 1976b. *Fish remains in archaeology and paleo-environmental studies.* London: Academic Press.

Cheynier, A. 1965. L'abri Lachaud à Terrasson (Dordogne). *Préhistoire* **16**.

Clark, J. G. D. 1947. Whales as an economic factor in prehistoric Europe. *Antiquity* **21**, 84–104.

Cockerell, T. D. A. 1910. The scales of European cyprinoid fishes. *Zool. Anz.* **36**, 475–80.

Cockerell, T. D. A. 1911. The scales of freshwater fishes. *Biol Bull.* **20**, 367–86.

Cockerell, T. D. A. 1913. Observations on fish scales. *Bull. U.S. Bur. Fish* **32**, 119–74.

Devereux, I. 1967. Temperature measurements from oxygen isotope ratios of fish otoliths. *Science* **155**, 1684–5.

Fitch, J. E. 1966. *Additional fish remains, mostly otoliths, from a Pleistocene deposit at Playa del Ray, California.* Los Angeles Co. Mus. Nat. Hist. Contr. Sci. no. 119.

Fitch, J. E. 1967. Fish remains recovered from a Corona del Mar, California, Indian midden (Ora-190). *Calif. Fish Game* **53**, 185–91.

Fitch, J. E. and R. D. Reimer 1967. Otoliths and other fish remains from a Long Beach, California, Pliocene deposit. *5th Calif. Acad. Sci. Bull.* **66**, 77–91.

Follett, W. I. 1965. Fish remains in the archaeological context. *Sacramento Anthrop. Soc. Cent. Calif. Arch. Found. Pap.* **3**, 36–46.

Follett, W. I. 1967a. Fish remains from coprolites and midden deposits at Lovelock Cave, Churchill County, Nevada. *Berkeley: Univ. Calif. Arch. Surv. Rep.* **70**, 94–115.

Follett, W. I. 1967b. Fish remains from Salinas la Blanca, an archaeological site on the Pacific coast of Guatemala. *Smithson. Contr. Anthrop.* **3**, 129–34.

Follett, W. I. 1970. Fish remains from human coprolites and midden deposits obtained during 1968 and 1969 at Lovelock Cave, Churchill County, Nevada. In *Archaeology and the prehistoric Great Basin lacustrine subsistence regime as seen from Lovelock Cave, Nevada*, R. F. Heizer and L. K. Napton (eds), 163–75. Univ. Calif. Arch. Res. Fac. Contr. no. 10.

Frizzell, D. L. 1965. Otoliths. In *Handbook of paleontological techniques*, B. Kummel and D. Raup (eds), 125–7. San Francisco and London: W. H. Freeman.

Gehlbach, F. E. and R. R. Miller 1961. Fishes from archaeological sites in northern New Mexico, *S. West. Nat.* **6** (1), 2–8.

Goodwin, A. J. H. 1946. Prehistoric fishing methods in South Africa. *Antiquity* **20**, 134–41.

Gregory, W. K. 1933. Fish skulls: a study of the evolution of natural mechanisms. *Trans Am. Phil. Soc.* **33** (2).

Heizer, R. F. and A. D. Krieger 1956. The archaeology of Humboldt Cave, Churchill County, Nevada. *Univ. Calif. Publs Am. Arch. Ethnol.* **47** (1).

von Ihering, H. 1891. Uber die zoologisch-systematisch Bedeutung Gehororgane der Teleostier. *Z. Wiss. Zool.* **52**, 477–514.

Irie, T. 1960. The growth of fish otoliths. *J. Fac. Fish. Anim. Husb. Hiroshima Univ.* **3**, 203–29.

Kishinouye, K. 1911. Prehistoric fishing in Japan. *J. Coll. Agric. Imp. Univ. Tokyo* **2**, 328–82.

Lagler, K. F. 1947. Lepidological studies 1. Scale characters of the families of Great Lake fishes. *Trans Am. Microsc. Soc.* **66**, 149–71.

Lagler, K. F., J. E. Bardach and R. R. Miller 1962. *Ichthyology.* New York: Wiley.

Mellars, P. and S. Payne 1971. Excavations of two Mesolithic shell middens on the island of Oronsay (Inner Hebrides). *Nature* **231**, 397–8.

Morse, D. F. 1963. *The Stenben village and mounds: a multicomponent Late Hopewell site in Illinois.* Univ. Mich. Mus. Anthrop. Anthrop. Pap. no. 21.

Napton, L. K. and R. F. Heizer 1970. Analysis of human coprolites from archaeological contexts with primary reference to Lovelock Cave, Nevada. *Univ. Calif. Arch. Res. Fac. Contr.* **10**, 87–129.

Olsen, S. J. 1968. *Fish, amphibian and reptile remains from archaeological sites. Part 1. Southeastern and southwestern United States.* Pap. Peabody Mus. no. 56 (2).

Olsen, S. J. 1971. *Zooarchaeology: animal bones in archaeology and their interpretation.* London: Addison-Wesley.

Payne, S. 1972. Partial recovery and sample bias: the results of some sieving experiments. In *Papers in economic prehistory*, E. S. Higgs (ed.), 49–63. London: Cambridge University Press.

Peabody, E. B. 1928. The scales of some fishes of the suborder Clupeoidei. *Univ. Colo. Stud.* **16**, 127–48.

Priegel, G. R. 1963. Use of otoliths to determine length and weight of ancient freshwater drum in the Lake Winnebago area. *Wisc. Acad. Sci. Arts Letters* **52**, 27–35.

Reibisch, J. 1899. Uber die Einzahl bei *Pleuromectes platessa* und die Alterbestimmung dieser Form aus den Otolithen. *Wiss. Meeresunters. Abt. Kiel* **4**, 231–48.

Ryder, M. L. 1969. Remains of fishes and other aquatic animals. In *Science in archaeology*, 2nd edn, D. Brothwell and E. Higgs (eds), 376–94. London: Thames and Hudson.

Sauvage, E. 1875. On fishing during the reindeer period. In *Reliquaie Aquitanicae, being contributions to the archaeology and paleontology of Perigord and the adjoining provinces of southern France.* E. Lartet and H. Christy (eds), 219–25. London: Williams and Norgate.

Shawcross, W. 1967. An investigation of prehistoric diet and economy on a coastal site at Galatea Bay, New Zealand. *Proc. Prehist. Soc.* **33**, 107–31.

Shumway, G., C. L. Hubbs and J. R. Moriarty 1961. Scripps Estate site San Diego, California: a La Jolla site dated 5460 to 7370 years before the present. *Ann. N.Y. Acad. Sci.* **93** (3), 37–132.

Starks, E. C. 1901. Synonymy of the fish skeleton. *Proc. Wash. Acad. Sci.* **3**, 507–39.

Templeton, W. and H. J. Squires 1965. Relationship of otolith lengths and weights in the haddock *Melanogrammus aeglifinus* (L.) to the rate of growth of the fish. *J. Fish. Res. Bd Can.* **13**, 467–87.

Trout, G. C. 1954. Otolith growth of the Barents Sea cod. *Rapp. Proc. – Verb. Reun. Cons. int. Explor. Mer.* **136**, 89–102.

Venner, T. (1620). *Via recta ad vitam longam.* London: Griffin, for Moore.

Wheeler, A. and A. Jones 1976. Fish remains. In *Excavations on Fullers Hill, Great Yarmouth*, A. Rogerson (ed.), 212–25. East Anglian Archaeological Report 2, Norfolk Archaeological Unit.

White, T. E. 1953. Observations on the butchering technique of some aboriginal peoples No. 2. *Am. Antiquity* **19**, 160–4.

Williams, D. 1973. Flotation at Sīrāf. *Antiquity* **47**, 288–92.

Witt, A. Jr 1960. Length and weight of ancient freshwater drum *Aplodinotus grunniens* calculated from otoliths found in Indian middens. *Copeia* (3), 181–5.

12 *Birds*

A wonderful bird is the pelican,
His beak will hold more than his belican.
He can take in his beak
Food enough for a week
But I'm damned if I see how the helican.

(Dixon Lanier Merritt, *The Pelican*)

12.1 Introduction

Bird bones on archaeological sites are generally collected by man, except in rare cases including the owl-pellet accumulations of palaeolithic cave sites. One needs to know the present and former distribution of the species, its range of ecological tolerance and the factors which are critical in determining that range, together with seasonal distribution of the species. The geographical range of many bird species is very wide indeed, stretching for thousands of miles, and since birds may also travel great distances during their seasonal migrations a very detailed knowledge of their behaviour is clearly a prerequisite of archaeornithological work.

Perhaps the main importance of bird remains in archaeology is that the biological and ecological requirements of birds are often very specific, but like some varieties of mammals birds will adapt themselves to new and sometimes man-made habitats. In recent years studies have been made on the changing distribution of small mammals, including the fox, which is becoming a regular dweller on urban sites, and similar work has also been started on changing habitat preferences of birds, especially the common urban birds such as the varieties of sparrow, in recent years. Bird remains have been primarily used in archaeological contexts to act as indicators of seasonal occupation, or to provide dietary evidence. The volume of background information available to aid in the interpretation of this material is increasing all the time, but the slow increase in the number of good archaeological bird bone reports which appears each year is no doubt due to the erratic retrieval of such bones on site and the paucity of specialists who are willing,

and able, to deal with them (Dawson 1969). In fact over 37 sites from Britain have published bird reports mostly done by one man (Don Bramwell), but these vary from the large Exeter report (p. 196) to one-line entries.

12.2 Identification

The skeletons of bird species are much more alike than those of mammal species; there are no keys to work from, meaning that a good reference collection is essential but will be difficult to obtain. Many species which are rare now were common in the past; some may even be extinct. Mammals have approximately 240 skeletal elements and birds only about 100, but they are small and more difficult to work with. The range of potential species is often much greater, but fish are, of course, an even worse problem since they may have 300 separate skeletal elements, some microscopic in size.

12.3 Interpretation

Bird remains from archaeological contexts can be grouped into food-producing and wild species. The most important use of birds has always been food, although, like mollusca, they seldom provide the bulk of the diet. There are, inevitably, exceptions to this generalization, for example, in New Zealand where the 3 m high ostrich-like flightless moas proved to be a very important source of food, causing their eventual extinction. Certain species (e.g. the domestic fowl) may be very important to the economy, but this importance will vary both diachronically and synchronically on the site. One family will never eat exactly the same amount of chicken as another down the road; they may also prefer different parts of the bird (these days of pre-packed chicken joints would completely change the picture of chicken consumption if it was calculated from domestic refuse), cook it in different ways and have preferred purchases, perhaps birds of specific size or weight. There will be little correlation between domestic bird remains and rural husbandry in the area, except in the very broadest sense. Birds do have other economic uses. Feathers were used by American Indians for costumes and by the Incas for ceremonial ornaments. Some birds provide much fat (the goose, for example; Riddell 1943) or were kept as pets (canaries), as sacred birds (ibis in Egypt) and for a wide variety of other reasons (e.g. pigeons for racing and communications).

Wild species on urban sites have been used principally as environmental indicators and their assemblages are affected by trade, hunting and fowling preferences, as well as the construction of or alteration of habitats. Fowling was a very important activity in the Middle Ages but is much less important now (Clark 1947). If the site is not a subsistence one, then the catchment area from which the wild bird fauna came is going to be restricted to the immediate area of the site. Interpretations of avian faunas proceed in a manner similar to that already described for large mammals (Section 10.5), establishing the MNI present for each species and then commenting on features of interest in the individual or the assemblage. An example (remarkable especially for its succinctness) might be the report of Bramwell (1979) on the two bird bones from the Iron Age and Norman riverside settlements at Farmoor, Oxfordshire (Lambrich & Robinson 1979):

F5, stockdove femur, F43, corncrake sternum. Both bones are Roman in date *c*. AD third to fourth centuries. The stockdove is a very edible bird favouring old parkland which usually nests in tree holes. The corncrake is a summer migrant once widespread in Britain on farmland such as cornfields and meadows. The sternum is slightly immature, possibly a bird captured during reaping operation in September.

12.4 Lovelock Cave, Nevada

A useful way of examining the structure of bird reports is to contrast two very different types of archaeological sites which yielded bird bones. Suitable opposites are caves and the type of complex stratigraphic series which are found, for example, in medieval urban situations. The comparatively restricted number of palaeornithological studies in archaeology does not permit large-scale general conclusions like those permissible with mammalian remains (Section 10.7).

At Lovelock Cave in arid west central Nevada (USA) one of the largest and most varied collections of bird remains in archaeology was reported by Napton and Brunetti (1969), including quills, skin, eggshell, several hundred bones, two dozen mummified heads of waterbirds stuffed with grass or tule (Loud and Harrington 1929, pp. 49–50) and a number of complete decoys made of bundles of bulrush culms bound together and covered with the heads, skins and feathers of ducks and geese and other waterfowl (Fig. 12.1). These form one of the earliest examples of taxidermy from North America and nothing like them is yet known from Europe. Human coprolite analysis from the cave showed that wildfowl was an important food source, taken from the littoral zone of Lake Humboldt which, at the time of occupation, was some two miles away. The excavation of the site, carried out in 1912 and 1924, produced at least 16 different species of bird, although no estimate of MNI for species was presented in the original report. A similar assemblage of 19 species was identified from the nearby Humboldt cave and both sites had a midden which produced identifiable feathers. Feathers (Allison 1979) are *very* scarce in archaeological contexts (Figs 12.2, 12.3) and optimum conditions are needed for their survival, generally extreme aridity. The identification of tiny feather fragments in coprolite is tricky and Messinger (1965) summarizes the problems and indicates the need for more research in micro-analytical ornithological identifications. A number of feathers have, however, been identified from other North American sites (Lockett & Hargrave 1953, Hargrave 1960, 1965, Guernsey & Kidder 1921). Over the years, wildlife research specialists have developed techniques for determining the age

Figure 12.1 Duck decoy made (a) of rushes and (b) skin covered (Lovelock cave, Nevada) (from Lapton & Brunetti 1969).

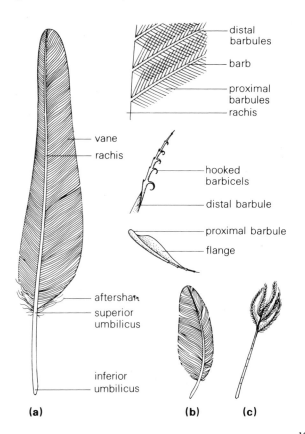

distal barbules

barb

proximal barbules

rachis

vane

rachis

hooked barbicels

distal barbule

proximal barbule

flange

aftershaft

superior umbilicus

inferior umbilicus

(a)   **(b)**   **(c)**

and sex of gamebirds by the size, shape and colour of their feathers (Taber 1963), and work on the Lovelock Cave coprolites was carried out by Ambro (1967). At this site fragments of bird leg skin were also obtained (from *Anas* sp.), although at first identified as snakeskin. The feather analysis shows that many were the contour or flight feathers of mature waterfowl (probably also *Anas* sp. or *Nyroca* sp.) – the identification being based on the examination of the down barbules. Lesser numbers of grebe (*Aechmophorus* sp.), at least one species of goose and a preliminary identification of heron (*Ardea* sp.) was made, but a very large percentage of the feathers found in the coprolite came from the common American coot (*Fulica americana*).

The bones from the site were on the whole in poor condition. About 100 bones of small to medium sized birds were found, including parts of vertebral column, synsacrum and ribs. A rail or a coot is suggested and it was noted that all the bones were adult, no nestlings are present, and some of the

Figure 12.2 Types of feather. (a) Quill; (b) contour; (c) filoplume.

Figure 12.3 Scanning electron photomicrograph of a chicken feather × 550. The pattern of the barbules may be used to identify the species of bird.

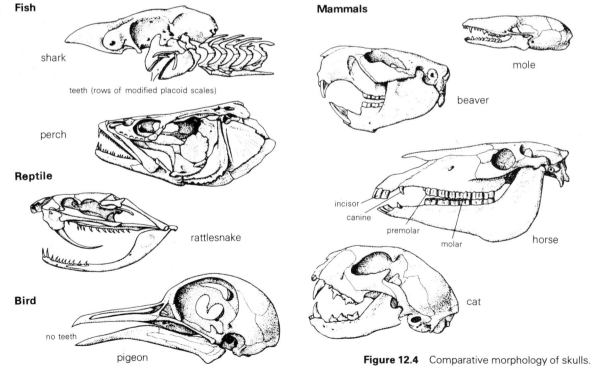

Fish

shark

teeth (rows of modified placoid scales)

perch

Reptile

rattlesnake

Bird

no teeth

pigeon

Mammals

mole

beaver

incisor
canine
premolar
molar
horse

cat

Figure 12.4 Comparative morphology of skulls.

material is charred. Coots live abundantly in the area at the present, especially in the autumn, rare only in May and June. The Great Basin Indians hunted many water species, including coots, by so-called 'mudhen drives', undertaken using fleets of balsas (boats of tule culms), 8–12 ft (2.4–3.7 m) long and able to carry four people. Most of the constituents of the Lovelock Cave coprolites had been obtained during autumn and it was then that the northern Paiute Indians had staged their annual mudhen drives; up to 100 birds would be taken on one occasion by driving them into nets. The presence of decoy heads proved that the birds were hunted, and it seems reasonable to postulate that the bulk of the avian fauna from Lovelock Cave was the result of this practice.

12.5 Exeter – birds from an urban context

Maltby (1979) produced an important report on some 4238 bird bone fragments from Roman–early modern contexts at Exeter, Devon, representing some 41 species. It is, unfortunately, difficult to make direct comparisons of the relative importance of birds at Exeter with bird bones from other sites due to different methods of recovery and quantitative analysis. However, at the Roman levels at Porchester Castle (Grant 1975), 378 bird bone fragments were recovered (0.13% of a total of 29 908 identifiable fragments which included ribs and vertebrae). If the numbers of ribs and vertebrae are removed (and many zoologists do not include them in such totals) the Porchester bird bones are seen to represent 2.02% of the total fragments, lower than Roman Exeter. Noddle (1975) tabled the bird remains from eight Saxon and medieval sites in southern England and found that bird bones averaged less than 7% of the samples, but it is not stated whether the total fragment count included vertebrae and ribs. In Roman and medieval contexts at Exeter a consistent and higher percentage of bird bones was found and this increased dramatically in the sixteenth and late seventeenth centuries until bird bones formed 16–30% of the total fauna (due to the high concentration of bird bones in two particular pits which biased the sample). There seems no doubt that bird remains are generally grossly under-represented in samples. Table 12.1 shows the bird fauna from Exeter. Domestic fowl dominate at all periods, ranging from 50% to more than 80% of the bird bones. This may again be compared with Porchester (where fowls represented 60.85% of the bird bones) and Fishbourne (75.12%; Eastham 1971). At the sites I, IV, V, VI and XX of the Melbourne Street excavations at Saxon Southampton (Coy 1977), fowl composed 67.03% of the identifiable bird bones; but at the medieval sites described by Noddle (1975) it was of less or equal importance to goose. In the Roman period at Exeter over 20% of the fowls eaten were under six months old and the large variations in the size of the domestic fowl suggested regular poultry farming, probably of more than one breed. Eastham (1971) tried to distinguish different breeds of domestic fowl from metrical analysis but this proved difficult. Greylag goose/domestic goose was the next most important bird, but even though the Romans are supposed to have domesticated it goose remains are comparatively insignificant compared with those of fowl. The age distribution of geese was also different from fowl; on post-medieval deposits the bones of young birds were very rare, suggesting that they were allowed to attain full maturity before fattening. It is uncertain whether the mallard (Table 12.1) was actually reared for the table or hunted, but the small number of bones actually found would tend to support the latter hypothesis. Woodcock, the most common wading species, was a winter food source and turkey does not, of course, appear until the post-medieval period. A wide variety of small birds suggest that 'diverse avian food' (Maltby 1979) was available but remained unimportant compared with mammals or fish. Sparrowhawks suggest falconry, but most of the other species were probably eaten. This is a situation rather analogous to that already described for fungi, where there is a reduction in the number of species eaten between the medieval period and the present day (Section 2.3). Here all but four of the bird species were eaten, although perhaps only 15% of the species consumed at Exeter would ever appear on a modern menu. Not that they were ever especially important; a wildfowling season in the winter seems likely, contributing a few birds to supplement the diet when there was less fresh meat or fish available.

Table 12.1 Bird species present at Exeter (data from Maltby 1979). Figures are minimum numbers of individuals.

Species	Roman (AD 55–400)	Medieval (AD 1000–1500)	Post-medieval (AD 1500–1800)
landfowl			
domestic fowl	78	215	132
turkey (*Meleagris galloparo*)	—	—	3
partridge (*Perdix perdix*)	1	2	3
swans, geese and ducks			
mute swan (*Cygnus olor*)	—	2	—
greylag goose/domestic goose (*Anser anser*)	9	62	21
small goose species	—	1	—
mallard/domestic duck (*Anas platyrhynchos*)	9	13	19
teal (*Anas crecca*)	1	1	3
widgeon (*Anas penelope*)	—	2	1
waders			
common crane (*Grus grus*)	1	—	—
grey heron (*Ardea cinera*)	—	—	1
oyster catcher (*Haematopus ostralagus*)	1	1	1
golden plover (*Pluvialis apricaria*)	—	1	1
ringed plover (*Charadrius hiaticula*)	—	—	1
green sandpiper (*Tringa ochropus*)	—	1	1
small wader species	1	1	—
curlew (*Numenius arguata*)	1	1	1
bar-tailed godwit (*Limosa lapponica*)	—	—	1
woodcock (*Scolopax rusticola*)	18	25	13
seabirds			
gannet (*Sula bassana*)	—	1	—
lesser black-back gull (*Larus fuscus*)	—	—	1
kittiwake (*Rissa tridactyla*)	—	—	1
black-throated diver (*Gavia arctica*)	—	1	—
auk species	—	—	1
pigeons and doves			
rock dove/feral pigeon/domestic pigeon (*Columba livia*)	5	7	4
stock dove (*Columba oenas*)	1	4	3
woodpigeon (*Columba palumbus*)	—	1	2
crow family			
chough (*Pyrrhocorax pyrrhocorax*)	—	1	—
raven (*Corvus corax*)	10	9	1
rook/crow (*Corvus frugilegus/Corvus corone corone*)	2	4	2
jackdaw (*Corvus monedula*)	3	2	4
birds of prey			
sparrowhawk (*Accipiter nisus*)	—	1	1
buzzard (*Buteo buteo*)	—	1	1
osprey (*Pandion haliaetus*)	—	—	1
barn own (*Tyto alba*)	—	—	1
passerines and other species			
thrush/blackbird/fieldfare (*Turdus merula/Turdus philomelos/Turdus pilaris*)	4	2	3
starling (*Sturnus vulgaris*)	—	—	1
cuckoo (*Cuculus canorus*)	1	—	—
skylark (*Alauda arvensis*)	—	2	1
large finch/bunting	2	—	—
Totals	148	364	230

References

Allison, E. 1979. Birds of a feather. *York. Arch. Trust Interim* **6** (3), 33–8.

Ambro, R. D. 1967. Dietary–technological–ecological aspects of Lovelock Cave coprolites. *Univ. Calif. Arch. Survey Report* **70**, 37–47.

Bramwell, D. 1979. The bird bones. In G. Lambrick and M. Robinson, 133. *Iron Age and Roman riverside settlements at Farmoor, Oxfordshire*, CBA Research Report 32.

Clark, J. G. D. 1947. Fowling in Prehistoric Europe. *Antiquity* **22**, 116–30.

Coy, J. P. 1977. *Bones of birds and non-domestic species from Melbourne Street sites I, IV, V, VI and XX of Saxon Southampton (Hamwih)*. Ancient Monuments Laboratory Report no. 2323.

Dawson, E. W. 1969. Bird remains in archaeology. In *Science in archaeology*, D. Brothwell and E. Higgs (eds), 359–69. London: Thames and Hudson.

Eastham, A. 1971. The bird bones. In *Excavations at Fishbourne 1961–9*, B. W. Cunliffe (ed.), 388–93, Reports of the Research Committee, Society of Antiquaries of London no. 27, Vol. II.

Grant, A. 1975. The animal bones. In *Excavations at Porchester Castle*, vol. I, *Roman*, B. W. Cunliffe (ed.), 378–408, 437–50. Reports of the Research Committee, Society of Antiquaries of London, no. 33.

Guernsey, S. J. and A. V. Kidder 1921. *Basket-Maker caves of northeastern Arizona: report on the excavations of 1916–17*, papers of the Peabody Museum of American Archaeology and Ethnology **8** (2).

Hargrave, L. L. 1960. Identification of archaeological features from Glen Canyon, Utah. *Univ. Utah anthrop. Pap.* **44**, 239–41.

Hargrave, L. L. 1965. Identification of feather fragments by microstudies. *Soc. Am. Arch. Mem.* **19**, 202–5.

Lambrick, G. and M. Robinson 1979. *Iron Age and Roman riverside settlements at Farmoor, Oxfordshire*. CBA Research Report no. 32: 152.

Lockett, H. C. and L. L. Hargrave 1953. *Woodchuck Cave: A Basketmaker II site in Tsegi Canyon, Arizona*. Museum of Northern Arizona Bulletin no. 26.

Loud, L. L. and M. R. Harrington 1929. Lovelock Cave. *Univ. Calif. Publ. Arch. Ethnol.* **25**, 1.

Maltby, M. 1979. *Faunal studies on urban sites. The animal bones from Exeter*. Exeter Archaeological Reports 2. Department of Prehistory and Archaeology, University of Sheffield.

Messinger, N. G. 1965. Methods used for identification of feather remains from Wetherill Mesa. *Soc. Am. Arch. Mem.* **19**, 206–15.

Napton, L. K. and O. A. Brunetti 1969. Paleoornithology of coprolites from Lovelock Cave, Nevada. In *Archaeological and paleobiological investigations in Lovelock Cave, Nevada*, L. K. Napton (ed.), 9–18. Berkeley: Kroeber Anthropological Society Special Publication no. 2.

Noddle, B. A. 1975. A comparison of the animal bones from eight medieval sites in southern Britain. In *Archaeozoological studies*, A. T. Clason (ed.), 332–9. Amsterdam: Elsevier.

Riddell, W. H. 1943. The domestic goose. *Antiquity* **17**, 148–55.

Taber, P. D. 1963. Criteria of sex and age. In *Wildlife investigation techniques*, H. S. Mosby (ed.). Michigan: Ann Arbor Press.

Appendix A *Latin names and their English equivalents, if available*

Acer	maple	*Cervus elaphus*	red deer
Aechmorphorus	grebe	*Ceuthophilus utahensis*	camel cricket
Alces alces	elk	*Chrysophrys auratus*	snapper fish
Alnus	alder	*Cicer arietinum*	chickpea
Allenrolfea occidentalis	pickleweed	*Clausilia*	doorsnail
Althaea	hollyhock	*Claviceps purpurea*	ergot of rye
Amanita caesarea	Caesar's agaric	*Cleome*	beeweed
Amanita muscoides	fly agaric	*Clonorchis siniensis*	Chinese liver fluke
Ancyclostoma duodenale	hookworm	*Clupea harengus*	herring
Anas	duck	*Conger conger*	conger eel
Anethum graveolens	dill	*Coriandrum sativum*	coriander
Anguiia anguiia	eel	*Corylus avellana*	hazel
Anobium punctatum	furniture beetle	*Crithmium maritimum*	sampohire
Anopheles	mosquito	*Cucumis sativa*	cucumber
Anthicus gracilis	narrow-headed beetle	*Cucurbita*	squash
Aphodius quadriguttatus	dung beetle		
Aplodinotus grunniens	freshwater drumfish	*Dama dama*	fallow deer
Ardea	heron	*Daphnia*	water flea
Arundo donax	reed	*Dicentracus labrax*	bass
Ascaris lumbricoides	roundworm	*Dicrocoelium dendriticum*	liver fluke
Atriplex	orache	*Dipylidum canium*	dog tapeworm
Avena	oats	*Drosophila*	fruit fly
Bacillus anthracis	anthrax bacillus	*Entamoeba*	a protozoan
Belone belone	garfish	*Enterobius vermicularis*	pinworm
Betula	birch	*Ensis*	razor shell
Bilharzia haemotobia	bilharzia fluke	*Equus*	horse
Bos	cattle	*Ephedra altissima*	a pine-like shrub
Boletus edulis	edible boletus	*Erinaceus europaeus*	hedgehog
Bothriocephalus latus	fish tapeworm	*Eriophorum*	cotton grass
Botrychium lunaria	moonwort		
Bruchus sp.	leaf beetles	*Fasciola hepatica*	liver fluke
		Felis	cat
Calluna	ling	*Ficus*	fig
Canis	dog	*Fistulina hepatica*	beefsteak fungus
Catharellus cibarius	chantarelle	*Foeniculum vulgare*	fennel
Capra	goat	*Fomes fomentarius*	tinder fungus
Capreolus capreolus	roe deer	*Fraxinus*	ash
Cardium edule	cockle	*Fulica americana*	common American coot
Castor fiber	beaver	*Gadus morhua*	cod
Centaura cyanus	cornflower	*Galium*	bedstraw

Helix aspersa	common (garden) snail	*Polytrichum commune*	common haircap moss
Helix pomatia	Roman snail	*Porphyra*	laver
Hesperophanes fasciculatus	southern European longhorn beetle	*Prunus avium*	wild cherry
		Prunus persica	peach
Heterogaster urticae	nettle groundbug	*Pteridium*	bracken
Heterophyes	a fluke	*Puccinia graminis*	wheat rust fungus
Hippoglossus hippoglossus	halibut	*Pulex irritans*	flea
Hordeum	barley		
Humulus lupusus	hops	*Quercus*	oak
Klebsiella pneumoniae	pneumonia bacterium	*Rangifer tarandus*	reindeer
		Rattus rattus	black rat
Larix sp.	larch	*Rattus norwegicus*	brown rat
Lecanora esculenta	lecanora	*Rickettsia prowazekii*	typhus rickettsia
Lens culinaris	lentil	*Rosa*	rose
Lepus	hare		
Littorina littorea	common periwinkle	*Salix*	willow
Lutra lutra	otter	*Sciurus vulgaris*	red squirrel
Lycopodium	clubmoss	*Somber scombrus*	mackerel
Lymnaea	pond snail	*Scophthalnus maximum*	turbot
		Selaginella	selaginella clubmosses
Martes martes	pine martin	*Senecio*	groundsel
Melanogrammus aeglefinus	haddock	*Setaria*	bristlegrass
Meles meles	badger	*Sialis*	alderfly
Merlangius merlangus	whiting	*Sitophilus granarius*	a grain beetle
Molva molva	ling	*Sole solea*	sole
Moniliformis clarkii	thorny-headed worm	*Sphagnum*	moss
Murex	winkle	*Squalus acanthias*	spur dog
Muscari	grape hyacinth	*Sus*	pig
Mustela erminea	stoat		
Mustela nivalis	weasel	*Taenia solium*	pork tapeworm
Mustela putorius	polecat	*Taenia saginata*	beef tapeworm
Myrica gale	bog myrtle	*Teredus cylindricus*	shipworm
		Thallia democratica	salp
Nucella lapillus	dog whelk	*Thymelaea*	dapne
		Trachurus trachurus	horse mackerel
Odobenus rosmarus	walrus	*Trichinella spiralis*	trichina worm
Olea europaea	olive	*Trichuris trichuris*	whipworm
Ophioglossum vulgatum	adder's tongue fern	*Tricholoma*	tricholoma
Opuntia	prickly pear	*Triticium diciccum*	emmer wheat
Oryctolagus cuniculus	rabbit	*Triticum spelta*	spelt
Osmunda regalis	royal fern		
Ostrea edulis	oyster	*Ulva*	sea lettuce
Oxyuris equi	horse threadworm	*Ursus arctos*	brown bear
Ovis	sheep	*Urtica dioica*	stinging nettle
		Ustilago hordei	covered barley smut
Patella	limpet		
Pecten maximus	scallop	*Variola*	smallpox virus
Pediculus humanus	head louse	*Vitis vinifera*	grape
Phragmites communis	common reed	*Vulpes*	fox
Phyllopertha sp.	chafer beetles		
Pinus	pine	*Xenopsylla cheopis*	a flea
Plantago	plantain	*Xestobium rufivillosum*	deathwatch beetle
Platichys flesus	flounder	*Yersimia pestis*	bubonic plague bacterium
Pleuronectes platesa	plaice		
Pollachius virens	saithe	*Zea*	corn
Polypodum vulgare	common polypody		

achene Dry one-seeded fruit formed from a single carpel.

actinomycete An order of bacteria.

aeolian deposits Laid down by the wind.

agar Gel obtained from certain seaweed which is used as a culture growth medium for micro-organisms.

aggradation The process of building up the land surface by, for example, river deposition.

allochthonous Sediments transported to the site of deposition from elsewhere: opposite of *autochthonous*.

anaerobic Capable of living without oxygen.

alluvium Sediments deposited by a river.

angiosperms Flowering plants.

Annelida Phylum of soft-bodied segmented worms.

annual ring Annual increment of secondary wood (xylem) in stems and roots of plants.

anther Part of the flower stamen which contains pollen.

attrition Mutual wearing down of rock particles during transport.

autotrophic Organism which makes its own food source using light or chemicals for energy.

axenic culture Of one organism alone.

bark Layer of dead, woody tissue on outside of old plant stems.

bedrock Solid rock under the soil or sediment forming the landscape.

berry Many-seeded fruit where the wall (*pericarp*) consists of an outer shell (*epicarp*), a fleshy *merocarp* and an inner *endocarp* (e.g. gooseberry, currant, tomato).

biocenosis Fossil assemblage of forms living together before death.

bog Wet spongy ground consisting largely of decayed moss and other plant material.

Brachipoda Phylum of molluscs with two-valved shells.

breccia Angular rock fragments cemented in a matrix.

brickearth Almost any fine-grained sediment suitable for making bricks (e.g. alluvium, loess).

cambium Layer of actively dividing cells between xylem and phloem.

carpel Female reproductive organ of flowering plant.

chemotrophic Organisms obtaining energy from chemical reactions.

chitin Nitrogenous polysaccharide of great tensile strength and chemical resistance present in the cuticle of insects.

chlorophyll Green pigment found in all algae and higher plants.

chroma Degree of greyness in a colour.

Coleoptera Beetles.

collagen Fibrous protein which forms the major constituent of bone.

colluvial deposits Weathered material transported by gravity.

conglomerate Rock composed of rounded pebbles cemented in a finer matrix.

Coombe rock Sediments resulting from solifluxion in periglacial conditions.

coprolite Fossil faeces.

Cromerian Stratigraphic name for a stage in the British and European basal and middle Pleistocene.

dehiscent Fruits which open to free the seeds (e.g. peas).

demography Numerical study of human populations.

dendrochronology Study and dating of past climatic changes from the annual growth rings of trees.

degradation Wearing away of the land surface.

deflation Wind lifting and transport of sediments.

deciduous Trees which loose their leaves annually.

Devensian Stratigraphic name for last glacial stage in Britain. Approximating to the European *Würm*.

Diptera Flies.

distal Away from the place of attachment: opposite of *proximal* (e.g. in a limb, away from the body).

drupe Fruit where pericarp consists of outer skin (*epicarp*), thick fleshy *mesocarp* and hard stony *endpcarp* with a single seed (e.g. plum, coconut).

ecology Science which considers the interaction of organisms and their environment.

eluviation See **illuviation**.

feral Domestic animal living in the wild.

Flandrian Stratigraphic name for British and European post-glacial Pleistocene (or *Holocene*).

fluvial Related to a river.

fluke Parasitic flatworm.

geoarchaeology Earth science applications in archaeology.

geomorphology The study of the arrangement and form of the Earth's crust.

gley soil A type of soil forming where the water table is near the surface.

gypsum Evaporite mineral $CaSO_4.2H_2O$.

heartwood Central dead xylem mass in tree-trunk.

'heavy' minerals Minerals whose relative density is greater than 2.9.

helminth Parasitic flatworm.

Hoxnian Stratigraphic name for interglacial between Lowestoft and Gipping cold phases in Britain.

heterotrophic Needing organic food.

humus Decomposing organic matter in the soil.

Hymnoptera Insect order including bees, wasps and ants.

hue Dominant spectral colour.

illuviation Deposition of mineral salts, etc., in B horizon of a soil which have been removed from upper (A) horizon by **eluviation**.

indigenous Native to a particular area.

Ipswichian British stratigraphic name for interglacial between Gipping and Devensian cold stages.

interglacial Relatively warm period between two cold (glacial) phases.

interstadial Warm pause in a glacial advance.

lacustrine Related to a lake.

Lammellibranchia Class of aquatic molluscs including mussels and oysters.

leaching Washing of soluble salts through the soil by rainwater.

legume Pod.

Lepidoptera Butterflies and moths.

lithification Formation of rocks from sediments.

loess Fine aeolian silt laid down in the Pleistocene.

mould Superficial fungus mycelium.

Nematoda Phylum of round-, thread- and eel-worms.

Orthoptera Insect order including cockroaches, locusts and grasshoppers.

pedology Soil science.

pericarp Wall of the flower ovary after it has developed into a fruit.

periglacial Region adjacent to an ice sheet.

Platyhelminthes Phylum of flatworms including flukes and tapeworms.

Pleistocene Geological epoch 1.6–0.01 Ma ago, often called the 'Ice Age'.

Quaternary Last of the four major divisions of the geological time-scale (see Appendix D).

raised beach Beach deposits now raised above present sea level.

saprophyte Organism which lives on dead organic matter.

sapwood Outer living xymen of the tree-trunk.

soil profile Section through the soil to show the different layers.

taxonomy Science of the classification of organisms.

tell Mound formed by successive occupations on same area where building debris mostly consists of mud brick.

Trichoptera Caddis flies.

value Lightness of a colour.

vector Organisms which transmit parasites.

weathering Disintegration of rocks by exposure to the atmosphere.

Würm Stage name for the last glacial period in north-western Europe (see Appendix D).

Appendix C Terminology of the Pleistocene glacial and interglacial stages

Common name	British Isles	Alps	Northern Europe	Central USA
last glacial	Devensian	Würm	Weichsel	Wisconsin
last interglacial	Ipswichian	Riss/Würm	Eemian	Sangamon
glacial	Gipping	Riss	Saale	Illinoian
interglacial	Hoxnian	Mindel/Riss	Needian	Yarmouth
glacial	Lowestoftian	Mindel	Elsetr	Kansan
interglacial	Cromerian	Günz/Mindel		Aftonian
glacial	Weybourne Crag	Günz		Nebraskan
interglacial	Norwich Crag	Donau/Günz		
glacial	pre-Crag	Donau		pre-Nebraskan

Note: This is a great oversimplification and implies that the glacial stages have their exact equivalents in different areas, which we now know not to have been the case. This is intended to be used as a framework only and should be compared with the findings of up-to-date research for a more precise nomenclature.

Appendix D The geological time-scale

Era	Period	Epoch	Time since start of epoch/period (Ma)
Cenozoic	Quaternary	Recent (Holocene)	0.01
		Pleistocene	1.6
	Tertiary	Pliocene	7
		Miocene	26
		Oligocene	38
		Eocene	54
		Palaeocene	65
Mesozoic	Cretaceous		135
	Jurassic		190
	Triassic		225
Palaeozoic	Permian		280
	Carboniferous		345
	Devonian		395
	Silurian		440
	Ordovician		500
	Cambrian		570

Author index

Subject index